English America and Imperial Inconstancy

ENGLISH AMERICA

and

Imperial Inconstancy

*The Rise of
Provincial Autonomy,
1696–1715*

J. M. Sosin

University of Nebraska Press
Lincoln and London

Publication of this book was assisted by a grant from the National Endowment for the Humanities, a federal agency that supports the study of fields such as history, philosophy, literature, and languages.

Library of Congress Cataloging in Publication Data
Sosin, Jack M.
  English America and imperial inconstancy.

  Bibliography: p.
  Includes index.
  1. United States—Politics and government—Colonial
period, ca. 1600–1775. I. Title.
E195.S77   1985   973.2   84-27865
ISBN 0-8032-4154-2 (alk. paper)

The paper in this book meets the guidelines for permanence and durability of the Committee on Production Guidelines for Book Longevity of the Council on Library Resources.

Contents

A Note on Dates and Quotations   vii
Preface   ix
Introduction   3
Part I   England and America: The Political and Economic Nexus   11
   1. Politics and Imperial Administration   13
   2. International War and Anglo-Colonial Political Relations   23
   3. War and the Disruption of Transatlantic Commerce   37
   4. The English Entrepôt and the Southern Colonial Staple Trade   45
Part II   The American Scene from the Ashley to the Delaware   55
   5. Virginia, 1696–1715: Royal Dominion and Local Oligarchy   57
   6. Maryland, 1696–1715: Royal Government in a Proprietary Colony   76
   7. The Carolinas: Autonomy through Proprietary Negligence   92
   8. Popular Politics and the Delaware Proprietaries   110
   9. New Jersey, 1696–1709: From Proprietary to Royal Government   132
Part III   Royal Government in the North: the Limitations of War, 1696–1715   151
   10. New York, Massachusetts, and the Captain-Generalcy of the Earl of Bellomont, 1696–1701   153
   11. War, Imperial Authority, and the Corporations of Southern New England   175
   12. Northern New England under a Governor ''of Our Nation''   192
   13. New York under Cornbury and Hunter: The Growth of Assembly Power, 1702–15   213
Conclusion   231
List of Abbreviations   237
Notes   239
Index   275

A Note on Dates and Quotations

ALL DATES UNLESS otherwise indicated (n.s. for new style) are in the Julian calendar, ten days behind those of the Gregorian calendar, adopted by some of the states of Western Europe in 1582–83. In England, where the Gregorian calendar was not adopted until 1752, it had become the custom from the thirteenth century to advance the number of the year on 25 March, the date of the Feast of the Annunciation. Not until 1750 did Parliament by statute provide that year numbers would change on 1 January in and after 1752 and that the day *following* 2 September 1752 would become 14 September. In the notes to this work I have followed the practice often used by contemporaries of writing dates from 1 January to 25 March to indicate both the civil and the Julian year, for example, 2 February 1696/7. In France and other regions where the new style, or Gregorian, calendar was in use, this date would be written as 12 February 1697. In 1700 the discrepancy between the Julian and Gregorian calendars had increased by one day, from ten to eleven.

In conformity with current editorial practice ellipses (. . .) have routinely been omitted at the beginning and end of direct quotations and initial capitalization and final punctuation regularized accordingly.

Preface

A RECENT STUDY on New England witchcraft succinctly sets forth one of the central "presumptions"—and it is just that: a presumption—of recent scholarship in early American history, the primacy of local experience. For the vast majority of Americans what most shaped their lives were not decisions made thousands of miles away across the ocean by the imperial government in London—these rarely or remotely, if at all, impinged on their lives—or even the enactments of the more proximate colonial governors and provincial legislatures but rather events in the "little community." More important than the imperial or provincial was the local scene, the informal structure of the immediate neighborhood where people confronted each other face to face.[1] This view has the great appeal of freshness and the further attraction of offering, at times, complex explanations integrating several academic disciplines. But two objections come to mind: no standard is offered to judge between the relative weights of local, provincial, or imperial influences, and the long-range consequences of decisions taken at the colonial and imperial levels of government may not be appreciated or even perceived, particularly by the rank and file, although their lives are indeed affected.

Perhaps a better case can be made that colonial governments, through legislation enacted by the provincial assemblies, were responsible for imposing a basic framework for local governmental, ecclesiastical, and even social arrangements, the bounds within which individuals and families carried on their lives. Provincial laws determined who could vote and the forms of town government. Laws enacted by the governments of the New England colonies, Carolina, and Maryland established the discipline and creeds of churches. That exceptions, for a time, existed—as in Rhode Island and the two New Jerseys—does not negate the rule. A critical question is how the provincial assemblies or, in the case of Connecticut and Rhode Island, the provincial corporations came to develop power autonomous from England. How did it happen that over the course of time the influence of English officials in Whitehall and the governors they appointed diminished and that of the locally elected assemblies—the House of Representatives, the House of Burgesses, the Commons House, as they were variously called—or that of the social elites sitting on the provincial councils increased?

To some readers this may seem an old-fashioned study concerned with questions already posed by scholars and employing conventional methods long used by historians. It is based on correspondence, governmental reports, and other literary evidence; it is concerned with power and the efforts of men, particularly those at the higher stratum of provincial society and government, to achieve it, although the focus is on the interaction of imperial and provincial governments, Whitehall and Westminster on the one hand and the various provincial capitals on the other. This is not intended as institutional history, but rather as a study in power and in the efforts of men to achieve their goals through political institutions, for in the early modern era government was the wellspring of power. Under rules, procedures, and institutions prescribed by the provincial legislatures and executives, commissions of the peace, town meetings, and boards of supervisors dealt with almost every facet of life.

This study does not deal with inarticulate data such as numbers, requiring the investigator to impose a frame of reference; it does not attempt to construct models of behavior or to recreate for what James Logan of Philadelphia referred to as the illiterate "meaner sort of people" a psychological frame of reference, rooted not in the social and economic circumstances of the seventeenth century but in the values of the late twentieth. Concepts derived from recent social science may indeed by useful tools to be employed in demography and anthropology, for example, disciplines for which literary evidence is lacking or scanty, but the conclusions derived from them, rather than being universals, applicable to all human societies, may well be reflections of the need to impose order on a complex and variegated past. This study seeks to understand men in provincial society in terms of their own time and values as far as the literary evidence will allow. It is concerned with power and the location of authority in provincial American society and how the locus of that power came to shift from officials and institutions extraneous to America to local legislative assemblies and councils consisting of and representing local interest and elites. The American scene was characterized by intense factionalism, instability, and competition among men who, although they employed the rhetoric of English liberty, were parochial, concerned with immediate goals of power, status, and influence.

The various American provinces reveal distinctive themes, with no type or paradigm of corporate, proprietary, or royal colony to do justice to the variety of experience. Several provinces — Massachusetts, Maryland, Pennsylvania — underwent reorganization so that they were not always one distinct type or another. Because of common religious affiliations and personal connections Quakers in Pennsylvania and men in New York often influenced events in neighboring New Jersey or in the Delaware counties. Decisions made in one colony bore on events in another. Developments in Connecticut and Rhode Island (corporate provinces) and in Pennsylvania (a proprietary colony) help to explain why the institutional arrangements, other than having the crown appoint a governor, failed to achieve imperial control and allowed provincial autonomy to develop. The Carolinas, different from each other in the ethnic composition of their populations and in economic develpment, serve well to illustrate the strong push toward localism in colonies under an absentee board composed of individuals with diverse interests. Maryland, technically the property of a single proprietor during the period covered by this study, was under governors appointed by the royal administration in Whitehall, but like Virginia, the province showed the weakness of Whitehall's simplistic formula. The home government on more than one occasion allowed significant intervals — as much as four or five years — to lapse without having a governor resident in the Chesapeake colonies, thus allowing local leaders to consolidate their power without opposition. And on three other occasions the home authorities failed to support men sent out as the representative of the monarch and removed royal governors at the behest of the local magnates on the council of the Old Dominion.

More than one road led to provincial autonomy. In New York and Massachusetts, provinces with different political and institutional heritages, the assemblies, rather than the upper houses emerged as the focus for local authority, as the government in London saw in these colonies a bulwark in the wars against France in America. Reliance on local financing for military efforts in an age of chronic war gave elected provincial representatives leverage against imperial administrators.

In placing this book within the perspective of early American history and the early British empire, another question is posed: When did the process of separation — one which ultimately, but not inevitably, ended in revolutionary war — begin? Where did its orgins lie: in London, or in the various provincial capitals, Williamsburg, Boston, Annapolis, Charles Town? In the respected tradition of imperial historians, J. P. Greene emphasized the growing maturity and political responsibility of the provincial assemblies.[2] Others, James Henretta and Thomas C. Barrow, following an equally distinguished tradition, have pointed to critical decisions made in England during the second quarter or third of the eighteenth century, when Robert Walpole, the duke of Newcastle, and later Whig ministries, by design and as conscious policy, followed a program of salutary neglect.[3] Under Newcastle particularly, effective administration of colonial affairs was subordinated to creating and manipulating a parliamentary majority for largely domestic political considerations. Henretta contrasted the lax years of the Walpole-Newcastle era with the more able, vigorous and expert administration which presumably prevailed earlier, particularly with the founding of a board for regulating plantation affairs in 1696.

Whatever the motive behind the laxity of imperial administration under Walpole, Newcastle, and the later Whig ministries, earlier imperial administration was not characterized by efficiency and expertness. As a consequence, the theme which emerges from this book is that the rise in power of the provincial assemblies and the growth of provincial autonomy came earlier than appreciated and resulted as much, perhaps more, from inconstancy, neglect, and parsimony in British administration as from colonial maturity. Provincial political, if not economic and cultural, autonomy was well developed by the time the first Hanoverian king came to the throne in 1714; it may well have been inherent in the instability and weakness of English national government from the time of the founding of the North American colonies. The development of a modern administrative apparatus in England in the late seventeenth and early eighteenth centuries — a consequence of the effort to wage extended war, primarily in Europe — did not substantially alter the loose administration of the overseas possessions; indeed, the financial drain on the crown acted to perpetuate this condition and to further the growth of provincial autonomy.

English America and Imperial Inconstancy

Introduction

T HE QUAKERS OF PENNSYLVANIA were an unruly, undisciplined people "who despise all Dominion & dignity that is not in themselves." So concluded John Blackwell, a Puritan of Old and New England commissioned by William Penn to administer public affairs in his American colony.[1] Blackwell's observation might well have applied to many other Englishmen who had crossed the Atlantic to lay the foundations of what became the most dynamic empire of the early modern era. The pattern and nature of settlement—private for the most part rather than public—created much of the confusion and lack of governmental system prevalent in America during the seventeenth century.

During the first two generations of colonization, not enough had been known in England of North America. Consequently, in sanctioning colonies the early Stuart monarchies had issued grants with overlapping boundaries. To add to the confusion, religious animosities had prevailed among the English settlers. Only three of the colonies in existence in 1660 had received sanction from the crown, but as a result of personal rivalries and religious differences other communities outside of Massachusetts Bay, Virginia, and Maryland had been founded. From the perspective of Whitehall, the seat of imperial government in London, the American settlements seemed scattered and loose, too independent of English control. Crown officials had sought to rectify the situation, but had proved themselves too indecisive and weak. Domestic discord, civil conflict, and war with the Dutch and French in Europe and across the seas had occupied the attention and strained the resources of the ministers of state. The financial weakness of the crown had further limited their choices of action.

By 1660 five distinct provincial governments—Massachusetts, New Plymouth, New Haven, Rhode Island, and Connecticut—whatever their legal status, were exercising authority over the English townsmen in New England. In the next quarter century two lost their separate identity as Connecticut absorbed New Haven and Massachusetts took over Plymouth. The Bay colony lost jurisdiction, however, over the small, scattered towns in the Piscataqua region, now called the province of New Hampshire, and that province became a royal colony. Charles II had granted charters to Connecticut and Rhode Island in an effort to win support in New England against the obstreperous Puritans of Massachusetts, men imbued with a sense of their own divine mission to establish a holy commonwealth free of outside interference.

During the two decades following the Restoration, the English crown had been unable to exercise control over the petty, sometimes squabbling jurisdictions in New England. Charles II had compounded the problem of governing the foreign plantations by allowing the formation of still more diverse colonies, provinces not subject to the immediate supervision of the ministers of state. The origin of several additional colonies — New York, New Jersey, Pennsylvania, the three counties on the lower Delaware, and North and South Carolina, communities diverse in their social composition and sometimes bizarre in their governmental arrangements — was laid during these years, the result of the king's propensity for rewarding his favorites, William Penn and a small coterie associated with the king's brother, James, duke of York. The decision had seemed immediately attractive: it offered an opportunity to displace competing foreign powers and to preempt portions of the North American continent claimed by the French and the Spanish. The early years of these proprietary colonies were dramatic, marred by an impractical, at times grotesque, division of governmental authority and seemingly irrepressible conflicts among settlers of diverse ethnic backgrounds and religious loyalties. The government of Charles II had played a limited role. In granting charters for these proprietary colonies the monarch had sanctioned the broad outlines of government and had required the consent of the settlers to the laws governing them, but otherwise had left the responsibility for the infant provinces to the proprietors.

Proprietary government — whether in the form of a single overlord such as Baron Baltimore in Maryland or William Penn for Pennsylvania and the Delaware counties, or that of a group of proprietors, either absentee or resident — had few supporters in America. Commanding little respect from the colonists and inspiring little awe, it further compounded the difficulties facing royal authorities in bringing order to the nascent American settlements. Taking advantage of the liberal provisions of the royal charters on freedom of religious conscience, proprietors, in order to sell lands, had welcomed — in some cases induced — the migration of various groups. The immediate effect in the new proprietaries was further to fragment the English community and to increase the number of diverse ethnic and religious elements resident there, as Presbyterian Scots, Quakers, French Huguenots, Baptists, and Welshmen responded to the opportunity to acquire land and to found their own churches.

Charles II had more latitude to act on the issue of religious toleration in the American colonies than he had in England, where a House of Commons dominated by vengeful Anglican gentry had vented their resentment over years of Puritan repression by enacting a code imposing Anglicanism as the national religion and depriving dissenters of political rights as well as the right to worship without a license. During his reign the king had issued six charters and concessions for new colonies; all contained a provision for liberty of conscience for peaceable Protestants. And for the province in New England already authorized, the king had urged on the Puritan government a similar policy. As a result of the royal program American society exhibited great diversity in religion, but this pluralism in turn contributed to political tensions.

Belated efforts by royal officials in England during the last months of Charles's reign and following the accession of his brother, James II, to bring the colonists to acknowledge dependence on the crown further heightened political tensions; while these efforts created avenues for those seeking honor, recognition, and profit, they also posed a threat to those who based their power on the sanctions of a local authority — in the Puritan commonwealths, for example, on the General Court — men who for more than a score of years had resisted any attempt to reach an accommodation with the crown or to admit that they owed more than minimal allegiance to the king as a titular head. They claimed virtual independence in church and state. These irreconcilable Puritans — commonwealthmen, they were called — had practiced systematic evasion for more than two decades in the hope that religious discord and political turmoil in England would lead to the collapse of the Stuart regime and save them from royal authority, as their fathers before them had been saved earlier in the century by the advent of the English Civil War and the Puritan Revolution.

Under Charles II royal officials had advocated gathering the loose and scattered colonial jurisdictions which had been allowed to form haphazardly into a more coherent body and rendering governments in America more directly dependent on the crown by appointing governors and allowing appeals from the provincial courts to the king's Council in Whitehall. After more than a score of years during which the commonwealthmen of Massachusetts, the most populous and the most powerful of the northern colonies, had refused to come to any accommodation or to accept any supervision, Charles and his ministers had instituted legal proceedings to have the royal courts at Westminster vacate the charter. Massachusetts Bay had become a royal colony. Coincidently, in 1684 several disparate developments in the southern proprietary colonies, developments unrelated to the situation in Massachusetts, had seemed to threaten the lucrative customs revenue accruing to the crown from duties imposed on colonial tobacco.

Ministers of the English crown when addressing themselves to the affairs of the overseas plantations following the Restoration had most concerned themselves with the obstreperous commonwealthmen of Massachusetts; with Virginia, a colony rent by riots and civil conflicts; and with the war-ravaged West Indies. Only in what proved to be the very last year of the reign of Charles II did they submit the proprietary provinces to close scrutiny. In the Carolinas bickering, petty jealousies, and instability characterized public life. Much the same situation prevailed in New Jersey, a territory divided by its English overlords into eastern and western sections, and in Maryland, where dissident elements capitalized on the religion of the Roman Catholic proprietary family and its cohorts, who constituted a narrow, privileged ruling elite. On more than one occasion the crown had warned the proprietors of Carolina to restore order and secure the revenue from tobacco. To no avail. And in 1684 the actions of the proprietor of Maryland and his appointed officials also seemed to threaten royal revenue. In that year ministers of state had acted to vacate the charter of Massachusetts, but before the winter of 1684–85 was out, Charles II died, and his brother, a convert to Roman Catholicism, became king. With the accession of James II the proprietary province of New York became a royal colony. James had already decided to grant the inhabitants — many of them of Dutch extraction with whom the English had waged war three times since 1650 — the privilege of electing representatives to meet with the governor appointed by London to enact laws.

The new administration in Whitehall followed no clear or consistent policy. James, determined to free his co-religionists from the legal restrictions of the religious code imposed in the early years of his brother's reign, at one point appeared on the verge of vacating the provincial charters by judicial action and issuing new patents to provide rights for Roman Catholics in the colonies, although Pennsylvania and Maryland, provinces where Catholics in law might already enjoy rights, seemed exempt from this decision. Other events in America and in Europe further influenced decisions relating to the continental colonies. With conflict with Bourbon France imminent in America, some men in New York and New England had urged consolidation of the English provinces better to meet the threat. As a result, the corporations of Connecticut and Rhode Island came under pressure to surrender their separate jurisdiction and accept annexation to Massachusetts Bay, now governed by an executive and a council appointed by the crown. Under a royal governor, Sir Edmund Andros, the Bay colony had been enlarged to include both the New Hampshire and Plymouth towns. And in 1688 the crown granted Andros a new commission with authority to govern the Dominion of New England, an amalgamation of all of the English provinces, including New York and East and West New Jersey, north and east of the Delaware River. As William Blathwayt, the secretary at war who for many years attended the committee of the king's Council responsible for plantation affairs, explained, "The French have occasion[e]d it by their incursions" into English territory. The union of all of the northern colonies "may make us more formidable" and would be "terrible to the French and make them proceed with more caution than they have lately done."[2]

Much to the surprise of some officials at the Plantation Office, when Andros had first been sent to Massachusetts in 1686, his commission from James II did not provide for an elected assembly to vote taxes and to enact laws. The new governor was himself apparently unhappy with the arrangement, complaining that a plantation government "without an assembly seems very mysterious." The ministers sitting on the committee normally responsible for colonial affairs had themselves noted that the crown law officers — the king's attorney general and his solicitor general — had both agreed that, notwithstanding the forfeiture of the charter, the inhabitants of the Bay colony yet retained the right to consent through elected representatives to taxes imposed on them and the laws under which they would live. James II had ignored this view, apparently relying on the advice of the lord president of the council, Robert Spencer, second earl of Sunderland.[3]

As a consequence, Andros was left to govern in America with little local support when war with France broke out and word came that James's subjects in England had overthrown their sovereign in the winter of 1688–89, following his heavy-handed attempt to dispense with the religious and civil disabilities imposed by Parliament on both Catholics and Protestant dissenters. Anglicans, both Whig and Tory, had called in William of Orange, the king's nephew and husband to his elder daughter, Mary, to save England for the Protestant cause.

In America of the seventeenth century, the potential for social disruption and political upheaval was inherent in ethnic and religious pluralism, social fluidity in the upper levels of the English communities, fragmented political authority, and institutional immaturity. The potential existed; its realization depended on events often fortuitous and men often weak. The spark was provided by the Glorious Revolution. Andros and other officials of the Dominion were quickly deposed as local leaders took control and established separate *de facto* governments.

For the inhabitants of the colonies decisions made in England during the reign of William and Mary would determine the political configuration of English America. Would Englishmen living in the plantations have some voice in determining the laws governing them? Would English America continue as a dozen or so petty, distinct provinces, discrete jurisdictions separate from each other and tied only nominally to the crown of England? Or would a strengthened monarchy finally reverse the trend of lax, haphazard administration which had so long prevailed during the seventeenth century and consolidate the particularistic colonies with civil administrations dependent directly on the crown and its ministers?

The answers to these questions and the key to Anglo-colonial relations during these years revolved about four related issues: provincial consolidation, representative government, religious toleration, and the subordination of the American communities to the crown of England.

The Revolution in the British Isles and the outbreak of a protracted international war in which William III brought England into a European coalition against France had doomed the projected consolidation of English America envisaged by James II and the earl of Sunderland. The failure of the ministers serving the new monarchs promptly and authoritatively to inform officials in Boston, Manhattan, and Saint Marys of the Protestant succession in England had presented dissident elements in New York, Massachusetts, and Maryland with the opportunity to overthrow the existing regimes and to assume power under the guise of protecting Protestantism from the menace of papist subversives and an invasion by the French and Indians. In the north the Dominion collapsed as the insurgents reestablished the jurisdictions which had prevailed in 1685. Once again English America consisted of a dozen distinct provinces. These dramatic events had had far-reaching consequences. In New York the assumption of power by the insurgents, their repression of many innocent loyalists, and the subsequent retribution imposed on the leaders of the rebellion condemned the Hudson River and Long Island communities to a generation of bitter animosities.

The assumption of power in Boston, Manhattan, and Saint Marys by local leaders had limited the alternatives open to London. William III and his ministers had accepted the principle that the colonists were entitled to some voice to their governments through an elected assembly, but occupied with the conflict against France in Europe and a French-inspired Jacobite uprising in Ireland and needing provincial support against Bourbon power in North America, they had had to accept the dismemberment of the Dominion. Yet they had not allowed Massachusetts to return to its former status of virtual independence under the old charter. By the terms of a new patent issued in 1691, Massachusetts had a governor appointed and instructed by the crown. So too did Maryland and, for a time, Pennsylvania, as the ministers of state adopted a formula suggested by the judges at Westminster. In case proprietary and chartered authorities failed to provide adequately for the protection of the king's subjects and in the face of imminent danger or invasion, the monarch was justified in taking the government into his own hands, that is, in appointing a governor.

Officials in England, and William himself, placed their faith in the abilities of governors to control their colonies while remaining financially dependent for their salaries and, more importantly, for military expenditures on revenue locally sanctioned in America. Struggles for power and status, parochial outlook, and pervasive factionalism made difficult the task of governing by officials armed merely with a commission from a distant king, a monarch occupied with apparently more complex and demanding problems. To ministers of state and even the few veteran bureaucrats familiar with colonial affairs, the solution had seemed simple: bring the colonies directly under the monarch, bring them to a closer dependence by having the king appoint the governors and by having his Privy Council review provincial legislation and entertain appeals for the colonial courts. Before the close of the seventeenth century the political and institutional forms prevailing in America prior to the attempt at consolidation by James II had been restored. The English in the overseas plantations remained divided under three distinct governmental arrangements: royal, corporate, and proprietary. In two of the chartered colonies—Maryland and Massachusetts—and in Pennsylvania at times, the king appointed and instructed the governors. Some officials in Whitehall—William Blathwayt, the long-time secretary to the Privy Council's committee on plantation affairs, for one—lamented the failure to adopt a systematic approach to governing the colonies. This failure, a legacy of the Restoration years, would continue into the eighteenth century. Some men in America would continue to look to Whitehall, but the more significant arenas for American leaders would now be Boston, Annapolis, Williamsburg, and the other provincial capitals, where the ambitious in the assemblies would wage their battles not only with the governors, but with each other for influence and status.

In following a simplistic formula, in seeking to render the chartered governments as well as the royal administrations in America immediately dependent on the crown by appointing a governor and requiring appeals from the provincial courts to Whitehall, successive English ministers of state misunderstood the problem of governing the overseas communities, of controlling events in America. They assumed that an executive appointed and instructed by the crown would veto objectionable bills coming from a local assembly and carry through decisions made in Whitehall for a colony across the Atlantic. For a royal governor to be free from local pressures, to be at liberty to execute policies and implement decisions made in England, he needed to be immune from financial pressure. In the last year of the reign of William III, the king and his ministers appreciated that depending on ''presents'' from the assemblies tended to render the governors ''precarious and dependent'' on the local populace. To support the dignity of the royal government they needed to receive adequate salaries.[4] But officials in Whitehall never consistently implemented this recommendation. Of even greater consequence during the coming decades, when war or the threat of international conflict was chronic, governors needed financial aid from England to provide adequately for military campaigns. Little was forthcoming for more than half a century. By leaving the representatives of royal authority in America dependent on the provincial assemblies for financing the civil and military establishments, English authorities provided the means for local leaders to coerce the governors and to enhance their own positions by exalting the status of the elected assemblies where they dominated.

No institutional reorganization, no simple constitutional formula rendering the plantations immediately dependent on the crown of Britain, would suffice. Money and political talent, liberally and wisely applied, was the solution. Neither would be apparent in adequate measure.

PART I

England and America: The Political and Economic Nexus

CHAPTER 1

Politics and Imperial Administration

Despite the failure over forty years to render the North American colonies more "dependent" on the crown of England, America did not exist in a political and commercial vacuum. Common ideas, economic interests, and political loyalties still linked people separated by a vast ocean. Anglo-colonial political relations at the close of the seventeenth century turned about several issues. At times, two of these conflicted: the search for stability in America and the tendency toward autonomy in the provincial world, toward making decisions independently of Whitehall and Westminster. The realization of both stability and autonomy depended on a complex of decisions and events relating to church and state, commerce, political rivalries in England and America, and the strengths or weaknesses of men in high office. Political instability and almost continual shifts in administration in England jeopardized the government's ability to follow a consistent approach to American problems. During the reign of William III partisan politics intensified with a reorientation of parties, Whig and Tory, and continued competition for high ministerial office.

The terms *Whig* and *Tory* had been current well before 1696; the first initially applied to members of a party favoring parliamentary restraints on the prerogative of the monarch and toleration for Protestant Dissenters. The Whigs arrogated for themselves the role of spokesmen for the "country," labelling their rivals a "court" party. But as the Revolution of 1688 had not restricted the power of the monarch to choose his servants, his ministers of state, rarely could an administration command a majority in Parliament. Nor could various factions in the House of Commons remain sufficiently united to coerce the monarch. The labels "country" and "court" soon acquired different meanings. After 1696 a reorientation of parties occurred, a reshuffling of factions and personal blocs. The same terms were used in America as in England, but in Massachusetts or New York, for example, colonists adopted the label "country party" to distinguish themselves from rival factions to whom they applied the perjorative "court," that is, men subservient to the administration of an appointed governor. In England, to be of the country party after 1696 was to be loosely connected, if at all, with either Whig or Tory bloc. In the House of Commons sat roughly 100 members who were placemen, appointed to administrative offices by the crown and subject to the wishes of the higher ministers of state. Two other groups consisted of members of the Whig and Tory parties; their leaders, on occasion and depending on the issue in question, could rely on the votes of a sizable number of independent country gentry. But not all questions, and certainly not matters relating to the colonies, were partisan issues. As the veteran House of Commons man, Robert Harley, appreciated, the key to control of the House lay not with the organized blocs, Whig and Tory, but with the 250 to 300 country members independent in fact whether styled Whig or Tory or neither. A manager for either the king's administration or the opposition needed to win over this mass of backbenchers.[1]

Since no group could command a majority for any sustained period, the king's administrations were usually mixed, consisting of men from each party. Only rarely did one group predominate and then for only a short time. The abilities of individuals and the wishes of the monarch also mattered, for while the logic of the Revolution dictated the supremacy of Parliament, until this could be realized by organized, disciplined parties commanding parliamentary majorities, the monarchs were left with discretion in choosing and dismissing ministers of state. And instability in the upper levels of administration made consistency in forming and executing colonial policy uncertain, if not impossible. Financial exigency, the need to establish and maintain the credit of the government during the long war with France, forced William III in 1696 to accept members of the Whig junto, a group with friends among the directors of the Bank of England. In the autumn of 1697 the Whig lords demanded that if Charles Talbot, duke of Shrewsbury, was forced to leave office because of poor health, their colleague, Thomas, Baron Wharton, replace him as a principal secretary of state and that Charles Montagu be admitted to the cabinet. But Shrewsbury was prevailed upon to remain for a time, and when the other secretarial position fell vacant with the resignation of Sir William Trumbull, Shrewsbury's assistant, James Vernon, obtained the post. In 1699 with the government's credit restored and a new coinage in circulation, the lords of the Whig junto appeared dominant. John Somers, now a baron, became lord chancellor, and Admiral Edward Russell was raised to the peerage as earl of Orford. Montagu, who allies among the directors of the Bank of England had been granted a banking monopoly, became a ranking member of the Treasury board. Only Baron Wharton, personally distasteful to the king, was not rewarded. A colleague of the Whig lords, Richard Coote, earl of Bellomont, then presided over the governments of Massachusetts, New Hampshire, and New York.

William III would have preferred being free of any organized group, but he clung to the Whigs because they seemed more willing than any others to forward his program. But with their followers only a minority in the House of Commons they depended on Robert Harley for passage of money bills. The Whig junto and Shrewsbury soon came under attack when word arrived in London that Captain William Kidd, Bellomont's protégé from New York and the privateer they had sponsored in an expedition against pirates, had himself turned marauder. The king sought a ministry of competent men and moderates. He restored Sidney Godolphin to the Treasury but resisted accepting Tory extremists such as Laurence Hyde, earl of Rochester, and Sir Charles Hedges. Yet as attacks on the Whigs mounted in the House of Commons in 1700, William looked to the leaders of the Tories provided they could guarantee a stable administration. The Commons voted to impeach Somers, Orford, and Montagu, and in 1702, with the accession of Anne, the shift toward the Tories continued. Sir Charles Hedges and Daniel Finch, second earl of Nottingham, became principal secretaries of state. But the Tories too were divided, between moderates and High Tories. Despite the efforts of Godolphin and John Churchill, earl (and later duke) of Marlborough, to maintain a balance in a coalition ministry, the government became unsettled, with the Whigs supporting the war against France which had broken out in 1702 and demanding more places. They sought particularly to force the queen to accept Charles Spencer, third earl of Sunderland, as a secretary of state. Over the next few years they were able to place their followers in office as attorney general and solicitor general and as commissioners for trade and plantations. By the close of 1709 the lords of the Whig junto had completed their comeback, with Somers as lord president of the Council, Sunderland as secretary of state, Wharton as lord chancellor of Ireland, and Orford as first lord of the Admiralty, and had forced the removal of the last of the Tories. Yet they were dissatisfied, resenting the need for managers in the Commons and for intermediaries, Godolphin and Marlborough, between themselves and the queen. Personal animosities also played a role. Charles Montagu, not yet back in the cabinet, disliked Godolphin and coveted his post as lord treasurer, and Somers' relations with Marlborough had been strained ever since he and the chancellor, Lord Cowper, had scotched Marlborough's attempt to secure life tenure as captain general.[2]

Godolphin fell from power in August 1710 when Anne was persuaded to put the Treasury into commission with Robert Harley (later earl of Oxford) as chancellor of the Exchequer. That year the queen was also induced to dismiss the Whigs and to appoint William Legge, earl of Dartmouth, and Henry St. John (later Viscount Bolingbroke) to replace Sunderland and Henry Boyle as secretaries of state. Somers gave way to Rochester as president of the Council, and Cowper relinquished the Great Seal to Sir Simon Harcourt. Harley emerged as the dominant figure in the administration, closely challenged by St. John. He resisted bringing in Nottingham into the cabinet, but under pressure had Nottingham's indigent cousin, Charles Finch, earl of Winchilsea, appointed to the Commission for Trade and Plantations.

The Tories came to power in the midst of an acute financial panic with their position made all the more difficult by the hostility of the financial interests in the City of London, especially the Bank of England, controlled by Sir Gilbert Heathcote, brother of Caleb Heathcote of New York. However, some financiers—the New England–born Sir Stephen Evance and John Drummond, an investor in colonial trade — were ranged against the bank and the East India Company. With Oxford they hoped to create a rival financial base oriented toward commerce in the Western Hemisphere and to free the Tories from dependence on Whig-dominated institutions for public finance. By a statute enacted in 1711 the government's short-term creditors holding debts of almost £9 million were incorporated as a stock company trading to the South Seas with a monopoly on commerce with much of South America. The project depended, however, on compelling, either by force of arms or diplomacy, commercial concessions from the Spanish and French crowns.[3] Throughout these turbulent years the conduct of the war and the terms for ending the conflict were divisive party issues, as was the question of the national religious establishment and the position of Dissenters both in England and in America.

As a result of the Revolution of 1688 religious dissenters had won but few concessions, for the Act of Toleration had been passed in 1689 on the assumption that most of the Protestant Dissenters would return to the established church — one so modified as to allow all but a relatively few Protestants in England to return to the fold. The assumption proved false, as a band of determined Anglican clerics in convocation effectively resisted efforts to modify the doctrines and liturgy of the national church. A significant number of Protestants remained unreconciled. By the provisions of the Test and Corporation Acts passed during the reign of Charles II, any person appointed to office had to receive the sacrament of Holy Communion according to the rites of the Church of England and present a certificate from an officiating priest so testifying. Although these requirements were intended to reserve office for practicing Anglicans, some Dissenters evaded the intent by conforming occasionally, that is, by taking the sacrament in the established church once a year to obtain the requisite certificate. In 1702 and 1704 bills against this practice were introduced into Parliament under the auspices of Rochester and Nottingham, but failed to pass.

In America, in the colonies initially established as proprietary ventures, tension between religious sects — as between Anglicans and Dissenters in South Carolina, or Quakers and Anglicans in North Carolina and on the Delaware — also prevailed. Protagonists would appeal to their co-religionists in England. For example, Dissenters in South Carolina, faced with a provincial law to establish the Church of England, dispatched John Ash and Joseph Boone to London, where they engaged the services of Daniel Defoe. His pamphlet, published in 1705, was based entirely on *ex parte* statements by the Carolina Dissenters and was calculated to appeal to partisan sentiment generally in England and particularly in the House of Lords.[4]

The English authorities had never clearly settled the status of the Church of England in America nor the authority of the bishop of London over the clergy in the plantations. Henry Compton, bishop of London, had claimed jurisdiction, but by the turn of the century had succeeded only in sending over a few commissaries — James Blair to Virginia, Thomas Bray to Maryland, and George Keith, a convert from Quakerism, to the Delaware communities. Several laymen in America, some governors among them—Francis Nicholson, Benjamin Fletcher, Caleb Heathcote, Lewis Morris, and Joseph Dudley—promoted the cause of Anglicanism in the colonies. Through the society for the Propagation of the Gospel, organized at the turn of the century, Anglicans sought to further their cause. John Talbot, a minister who served in Virginia before settling in Burlington, New Jersey, among others, urged upon the secretary of the SPG the appointment of a suffragan for America.[5] In response to these solicitations the SPG in 1704 presented a case for the law officers of the crown on consecrating suffragans in the overseas plantations. A convocation of more than a dozen Anglican clerics in the middle colonies supported the proposition. No action followed, but as late as 1709 rumor had it in America that Dean Jonathan Swift, the Tory writer, was under consideration. Swift may have had some interest, but John Sharp, archbishop of York, persuaded the queen not to grant him preferment.[6] Francis Nicholson, who had served as governor in several of the colonies, continued to push the issue, as did Bishop Compton with the newly appointed Tory secretary of state, the earl of Dartmouth. Compton also forwarded to the queen a petition from seventeen missionaries of the SPG asking for a bishop to confirm communicants baptized in the church, to ordain ministers, to consecrate churches, and to oversee, govern, and direct them in the instruction of the "ignorant" and to recover those "seduced" from Anglicanism. In 1712, on the motion of the earl of Clarendon, a former governor of New York, the SPG presented a bill to be brought into Parliament, but Sharp of York, to whom the matter was referred, failed to pursue it.[7] That same year Anglicanism infected Puritan Massachusetts. A discontented minority of the congregation in Newbury was induced to declare that they would no longer persist with their mistaken brethren in the separation from the Church of England. Compton took up their cause.[8]

Despite gains in the colonies the episcopal bench was divided on appointing prelates for the plantations. Winchester and London, joined by the earl of Clarendon, solicited the queen to send bishops across the Atlantic to Barbados, the Leeward Islands, Jamaica, and Burlington and Williamsburg in North America, there to convert the infidels and better regulate "such Christians in their faith" and practice "as are already Converted thereto." But as Clarendon reported to the SPG, Anne would not commit herself. Although pressed by others on the episcopal bench Archibishop Sharp too held out, apprehensive that the leading men in the SPG had been "much imposed" on by the clamors of some "indiscrete missionaries abroad."[9]

By the second decade of the eighteenth century relations between church and state had become an explosive political issue in England, one colonials followed closely, as the more extreme Tories and High Church adherents pressed their attack against occasional conformity. When the Whigs made an ill-advised attempt to prosecute Henry Sacheverall for an intemperate speech attacking Dissenters, they presented the High Churchmen with a public cause. As a consequence, the House of Commons returned in the general election of November 1710 contained backbenchers zealous for Anglicanism; Nottingham's Occasional Conformity bill became law the next year. Prosecutions under the act were rare, however. On the advice of Oxford, Anne appointed to the episcopal bench men of moderate Tory persuasions. Francis Atterbury, bishop of Rochester, then broke with Oxford, the lord treasurer, and with the support of Henry St. John, now Viscount Bolingbroke, pressed in Parliament for a schism bill. Passed by both houses in a demonstration of religious zeal the measure barred any person from teaching without signing a declaration of conformity and obtaining a license from the bishop of his diocese, a permit he could not secure unless he could produce a certificate that in the previous year he had received the sacrament according to the rites of the Church of England. Bolingbroke and the High Tories seemed triumphant. On 27 July 1714 the queen dismissed Oxford, but the victory of the Tory extremists was short-lived, for on 4 August Anne died. With the accession of the elector of Hanover as George I, the Whigs dominated the administration and proscribed many of their opponents as Jacobites.[10]

Continuous party strife and the resulting turnover in ministries had made it difficult to devise and implement a consistent policy for the overseas plantations. Among the higher officers of state, the secretaries' offices and the Commission for Trade and Plantations, commonly called the Board of Trade, were particularly affected.

The reigns of the last Stuart monarchs witnessed a shift in the highest level of governmental administration, as work done formerly by the large, unwieldy Privy Council now fell to the purview of the cabinet, or as they were formally known, the Lords of the Committee of the Council. The full council was becoming a body whose function was merely to ratify reports and sanction decisions made by departmental boards or other officers of state. The Lords of the Committee—the cabinet when they met in the presence of the monarch—included as a matter of course certain ranking ministers and, as the occasion warranted, other officials of sufficient political influence.[11] During the reign of William III when the king was absent from England, the leading members of the administration sitting as the Lords Justices in Council presided over the government.

Almost all decisions made at the uppermost level of government were translated into action by orders passing through the principal secretaries of state. They authenticated almost all patents, orders, proclamations, and warrants. Through their offices passed all petitions, letters, and information to the monarch. In Anne's time the only other minister normally to manage his department directly with the monarch was Godolphin, but the lord treasurer's position was exceptional. Control over foreign affairs—including the overseas plantations—also fell to the two principal secretaries of state. By 1689 the northern department of the secretariat had jurisdiction over relations with Russia, the Baltic and Scandanavian states, and Germany; the southern, over those with the rest of Europe, Ireland, and the overseas colonies. Initially the southern department was senior, but as the diplomatic balance shifted, the positions of the two departments changed. When Sophia, electress of Hanover, became the heir designate to the throne of Britain in 1701, German affairs became more important, but only after 1714 did the northern department definitely become the senior of the two divisions. Until 1706 a newly appointed secretary ordinarily occupied the northern post while the more experienced minister transferred to the southern.[12]

William III, personally involved in leading a European coalition against Louis XIV, had insisted on keeping control of diplomatic affairs in his own hands and, for a time, had allowed one secretary's office to lie vacant. Often he appointed lesser men, bureaucrats concerned merely with implementing rather than formulating decisions. In the later years of the reign the duke of Shrewsbury had the southern department, and his undersecretary, James Vernon, the northern. But as Shrewsbury was often ill and absent from London, Vernon, a minor political figure, in effect presided over both departments of the secretariat.[13]

The practice of appointing a ranking peer to the senior department and a political and social inferior to handle routine administration through the other office continued under Anne. In 1702 the earl of Nottingham and Sir Charles Hedges became the principal secretaries. Nottingham insisted on controlling colonial affairs, as did the third earl of Sunderland, the Whig appointed to the southern department late in 1706. For example, Sunderland sharply reprimanded the commissioners for plantation affairs for presenting to the queen a recommendation without consulting him.[14] Sustained political warfare resulted in an unstable bureaucracy. Sunderland's dismissal from office in 1710 marked the decline of the Junto. Henry Boyle, who had replaced Robert Harley, resigned the northern department in September 1710. The Tories Henry St. John (created Viscount Bolingbroke in 1712) and William Legge, earl of Dartmouth, then took over the secretariat until the Whigs swept all before them at the accession of the Hanoverian elector in September 1714, when Charles Townshend and James Stanhope came into office, the former for the northern department, now the more important of the two.

Little continuity in administration existed, as instability extended to the undersecretaries of state, the men responsible for carrying on the day-to-day routine. They generally came and went with their patrons. The positions of undersecretary and clerk of the council were posts of patronage, contended for as prizes in the partisan struggle for office.[15]

For a time the Treasury became important in the administration of plantation affairs because of the powerful position enjoyed by Sidney Godolphin when he became lord treasurer in 1702. Hitherto the Treasury had had only a marginal role in the machinery of colonial administration. Having served for many years as a member of the Treasury commission, Godolphin, once he became lord treasurer, moved quickly to expand his powers over colonial affairs. By his orders whenever any doubt in point of law arose before the Council for Trade and Plantations, the solicitor for the Treasury was to be called in to advise on the matter.[16] Godolphin's power was political as well as institutional. As the queen's adviser—at least until 1711—he had a voice in appointments to the Commission for Trade and Plantations; and as the confidant and ally of the duke of Marlborough, after 1704 he guarded closely the captain general's claim to nominate colonial governors against the pretensions of party chieftans. Marlborough jealously reserved governorships as rewards for army subordinates he thought deserving. When vacancies appeared imminent in South Carolina, Maryland, and Virginia, Godolphin assured Marlborough that the queen would be careful not to let the duke of Newcastle "or anybody else make you uneasy about governments."[17]

Particularly vulnerable to the vicissitudes of politics were the Commissioners for Trade and Plantation, advisers to the crown on matters of commerce and overseas colonies. The Board of Trade, as the commission was commonly called, was misnamed, for its records reveal clearly that its attention was devoted primarily to plantation affairs, not trade. Created by royal commission in 1696, the board constituted an effort by William III and, ironically, his Whig ministers to prevent members in the House of Commons indignant over the ruinous state of trade and the failure of the administration adequately to protect overseas commerce from establishing a council independent of royal control. After its creation the board was subject to frequent parliamentary criticism. As late as the summer of 1701, one commissioner, the diplomat George Stepney, reported to a colleague his relief that the board had managed to survive another parliamentary session. As a junior board with little support and an uncertain future, the Commission for Trade and Plantations had little attraction for ambitious men. During the interlude between the wars with France, it served as a convenient, lucrative abode for members of the diplomatic corps. George Stepney, envoy to Berlin and Vienna, was content with the post, but John Methuen, the veteran diplomat who represented William III in Portugal, preferred bigger game.[18]

The peers who served on the first board appointed in 1696 soon departed for more prestigious posts—the Admiralty and the Treasury. During the initial years of the board William Blathwayt, a long-time clerk and secretary to the Privy Council's committee for plantation affairs, served as a commissioner, but his tenure was interrupted by trips to Holland when he served as secretary to the king. With the accession of Anne in 1702 Nottingham became secretary for the southern department on condition that both his kinsman, Thomas Thynne, Viscount Weymouth, and Dartmouth go to the Board of Trade. For a time Godolphin restrained Nottingham's hunger for patronage and protected the other commissioners. When Nottingham departed in 1704, Weymouth too left office. Although Dartmouth remained for some time, he did not often attend meetings of the board. Until 1707 William Blathwayt, John Pollexfen, and Sir Philip Meadows as commissioners and William Popple as secretary provided some continuity and experience on the board, although Weymouth had objected in 1702 to the continuation in office of six of the commissioners, particularly Pollexfen.[19] Popple—an old Whig, an associate of William Penn, and a known opponent of the Church of England—finally resigned in 1707 because of age and infirmity, but not before securing the secretary's post for his son, William Popple, Jr.

That year the Board of Trade and Plantations again became a bone of contention as Marlborough and Godolphin jousted with Sunderland, one of the lords of the Whig junto, for control of the commission. In April Robert Cecil, John Pollexfen, Matthew Prior, and William Blathwayt all left the Plantation Office, Cecil's departure being the least significant, Blathwayt's the most. He had been the most experienced and the best informed commissioner on plantation affairs. His friend Stepney died a few months later. Only Sir Philip Meadows and Dartmouth remained, but the Tory peer never made policy, even as presiding officer. William Byrd of Virginia was registering more than a sycophant's note when he wrote Blathwayt of his great regret at the commissioner's dismissal: "The plantations I'm afraid will have cause to lament your absense from the board."[20] The new appointments were not distinguished. Henry Herbert, Baron Herbert, an impecunious Whig noble, and Robert Monckton owed their nominations to the duke of Newcastle. John Pulteney was a Whig M.P. connected with Sunderland, and Sir Charles Turner, a member of a leading Norfolk family, was Robert Walpole's brother-in-law. These appointments were made to secure parliamentary votes, not to add to the efficiency or competency of the Plantation Office.

The majority of commissioners who sat on the Board of Trade and Plantations after 1707 were politicians who had little intention of burdening themselves with daily business. Attendance fell off sharply. For several months in 1709 the board failed to act on several matters referred to it by the Privy Council. Sunderland had to order the commissioners to take turns in attending to their private affairs so as to have a sufficient number present for a quorum. Nonetheless, on several occasions Meadows presided with only a single other member of the board attending.[21] Politics took its toll again in 1710. Within two weeks after Henry St. John received the seals of office for the northern department, his friend Arthur Moore, an ingenious financial manipulator, came to the Board of Trade. The next year Francis Gwyn and Winchilsea, now under a fresh commission, joined the Plantation Office, but the indigent peer, a cousin of Nottingham who had served as envoy to Hanover, took the post reluctantly; it was inferior in both profit and honor to his previous employment. He demanded an advance of £1,000 on his salary. The impecunious earl did not have to suffer long. He died in August 1712. Harley, now earl of Oxford, yielded to Tory pressure and removed the last of the Whigs. Named in their place were Thomas Foley, Francis North, second Baron Guilford, and the Jacobite John Hynde Cotton. Tory followers of Oxford and St. John now staffed the Plantation Office.[22] Bolingbroke seemingly prevailed as Oxford's appointees gave way to the nominees of the aggressive secretary of state: Samuel Pytts, a shareholder in the United East India Company and the South Sea Company; Thomas Vernon, a trader to the Levant and a director of the South Sea Company; and John Sharp, son of the archbishop of York and a member of Parliament for Ripon. The ascendancy of the Tories was short-lived. With the accession of the elector of Hanover the Whigs swept their rivals from office. Under Townshend and Stanhope, the two principal secretaries of state, the board for plantation affairs underwent another thorough purge.

Such repeated changes in personnel and the lack of experienced and informed members meant the board provided little to the administration of the colonies. At times the Plantation Office was hard-pressed with other work. Occupied with various proposed treaties of commerce and requests for the state of trade, late in 1714 the newly appointed commissioners had had little time for colonial business. As Townshend informed a harrassed Robert Hunter, governor of New York, the newly appointed commission was in no position to consider the state of the North American colonies.[23]

Poor communications constituted a further handicap, particularly in time of war. Travel across the Atlantic was slow and uncertain. At the outbreak of hostilities with France in 1702 the secretary to the Admiralty board had been forced to confess to being at a loss as to how to send dispatches to the governors in America and the West Indies. No vessel was scheduled to leave at that time.

CHAPTER 2

International War and Anglo-Colonial
Political Relations

ENGLAND AND HER overseas colonies were at war with France for twenty-one of the twenty-five years of the reigns of the last two Stuart monarchs. Sustained, widespread conflict threatened the role of the mother country as the commercial entrepôt and jeopardized the authority of the governors sent out by the crown to preside over the plantations, for war provided leaders in elected assemblies in America with an opportunity to further their claims and to enhance their power in the critical sphere of finance, and thus to lay the foundation for the growth of provincial autonomy.

For decades the requirements of the parliamentary navigation code had proved a source of tension and controversy between royal officials and trading interests in the colonies as well as in England. Englishmen within and without the realm did not hold the authority of the state as sacrosanct; petty smuggling was rampant. The great attention paid to violations of the acts of trade could have created the impression that the code was entirely inappropriate for the American economy and reflected merely the needs of the English mercantile and manufacturing communities as against the interests of the colonies. Actually the great bulk of American overseas commerce was conducted within the provisions of the navigation code. English merchants, shippers, and importers were themselves not averse to smuggling or otherwise violating the provisions of the laws if such activities were sufficiently remunerative. English as well as provincial ship captains, for example, engaged in illicit trade with foreigners in the Newfoundland fishery and ran tobacco and other goods from the Isle of Man to out-of-the-way harbors in England, Ireland, and Scotland to avoid paying customs duties.[1] Some offenses consisted of traffic prohibited during war but legal in time of peace. London merchants sent tobacco to France under cover of trade to the Mediterranean and shippers in the English West Indies and mainland colonies supplied provisions to the French enemy in the Antilles. The English code required certain products of the colonies—enumerated produce such as sugar and tobacco—to be carried from America through the English entropôt, where duties were collected and stipulated that European manufactures be shipped through English ports to the colonies. This traffic had to be conducted in vessels owned and manned predominately by English subjects. Until the Union of England and

Scotland in 1707 Scots were allowed as merchants in the colonies, but Scottish ships could not legally carry enumerated commodities across the Atlantic—a prohibition much ignored in the Delaware River ports—nor could Scottish ports receive them directly from America. Even a vessel properly owned, captained, and manned might fall into the clutches of customs officials if it lacked proper papers. The galley *Cole and Bean* of London fell afoul of the authorities and had her cargo condemned in the Court of Vice-Admiralty in Carolina for having improper registration. The owners and shippers in England had to appeal to the Privy Council for relief.[2] Trafficking with pirates was illegal, as was trading to regions such as the East Indies reserved to chartered monopolies. Nonetheless, merchants in New York established a small but lucrative trade with buccaneers based at Madagascar who preyed on commerce in the Red Sea and in the Indian Ocean, much to the anger of the officials of the East India Company and the eastern potentates with whom they were allied.

The paucity of records makes it difficult to estimate the extent of this illicit trade, particularly in the Newfoundland fishery, where no officials resided and where shippers exchanged tobacco and other colonial produce for European manufacturers.

In the last years of the seventeenth century the English government imposed elaborate procedures to enforce the code on foreign and colonial commerce. The Act for Preventing Frauds and Regulating the Plantation Trade (1696) charged governors in the colonies specifically with the responsibility for enforcing the acts of trade and allowed for courts of vice-admiralty staffed by judges, registrars, advocates, and marshalls. Yet the ambiguous wording of this statute made it possible for violations of the navigation code to be tried in the common law courts of the colonies, where verdicts were rendered by juries often sympathetic to the accused. The proprietors of several of the chartered colonies—the Carolinas, Pennsylvania, and the Jerseys—as well as elected officials of Connecticut, fearing that new officials not responsible to them would exercise power, asked that governors appointed by the proprietors receive commissions of admiralty comparable to those held by their counterparts in the royal provinces. Naval officers appointed by them had the responsibility of recording the bonds required for vessels to load enumerated produce and the certificates for entering and clearing ships.

These new procedures and requirements notwithstanding, reports continued to reach the Customs House in London of widespread violations of the acts of trade and navigation. The governors and naval officers appointed by them were not fulfilling their duty. In attempting to enforce the laws in admiralty courts, customs officials in America found themselves charged in the common law courts of some provinces. At times, royal officials in America, antagonistic to each other, worked at cross-purposes. Robert Quary, the surveyor general of the customs for the southern district, complained of the obstructionist tactic employed by Roger Mompesson, judge of the admiralty court with jurisdiction in the middle colonies but an associate of William Penn.[3] Even at the close of the Stuart era reports indicated the provincial governors were still not enforcing the laws, while judges in the local courts of New England were yet granting "prohibitions" against officers of the vice-admiralty courts.[4]

Although the enforcement of the navigation code and the collection of customs duties left much to be desired in the provinces where governors commissioned by the crown presided, the Commissioners of Trade and Plantations consistently attacked the chartered colonies, the corporations of Connecticut and Rhode Island, as well as the proprietaries of East and West New Jersey, the Carolinas, Pennsylvania, and the lower counties on the Delaware River, the property of William Penn. In these governments the crown did not appoint the chief executive. Responding to complaints by officials of the Customs establishment, the House of Lords in 1697 had insisted that governors in the chartered colonies assume the same legal and financial obligations to enforce the acts of trade as did the royal appointees.

The legal status of the colonies differed, however; some were clouded. The proprietors of the Jerseys had never received a royal charter. The crown later merged the two divisions and assumed control of the government. In New Hampshire, a royal executive presided over the government, and a proprietor claimed the right to the soil and, at times, the title of governor. Under the charter granted for Massachusetts Bay in 1691 the crown appointed the governor. Connecticut and Rhode Island still enjoyed their original charters. Pennsylvania and the lower counties on the Delaware were the propriety of William Penn, and the Carolinas, of a board resident in England. In 1690 the crown had assumed for the time being the right to name the governor and councilors of Maryland, a colony still the property of Baron Baltimore under a charter granted in 1632. The remaining colonies, Virginia and New York, were royal provinces. For a time during the reign of William III, William Penn too had lost the right to name the governor and councilors of Pennsylvania, and as late as 1697 crown officials had warned that failure to enforce the acts of trade in Pennsylvania and the lower counties might result in forfeiture of the charter.[5] Yet the ministers of state failed to carry out this threat.

During the first years of the eighteenth century the Commissioners of Trade and Plantations sought to have Parliament by law annex all of the chartered colonies to the crown. The commissioners were in a weak position, however. Neither the higher ministers of state nor the Lords and Commons held the matter in great importance; other issues — the potential conflict with France and the impeachment of the Whig lords, for example — loomed larger. Despite the charge by Penn that Anglican zealots were behind the move, the issue of the charters did not reflect religious or party divisions.[6] The Commission for Trade and Plantations, newly founded by the administration just a few short years before to head off parliamentary discontent over the state of trade, was but a junior board with little prestige or influence. Whether staffed by Whigs or Tories the board received support neither from the administration nor from the Parliament in its quest. Following the establishment of the body, both houses of Parliament routinely had required reports from the commissioners as to their success in furthering English trade. In March 1700 and again twelve months later the commissioners had condemned the chartered governments for failing to enforce the acts of trade and for condoning breaches of the code. In 1701 they went further, charging the chartered governments with assuming for themselves power to make laws contrary to those of England and directly prejudicial to the trade of the mother country. Some provincial governments had refused to submit their laws to England for review; others reported them imperfectly; while some denied appeals from their courts to the king in council, thus depriving the king's subjects there of the privilege enjoyed by others residing in the royal colonies. Aggrieved parties were left without remedy from arbitrary and illegal proceedings of the courts established under proprietary and corporate authority. Nor had these "independent" colonies, as distinct from those immediately under the king, proved capable of defending themselves from foreign enemies. Their ill-equipped and poorly trained militia were in a state of confusion, indeed, of anarchy. For these reasons the Commissioners of Trade proposed that Parliament take up the charters but without prejudice to any man's property or freehold.[7]

At the time of the board's attack William Penn was in America. Through his son, William, he managed to have a bill to vacate the charters that had been introduced in the spring of 1701 put off until the next Parliamentary session. With the aid of a Quaker lobby in London, he then orchestrated an elaborate campaign among two dozen politicians, nobles and commoners, Whigs and Tories, to block any action as detrimental to the political and religious interests and the rights in property of the proprietors. Later that year he left America for England to conduct the campaign himself. The ubiquitous Penn had extensive connections within a wide circle of politicians, including Robert Harley, then Speaker of the House of Commons, and Sidney Godolphin. Not long after, it was known among the bureaucrats that Penn "had the favor of my Lord Treasurer."[8]

In February 1702 the Commissioners of Trade and Plantations returned to the attack. In reports to both houses of Parliament, Stamford, Meadows, Blathwayt, Pollexfen, and Matthew Prior once more urged the assumption of the provincial charters. During lengthy, extended testimony Penn contested the issue with them, but the Board of Trade simply could not marshall enough support for a bill. More dramatic events soon occupied the attention of men of affairs. William III died the next month, and Anne succeeded to the throne. A declaration of war against France followed when Louis XIV recognized the Pretender, James, as king of England. Anticipating another attempt by the Board of Trade, lobbyists for several of the chartered colonies — William Wharton of New England, now a solicitor in London, Governor Fitzjohn Winthrop of Connecticut, Penn, and the proprietors of the Carolinas — began to organize.[9] Again the press of other parliamentary business prevented any action on the charters. By January 1703 the commissioners for plantation affairs had given up any hope of action that parliamentary session. Another year passed and still Parliament did not act, although much to Penn's chagrin, the British-based proprietors of the Jerseys had decided not to contest with the crown over the government of their proprietary.

At the end of 1703 the Plantation Office again took up the issue, but concentrated its attack on a single colony, the corporation of Rhode Island, a provincial regime which had established its own court of admiralty. Unhappily for the commissioners for plantation affairs the attorney general, Edward Northey, concluded that no sufficient cause to prosecute the charter existed, inasmuch as the statute of Rhode Island establishing the court was provisional, pending a determination by the crown. However, should the authorities in Rhode Island persist, the passage of similar acts in the future would be grounds for rendering their charter void.[10] Notwithstanding the repeated failure of the Plantation Office, spokesmen for the chartered colonies remained active. Penn insisted with the Speaker of the House of Commons that these provinces were better behaved than were the royal colonies; petty bureaucrats and other "turbulent persons" in America had misrepresented the situation.[11]

Rather than moving precipitously and arbitrarily on the complaints against Rhode Island and Connecticut, the queen in council on the advice of the law officers of the crown offered agents for the two corporations an opportunity to answer the charges. Sir Henry Ashurst, a dissenting merchant and Whig politician of London representing the regime at Hartford, then undertook a campaign of procrastination and evasion. Ironically, among those in England complaining against the regime in Connecticut were Quakers. Although Pennsylvania was not then under attack, Penn believed a threat still existed against all chartered governments. Pessimistic of the outcome and unhappy with the opposition to him in Philadelphia, he was negotiating with the crown to relinquish the government of his colony. Over the next few years the sum of money he demanded and the conditions he proposed to safeguard the privileges of the Friends proved stumbling blocks.[12]

By the close of 1705 the Board of Trade had a stronger case, complaints having arrived from inhabitants in the Carolinas against their proprietors. The following January the commissioners for plantation affairs represented that the proprietary and chartered colonies in no way had merited the privileges and immunities granted them. They had not conformed to the various parliamentary acts of trade and had assumed for themselves powers of making laws contrary to those of England and directly prejudicial to legal commerce; they had denied the queen's subjects the benefit of appeals to the crown and had been notoriously remiss in contributing to the common defense. They ought to be reunited to the crown. On 7 February the queen in council referred this report to Parliament, the matters therein contained ostensibly being thought proper for the consideration of the Lords and Commons. A week later the lower house granted Secretary Hedges and Blathwayt leave to bring in a bill for the better regulation of the corporate and proprietary governments, the chartered colonies. Presented on 23 February, the measure was the work of the attorney general, Hedges's office, and the Commissioners for Trade and Plantations. New Jersey and the three lower counties were not mentioned, for the proprietors of the first had capitulated to the crown and the ministry had not recognized Penn's title to the lower Delaware counties. The proposed bill would grant to the queen the power of government in Massachusetts, Connecticut, Rhode Island, Pennsylvania, Maryland, the Carolinas, and the Bahamas, and authority to appoint governors, councilors, judges, and all officials for the administration of justice, any charters previously granted notwithstanding. Laws then in force and approved by the crown would remain in force; all future laws would be made by an assembly with the consent of a governor appointed by the crown and with appeals from the provincial courts to the crown allowed.[13]

The bill for the resumption of the provincial charters failed to pass. On the motion to read a second time, a thinly attended House of Commons rejected the measure. Ashurst claimed credit through his influence with the leading men in the house.

Apparently loathe to learn the lesson, the Commissioners for Trade and Plantations persisted. The annual request in 1707 for a report on the state of the nation's commerce gave them another opportunity. In the long report submitted to the House of Commons on 19 November they again cited complaints from the governors of New York and Massachusetts on the failure of Connecticut and Rhode Island to prove military assistance. The two corporate provinces were a refuge for deserting sailors and militiamen. Precedent existed for the crown to assume the governments of the chartered colonies without recourse to Parliament or even to the courts. Lord Baltimore and, for a time, William Penn had lost the power to appoint officials through default, neglect in protecting the inhabitants of Maryland and Pennsylvania in time of danger. As recently as 1704 Attorney General Edward Northey and Solicitor General Simon Harcourt had concurred in this judgment, a proposition advanced to the crown more than a decade before by Lord Chief Justice John Holt. The Commissioners of Trade and Plantations pressed the same argument in a report submitted nine days later to the House of Lords. Apparently it impressed some peers. Early in January 1708 the Lords requested the Board of Trade and the law officers to present their charges,[14] but again the matter was allowed to lapse.

As long as Parliament did not act, the administration would do nothing. In commenting to the Plantation Office on laws enacted in the chartered colonies, Edward Northey in 1714 remonstrated that the proprietors and corporations had a power vested in them by charter to make laws. They could not be put under any restraints other than those specified in the patents, but by an act of Parliament.

Except for the charter to Penn—and his health hindered concluding an agreement to give up the patent—the charters to the corporations did not require provincial officials to submit their laws to the crown for approval. Such a requirement must come through an act of Parliament. [15]

Across the Atlantic, too, men were unhappy with the corporations. Caleb Heathcote—merchant, Anglican communicant, councilor of New York, and brother to the great London financier—had complained to Lord Treasurer Oxford that "one of the greatest mischiefs which attends America . . . is the many little charter Governments." With the war against France coming to an end, parliament ought to act, "for they are so vain and great in their little commonwealths" as to make laws without any regard to their being repugnant to the laws of England. Heathcote cited Connecticut specifically for discriminating against Anglicans and for imposing fines on persons attending any but an established Congregational church. [16]

The reign of the Stuarts came to an end without action by Parliament to take up the charters of the proprietary and corporate colonies, to bring them directly under the crown. Indeed, in 1715 the Hanoverian administration returned to the proprietor of Maryland the authority to appoint a governor and council. The last attempt in Parliament to vacate the patents came in the summer of 1715 in response to a plea from an agent of South Carolina and from London merchants trading to Charles Town. With the inhabitants facing an Indian uprising their agent proposed that in exchange for military assistance from the crown the charter be surrendered. But the Carolina proprietors claimed that several of their number were minors and thus could not legally act. A bill to take up the charters was brought into the Commons in August but did not survive the opposition of the proprietors, particularly the strong objections of the influential John Granville (Lord Carteret), or those of Jeremiah Dummer, agent for Massachusetts and Connecticut; Richard Partridge, agent for Rhode Island; and several Quaker merchants of London, trustees for William Penn's mortgaged holdings in America. [17]

An act of Parliament taking up the charters would not have substantially increased the authority of the crown in the proprietary and corporate colonies or made for more effective control by the royal administration. For decades bureaucrats and ministers of state had held it as an article of faith that the means to render the foreign plantations dependent on the crown was to have an executive appointed and instructed from England preside over the provincial governments. Past experience in the royal colonies had not borne out this assumption; neither would future developments.

During the later years of the reign of William III the crown attempted to tighten its control over the administration of government in the colonies. In 1699 an order had gone out to eliminate absentee office-holding by officials holding patents from the crown. At times men appointed to posts in the colonies remained in England and drew their salaries while allowing a deputy in the province to

execute the duties of their office—and underpaid deputies sometimes succumbed to the temptation of bribes. This regulation, like others, some governors
failed to enforce.[18]

For several years during the reign of Anne, the choice of governors for the
royal provinces was limited; nominations were the prerogative of the duke of
Marlborough, the ally of Lord Treasurer Godolphin. His duchess was the confidante of the queen. The captain general jealously guarded these posts, reserving
them for officers who had served under him in the campaigns in Europe. William
Byrd once sought to procure the post of deputy to the absentee governor of Virginia, George Hamilton, earl of Orkney, a favorite general of Marlborough. An
agent for the Virginian soon disabused him of the notion: Marlborough had declared that "no one but soldiers should have the government of a plantation."[19]
Even before the rise of Marlborough, William III had thought it essential to have
capable, experienced military officers to preside over the governments in North
America and the West Indies because of the chronic threat from the French and
hostile Indians.

Through commissions, instructions, and circulars dispatched to the governors, Whitehall sought to determine policy. The king's representative, the
councilors, and other officials appointed by the crown were required to take an
oath to enforce the parliamentary statutes relating to the colonies and to overseas
trade. At times the administration found it necessary to admonish the provincial
councilors; absence from the board might prevent a quorum for the conduct of
business. Willful or continued absence by an individual might lead to his suspen-
sion or dismissal. In the case of the death of a governor or his deputy the senior
resident councilor presided over the board; as it happened, for extended periods
of time in some colonies no governor resided, much to the detriment of royal
authority. Four years passed in Williamsburg without the appearance of a governor or deputy appointed from England. The crown generally filled vacancies on
the council board from the more prominent men in provincial society on the
recommendation of the governor, but at times councilors so commissioned
clashed with the chief executive to whom they owed their places. By virtue of
their offices, collectors and surveyors of the customs in a colony often had seats
on the provincial boards, but their votes were not decisive.

Whatever had been the inclination of James II before the Revolution of 1688
to govern America without representative assemblies—a view shared by only a
very few of his ministers[20]—after 1689 the commissions and instructions issued
to governors contained a provision for calling elected assemblies to enact laws
with the consent of the upper house—boards appointed in all the colonies except
Rhode Island, Connecticut, and Massachusetts—and the governor. Through
these instructions Whitehall sought to control the content of provincial laws.
Governors had orders not to assent to bills of an unusual nature or to measures
thought contrary to the prerogative of the crown or injurious to the interests of
inhabitants (often merchants) of England.

Despite these injunctions governors were frequently remiss in following instructions or failed to foresee that Whitehall would find the laws they signed objectionable. At times they even failed to transmit laws to London for review.

The colonial laws that were transmitted to Whitehall for review were sometimes disallowed by the king or queen in council if thought objectionable after reference to an appropriate legal officer or administrative board. In 1709 the queen in council rejected an act passed in New Jersey for regulating Negro, mulatto, and Indian slaves on the ground that the harsh punishments prescribed in the provincial statute were such as had never been known in the laws of England. When recommending disallowance the Commissioners of Trade had protested that the colonial statute inflicted inhumane punishment.[21] To circumvent royal disallowance a provincial legislature could enact laws to run for a limited period of time and then, before they were scheduled to be sent for review, renew them as "new" laws. To guard against this practice Whitehall instructed governors to see that certain types of laws contained clauses suspending their operation until approved by the crown or required that they take care against extraordinary bills, undesirable measures not foreseen when a governor received his instructions. The Commissioners of Trade regretted that they could not so instruct governors of the proprietaries and corporations, protected as they were by the charters. And only Parliament could rescind that privilege.[22]

Throughout the reigns of the last two Stuarts the ability of the crown to govern in America was also hindered by poor communications. By 1703 a regular packet service had been established between England and the West Indies, but not with North America. Nothing came of a proposal advanced by the tobacco merchant Jeffrey Jeffreys to establish regular sailings between New York and the Isle of Wight.[23] Only the proprietor of Pennsylvania was required by charter to maintain an agent in England to answer for the administration of his colony. Branches of government in the other provinces—the council, the assembly, the governor, or any combination of them—maintained agents, but only on an *ad hoc* basis. As the Commissioners of Trade and Plantations complained to the attorney general in 1703, very seldom did agents appear at the Plantation Office when laws enacted by their assemblies were under consideration, unless in relation to some private matter.[24]

The ability of ministers of state in Whitehall to control the courts and the administration of justice in the colonies through royal governors was also limited. English officials were at times unhappy with the competency of men professing law and occupying the judicial benches in America. In their view the colonies attracted few competent lawyers; most, they thought, were clerks and "other such small dealers" in the law from England. The paltry salaries and skimpy fees allowed by the provincial governments offered little incentive. Not only were judicial offices of little profit, but tenure was precarious. In order better to decide on appeals from the provincial courts, the lords justices in council in 1700 ordered an account sent from each colony of the procedures used in various legal actions. Yet complaints continued to come in of great delays and irregularities in the provincial courts. In 1713 a sharp reprimand went out to the governors for allowing prisoners accused of crimes to be sent to Britain without any evidence as to their guilt.[25]

The most glaring defect in the procedures for controlling America from London lay in the failure adequately to finance the civil and judicial establishments and to provide funds for military operations in America against French, Indians, and Spanish, independently of the provincial assemblies. The governors of New York repeatedly had to borrow money from private persons to help finance the defense of the colony. One such creditor, Robert Livingston, on more than one occasion traveled to London seeking reimbursement. In 1705 he complained, "It's a miserable thing to solicit ye Treasury for money at this juncture."[26] With royal governments suffering from mounting debts, the keys to the exchequer were closely guarded. More than any other man, William Blathwayt knew how troublesome was the problem of financing English military needs in America. For years he had served as clerk of the committee of the Privy Council charged with colonial affairs, as auditor for the plantation revenue, and as secretary at war. More recently he had functioned as an unofficial secretary of state when he accompanied William III on annual campaigns in Europe during the War of the League of Augsburg. In America too war had raged between the French supported by Indian allies and the English of New York and New England. But Blathwayt's concerns were more with holding down expenditures than with expanding empire in America, much to the chagrin of the earl of Bellomont, the peer sent out as governor of New York, New Hampshire, and Massachusetts during a lull in the hostilities following the Peace of Ryswyck. Saddled with the responsibility of presiding over the three provinces expected to carry the brunt of the war against the French and Indians, Bellomont complained bitterly against Blathwayt, whom he blamed for reducing the already depleted number of English soldiers on the northern frontier from 400 to 200 men. The four companies of troops, nominally set at 100 soldiers each, never had more than 75 effectives. Death and desertion had reduced the total to fewer than 200 troops. By a new establishment for which Bellomont held Blathwayt responsible each company was allowed only 50 men.[27]

William III and the Whig ministers of state who served both him and Anne generally saw Europe rather than America as the critical arena in the war with France. Consequently, except for one ill-fated expedition against Quebec, launched in 1711 by a Tory ministry, the English administrations committed the great bulk of English troops and resources to campaigns in Europe, relying on the great numerical superiority of the English colonists in North America to ensure victory over the Canadians and their Indian allies.

The division of the English into a dozen discrete provinces posed a near insuperable problem in coordinating the common effort in North America, particularly since there was little sense of commitment to the larger community.

Nominal unity of command for the forces of the northern colonies came with the appointment in 1697 of Richard Coote, earl of Bellomont, as governor of Massachusetts, New Hampshire, and New York. His commission also gave him command of the militia of neighboring Connecticut, Rhode Island, and East and West New Jersey during time of war. This arrangement fell far short of the plan proposed by William Penn for the appointment of a commander-in-chief and an intercolonial congress to assign a quota of men and the financial charge for each colony.[28] Limited as it was, the captain-generalcy met strong opposition from the neighboring colonies. Fitzjohn Winthrop, as major general of the militia of Connecticut, entered heated protests in Whitehall. Only on occasion could Bellomont arrange meetings with the executives of Virginia and Maryland to consult on matters of common concern.

The experiment of a captain general to command the forces of the northern colonies did not survive the death of Bellomont in 1701. Joseph Dudley succeeded him in Massachusetts and New Hampshire, and Edward Hyde, Lord Cornbury, in New York. By 1702 East and West New Jersey became a single royal colony with Cornbury as governor. William III died that same year and war with France broke out when Louis XIV, having allowed his grandson to accept the crown of Spain, recognized the young pretender, the son of James II, as king of England. In April agents and inhabitants of the northern colonies who then happened to be in London were called to a meeting with the Commissioners of Trade and Plantations held at Secretary Vernon's office to devise some arrangement for coordinating military operations in America. They agreed to a quota of men to be raised by each of the provinces—Rhode Island, Connecticut, New Jersey, Pennsylvania, Maryland, and Virginia—to assist New York, Massachusetts, and New Hampshire.[29]

The response of the provincial assemblies was disappointing. A successful French attack down the Connecticut Valley against Deerfield in 1704 should have brought home, once and for all, the lesson which a similar raid against Schenectady fourteen years before had taught: static defense by the forces of individual colonies was inadequate. The raiders butchered thirty-eight inhabitants and carried over one hundred off into captivity. Fitzjohn Winthrop of Connecticut now appreciated that the several provincial governments had to cooperate to take the offensive.[30] Dudley too sought a campaign against the French at Port Royal, but with the neighboring colonies slow to respond he joined with the assembly of the Bay colony in imploring the crown for large guns, powder, and shot. Ever concerned about cost and precedent, William Blathwayt reminded the lord treasurer that the queen had no revenues in Massachusetts for ordnance. To divert money from the other colonies for this purpose would provide a pretense for the assembly not to comply with requisitions.

The crown continued to press on the colonies a campaign against the French. Attacks planned against Port Royal failed, some charged, because of the laxity of the provincial assemblies.[31] In 1709 Colonel Francis Nicholson, with some 1,500 men, was poised to move from Albany against the St. Lawrence; but the difficulty of moving supplies, as well as the toll from disease and desertion, caused him to abort the campaign. An English fleet was planned to carry redcoats and volunteers from New England in a separate seaborne attack on Quebec, but the English forces were diverted to the Iberian Peninsula. While Nicholson did lead a successful assault on Port Royal in 1710, its capture was the only Anglo-colonial victory of any consequence. Canada, the seat of French power, remained in enemy hands.

The Western Hemisphere did not seem strategically important to Godolphin, Marlborough, or the Whig junto. The duke opposed diverting troops for a West Indian campaign; it would only serve to incite the soldiers to plunder, increase the debt of the government, and place Godolphin at the mercy of the politicians in the House of Commons. But Harley's wooing of the queen from Marlborough's duchess rather than partisan opposition in parliament led to the downfall of Godolphin and Marlborough. When the Tories came to power, they increased the weight of the British effort in the colonial arena. Henry St. John pushed vigorously for an expedition against Canada, a venture Harley at the Treasury thought too expensive and precarious. When it became apparent that St. John's views would carry, Harley absented himself from the meeting that decided on the expedition against Quebec as a means of signifying his opposition, or possibly to disassociate himself from the venture should it fail. In June 1711 a powerful fleet commanded by Sir Hovenden Walker and carrying over 5,000 British soldiers arrived in Boston. They were under the command of General John Hill, brother of Mrs. Abigal Masham, who had displaced the duchess of Marlborough as the queen's intimate companion. A brief stay in the capital of the Bay colony was enough to turn some British officers against the colonials. One, Colonel Richard Hill, was outraged by the "sourness" of the Bostonians, by their "hypocrisy and canting"; until Parliament took up the charters and settled the New Englanders under one government, but with an "entire liberty of conscience," they would grow more stiff and obstinate. Whatever the difficulties, at the end of July the expedition, augmented by about 1,000 colonials under Samuel Vetch, left for Canada. Disaster struck the ships, driven upon the rocky shores of the St. Lawrence some 300 miles short of their goal. Walker then withdrew his force. Nicholson, at the head of several hundred men gathered north of Albany for an overland push, disbanded his force in disgust. To finance the drive from New York the governor at Manhattan had drawn bills totaling £24,500.[32]

Unwilling to pursue the war any further in America or in Europe, the Tory ministry then concluded a peace with the Bourbon monarchies. The French were left secure in Canada. With the immediate need to finance military campaigns in North America at an end, the British government did not press for a new financial arrangement, a program which might have altered the constitutional and political balance in the American colonies. Such a scheme had already been proposed to meet the military needs of the royal administration in New York. For decades successive English administrations had sought to control the governments of the overseas colonies but without incurring any significant financial liability or burdening the financial establishment of the mother country. The reign of Charles II had begun in debt and had ended in greater debt. This had also been the case under William III and Anne.

Governors appointed by the crown but dependent on the assemblies for "presents," or short-term appropriations, were subject to the whims of the representatives of the provincial populace, as ministers of state had appreciated.[33] To free the civil and military establishments from the vicissitudes of colonial politics an alternative existed, as Lord Treasurer Godolphin had discovered when Blathwayt submitted a return of the sources of revenue available in the West Indies and North American colonies. By the terms of the settlement transferring the proprietary Leeward Islands and Barbados to the crown, one agreed to shortly after the Restoration, a duty of four and one half percent *ad valorem* was paid on commodities exported from the islands. Except for quitrents on land in the royal colonies — and these proved difficult to ascertain and even more so to collect — no other significant sources of revenue existed other than the money voted from time to time by provincial assemblies. And when voting these short-term appropriations, the provincial representatives insisted that they be dispensed by an official accountable to them and for purposes they specified.[34] In 1673 Parliament had imposed a duty on enumerated commodities shipped from the plantations on vessels arriving in a colony without having bonds to carry these products directly to some English port. Since the great majority of the vessels did have bonds and little tobacco or other enumerated commodities were shipped in the intercolonial traffic, the money from this "plantation" duty did not amount to much. Nor did the sums collected from quitrents, a tax paid by landholders in commutation of feudal service. In New York the state of the rents was deplorable; only in 1703 did a newly appointed auditor, Thomas Byerly, begin to draw up a rent roll. Most landholders had not paid rents since the time they took out patents for their land, and some were sixteen or more years in arrears. The situation in Virginia was somewhat better. In 1703 £1,843 had been collected, but £429 was still owed the crown.[35]

Almost everywhere in the provincial world governors were at the mercy of the assemblies. In 1708 Robert Quary, the surveyor general of the customs for the southern district of America, charged the Quaker assemblymen of Pennsylvania with attempting to deny the authority of the crown and the proprietary governor and to arrogate all power to themselves. If not reversed, this situation would be repeated throughout the continent. The following year Quary cited the behavior of the assemblymen of New York. The problem was not restricted to the mainland. In Barbados for years the assemblymen had insisted on their right to appoint the provincial treasurer. In the face of these persistent demands the governor and council of the island had acquiesced. In 1710 the law officers of the queen, James Montagu and Robert Raymond, advised the governor not to dispute the issue; they had found nothing in the instructions issued him to deny the assembly.[36]

That same year a dispute over the powers of the governor and assembly on finances reached a point of crisis in New York. Political talent, tact, and intelligence—attributes rarely found in one governor, but possessed by Colonel Robert Hunter—proved not enough to end the crisis quickly. In the past the assembly at Manhattan had granted money for the support of government for brief, set terms, the revenue to be raised by import and export duties. In 1708 the last such act had expired and the governor had not been able to prevail on the assembly to settle a revenue or to continue the statute. The representatives had insisted on determining how and by whom the money was to be spent. Except for the funds from quitrents (no more than £300 a year), no other revenue was available. To finance military operations the governor had to borrow extensively, pledging the credit of the government. On several occasions the Plantation Office in London had seemed to recommend an act of Parliament to impose import duties in the colony for the support of government there. The Commissioners of Trade and Plantations had held the pretense of the provincial representatives to have an inherent right to dispose of the money of the freemen of the colony as altogether groundless: they sat only as an assembly by virtue of the authority of the commission granted by the monarch. Apparently Lord Treasurer Oxford took the matter seriously in 1712, and the next year Hunter pressed the matter with him. "I am persuaded that by this time the distracted state of this province calls for a speedy and effectual remedy, which is not to be hoped on this side." Finally after two years the queen in council in May 1713 referred the matter to the House of Commons.[37]

But the legislature in Westminster took no action. Blathwayt predicted to Oxford that the measure if passed would have satisfied the just demands of the royal administration. Years before—at the turn of the century—he had complained that the proper course in dealing with the colonies had been recognized for some time, but not followed. He regretted that now again the ministry had fallen back on "the more regular and usual manner" of raising revenue in America.[38] In 1714 Anne died, the Tories went out of office, and a new administration took power. In New York, Governor Robert Hunter, complaining bitterly that the bill in Parliament for enacting a revenue in New York was never intended to be passed, capitulated to the assemblymen.[39]

In the end, the monarch's governor and ministers of state at Whitehall had backed down before the provincial politicians at Manhattan. Much the same happened elsewhere in America.

CHAPTER 3

War and the Disruption of Transatlantic Commerce

Before the British navy rose to dominance later in the eighteenth century, years of protracted war disrupted the pattern of trade between England and the colonies and jeopardized the navigation code by which English officials sought to reap a financial harvest from duties imposed on American tobacco, West Indian sugar, and other "enumerated" or listed produce of the Western Hemisphere required under parliamentary law to be sent to England before being reexported to other markets. To increase revenue and promote Anglo-colonial shipping the government between 1660 and 1697 had enacted various statutes governing overseas trade and navigation. These laws reflected the needs of the state for revenue and for potential naval power more than the economic interests of merchants, shippers, and manufacturers in England. No consolidated interest group existed, even among those engaged in foreign commerce, as was realized in bureaucratic circles. As the Commissioners of Trade appreciated in 1707, "Some traders interfere with one another. It has frequently been found by Experience, that in the Management of one and the same Trade Merchants have differ'd in opinion, according to their respective private Interest or way of Trade." The needs of manufacturers and merchants engaged in overseas commerce often conflicted with each other and, at times, with the requirements of the government. In 1693, when the House of Commons was considering a proposal to increase import duties on indigo, some members objected that this was in effect a charge on English manufactures, since indigo was used as a dye in domestic textile manufacturing.[1]

Two laws passed early in the reign of Charles II set down the basic requirements of the carrying code. Another statute enacted in the reign of William III, an Act for Preventing Frauds and Regulating Abuses in the Plantation Trade (7 & 8 W. & M., c. 22), provided little new in substance but sought to impose more effective enforcement in the colonies. By an Act for Encouraging and Increasing Shipping (12 Car. 2, c. 18) certain commodities grown in the colonies, tobacco and sugar among them, had to be shipped to some port in England, Wales, or Ireland (a later act passed in 1671 excluded Irish ports), where a duty was paid, before being eligible for reshipment to European markets. Because tobacco was considered a luxury, commodity taxes were increased from time to time as the government felt the need for revenue. But much of the duty was rebated on reexported tobacco so as not to interfere unduly with trade. By the close of the century about two-thirds of the tobacco imported into England was reshipped. Owners of vessels sailing from England for the colonies had to give bond that if any of the enumerated commodities were loaded there, they would be brought to an English port where the required duty would be paid. Vessels arriving in the Chesapeake without such bond had to pay a duty in the plantations to load tobacco. This requirement was imposed in 1673 to frustrate direct commerce between the colonies and Europe under the guise of an intercolonial or coasting trade. Vessels eligible for the carrying trade were those owned and commanded by English subjects and manned predominately by English seamen. By the Staple Act of 1662, an act for the Encouragement of Trade, England was made the entrepôt through which, with few exceptions, goods of European nations passed when carried to the colonies.

This code aimed to stimulate the English shipbuilding industry and to increase revenue for the government, not to restrict the sale of colonial produce — even of the enumerated commodities — to England or to force the colonists overseas to purchase goods finished or manufactured in the mother country. For the government, a trade in foreign goods to the colonies bypassing England and a direct traffic from the plantations to foreign markets were objectionable because the crown lost revenue. Before the close of the century, the duties owed on tobacco alone came to over £300,000 a year.[2]

What English authorities hoped to eliminate was the carrying of enumerated commodities from the colonies without duties' first being paid in England. Inasmuch as the West Indian islands and the Chesapeake provinces produced sugar and tobacco from which much revenue was derived, these colonies were highly prized, but the New England provinces were also valued, for they supplied Barbados and the Leeward Islands with essential foodstuffs, livestock, and lumber.[3]

During periods of economic or financial difficulty, and especially when war disrupted normal oceanic shipping, particular interests groups — some engaged in Anglo-colonial ventures — sought relief from the government. Iron manufacturing involved a variety of competing interests: providers of raw materials, including owners of woodlands who supplied the timber from which charcoal was obtained; merchants importing colonial and Swedish iron; and manufacturers of wrought iron. By the close of the seventeenth century the English iron industry was still scattered and migratory, its operations intermittent and probably declining. Domestic production of pig iron went to manufacture cast-iron commodities; most of the wrought iron produced in England was made from bar iron imported mainly from Sweden. English pig iron was too brittle for making steel. The local industry faced a chronic shortage of high-grade ore and a dwindling supply of charcoal as woodlands and copses were exploited. As a consequence of these conditions various interests in the industry came into conflict. Smelters of pig iron and owners of woodlands feared competition from cheaper colonial iron, but manufacturers of finished goods who needed cheap supplies welcomed the colonial product while at the same time they sought protection against Swedish competition. On several occasions during the first half of the eighteenth century the various groups clashed when seeking aid from the government.[4] The contest was long and protracted, with no significant legislation coming until 1750.

More immediately successful were proponents of the English woolen industry. For centuries wool had been the backbone of English overseas trade, ventures in the main conducted directly with northern Europe. During the seventeenth century, however, English overseas trade had become more widely dispersed and varied as England became a European entrepôt for goods from the East Indies and commodities from the Western Hemisphere. Three principal factors led to chronic difficulties for the English woolen industry: competition from foreign textiles, industrialization in European areas traditionally relying on English woolens, and the changing character of the English cloths. Late in the century war brought on an acute crisis. The industry was in a state of depression as trade with Flanders was disrupted, and several industrial centers suffered from severe unemployment. As solutions to the immediate problem, the cloth industry sought to have government prohibit the export of raw wool to foreign manufacturers and, wherever possible, to eliminate producers under English control, those in Ireland and America, from competing in the export market.[5]

In the last years of the century the weakness of the Whig ministry allowed a coalition of special interest groups, in a rare display of unity and against the better judgment of the administration, to secure legislation. John Cary, Sir Joseph Tily, and Sir William Ashurst, spokesmen for manufacturers in Bristol, Leeds, Exeter, and Colchester, launched attacks in the House of Commons against Irish exports. The Tory opposition, led by Sir Edward Seymour, also took up the issue: it became a political matter decided not on economic but on political grounds. By the beginning of 1699 the much weakened Whigs no longer controlled the House of Commons. In January a bill to restrain the export of woolen cloth from Ireland and the colonies passed without difficulty as the administration offered no resistance; indeed, it was on the recommendation of the Board of Trade that North American woolens were added.[6] The Act to Prevent the Export of Woolens (10 Will. 3, c. 10) was not designed to prevent colonists from manufacturing cloths similar to those produced in the mother country or to preserve the American market for English weavers.[7] Some sentiment existed in the House of Commons for preventing the setting up of manufactures in America, but the bill as adopted with a clause recommended at the Plantation Office did not forbid the making of fabrics in America for local consumption, merely the carrying of woolen cloth out of a colony.[8] For some financiers and investors the act fell far short of what they desired. In 1700 a group of merchants petitioned to be incorporated as a joint stock company for carrying on a trade in woolens. Nothing came of the petition.[9]

The ban on exporting woolens from Ireland and the American colonies apparently had little immediate effect on the consumption of English manufactures in America. The use of locally produced cloth increased, as dislocations induced by wartime limitations of trade probably led to a shortage of the finer English textiles and stimulated local production of coarse woolens. As the Commissioners of Trade and Plantations had predicted in 1696, "The Plantation Trade suffers, and always will, by Warr."[10]

The ability of the Royal Navy to protect the various branches of overseas trade and the supply of needed naval stores (masts, planks, spars, pitch, tar, and hemp) from enemy privateers was critical to the well-being of the nation and the colonies as well as the revenue of the state. To free England from entire dependence on the Baltic lands—at best, an uncertain source—the ministers of state had turned to America. But the traffic in naval stores was a complex trade, one in which several competing Anglo-colonial syndicates or gangs emerged.

Various groups seeking a monopoly, an exclusive contract to supply stores for the Royal Navy, bombarded the government with petitions. The most ambitious venture was that organized by Richard Wharton, a New England entrepreneur, a syndicate of investors from Old and New England. Following Wharton's death, leadership passed to Sir Matthew Dudley. Dudley and Associates—as the gang was known—met intense opposition from rivals, among others, Sir Joseph Herne and his partners and Sir Henry Ashurst and Sir Stephen Evance. Ashurst, a member of a well-known Dissenter family, had close religious and commercial ties with Massachusetts, while Evance, Connecticut born, was a prominent financier in London. Another syndicate opposed to the Dudley Associates was led by John Shippen and David Waterhouse. Among the independents were John Taylor and William Wallis, contractors with their own connections in New England. The rivalry among these groups had ramifications for local alignments in northern New England.

Several years of protracted lobbying resulted in no decision favorable to any of the gangs. Since no syndicate was willing to pledge to import minimum quantities, the Commissioners of Trade concluded that stores imported from the colonies would never be sufficient to meet the needs of the government until it offered subsidies to compensate for the extraordinary charges of freight across the Atlantic and the high cost of labor in the northern plantations. They also concluded that competition among the various groups of merchants rather than a monopoly to a chartered company would allow the government to buy at lower prices. "Charters cannot remove nor decrease the Cloggs that lye on this trade."[11]

Events in Europe prompted the English government to take a more active role. Following the overrunning of Finland by forces of the Muscovite czar, prices for naval stores rose considerably, and when merchants in Stockholm obtained from the Swedish crown the sole right to deal in pitch and tar, the price they demanded of English buyers doubled. Following the renewal of war between England and France in 1702 the situation became precarious. The Swedes refused to negotiate a contract for stores, and in 1703 the Stockholm company excluded English vessels from the trade. Thereafter Swedish ships would carry stores sold at prices determined by the Swedish monopolists.[12]

The commissioners of the navy entrusted with the responsibility of providing for the queen's fleet saw the advantage of securing stores from America, but were unwilling to burden their budget by paying the higher prices imposed by high labor costs and freight rates. Employing the arguments advanced by John Bridger, a surveyor of the woods in New England, and Stephen Mason, an Anglo-colonial merchant, the Board of Trade suggested that the government subsidize the importation of naval stores from the colonies by paying bounties when stores were carried to England. Late in 1704 the queen in council rejected the petition of Thomas Byfield and other investors in the Pennsylvania and Carolina Company for a monopoly, and a few days later the House of Commons gave leave for a bill to grant subsidies for the importation of stores from the colonies.[13] Sitting on the committee considering the bill were Sir Matthew Dudley and Sir Gilbert Heathcote, a lobbyist for the Pennsylvania and Carolina Company, but the act awarded bounties to all merchants importing naval stores from all of the American colonies. Following passage of the bill the administration instructed the governors in the Chesapeake colonies to recommend to their assemblies regulations for producing stores, but warned them ''to take care not to Suffer'' people employed in the raising of tobacoo to be diverted by this or any other undertaking.[14] Customs revenue from tobacco entering the kingdom had the higher priority.

As the Plantation Office advised in response to a proposal from the syndicate lobbyist, Sir Gilbert Heathcote, the act for encouraging the importation of naval stores was designed as a general invitation to all merchants; for the government to conclude an agreement with one group would run counter to the intention of Parliament.[15]

The experiment of subsidizing the importation of pitch and tar from America had yielded few results by the close of the war with France. From 1711 through 1715 the navy had purchased through contracts made with merchants having colonial connections—Francis Collins, Richard Letchmore, Richard Mico, James Dean, Samuel Baron, Charles Lodowyck, John Lloyd, William Harkins, and James Mark—about 70 lasts of tar and 104 tons of pitch, and the tar was judged defective, not fit for use on cordage. The Admiralty had received little value for the premium paid.[16]

The experience with masts from New England was somewhat better, but procurement was handicapped by two problems: protecting the woods from wasteful cutting by private interlopers and the fierce rivalry among competing contractors, Londoners who operated through factors in New England. Francis Collins employed John Mico and John Plaisted, the latter a judge and councilor of Massachusetts. Plaisted's brother, Ichobod, served John Taylor. Some local officials in New England accused the factors of abusing their licenses to procure masts by overcutting of pines and wasting potential mast timber; but Joseph Dudley, the governor appointed by the crown for Massachusetts and New Hampshire, sided with the factors and their principals rather than with the royal officials appointed to protect the woods. John Bridger, the surveyor general of the woods, was himself under attack in London for allegedly taking bribes from the common settlers to cut what trees they pleased.[17] The charter granted Massachusetts in 1691 reserved trees of a certain size growing on lands hitherto not granted to any private person, but confirmed all lands previously granted to private individuals. Yet as the queen's solicitor general, Robert Eyre, defined "private," the crown had no more power to reserve trees on lands granted to public institutions than on lands given to private individuals. Moreover the charter applied only to lands granted after, not before, 1691. In November 1710 Robert Monckton, a commissioner of trade, brought into the House of Commons a bill for the preservation of white pines in New England, New York, and New Jersey. The law, 9 Anne, c. 22, provided a penalty of £100 for cutting or destroying any pine not the property of a private person, with a diameter of twenty-four inches or more measured one foot above the ground.[18]

With a handful of poorly paid deputies recruited in New England, John Bridger, the surveyor of the woods, found it impossible to enforce the law. Even when he obtained convictions and local officials distrained the estates of men convicted for violations to pay their fines, no neighbors would buy them. Too many men on the Piscataqua were engaged in the same practices. Bridger himself came under attack from the principal inhabitants of New Hampshire, the Wentworths and the Vaughans, for extorting bribes from the townsmen to be allowed to cut timber.[19]

In 1715 the Board of Trade was still pleading for support for American naval stores. Little had been accomplished in the decade since the passage of the act to encourage imports from the colonies despite the high priority given for regular convoys of the Royal Navy to escort the mast ships and to exempt their crews from impressment.

Protecting overseas commerce and reconciling the claims of the oceanic traders was a chronic problem during wartime. Various trades—those with the Mediterranean, the Baltic, the East and West Indies, Africa, and North America—all had to compete for the limited number of convoys, the escort vessels accompanying the merchant fleets, and for the pool of seamen to be alloted to man naval vessels and commerce carriers. Protection for the plantation fleets ranked high among the priorities of the Commissioners of Trade. Seaborne commerce fell into three categories: coastal traffic and interisland trade in the West Indies; foreign trade carried on by merchant vessels sailing together in fleets periodically to various destinations and returning in the same manner; and foreign commerce conducted by single ships. To protect waterborne commerce from enemy warships and privateers, cruisers patrolled the coasts of the home islands and in colonial waters, convoys escorted the fleets of merchantmen, and squadrons of the Royal Navy covered the departure and arrival of merchant fleets in the narrow waters of the North Sea and south of the English Channel, where French corsairs based in the Channel and Biscay ports prowled.[20] When war had broken out with France in 1689, shippers engaged in the various trades had competed for the limited number of vessels and seamen to be assigned to the respective trades. Because of its bulky cargo and the valuable customs duties it had to pay to the crown, the tobacco fleet destined for the Chesapeake fared well in the allocations. But not all merchants engaged in overseas commerce or even in the tobacco trade agreed on procedures, so varied were their interests. Tobacco dealers in London and the various outports and those residing on the Chesapeake could not agree on how many fleets should be sent out in a year, at what times, or whether single vessels ought to attempt the passage. Similar disagreements were evident among those engaged in the provision trade from New York and New England to the West Indies.[21]

The government had particular interest in the Chesapeake trade: when imported into England, tobacco paid a very high duty. By the impost voted in 1685 the duty was raised from two to five pence. Another penny and a third was added in 1697 and 1704. All but one-half penny was drawn back on tobacco reexported from England. Receipts from tobacco imports ranged from £200,000 to £300,000 annually.[22] But on the question of protecting the merchantmen returning from the Chesapeake there was little agreement. William Byrd of Virginia thought it advisable not to rely on a single, large annual fleet. Should it arrive on the Chesapeake when tobacco was plentiful and a glut on the market, the planters and shippers would have to send off their crops when tobacco was worth little. Risking a winter passage by a single vessel so as to obtain a higher price was preferable, so Byrd advised when urging the London house of Perry and Lane to hire small ships in the West Country ports. Robert Anderson, a planter and merchant of Virginia, saw another disadvantage in shipping by vessels operating in fleets and restricted to a schedule determined by the need to sail with the convoys: shipmasters would not have sufficient time to dispatch their sloops to collect cargo from the remote plantations.[23] Among the dealers in England also there was no agreement: merchants in the outports of Bristol and Liverpool differed from the Londoners, who were themselves not of one mind, some trading on their own account, while others, agents and factors for planters, received shipments on consignment. The latter would have been satisfied with sending out one great fleet a year.[24] By such an arrangement, however, the market would be glutted and the financial resources of the importers strained when the vessels returned with a full year's supply. The traders in the outports preferred few, if any, restraints. Those Londoners trading on their own account wanted at least two yearly voyages rather than a single great fleet.

After sounding out the various mercantile interests in England as well as Virginians and Marylanders then resident in London, the Commissioners of Trade and Plantations recommended that beginning in 1703 the Admiralty send a convoy from the Downs to call at ports between the Isle of Wight and Land's End for merchantmen bound for the Chesapeake. The convoy was to leave from the Capes of Virginia early in July escorting as many of the eighty or so merchantmen then in Chesapeake waters as were ready to return. Another convoy would leave England about the first of July with another fleet and not return from America until the following spring with another crop. Thereafter only one convoy would be assigned. This arrangement was protested by Peter Paggen, Edward Haistwell, and other merchants of London who traded on their own account.[25] Other trades put in claims on the limited resources of the navy. In 1703 the West Indian merchants asked for six men-of-war.

Due to the great distances involved, sailing schedules and rendezvous could not be coordinated precisely. For want of reliable news on departures many vessels in the plantations trades were lost in 1704, when the fleet arrived two months later than expected. The French took eighteen merchantmen. Better to inform traders, merchants engaged in American commerce petitioned the Treasury to establish a packet service between London and New York, but Godolphin wanted the traders themselves to defray the cost.[26]

Despite the hazards involved in solitary sailings, merchants trading on their own account preferred to have their vessels run the risk rather than remain in port when convoys were not available. After four years of debate the Londoners remained divided as between the benefits of one or more fleets annually while the merchants of Liverpool, Bristol, and Whitehaven argued for liberty to have their vessels sail without time restrictions.

At this point the surveyor general of the customs in America, Robert Quary, entered the debate to raise another issue: the prospect of enlarging the market for Chesapeake tobacco in Europe. Due to the disruption of the carrying trade, the market for English colonial tobacco in Europe had suffered as Dutch and German growers took advantage of the situation to increase their production. As a result the Dutch were now supplying Spain, France, Flanders, and even the Baltic lands. Quary suggested widening the market for Chesapeake tobacco through diplomatic negotiations with Russia, Spain, and Portugal and by allowing English merchants to carry tobacco directly from the colonies to Europe.[27]

CHAPTER 4

The English Entrepôt and the Southern Colonial Staple Trade

THE MARKETING OF colonial tobacco affected not only an important source of revenue for the English government, but also the prosperity of dozens of English merchants and the welfare of thousands of planters, farmers, servants, and slaves in four of the American colonies—Virginia, Maryland, and to a lesser extent North Carolina and the lower counties on the Delaware. To the planters on the Chesapeake, tobacco was the foundation of their economic well-being, and in turn, the close connection between America and the Western European markets for tobacco was well appreciated in English governmental and commercial circles.

Soil and climate allowed for the growing of tobacco in England and in northern Europe, but to secure the revenue of the crown from American imports, the English government in the decades after the Restoration had stamped out tobacco planting in the home counties. Provided the price was not too high, many dealers on the Continent preferred to purchase, via England, higher-quality Chesapeake leaf, a better grade of tobacco than that grown in northern Europe, and to pay by remitting local manufactures. Tobacco planting in Europe was limited, if only to preserve the market for finished goods in England.[1] But war warped and disrupted trans-Atlantic commerce.

Planters on the Chesapeake grew two principal varieties of tobacco, oronocco and sweet scented. Oronocco was the coarser and stronger in flavor of the two; sweet scented, requiring different soil, was confined largely to the banks of the great rivers, James, York, Rappahannock, and Potomac. Considered the better of the two, it was consumed largely in England, where it commanded a higher price. Oronocco had a wider market in eastern and northern Europe except in time of war, when privateers and warships interdicted commerce.[2] From the start of tobacco planting by Europeans on the Chesapeake down to the outbreak of the major wars in 1689, the trade was characterized by expanding production, first rising and then declining prices, and widening markets in the British Isles and in Europe as the taste for tobacco spread to include almost all social classes. Years of prolonged war (1689–97 and 1702–13) led to relative stagnation as high freight and insurance rates and the hazards of wartime sailings discouraged the dispatch of merchantmen to the Chesapeake. These conditions depressed the price offered planters in America but raised them in Europe; as the supply of the superior Chesapeake product dwindled, European farmers were encouraged to cultivate coarser plants. Before 1689 Continental markets other than those in France—where tax farmers, a syndicate granted a monopoly to import tobacco and levy duties, restricted importation—took some of the Chesapeake leaf available for reexport from the English entrepôt. Demand for Chesapeake tobacco in France dated only from the 1690s, when Virginia tobacco was introduced by dint of capturing English merchantmen returning from America, a method of marketing that brought losses, not gains, to English traders, factors, and planters. If the French captured one Chesapeake merchantman out of ten risking the return voyage, they obtained more tobacco than they had imported from the entire world before 1689. In the long run the English planters and merchants engaged in growing and marketing tobacco would benefit, as captured Chesapeake leaf introduced into France during the war altered French tastes and created a new market.[3] But the immediate result of French captures was to restrict the movement of the merchantmen to and from the Chesapeake and to jeopardize the reexport trade from England to European markets.

As increased production in the colonies far outdistanced demand partially because of war, and prices fell, the need to widen the market for American colonial leaf became more evident. An opportunity for opening a new market came in 1697, following the Treaty of Ryswick, with the visit of Czar Peter to the Low Countries. Merchants of the chartered Muscovy Company, who had lost their trading privileges in Russia, now petitioned William III seeking restitution of their rights and liberty to import tobacco duty free into the czar's dominions. Russia had been closed to tobacco since 1648, but following Peter's visit, Dutch merchants had obtained the right to bring in tobacco for one year. Both the English Commissioners of Trade and London merchants importing tobacco from America welcomed any attempt to open a market in Muscovy, but Micajah Perry, John Cary, and almost fifty more Virginia merchants in testimony before the House of Commons opposed any monopoly for a particular group. The trade should be open to all.[4]

This argument notwithstanding, the Muscovy Company and the independent traders to the Chesapeake lost out to a new group of investors, about a dozen men related by kinship and prior business ventures who signed a contract with Russian officials to import tobacco into the czar's dominions for a period of seven years. Subsequently they brought in some sixty other men to form an unincorporated company. Among the investors were Sir Gilbert and Samuel Heathcote, Edward Harrison, and Edward Haistwell, the only member with connections in the Chesapeake trade. The Tobacco Adventurers—more formally, the Company of Contractors with the czar for the sole importation of Tobacco into Russia—was no chance grouping, but part of a definite new "gang" centering on Sir Gilbert Heathcote, one of the richest men in the country, and investors active with him in the trade to the Baltic, in the management of the Bank of England, and in the East India Company, one of several gangs of London entrepreneurs who hunted together in packs.

During the last decade of the seventeenth century the metropolis had three such groupings: an "old gang" centered on the chief joint stock companies—the old East India Company, the Africa Company, and the Hudson's Bay Company—in addition to the closed, regulated Russia and Levant companies; a "new gang" centered on the New East India Company but also active in the Bank of England, various European traders, and the open, regulated companies trafficking to Hamburg and the Eastland; and, finally, a more amorphous third group of independent merchants trading individually with America and the West Indies, men whose commercial activities were not subject to corporate regulation. Some overlapping among these groupings existed. The contractors with the czar generally belonged to the new gang.

Which group would receive governmental support in exploiting the new market in the czar's dominions: the old Muscovy Company, the free merchants importing tobacco from the Chesapeake, or the new gang of would-be monopolists? In Parliament the latter successfully assailed the old in the name of free trade. In 1698 victory went to Heathcote, Haistwell, and their associates; their rivals in the Muscovy Company could do little more in the coming years than snipe from the flanks. The independent traders dealing in American tobacco were in a stronger position as spokesmen for a ranking national as well as colonial, a mercantile as well as fiscal, interest. Micajah Perry and the Londoners involved in the Chesapeake trade reopened the question early in the eighteenth century: would English commerce benefit more from free trade to Russia than from monopoly?[5]

For the English government the immediate need was to find markets for the great quantities of tobacco grown on the Chesapeake, a requirement reinforced by the decision of the Spanish crown in 1701 to prevent the further introduction of Chesapeake tobacco into its territories. With the succession of the grandson of Louis XIV to the throne of Spain, action soon followed against English merchants. War with France and Spain broke out the next year after Louis recognized the young Stuart pretender as king of England.

Under pressure from the Russian authorities the Tobacco Adventurers in 1704 committed a blunder, one the more than sixty independent traders with the Chesapeake and the processors of tobacco quickly seized upon. Not content with reasonable profits and finding Circassian tobacco much cheaper than the leaf imported from England, the Adventurers had sent out to Russia two operators, Peter Marshall and his wife, with the necessary machinery to spin and roll tobacco in the czar's domain. Following protests by independent traders, the English Privy Council ordered the recall of the artisans from Moscow and the destruction of any machinery for rolling and cutting tobacco the contractors had shipped to Russia. The administration further ordered the queen's envoy to assist all of the monarch's subjects in a free trade to the czar's territories.[6] Hoping to minimize their losses, the contractors offered to sell their holdings for 190,000 rubles, but Aleksei Kurbatov, whom Peter had appointed as director of a department of industry and commerce, demurred. He could purchase the same quantity of Circassian tobacco for only 17,000 rubles. Kurbatov later died while awaiting trial on a charge of embezzling public funds.[7]

Despite the collapse of the Russian venture, other markets on the Continent offered promise. The French had acquired a taste for the higher-quality Chesapeake leaf seized from English merchantmen during the war of 1689–97. Tobacco planting on the French Antilles was declining, and superior tobacco imported from Spain and Portugal was several times more expensive than any other on the European market the French might use for mixing in luxury snuff. In the interval between the close of the War of the League of Augsburg in 1697 and the onset of the War of the Spanish Succession in 1702, England for the first time became a major supplier of tobacco for France through the open market.[8] With the resumption of war against France the English government prohibited dealings with the enemy. England's Dutch ally, however, was not as rigorous in banning trade when, in 1705, the French government was prepared to permit some exchange with the Netherlanders. With the Dutch already supplying tobacco to France, in 1706 several English merchants applied for permission to dispose of English colonial tobacco through neutral shippers.

The request brought under review a broad range of problems on the trade, including marketing and shipping. Various men in the English trading community involved in the Chesapeake, merchants and consignees in London and in the outports, still had not agreed on the schedule and number of fleets to be sent to America. Robert Quary, surveyor general of the customs for the southern district, had plumped for a single flotilla and had advised Lord Treasurer Godolphin to allow reexport of colonial tobacco to France on neutral ships and to exert pressure on Sweden, Spain, and Portugal to permit the free importation of English tobacco.[9] Dealers in the Chesapeake trade and John Linton, a processor of tobacco, also supported the recommendation to open new European markets and to allow reexport to France in neutral vessels. Micajah Perry, Thomas Lane, and twenty-five other importers pressed the issue.

Reaction in the Plantation Office was favorable, but in the House of Commons doubts prevailed. Quary, who was waiting in Plymouth to take ship for America, left it to Linton to present the case to the administration. Not for the first nor the last time matters other than colonial affairs occupied the attention of the higher ministers of state. Marlborough and Godolphin were busy altering the ministry to placate the Whigs. Not until May 1707 did a reconstituted Board of Trade packed with Whig placemen take up the question of the tobacco trade raised thirteen months before. In July, on the basis of the testimony of the Virginia traders, the full council accepted a recommendation from the Plantation Office that the queen's envoys to Portugal, Sweden, and Russia exert themselves to secure the importation of tobacco from Britain. Nothing would come of these diplomatic efforts, however. And resistance from the British Customs Board and the distracted state of affairs of the monopoly controlling tobacco imports in France frustrated efforts to export Chesapeake leaf to the Bourbon kingdom in neutral carriers.[10] According to Linton, opposition to allowing exports to France came from the mistaken belief that drawbacks paid out on re-exported tobacco prejudiced the royal customs revenue, a notion used by vendors selling in the home market and "improved on" by their friends in the London Customs House. The Commissioners of Customs made it a point with Godolphin: on reexport, the crown paid back all but a half penny of the six pence due on tobacco entering England.[11] To offset this argument John Cary, Richard Lee, and other English merchants with interests in the Chesapeake proposed that vessels carrying tobacco to France be allowed to bring back French wines, commodities on which duties would be paid. The Commissioners of Customs discounted the idea—the increase in revenue would be minimal—while British merchants importing wine from Portugal objected more strongly, arguing the importance of the Iberian market for English woolens. The cause of the Virginia traders was not helped by the suspicion that three of their number—John Cary, Jonathan Searle, and Cornelius Denne—had been secretly sending tobacco to Dieppe under cover of shipments through the Straits.[12]

In 1709 a bill intended to offer relief to the tobacco trade encountered strong resistance in the House of Commons from merchants exporting cloth to the Iberian Peninsula and importing Portuguese wines. As the crisis in the tobacco trade deepened the following year, many of the firms were pressed to the wall and some went bankrupt. When the queen dismissed Godolphin and the Whig ministers, some men took hope that the change in administration might bring relief as Robert Harley, soon to be raised to the peerage as earl of Oxford, took over at the Treasury. He and the other Tories, eager for peace and a treaty of commerce with France, were not as solicitous as their predecessors had been of the Portuguese connection. With little fanfare, early in 1711 the new administration put through Parliament a bill repealing the prohibition on imported French wines. British ships might now bring in French wines up to the value of British commodities exported to France. But since the government of Louis XIV did not allow the importation of most English goods or the export of French wine in alien vessels, the measure would do little to stimulate the traffic in tobacco.[13] Hoping to include a treaty of commerce in the negotiations to end hostilities, the Board of Trade in 1709 had drawn up a proposal calling for the importation of English tobacco into France free of restrictions from any monopoly appointed by the French crown to farm customs. Duties would not exceed those imposed on tobacco grown in Europe. The negotiations that year fell through, and during later discussions at Utrecht in the fall of 1712, the British plenipotentiaries, in the face of French intransigence, had to abandon their call for the abolition of the monopoly of importing tobacco enjoyed by the tax farmers to the French king.[14]

Throughout these years the merchants in England and the planters on the

Chesapeake had found, not new markets, but fresh competition as European-grown tobacco displaced Chesapeake leaf due to the dislocations and restrictions on transatlantic shipping imposed by war.

During the conflict, to ease the burden on their trade English merchants had sought relief in the manner in which they paid duties to the government when they imported tobacco into the realm. Since the reign of Charles II tobacco paid on importation one penny per pound Old Subsidy and another penny as additional duty, with half of the subsidy and the full additional duty drawn back on reexport. Even more taxes were imposed in 1685, in 1697, and in 1704. By 1706 six and one-third pence was paid on a pound of colonial tobacco imported into England, of which all but one-half penny was rebated by debentures on reexport. For a government concerned with revenue, the elimination of smuggling—a practice made easier by the shipment of tobacco loose or in bulk rather than packed in hogsheads—was highly desirable. To merchants chronically short of cash, the method of paying customs was as important as the amount of tax owed. "In fact, the credit allowed in paying the duty was probably more important to the average tobacco merchant than the actual level of the duty."[15] As one undersecretary had noted, the large Virginia fleet arriving in 1698 would bring a great sum into the Exchequer, "but the merchants are much too seek where to find ready money to pay so much customs." Five years later one Liverpool dealer on learning of the arrival of a ship in which he had an interest found himself strapped for "moneys to clear the Dutys." He was forced to write to a London correspondent for payment of a past due bill of £60. Merchants also squabbled with customs officials as to how much would be allowed them as discount for spoiled or damaged tobacco. In Liverpool "pretty sharp disputes" were frequent between the surveyors and the importing merchants on the amount of damaged tobacco and the weights by which duties were reckoned.[16]

The government did not require importers to pay full duty at once: it allowed them to post bond to reexport within a specified time. Few merchants had sufficient capital to pay cash at the time of importation and thus receive a discount on the duty due. For almost a quarter of a century after the accession of James II, personnel in the Treasury and customs establishments were apparently unaware of the full implication of the high duties on the entrepôt trade. They let the number of overdue bonds on tobacco duties get out of hand. In 1711 almost half a million pounds sterling were due. Operating on credit and overextended, many of the British merchants in the trade were hard hit when panic struck the international credit markets in 1710. Fortunately for the tobacco traffic a political realignment had brought to the Treasury Robert Harley, "probably the greatest friend in office that the tobacco trade ever had." The financial failure of many merchants, particularly the Londoners, troubled the new treasurer. Legislation enacted during his tenure of office "so liberally amended the rules relating to tobacco revenue that, for all practical purposes, it as much as gave a reduction to the duties." Relief for the distressed traders was not immediate, however. The debacle in the traffic and the ensuing bankruptcy of many of the merchants during the years 1711–13, more than any action taken by the government, may have ended the reign of the fly-by-night, whether large or small, in the London trade. It also brought under scrutiny for the first time the bonding system, particularly as it influenced the trade in tobacco.[17]

At the onset of the crisis, with many merchants unable to export or redeem their bonds, the Commissioners of the Customs instructed the receiver general to call on the merchants to clear the bonds taken out eighteen or more months before or face forfeiting them. Vigorous prosecution of the bonds as they became due would impose great hardship on the trade, yet only Parliament could offer relief to the merchants unable to pay.[18] But with the importers themselves unable to agree—some had even fled the kingdom—not until the spring of 1713 did the London-based merchants trading to the Chesapeake present their plight to the House of Commons: the heavy duty—more than six pence on a pound of colonial tobacco—was more than the trade could bear. As a consequence planting in Europe had so greatly increased that the tobacco of the British colonies sold in foreign markets for less than the cost of freight and customs. Many dealers had been forced out and many planters in America, allegedly, compelled to turn to other pursuits, manufactures. The merchants asked for a reduction of the duties on tobacco and any other relief Parliament might give. As finally passed by the Commons, the bill for the aid of the tobacco trade contained provision for destroying spoiled tobacco, but without compensation for prime cost or transportation charges incurred by the shipper. The Commissioners of Customs had differed sharply with the merchants on allowances for damaged tobacco, for which the traders had refused to pay duty. The Customs Board had also proposed the establishment of royal warehouses in which all imported tobacco would be stored until duties were paid and would not be removed until ready for export. The merchants had objected: it was impractical to distinguish betwen tobacco intended for the inland trade and that destined for export. They opposed even an optional warehousing scheme. The bill did grant merchants additional time for redeeming bonds due in June 1713 and continued the allowances for shrinkage and wastage. All duties were payable within eighteen months after tobacco was landed, but a discount of 10 percent was allowed if duties were paid within fifteen months. The Commons passed the bill for encouraging the tobacco trade on 11 July, but two days later the Lords rejected the measure, ostensibly because it contained too many extraneous matters.

Anticipating some relief by Parliament some London traders had not entered the cargoes of their ships with the customs officials. For months several vessels had lay at anchor in the Thames with over 6,000 hogsheads holding almost five million pounds of tobacco on which was due over £120,000. Under the existing law customs officials had to insist that the traders take out bond to secure payment.[19]

A bill for the relief of the trade passed both houses of Parliament the next year, a measure allowing some compensation to the merchants for damaged tobacco and providing for the optional use of warehouses. If the importer was unable to pay full duties or could not find surety for his bond, after paying the Old Subsidy of one penny per pound he would place his tobacco in an approved warehouse. If not withdrawn after fifteen months it would be sold at auction, by inch of candle. This provision came to nothing, for the customs officers did not force the merchants to use the optional system; it was ignored.[20]

During the years of war yet another staple of the American colonies was brought within the English entrepôt. Before 1705 rice was not enumerated — not one of the commodities of America and the West Indies required by law to be shipped to England before being carried to European markets. Not long after the cultivation of rice was begun in South Carolina, merchants began shipping rice directly to English factors and traders resident in Spain, Portugal, and Italy. Such routing did not allow the English customs service to collect duties normally imposed on rice entering England. A shipmaster engaged in the Carolina trade, Michael Cole, first brought this direct traffic to the attention of English officials. In 1704 he complained to the Treasury that three years before, Richard Cock, master of the *Dove,* a vessel of ninety tons, had given bond in Charles Town, but then sailed directly for Holland. Two other ships then followed suit, one to Holland and the other to France. In 1704 five more vessels had sailed directly to northern Europe with, Cole conjectured, great loss to the royal revenue. The government then took action. The following February in the House of Commons a clause was added to a bill granting further subsidies on wines and other imports, one adding rice and molasses (a by-product of processing West Indian sugar cane) to the list of enumerated commodities of the plantations to be shipped to some English port before being carried to Europe.[21]

Planters and traders in Carolina and British merchants involved in the rice trade objected to the new requirement. In 1711 the British consuls and merchants resident in Oporto, Lisbon, and Leghorn complained that French, Italian, and Dutch competitors could import rice directly from Curaçao and Martinque. Carolina rice deteriorated when shipped through the British entrepôt and cost more to market. The English factor at Lisbon recommended eliminating the requirement to ship through British ports and instead imposing a duty in Carolina when rice was exported. The following year the assembly of South Carolina sent an agent, Abel Ketterby, to London to solicit permission to ship rice directly to ports in Europe south of Cape Finisterre.[22] Neither Ketterby nor the London merchants involved in the Carolina trade had any success in 1711 or ten years later. Not until 1730 did shippers receive liberty to carry rice directly from the colonies to ports in southern Europe.[23]

The marketing of rice and tobacco, two crops critical to the economies of the southern colonies of America, suffered from the restrictions imposed to meet the financial needs of the British government, strictures injurious both to the merchants of the metropolis and the planters in the colonies. To protect the financial interests of the crown, successive administrations in London sought to curb smuggling and to prosecute violations of the acts of trade. These efforts became a critical issue as Whitehall sought to control directly the provincial regimes in America. And in Virginia an effort to improve the marketing of tobacco led to an open confrontation between governor and assembly, a rift which brought to the forefront the provincial House of Burgesses as an institution to be reckoned with.

Sustained periods of war in Europe and in the American and West Indian dependencies of the belligerent imperial powers as well as partisan politics in London weakened and distorted the Anglo-American commercial and political nexus. As English officials and party chieftains occupied themselves with partisan squabbles at Westminster and bloody battles in Europe, the formulation and implementation of colonial policy suffered greatly. The commercial relations of New England and the Chesapeake provinces with the mother country were particularly affected. Against this backdrop the struggle for power between local leaders in the American colonies and royal officials in each of the diverse mainland provinces was waged.

PART II

The American Scene from the Ashley to the Delaware

THE POLITICAL HORIZON of the great majority of the inhabitants of English America was no wider than that of the petty gentry or the common folk of England. Although the early emigrants had left England they brought with them to America the strong sense of localism tenaciously held by their countrymen, a resentment against outside interference. They gave their loyalty to the immediate community; they also retained traditional English values regarding social status and its relation to political authority.

Customarily in England, even at the local level, governmental office was identified with social status, and political contests in the counties were struggles among local leaders for prestige and influence. The sons and nephews of the lesser gentry and merchants who crossed the Atlantic and the men who rose in America from humble beginnings continued in the belief that social rank must be recognized by the conferring of political authority. But the colonial scene was characterized by greater economic opportunity, more social mobility, and more fragmented governmental authority than existed perhaps in England. In the individual provinces governmental power was divided. Men might seek to enhance the elected assemblies; they might attempt to better their position through the patronage and authority of an appointed governor and council, or if denied gratification on the provincial level, an aspirant for office and influence could appeal to Whitehall and Westminster to reverse an unfavorable decision in the colonies. American society exhibited marked instability and friction brought on not only by the pursuit of economic advantage and religious and ethnic pluralism but also by the disparity between social status and political power at the upper levels and competition between those who held power and those who aspired to it as a mark of recognition, as a symbol of having arrived.

That men commonly resorted to the rhetoric of liberty or the rights of Englishmen in the local legislative assemblies or preached the virtues of prerogative government often indicated no more than that they needed to appear high-minded and disinterested even while pursuing their own goals. Anti-popery at times served the same purpose. Rarely did ordinary men even express themselves on political issues. As for those at the upper levels of provincial society who did profess beliefs, they were not impelled to transform their rhetoric into action and thus create situations dictated by the logic of the ideas they professed. Politics, the quest for office and status, was a passion with the ranking elements of colonial society in the seventeenth century. William Penn once described America as "this licentious wilderness" and the Friends in Pennsylvania and New Jersey as men infatuated with a sense of their own importance. "Be not so *govermentish*, so noisy and open in your dissatisfactions," he implored them. Avoid "factions & partys, whisperings and reportings, & all animosities."[1]

Attempts by royal officials in England to bring the colonists to acknowledge dependence on the crown added but one more dimension to the political scene; it created yet another avenue for those seeking honor, recognition, and profit, but it also posed a threat to those who based their power on the sanctions of a local authority—in New England, for example, on the provincial corporations, or elsewhere in the royal and proprietary provinces, on the locally elected assemblies.

The majority of the American colonies, those south of New York, were more remote from the conflict with the French than the New England provinces; their governments were not as immediately or consistently involved in the problems engendered by chronic war. Different political arrangements further divided the middle and southern provinces. Only Virginia was a royal colony—one directly dependent on the crown, as the monarch appointed the governor and the council—although in Maryland and, for a time, in Pennsylvania the authorities in Whitehall had interfered, ostensibly because the proprietary administrations of William Penn and the Calvert family had jeopardized the safety of the king's subjects.

CHAPTER 5

Virginia, 1696–1715: Royal Dominion and Local Oligarchy

Since the days of the Restoration it had been a commonplace in English administrative circles that authorities in London could best control the overseas plantations, could render them directly dependent on the crown, by a governor commissioned and instructed by Whitehall. The experience with two colonies in the American South offered an opportunity to test this assumption. Both Virginia and Maryland were far enough removed from the conflict with French Canada that their governors were not forced to make certain concessions to satisfy the almost continuous need, common in New York, New Hampshire, and Massachusetts, for military appropriations from the local assemblies.

Except for the Commonwealth and Protectorate interludes, royal appointees had presided over the government of Virginia since 1625, yet the experience of these officials both before and after the Glorious Revolution offered concrete evidence that the simple formula espoused by the ministers of state had serious shortcomings. A rebellion in 1676 had nearly toppled Sir William Berkeley; his successor, Thomas Lord Culpepper, had demonstrated more concern for his own ease and purse than for fulfilling his orders from Whitehall; and Baron Howard of Effingham had shown neither the physical nor the mental toughness needed to preside over the colony. A coterie of contentious, self-assured planters from the upper stratum of Virginia society, related by blood and marriage and, for the most part, native born, during the next two decades effectively challenged the royal appointees subsequently sent out from England. Dominating in the council, if not then in the elected House of Burgesses, they laid the foundation for provincial autonomy.

Several factors worked to undermine the royal governors. Various ministers and officers in Whitehall, Lambeth Palace, and Fulham Palace—the last two, seats of the primate of England and the bishop of London—often were at cross-purposes; as a result they thwarted the monarch's deputy at James Town and Williamsburg and encouraged contentious local magnates seeking to circumvent the governors. The revenue available to the governors was limited: the hazards of transatlantic traffic during the war years led to stagnation in trade as too few ships arrived in the Chesapeake to carry the colony's staple crop to market. In some years no fleet arrived. The price for tobacco sold in Virginia remained low.

As exports fell, so too did revenue. A tax of two shillings per hogshead of tobacco shipped out of the colony, voted by the provincial legislature, went to help defray the cost of government for the province. Quitrents constituted another potential source of revenue, but the Culpepper-Fairfax families, not the crown, received the revenue from a portion of Virginia, that lying between the Rappahannock and the Potomac rivers. This enormous tract, the so-called Northern Neck, consisting of more than a million acres, was an entity within the larger unit of Virginia. Initially granted in 1649 by the exiled Charles Stuart to a group of royalist supporters, by 1696 it had become the property of the Culpepper-Fairfax clan in England. These proprietors collected their rents in the Northern Neck through deputies in Virginia—Philip Ludwell, George Brent, and William Fitzhugh.

The idiosyncracies and personal ambitions of the leading Virginians were also critical to the success of an administration. The problems faced by governors coming out from England ranged from the profound to the petty and involved questions of local privileges and parochial desires as against royal authority and imperial needs. Ranking Virginians, masters in their own estates over family, servants, and slaves, were jealous of their position and prestige. Contentious personalities, they often clashed with governors and with each other. Ralph Wormeley once complained of having been replaced as collector for the Rappahannock district after serving for twenty-odd years. Not the loss of salary, but of honor and the implication of censure rankled.[1] At times contentiousness seemed to run in a family, as with the Beverleys, who established a tradition of opposition to royal governors.

Cohesive political groupings had not as yet formed as the last decade of the seventeenth century opened. Among the leading families, some supported whoever might occupy the governor's chair—he was still the source of high-level patronage—but rewards in the form of office did not always bring support for a governor. For every successful office-seeker there was at least one disgruntled aspirant. As Lord Chesterfield was to comment on the English political scene a half century later, there was not enough pasture to feed the beasts. A potential for faction existed within the governor's council, among the men who sought financial as well as moral support from the crown for the Anglican college at Williamsburg and in a coterie of men at the highest level of provincial society, magnates related by blood and marriage.

A member of both groups was James Blair, a contentious, opinionated, and unscrupulous Scot who had taken orders in the Church of England before coming to Virginia in 1685 as the protégé of Henry Compton, bishop of London. Four years later Compton had appointed Blair his commissary for the colony. The Scottish-born cleric immediately formulated plans to establish an ecclesiastical court, challenging the authority of the vestrymen and the church wardens in the local parishes to employ priests. Hitherto the laymen had decided whether or not to present ministers to the governor for induction into office. Through the House of Burgesses the vestrymen sought to thwart Blair, initially on the issue of augmenting clerical salaries. The amount of money agreed upon failed to satisfy the commissary, who accused the incumbent governor, Sir Edmund Andros, of failing to use his prerogative in inducting priests into the parishes and in not applying the revenue from quitrents for clerical stipends. Blair was in a strong position because of support in Fulham Palace and because of his marriage to Sarah Harrison, daughter of Benjamin Harrison II.[2] Through the Harrisons he was also related to the Burwells and the Ludwells, who formed an inner ring among the more prominent clans of Virginia. Blair's brother-in-law, Benjamin Harrison III, was also a close friend of Robert Carter, a magnate in the Northern Neck. Vain men, used to dominating people on their estates and in their local communities, and possessed of a strong sense of their own worth, the Harrisons, the Ludwells, and Carter and Blair viewed high office and the exercise of power as nothing more than the consequences of their ability, their wealth, and their social position.

The contentious Blair, secure in the favor of the episcopal bench in England and in his family relations in Virginia, was a particular problem for any governor sent out from London. No man could oppose him without earning his enmity. The first to feel the wrath of the commissary was Sir Edmund Andros. An experienced army officer, he had served as governor of New York from 1674 to 1681 and had presided over the Dominion of New England with another officer, Francis Nicholson, as his deputy in Manhattan. Both men had fallen victim to insurgent propaganda in 1689 when news of the overthrow of the Catholic James II arrived in America. Nicholson had fled New York in 1689 but then had gone on to serve briefly as deputy governor in the Old Dominion before Andros arrived there in 1692 with a commission as governor. Nicholson was transferred to the less important post in neighboring Maryland. Ambitious, and resentful of Andros, Nicholson allied himself with Blair. London and the Chesapeake were treated to the spectacle of one royal governor attacking another. From Annapolis Nicholson complained to the archbishop of Canterbury of "being kicked upstairs" and prevented from righting the affairs of the churches, schools, and college in Virginia.[3]

Blair sounded the same theme. For some time he had been contending with the governor over money to be allotted for the support of the college, funds Andros preferred to spend on defense. An open break between the two occurred in 1695 with Andros suspending Blair from the council. But the Board of Trade in Whitehall ordered Blair reinstated, until such time as he forfeited the king's trust. The governor's judgment mattered little. By the end of 1696 Blair and Nicholson were collaborating to oust Andros. Blair's own position on the provincial council had been put in doubt, for under the provisions of the Act to Prevent Frauds, passed in 1696, as an alien Scot he might not be eligible to hold public office in an English colony.

For some time officials in Whitehall had been unhappy with the situation in Virginia, particularly with the claim of the councilors to an exemption from prosecution in the local courts. Residents in Virginia had complained that under the rules promulgated by the General Court of the colony, a would-be plaintiff in any action against a councilor had no remedy at law. The councilors were also among the largest land speculators in the province.[4] Officials in London also frowned on plural officeholding by the councilors. To facilitate the administration of the regulations on trade and the collection of duties, six districts had been established in the colony, with a naval officer to maintain records of ships entering and clearing and a receiver to collect duties. Contrary to the wishes of the administration in London the governors had acquiesced to the council board and had appointed the same man, often a councilor, as naval officer and receiver of the customs.

By the spring of 1697 the administration of government on the provincial level was in disarray. Nicholson spent much of his time not in Maryland but in Virginia, where he and Blair kept up a steady attack on Andros. Both governors appealed to London, Andros to the duke of Shrewsbury, Nicholson to, among others, John Locke, a member of the Board of Trade. In a fawning letter to "ye most ingenious and learned author of Human Understanding" (Locke had published his *Essay Concerning Human Understanding* in 1690) Nicholson suggested that Blair, then on his way to London, might give the commissioner of trade a full account of the situation in Virginia. Not content with letting Blair carry the burden alone, Nicholson wrote to Archbishop Edward Tenison that had he, as governor of Maryland, done but half of what Andros had committed in Virginia, he would have been turned out of office.[5]

Andros was not without defenders in Virginia and in London. In the spring of 1697 William Byrd, the receiver and auditor of the royal revenue in the Old Dominion—posts he held as deputy to William Blathwayt—sent his son off to England. Having resolved to pursue a career in law, the younger Byrd intended to settle at one of the Inns of Court. Andros might also benefit—if only indirectly—from the enemies Nicholson had made in Maryland, particularly the relations of John Coode, a malcontent with a reputation as a perennial rebel. From Plymouth, Coode's stepson, Gerard Slye, a merchant who traveled often between England and the Chesapeake, sent in a damning assessment of Nicholson to Godolphin at the Treasury, accusing him of being "furiously jealous" in his zeal for erecting churches and colleges at such great expense that the populace was unable to bear the cost. Nicholson was "mad" at those who had first supported the Protestant king during the late revolution, calling them "rebels" and threatening to try them by a file of musketeers and then to "hang them with the Magna Carta about their necks." So Sly professed himself compelled to relate. The Lords Justices in Council—with Tenison among them—resolved to hear Slye when next he came to London and, if necessary, to have him testify at the Plantation Office.[6]

Evidently Slye did not put in an appearance for some months, too late to influence the decision on Andros. The governor of Virginia had already fallen into disfavor with Bridgewater, Meadows, Pollexfen, Hill, and John Locke at the Plantation Office; he had failed, as ordered, to secure from the council and

Burgesses a complete body of laws of the colony. For some time, so it had appeared in London, the statutes of Virginia had been in disarray. In the summer of 1697 Locke cooperated with the opponents of Andros to orchestrate the case against the governor. To this end Blair composed a paper, "Some Cheif [*sic*] Greivances [*sic*] of the present Constitution of Virginia with an Essay towards the Remedies thereof."[7] With this as a guide Locke set down a list of questions to be put to Blair and two other Virginians then in London, Henry Hartwell and Edward Chilton. The three Virginians then drew up a "full and plain " account of the government of the colony, a document they submitted at the Plantation Office on 20 October.[8]

In their account of the state of Virginia, Hartwell, Blair, and Chilton found the Old Dominion to be the poorest, most miserable, worst country in America. They found particular fault with what they saw as the concentration of power in the royal governor: he granted lands; appointed officials; called, prorogued, and dissolved assemblies; and either approved or rejected bills. As commander in chief he appointed officers of the militia; as treasurer he issued warrants for paying out public moneys; as president he directed and managed the council; as chief justice he presided over judicial affairs; as ecclesiastical ordinary he granted licenses for marriages and for the induction of ministers and decided all church causes. The means to limit the power of this single official, once effective, were now weakened. Although the governor could not act without the express advice and consent of the council, the present incumbents of the board were at the "devotion" of Andros, ready instruments to do his will.[9]

Blair extended the campaign to remove Andros and weaken the power of royal governors in Virginia to the ecclesiastical authorities. He submitted to Archbishop Tenison and Bishop Compton accounts of Andros's character, attacking his conduct toward the clergy of Virginia and his actions relating to the college.[10] These defects he stressed at a conference held on 27 December 1697 and attended by Tenison and Compton. John Povey, one-time clerk of the committee of the Privy Council for plantation affairs, and the younger Byrd sought to defend Andros, but in vain. The decision was never really in doubt, although Tenison terminated the session by turning to Compton with a cryptic "We must take a time to consider what is fit to be done upon all this." Andros was not inclined to continued the struggle. He had already informed Blathwayt of his inclination to leave Virginia on account of "great sickness." In March 1698 he asked for permission to return to England.[11] Locke was pressing the case for Nicholson with the king's "great ministers of state," Somers and Shrewsbury, as was Tenison. According to the prelate, no man was so well inclined as Nicholson: "He will be true to his God and his King." Blathwayt preferred not to contest the matter, and William III was brought to accept the transfer of Nicholson, Andros ostensibly having desired to resign the government of Virginia to attend to private business in England.[12]

Bishop Compton now sought to secure the financial position of his commissary, but his argument that Blair sit on the provincial council so that his colleagues might not reject his authority met with no success initially. His characterization of Blair as a "discreet man" may have amused some at Whitehall.[13]

The successful attack on Andros had serious consequences for the position of a king's governor in Virginia—consequences perhaps not appreciated at Whitehall. Accepting the arguments of Blair, Chilton, and Hartwell in drafting the instructions to the new governor, Bridgewater, Pollexfen, Meadows, Locke, and Abraham Hill struck hard at the power of the official through whom the colony was to depend directly on the crown. The Commissioners of Trade objected to the administration of government depending entirely on the governor's will and pleasure. Hereafter the council had to approve all orders issued in the name of the governor and council, and when suspending a member of the board, Nicholson had to transmit to England a full transcript of the proceedings. The councilors also lost some privileges: they would no longer be exempt from civil suit and no longer hold the posts of collector and naval officer at the same time. The positions of auditor and receiver of the revenue would also be kept separate.[14] Nonetheless, in seeking to correct the defects and abuses in the government alleged by Blair and his colleagues, the Commissioners of Trade were weakening the power of the king's governor. The Lords Justices in Council—Tenison, Dorset, Marlborough, and Charles Montagu—approved the instructions to Nicholson.

At the close of the summer of 1698 Blair was preparing to leave England for the Chesapeake. His brother-in-law, Benjamin Harrison III, was able to inform Nicholson, then in Maryland, of the alterations proposed for the government of Virginia, but advised the governor-designate to keep these instructions secret so as to maintain an advantage over the provincial magnates. Nicholson could thus rid himself of anyone on the council who displeased him.[15] So much for the complaints of arbitrary rule by the governors. Before Andros left Virginia he had taken the opportunity to place his supporters in office: Colonel Dudley Digges on the council, William Byrd II as agent for the board in London, and Bartholomew Fowler as provincial attorney general.

On 9 December 1698 Francis Nicholson took over the government of Virginia, an administration much in debt. One of his first acts was to pay his respects to his patrons. To John Locke he sent a bottle of brandy and some gloves, products of Virginia. Locke acknowledged the gifts: "The flourishing of the plantations *under their due & just regulations* being that w[hi[ch I doe & shall always aim at whilst I have the honour to sit at the board I now doe."[16] The new governor also moved quickly to confirm James Blair and his friends in power and to remove Andros's last appointments. He raised Robert Carter and John Custis to the council board and allowed Nathaniel Harrison to serve as collector and naval officer for the upper district of the James River. When Richard Lee resigned from the council because of old age, Nicholson named another of the Blair clan, Lewis Burwell. Benjamin Harrison II and his son also won office, as clerk of the council and provincial attorney general. During the first two years of the administration James Blair and his allies dominated. When the governor was ill, not the ranking member of the council or the provincial secretary but Blair communicated with the Plantation Office. The commissary, Philip Ludwell, Jr., the Harrisons, and Robert Carter formed an inner group in power.

Francis Nicholson soon became unhappy with the situation, complaining repeatedly that as the business of government increased it was more difficult to fill offices with qualified men. The English gentlemen of quality who had fled to the Old Dominion during the Civil War were now almost all dead. As opportunities to amass a fortune in the province through land speculation narrowed, the local magnates were monopolizing the process; the migration of educated men from England consequently had fallen. Within a generation the government would lack qualified officials should the "Natives," those born in Virginia, prove incompetent. By the opening of the new century, men of tolerable parts in England would have little encouragement, if any, to emigrate. Formerly there had been lands to take up and widows with good fortunes to marry. Now most of the good soil was claimed, and if widows or maids of fortune remained, the natives got them. The governor professed to see in the Virginians an aversion to outsiders, "strangers," they called them.[17]

Governor Nicholson himself ardently pursued one of the most eligible young maids of Virginia, Lucy Burwell, much to the disgust of her father, Major Lewis Burwell. The middle-aged governor's crude attempt to force himself on the girl won him only the enmity of the Burwells and their relations, the most powerful clan in the Old Dominion. Nicholson's alienation from the Burwells and the need to maintain a quorum of councilors who lived within easy traveling distance of the provincial capital weakened the governor and strengthened Blair's position. Nicholson showed poor judgment in pressing his suit with Lucy Burwell and in nominating men to the council board on the basis of their convenient residence without fully considering family and political attachments. Soon after Nicholson had assumed the governorship, the balance on the council shifted. Of the men who had sided with Andros in his dispute with Blair, by the spring of 1703 only John Lightfoot and William Byrd remained. The majority of the new appointees were young men, native to Virginia, on the threshold of great wealth and jealous of their personal interests. Unfortunately for Nicholson they were also related to the strong-minded commissary and to Benjamin Harrison II, the dominant political figures south of the James River. And James Blair regarded himself as the unofficial ruler, the power behind the governor's chair, the man who made and unmade governors.

To carry out the reforms and changes demanded from Whitehall, Nicholson had to transgress on the vested interests of the family alliance dominating on the council. And in his efforts to obtain a revision and codification of the provincial laws, the governor failed, although his criticism of the arrogant aristocrats may have endeared him to the rank and file, the freeholders, smaller planters, and farmers who elected the burgesses. Nicholson was popular among the smaller planters and received support from many of the burgesses, as the lower house and the council were often at odds.

The provincial legal code was one of several issues dividing the government; others included domination of office by the councilors, the method of disposing of public land, and money for the civil establishment and for the defense of Virginia and other English colonies. Administration of revenue came within the offices of receiver and auditor, posts sought by the younger William Byrd. When Nicholson, following the lead of the Plantation Office, suggested one man not fill both positions, he precipitated the opposition of Byrd, who hoped to succeed his father. Nor did Nicholson have much success in inducing the Byrds and the councilors to draw up an accurate roll to ascertain the quitrents due the government. The speculators on the council were among the officials who determined the procedures for surveying and distributing land and for registering patents. The entire system as already established operated to benefit those at the uppermost level of Virginia society and government.[18] In challenging this system Nicholson was striking at their source of potential wealth, and in seeking to name justices of the peace, sheriffs, and militia and naval officers he was undermining their social and political influence.

By the summer of 1702 the break was open. "We live in a storm and continual hurry," the younger William Byrd complained.[19] Blair and his cohorts on the council had fired the opening shot with publication of *An Essay on the Government of the English Plantations*. Robert Beverley followed this with his *Present State of Virginia* in which he accused the governor of violently attacking Andros's appointee as provincial attorney general when Bartholomew Fowler had protested that some action of Nicholson was contrary to law. As Beverley told it, Nicholson, in a fury, had seized the attorney general and swore that "*he knew no laws they* [the colonists] *had, and that his Commands should be obey'd without Hesitation or Reserve.*" When men claimed the protection of the laws of England and protested the governor's arbitrary actions, Nicholson allegedly retorted: "*They had no right at all to the Liberties of English Subjects, and that he would hang up those that should presume to oppose him, with Magna Carta about their Necks.*" He openly professed that he knew how to govern without assemblies, and if the Virginians should deny him anything, he would secure a standing army to bring the obstreperous provincials to reason, with halters about their necks. So Beverley alleged.[20]

James Blair was more direct, if not more circumspect, in his attacks on a governor he could no longer manipulate. Through Stephen Founce, a local clergyman, the commissary protested to Archbishop Tenison: "He governs us as if we were a Company of Galley Slaves," continually roaring and thundering, cursing and swearing with such abusive "Billingsgate Language" as to be beyond belief of anyone who had not heard him. Blair professed to speak for the clergy of Virginia, but when he and his relations on the council formally complained against Nicholson, twenty of the clerics, a majority of those resident in Virginia, defended the governor.[21] The support of the provincial clergymen notwithstanding, in London Nicholson had been compromised. Rumors circulated in the coffeehouses and on the Exchange questioning his mental state.[22]

In the spring of 1703 the Blair-Burwell-Ludwell-Harrison clique on the council openly called for the recall of the governor. Objecting not only to Nicholson's crude mannerisms and his alleged bullying, six councilors charged him with attempting to promote a scheme to alter the government of the colony; ironically it was the plan inspired by Blair, Hartwell, and Chilton several years before in the campaign against Sir Edmund Andros. The sheer number of accusations placed Nicholson on the defensive. Emphasizing his personal indiscretions as evidence of unfitness for office, the dissident councilors devoted much of their memorial to a series of vague charges called ''Other Public Abuses''—recriminations ''little more than gossip mongering''—and resorted to half-truths, innuendo, and guilt by association. In the following months they substantiated these allegations only by repeating them. The dissidents were not disinterested men: directly or indirectly they stood to lose from the governor's efforts to end plural office holding and to check the acquisition of large tracts of land. At this time, the other councilors on the board—John Custis, Henry Duke, and Edmund Jennings—did not join in the attack, but neither did they defend Nicholson.[23]

In England developments unrelated to the contest in Virginia led to Nicholson's dismissal. With the support of Lord Treasurer Godolphin, Marlborough, even before his smashing victory at Blenheim, was moving to preempt the governorships in the colonies for favored officers of the army. James Blair and Stephen Founce arrived in London in the fall of 1703 but waited until the tobacco fleet had departed for the Chesapeake the following spring to present their protests against Nicholson. Since communication was usually restricted to the tobacco carriers, the governor would not learn of the official charges against him until the arrival of another fleet, perhaps the following year. Late in April 1704 the Plantation Office received affidavits from the Reverend James Wallace of Elizabeth City County; George Luke, a collector of customs; Robert Carter; John Lightfoot; Philip Ludwell, Jr.; the Harrisons; and Lewis and Nathaniel Burwell. On 1 May Blair offered further charges of maladministration. Other Virginians were present—Robert Beverley and Edmund Jennings—but the provincial secretary failed to support the governor; he was more concerned with private family matters in England. It fell to John Thrale, acting as a private agent for Nicholson, to point out that the charges by Blair, Beverley, and Founce were either too vague to be answered or malicious insinuations submitted without proof.[24] Thrale was of no further use; he died suddenly while the hearings were in progress.

Any reply Nicholson might have offered would probably have been useless. His reputation had suffered from the rumors circulating in London, and Marlborough had already promised the governorship of Virginia to one of his favorites in the army, George Hamilton, earl of Orkney, when the position became vacant. Marlborough professed to his duchess that he would not pretend to judge whether or not the incumbent ought to go, that he would leave to others who were hearing the evidence, "for if he be not madd, as thay [sic] say he is, he is a good officer." Rumor in London also had it that Colonel Daniel Parke, a Virginian who had won the favor of Marlborough and who had received the honor of bringing to London the news of the victory at Blenheim, would return to the Chesapeake, perhaps as Orkney's deputy.[25]

Nicholson was not a man to accept his fate passively. From private sources he had received copies of letters and a "Narrative" composed in England by Beverley in which he had accused the governor, "our Duke," of aiming at despotic power, of seeking to impose martial law by military force. A grand jury in Virginia condemned Beverley's paper as false, scandalous, and malicious and concluded that, contrary to what he claimed, the people generally were well satisfied with the government under Nicholson. The justices of Beverley's own county—he was clerk of the commission of peace—condemned him for stirring up sedition and asked that he be removed from office.[26] Not until 1 March 1704/5 was Nicholson able formally to reply to the charges made against him in London. He gave as good as he got, and in kind. By written records and the evidence of living men, most of the charges sworn by Blair and Beverley were not true; other actions he had simply taken in carrying out his duties as instructed. Three of the "Affidavit Sparks" were "extra-Tweedians"—that is, Scots—and another, a Frenchman. As for Beverley, the Virginians themselves would not own him. John Lightfoot was merely a tool of the Harrisons, Ludwell, and Robert Carter to inflate the number of the dissident councilors. Blair he dismissed as a man dissatisfied with every administration.[27]

But well before Nicholson sent off his justification the decision had gone against him. Two months before, Blair had sent word from London to Philip Ludwell, Jr., that "it is in everyone's mouth" that the earl of Orkney would receive the government. Only parliamentary business in Scotland delayed the appointment. But Orkney would be an absentee governor, and since Daniel Parke was to go to Leeward Islands, several hopefuls had put in for the post of deputy governor at Williamsburg. Marlborough and Godolphin had settled on Major Edward Nott, the deputy governor of Berwick, who had married the sister of Nathaniel Blakiston, once governor and now agent for Maryland. The son of a royalist follower of Charles I, Nott had served for twenty-eight years in the army and had spent some time in the West Indies. As Blakiston put it, Blair "has effected his conquest at last."[28]

Nicholson had suffered defeat in Whitehall, but it was a defeat inspired from Virginia. The royal governor commissioned to carry out the wishes of the ministers of the crown, to insure that the government of the colony would depend on the monarch, had been repudiated by the crown at the call of provincial magnates seeking to maintain and advance their own power in the colony. Nicholson had lost in London, but not in Virginia. When the assembly met in April, Nicholson's supporters were in the majority; his staunch friends Gawin Corbin, Miles Cary, and William Randolph led the key committees. On 4 May when John Lightfoot, Robert Carter, and Philip Ludwell appeared at the door of the House of Burgesses asking permission to present their side of the dispute with the governor, they met with a refusal. The majority in the burgesses would not even allow a letter submitted by the councilors to be read, and at the end of extended debate Cary carried a resolution by a vote of 27 to 18 that it was the opinion of the house that Nicholson had great respect for the welfare and prosperity of the country and that the better part of the queen's subjects in Virginia did not share the sentiments of the dissidents on the council who had accused Nicholson of maladministration. A week later four of the council—John Lewis, John Custis, John Smith, and Henry Duke—formally adhered to the position taken by the majority in the burgesses. Before Nicholson left the Old Dominion, twenty-three of Virginia's clergymen also acknowledged his services as governor and repudiated Blair's accusations as scandalous and malicious.[29] Nicholson had the further satisfaction of seeing Robert Beverley suffer political ruin. As a result of his intemperate attacks on the crown Surveyor General of the Customs Beverley lost credibility both in England and in Virginia.

Well aware that James Blair had engineered the fall of the two previous governors of Virginia, Edward Nott was hardly anxious to contest the position of the commissary, his relations, or his allies. After a tedious voyage across the Atlantic, Nott and Blair arrived within the capes of the Chesapeake on 11 August 1705. Four days later the deputy governor met with the councilors. At their urging he agreed to recommend that William Byrd, Jr., succeed his dead father to the posts of auditor and receiver of the revenue, since the elder Byrd had held these positions for some years and it was essential to place the revenue in the hands of a capable man. Although Nott was well aware that his instructions prohibited one person's executing both offices, he gave way. The decision was reversed in Whitehall, however, despite the further support of Micajah Perry and Thomas Lane, a prominent tobacco firm in London. The younger Byrd had to content himself with the post of receiver. The office of auditor went to Dudley Digges.[30]

The deputy governor's instructions also prohibited councilors from concurrently holding the positions of collector of the duty on exported tobacco and naval officer, but the members of the board prevailed on Nott to waive this rule. They also sought a role in nominating and commissioning clerks of the county, thus encroaching on the prerogative of the provincial secretary. The magnates on the board further resisted implementing the instructions to Nott for revising procedures in granting lands, for securing a bill to establish ports for vessels in the transatlantic trade, for compiling a roll of quitrents, and for codifying the provincial laws. An assembly elected shortly after the arrival of Nott had revised many of the statutes, but of the twenty-two sent up to the council, the board passed only seven without amendment, sending the others back. After a month, later in November 1705, the Burgesses complained of having to meet during cold weather and asked for a recess. Nott complied, allowing them to adjourn until the next spring.[31]

Within a few months after the Burgesses reconvened, in August 1706, Nott died of a fever. The administration of the government then devolved on the councilors, Dudley Digges, Benjamin Harrison, Robert Carter, James Blair, Philip Ludwell, William Basset, Henry Duke, and Edmund Jennings as president. The fortunes of war, English politics, and bureaucratic ineptness all combined to favor Blair and his relations on the council of Virginia.

Four years passed before a new deputy governor commissioned by the crown arrived in Williamsburg. During the hiatus the magnates in Williamsburg took charge of revising and codifying the laws of Virginia. The attorney general and solicitor general of the crown had objected particularly to the method of enacting laws in the colony, in which the general assembly assumed a liberty to pass such measures as thought convenient, laws to be in force until the monarch might choose to disapprove. They preferred a method previously incorporated in the commission issued to Thomas Culpepper a quarter of a century before whereby the governor would submit proposed legislation to the king in council. If found satisfactory in England the legislation would be returned to the colony under the Great Seal to be enacted by the provincial assembly.[32] Such a procedure, one fundamentally altering the locus of power and dependent on a strong-willed governor, had not worked in the past.

Not until the end of 1706 did the Commissioners of Trade inform the ministers of state of Nott's death and the need to send out a replacement, and not until April 1707 did the Plantation Office receive orders to prepare a commission and instructions for Colonel Robert Hunter, another of Marlborough's favorites. But while on his way to his new post, Hunter fell victim on the high seas to French marauders and was taken captive to France. The British authorities failed to appoint a successor, and when Hunter was finally exchanged, he was sent as governor not to Virginia but to New York. In the absence of a governor or his lieutenant the clique on the council who had railed against Andros and Nicholson dominated the government of the Old Dominion free of restraint both from the local assembly and the ministers of state at Whitehall. Although Jennings, the president of the council, had instructions allowing him to call an assembly, he and the other members of the board governed for four years without the burgesses. Almost two years after Nott's death, Jennings revealed to the authorities in London that since the assembly had been prorogued before the demise of the deputy governor, the councilors thought fit to continue the prorogation until a successor to Nott arrived. Jennings simply continued to prorogue the house from one scheduled meeting to another so that some among the burgesses surmised that the assembly was "ipso facto" dissolved. The country being quiet, no need existed to call another. On the advice of the other councilors the next year, Jennings held off meeting the burgesses, ostensibly to save the taxpayers money. By 1709 the councilors had regained all of the authority they had lost to previous governors over the appointment of officers of the militia, justices in the counties, and the distribution of land.[33]

In the spring of 1709 Robert Hunter was back in London following an exchange of prisoners with the French. But doubt arose as to when, if ever, he would take up his duties in Virginia. Several vacancies now existed in the American and West Indian colonies. Death had created an opening at Manhattan, and dissatisfaction with the incumbent in Boston was evident. At one time Godolphin and Marlborough gave some thought to reinstituting the arrangement used when Bellomont had gone to America, by appointing Hunter governor of both Massachusetts and New York, but Joseph Dudley managed to hang on in Massachusetts, and Hunter received only the appointment for New York and New Jersey.

Who would succeed Nott as Orkney's deputy at Williamsburg? William Byrd II had aspirations. Through Nathaniel Blakiston, former governor of Maryland and now agent for Virginia in London, he hoped to purchase the post from Lady Orkney for £1,000. Blakiston quickly disabused him of the notion: the duke of Marlborough had declared that no one but a soldier should have the government of a colony. The choice fell on another of the duke's favorites. In 1710 Secretary Sunderland issued a warrant for the appointment of Alexander Spotswood as lieutenant governor of Virginia. Blakiston thought him to be a man of honor.[34] The son of an army physician and grandson of a distinguished lawyer executed for his loyalty to Charles I, Alexander Spotswood had entered the army as a youth. He had been wounded at Blenheim and captured at Oudenarde and finally exchanged. At the age of thirty-four he arrived in Virginia to begin what proved to be a long and eventful career.

For four years Blair and a coterie related to the Burwells had dominated the council and higher levels of government in Virginia. The commissary had already undermined two governors appointed from Whitehall. The latest appointee arrived on the last day of the spring of 1710. His first weeks in office were deceptive; that summer he wrote from Williamsburg: ''The life I am now likely to lead here is a perfect retir'd Country life.'' He saw a ''fair prospect of a good Agreement with the People,'' and thought he would ''live very contentedly here; for I have not the Diversions of London (which I do not in the least hancker [*sic*] after) neither have I the perplexities of that Town.''[35]

Such was not to be the case, as relations with the councilors soon demonstrated. A majority of the board, seven of the twelve members, belonged to one extended family: Blair, Philip Ludwell II, Benjamin Harrison II (Blair's father-in-law), William Byrd II (husband of Ludwell's half niece, Lucy Parke), William Basset and Edmund Berkeley (husbands, respectively, of Joanna and Lucy Burwell), and Robert Carter (father-in-law of Nathaniel Burwell). Personal rivalries set this clique against other members of the council. Ludwell coveted

Jennings's post as secretary. Jennings had persuaded Lady Fairfax, proprietor of the Northern Neck, to drop Carter as her fiscal agent in favor of his nephew, Thomas Lee.

After the initial weeks of tranquility Spotswood began to discover the difficulty of administering a colony handicapped by factionalism on the council and the obstructionist mentality of many men chosen for the House of Burgesses by a fickle and poorly educated electorate. As did Robert Hunter, his colleague in New York, Spotswood determined to create a party in the assembly supporting the governor,[36] a tactic immediately to the advantage of the executive, but one potentially dangerous in that it enhanced the prestige and authority of the elected representatives. In setting up a court of oyer and terminer to deal with criminal cases when the General Court was not in session, Spotswood went outside the council to appoint the speaker and two burgesses as judges. Still the assembly proved stubborn over appropriations for military expenditures. Spotswood had to ask several of the councilors to advance money on the credit of the provincial revenue to make good a treaty with the Tuscarara Indians. The deputy governor also sought to win the favor of certain of the councilors. In 1711 Spotswood, despite the plea of "Divers pretenders," recommended Ludwell to succeed to the posts of auditor and provincial secretary, Dudley Digges having died and Jennings having retired from the struggle and returned to England to manage his family's affairs. These were among the most prestigious positions in the provincial government.[37] What Spotswood did not foresee was that Ludwell and William Byrd II would unite against him when he made clear his unhappiness over the method of collecting quitrents by deputies, under officials who had put in the highest bids for offices. After a protracted battle Byrd departed for England in 1715 to present the case against the lieutenant governor. Personal animosities and a heightened sense of *amour propre* turned others against Spotswood. Gawin Corbin too hurried across the ocean to protest his removal as naval officer for the Rappahannock District for alleged complicity in forging ships' papers. He arrived in London "full freighted to retrieve his honor."[38]

The magnates who sat on the council had a well-developed sense of their prerogatives. In filling one vacancy Spotswood recommended William Basset, a planter who had formerly sat on the board, but Basset refused to take his place, not having been given the precedence he thought his former tenure allowed. Basset asked Ludwell, then in London, to present his case at the Plantation Office. When the Commissioners of Trade would not restore Basset to his former rank, he refused office.[39] In 1714 Spotswood called Edmund Berkeley, Nathaniel Harrison, and Mann Page to the board, but Berkeley in a pique of temper refused to serve, alleging that Spotswood had prevented him from presenting his warrant for office in time, thus allowing Harrison and Page to have precedence over him. Berkeley then had Micajah Perry, the London merchant and close associate of Nathaniel Blakiston, plead his case at the Plantation Office. Spotswood was indignant at "Old Perry's" impertinence; it did "little honor to the

Government to have its Council appointed in the Virginia Coffee House." A governor was at least as capable of ascertaining the qualifications of candidates for the board as a "Merchant in London who has no other rule to judge a man's merit than by the Number of his tobacco hogsheads."[40]

Although Spotswood appreciated the consequence of having Basset and Berkeley on the council—it would increase the number of adherents of the Burwell clan—his choice of suitable men unconnected with the clique was limited. He was particularly loathe to promote John Robinson from the House of Burgesses, where he had done noteworthy service for the administration. For him Spotswood reserved an office of considerable profit, a recently created post of tobacco inspector. To another of Christopher Robinson's sons, the lieutenant governor gave the office of deputy clerk of the county. To carry a majority of the House of Burgesses on controversial matters—granting lands, collecting quitrents, appropriating funds for military expenditures, and reforming the system for shipping tobacco—Spotswood needed the support of the Robinsons and other burgesses willing to join a governor's party and do his work.

For years officials in Whitehall had instructed governors to check the engrossing of large tracts of land and to provide for systematic collection of quitrents. Traditionally, persons acquiring headrights—fifty acres of land for each immigrant entering the colony—had not been limited in the amount of land acquired or forced to make the requisite improvements, which consisted of cultivation of at least three acres and the erection of a house or hut for each headright. The Board of Trade had incorporated these requirements into the eighty-fourth instruction to Spotswood. Yet in passing a law for granting lands the Burgesses in 1711 failed to include these provisions. They had been willing, however, to allow the failure to pay quitrents for three consecutive years to constitute cause for forfeiture of title. In the past great tracts of land had been taken up and allowed to remain uncultivated with the owners not paying rents, for the sheriffs had found nothing on such properties to distrain. In 1711 Spotswood issued a proclamation embodying the terms of his instructions and an order prohibiting the granting of rights for more than 400 acres until he was satisfied as to the qualifications of the grantee to take up additional land. In London, the Commissioners of Trade insisted that the provincial assembly enact legislation incorporating into law the requirements stipulated in the royal instructions to the governor.[41]

As Spotswood feared, the burgesses rejected a procedure limiting their role merely to ratifying policy set in Whitehall. As the lieutenant governor explained, the "license" to which they had been accustomed was fresh in their minds. The entire country was averse to limitations on grants of land as imposed by Spotswood's instructions. Such limitations had not prevailed during the interim of the administration by the council or even under Nott when the General Court, a body where the governor had no veto, had passed on land grants.

The lieutenant governor did not press the matter, an issue uniting the councilors and the burgesses, but contented himself with devising means more effectively to collect quitrents. The need for additional money for the defense of the colony prevented Spotswood from antagonizing the burgesses, particularly when a war with the Tuscarara Indians broke out on the southern frontiers a little more than a year after he arrived on the Chesapeake. So fearful were the planters of a head tax that they refused even to reveal the number of persons in their families when Spotswood attempted to have a census compiled. This attitude carried over to the elections for the assembly. The governor had little hope for the session called for October 1712 because the qualifications for voting were so low that the vulgar sort among the voters — as Spotswood called them — had returned poorly qualified burgesses, candidates whose principal recommendation had been their pledge to impose no tax no matter what the occasion. Governor Robert Hunter was to find a similar attitude prevailing in New York. The disruptions of trade caused by the war were having their impact, depressing the economy of the Chesapeake. When the burgesses met on 22 October, Spotswood put before them a state of the annual charges to the government for the past twenty-two years, together with the returns for the established revenue over the same period. Since 1689 the funds raised by appropriation acts had fallen each year about £700 short of what was needed to pay salaries and the contingent charges of government. Money paid in the colony to the account of the crown had made up deficiencies.[42]

This last point became a bone of contention following the cessation of hostilities with the Tuscararas and the close of the war with France, when the assemblymen and the councilors joined in an address remonstrating against the practice of crediting revenue from quitrents to the Exchequer in England. The funds should be returned to their "old channel" to pay public expenses. Quitrents were all the more important with the drop in revenue from the duty on exported tobacco as a result of depressed conditions in transatlantic trade.[43]

Spotswood was able to secure two important pieces of legislation from the Virginia legislature, one for regulating trade with the Indians, the other for marketing and shipping tobacco. Both were potentially disruptive for his administration and his relations with the burgesses and councilors. For years fraudulent practices by unscrupulous traders had threatened the traffic with the Indians, leading the outraged natives to vent their wrath on the nearby white settlers. To prevent future antagonism the Virginia legislature in 1714 passed an act for the better regulation of the Indian trade, a law providing for a company of men with sufficient capital to manage a central trade. The group received a monopoly of the traffic to the south of Virginia on condition that it provide forts for the protection of the colony, thus relieving the taxpayers of Virginia of the burden. The venture did not progress well because independent traders already engaged in the traffic and private investors regarded the requirement to fortify the borders as too great a financial burden and hesitated to buy stock in the monopoly. The shares in the company were finally subscribed, but an undue number went to friends of the lieutenant governor and to Spotswood himself, leading to charges that the company was a private monopoly secured by the administration for the benefit of Spotswood and his cronies.

The program the lieutenant governor put through to reform the method of paying public duties and shipping the colony's staple export brought similar charges. For years overproduction and inadequate shipping facilities had led to a glut of tobacco. Not only was tobacco the chief commodity for export, but it was also the principal means of paying taxes. Regardless of quality and current price, tobacco was tender by weight. Often planters paid their taxes with inferior leaf, but enough damaged tobacco or inferior leaf remained to swell the total volume for sale and detract from the reputation of the Chesapeake produce in the overseas market.

In November 1713 Spotswood secured from the assembly an act for improving the shipment of tobacco, a law providing for warehouses at convenient locations for loading. Here agents appointed by the government inspected tobacco brought for export or offered as legal tender; if they found the leaf to be of sufficiently good quality, they would issue certificates specifying the weight and type, whether oronocco or sweet-scented. These certificates were legal tender for all debts and public dues payable in tobacco. A holder presenting these certificates for redemption was entitled to any hogshead of the proper type of tobacco. The law offered several advantages. It would ensure payment of dues owed the government in tobacco of marketable grade rather than in trash and would prevent the export of inferior produce, tobacco which reduced the price and reputation of Virginia leaf. With trash eliminated and the crop offered for market reduced in size, prices would climb. Finally, bringing tobacco to centrally located warehouses rather than having it picked up at the scattered individual plantations would reduce the number of collecting points and the time needed for ocean-going carriers to gather their cargoes, thus lowering freighting charges. Passed over the opposition of some burgesses, the law, providing for inspection for three years, was scheduled to go into effect in November 1714.

The system was potentially open to corruption and abuse by the forty inspectors appointed by the lieutenant governor. Moreover, the disposal of two-score inspectorships, each with an annual salary of £250, gave Spotswood a potent source of patronage. In appointing members of the assembly or their relations Spotswood hoped to create a party to carry "any reasonable point" in the lower house. He named twenty-five burgesses as inspectors, and of the twenty-two in the house not so honored, four had sons or brothers appointed. Every first-term member except two was appointed, and the two passed over had brothers who were named. But adverse weather conditions and the passions of men intervened to frustrate Spotswood's plans. The following summer Robert Anderson, a planter and merchant who served as agent for several London tobacco houses, wrote to Micajah Perry with news of the effects of drought: the crop had been reduced by half. The shortness of the crop when word reached England "must doubtless r[a]ise the tobacco to a good price."[44] Even damaged tobacco, slated for destruction under the provisions of the act scheduled to go into effect that fall, would now be worth some money.

The meeting of the House of Burgesses that autumn inaugurated an interlude of half a dozen years of strife. In the ensuing controversy dissidents made Spotswood the focus of their discontents; their rallying cry was improbity, corruption in the system of tobacco inspection, and the monopolistic company for trade with the Indians. Just as the act for warehouses was to go into effect, opposition to implementing the measure mounted, for much of the crop that year was trash, and many of the smaller planters were near ruin. In the past planters could have sold their inferior tobacco; now it was to be seized and burned under the requirements of the new law. Some planters, better off than most, had assumed that the law would apply only to tobacco used to pay public debts. They now learned otherwise. Others who had used their own wharves for loading and shipping on ocean-going vessels now resented having to transport hogsheads to the warehouses. The planters in the far Northern Neck were opposed to any type of inspection. Reacting to the rising opposition, the assembly passed a bill deferring the operations of the law for another year but coupled it with a measure excusing the poor from levies and permitting them to export freely what tobacco they had.

The outbreak of war with the Yamassee Indians followed by the plea of South Carolina for aid forced Spotswood to call an assembly in 1715 in order to raise men and money. Opposition again centered on the tobacco inspection law as demands for repeal came in from all but four of the twenty-five counties. The elections had resulted in a massive turnover in assembly membership and a rout of the governor's supporters, for the freeholders had returned but sixteen of the fifty-one representatives. Of these sixteen many were burgesses opposed to Spotswood. Successful candidates had appealed to the tax-conscious planters with promises to serve in the assembly without pay. Spotswood placed the blame for the debacle on unprincipled candidates and an uneducated electorate, the meaner sort among the freemen. Whatever the cause of their election, the majority among the burgesses tacked onto a bill repealing the inspection and warehouse law a clause granting a duty to furnish money for the relief of South Carolina. By another bill, one barring all persons from holding offices of profit under the government while sitting in the assembly, they hoped to prevent burgesses from holding inspectorships. In a reversal of roles the councilors rejected both measures.[45]

The burgesses grew even more independent. In the summer of 1715 the group dominating in the lower house refused to make good the deficiencies from the duty on tobacco exported from the colony until the crown allowed revenue from quitrents to be used for the payment of the provincial debt. Spotswood complained to Whitehall that a government without money was helpless. A new administration under the Hanoverian monarch gave in, allowing the revenue from rents to be applied to the charges of the provincial regime.[46]

The next election brought Spotswood no relief in the House of Burgesses, however. To make matters worse for the lieutenant governor, in 1715 several councilors came out against him. William Byrd II and Philip Ludwell II, the receiver and the auditor, broke with him on the question of the Indian trade and a new procedure for administering the collection of quitrents, complaining that the governor proposed to reduce their offices to mere sinecures. Byrd traveled to London, where, with the support of several merchants, he lobbied successfully for the repeal of both the tobacco inspection and Indian trade acts. The breach between the lieutenant governor and the magnates widened when Spotswood dismissed Ludwell and challenged the right of the other councilors to sit as sole judges of the court of oyer and terminer. He thus reinforced the resolve of the majority of the board, men already closely tied by blood and marriage.[47] As Spotswood reported the incident to Whitehall by way of mitigation, Ludwell and his adherents were setting themselves up as "patriots" charging the king's representative with oppressing the people by extending the prerogatives of the crown. Ludwell had made it a merit to oppose all governors.[48]

Despite local opposition, Alexander Spotswood continued as the king's representative in the Old Dominion for a few years longer until 1722, when James Blair again intervened to offset Spotswood's personal connections in London. Apprehensive over the consequences of a test case on collation—the bestowal of a benefice on a clergyman—Blair, through Bishop John Robinson, engineered the dismissal of the lieutenant governor. Major Hugh Drysdale, a friend of Sir Robert Walpole, replaced him. For the third time in a generation the ministers of state and bureaucrats in London, succumbing to the temptation to reward favorites, had acquiesced to pressure from the provincial magnates on the Chesapeake and undermined the royal official entrusted with the duty of rendering the government of the colony directly dependent on the crown.

CHAPTER 6

Maryland, 1696–1715: Royal Government in a Proprietary Colony

THE ABILITY OF ministers of the English crown directly to control government in Maryland came down to the capabilities of a single individual. In an age when lifespans were short and sudden death not uncommon, such control was precarious.

Government directly dependent on the monarchy of England had come to Maryland in the wake of a coup carried out in 1689 against the proprietary regime of Charles Calvert, Lord Baltimore, following receipt of the news from England of the overthrow of James II and the succession of William and Mary. Although Lord Baltimore dispatched a messenger to order the provincial government to proclaim the Protestant monarchs, that messenger died while waiting for a ship to cross the Atlantic, and Baltimore failed to send out another. A small coterie of men headed by John Coode, dissatisfied with the concentration of power in the hands of a clique of Roman Catholics and relatives of the proprietor, then seized control, claiming that the relatives of the Calverts and the Catholics were plotting with hostile Indians to destroy the Protestants of Maryland. The beneficiaries of the coup were not Coode and his disgruntled relations, however, but about three dozen of the more prominent Anglican residents, many of them recent immigrants from England, who, as the Protestant Associators, took upon themselves legislative and administrative functions. They received the favor of the crown when the ministers of state at Whitehall, without calling into question the charter to Baron Baltimore, assumed the authority to appoint a governor and council for the province on the ground that the proprietor, by failing to provide adequately for the protection of the colony, had endangered the lives and property of the king's subjects. They applied the same rationalization against William Penn, although Penn, enjoying much more influence than Baltimore, was able to have the government of Pennsylvania restored to him after only two years, in 1694.

In the government established in Maryland under the royal aegis, members of the Protestant Association, men who had been excluded from higher office and power before 1689, predominated in the appointed council and the elected assembly. But the administration of the first royal governor, Lionel Copley, a petty man concerned solely with his own comfort and profit, provided little stability. Copley's death in September 1693 had further intensified competition for power and the perquisites of office among the leading Protestant Associators and other royal appointees—among them, Sir Thomas Lawrence, Nehemiah Blakiston, Henry Jowles, Kenelm Cheseldyne, and Nicholas Greenberry. Lawrence, the provincial secretary sent out from England, had been involved from the outset of the royal administration in a struggle with Copley and his sycophants over the fees and perquisites of the secretary's office. This contest over Lawrence's post became a test of strength among the contending personalities in the elected House of Delegates and an element in the effort to restore the administration to the proprietary Calvert family.

During these years the proprietor was Charles, third Baron Baltimore, of the Irish peerage. From 1661 he had acted as governor of the province for his father until he himself succeeded to the proprietary in 1676. Although a Catholic he served as a brigadier under William III in 1696 and in the succeeding reign commanded a regiment, winning promotion to major general in 1704.[1] It was a sign of hypocrisy or perhaps merely an indication of the nature of the political world of Whitehall that although Baltimore could be entrusted to command the monarch's troops, he was not allowed to preside over the government of Maryland.

The Catholic supporters of the proprietor in the colony presented a more immediate problem for royal governors when they formed an alliance of convenience with two of the more obstreperous assemblymen. John Coode, a chronic malcontent, had led the insurgent movement in the name of anti-popery half a dozen years before when the proprietary clique was overthrown. But in the subsequent awarding of offices following the assumption of government by the crown, Coode went unrewarded. Indeed, Copley's successor publicly excluded him. Coode then joined forces with the very Catholics against whom he had railed and with Philip Clarke, a rising newcomer in the assembly. As yet, the elected House of Delegates was not a powerful base; it met but once or twice a year and sat for twelve to twenty-one days at a session.

Governor Francis Nicholson had arrived in Maryland in 1694 to find a provincial populace wracked by animosities, its laws unsettled, and its government in disarray. A staunch adherent of the Church of England, he was distressed to learn that an act for supporting the church by a tax of forty pounds of tobacco per poll was little obeyed. Both Catholics and Protestant dissenters, especially Quakers, opposed the law, so that the few Anglican clergymen in the colony subsisted only through voluntary contributions. Nicholson professed to see and hear much Sabbath-breaking, cursing, swearing, whoring, and drinking in evidence. Some men had two wives and some women two husbands. The brief administration of Copley had done nothing to end the chaotic conditions prevailing after the overthrow of the proprietary regime, and money for the support of the provincial administration was short because Baltimore still claimed a portion of the revenues from lands, tobacco exports, and ship duties. From the outset of his administration Nicholson sought to build support through patronage, and in forming a party in the House of Delegates he reserved appointments as sheriffs in the counties to reward men who had done the king's—that is, Nicholson's—service and to encourage others to do the same.[2]

Although the governor was able to prevail upon the delegates in the lower house to enact two laws to supplement the statute for supporting the Anglican church, these enactments fell victim to a disallowance by the king in council after Quakers, in combination with Roman Catholics in the colony, petitioned in London against establishing the Church of England. The English attorney general, Thomas Trevor, found a clause in one of the statutes particularly unacceptable, that proclaiming that the people of Maryland "shall enjoy all their rights and liberties" according to the laws of England where the statutes of Maryland were silent. For all acts of Parliament to be made laws of the colony by this clause was unreasonable. If the assemblymen of Maryland wished to enact any particular statutes of England, they would do better to send over a list so that the king might declare which were fit to be made law and which not. Despite the disallowance, when the House of Delegates was considering an alternative bill, Philip Clarke insisted on tacking on a clause concerning the liberties and properties of the subject. Clarke, Nicholson charged, was a "mighty pretender" to the law, especially to Magna Carta, and one of the most outspoken critics in the assembly. From working with a hoe he had presumed to take upon himself the noble profession of the law, and in pleading cases he took on a confident, impudent, and "balling" (bawling) style.[3]

Clark and his allies—Robert Mason, John Coode, and Coode's stepson, Gerard Slye—did not confine their opposition to the assembly. At Saint Marys in 1698 they instigated a series of disturbances, tending, as Nicholson described it, to rebellion. Slye, Clarke, and Mason were tried, found guilty, and sentenced to confinement for six months. The chief "incendiary," Coode, escaped to Virginia, as he had once before, in 1681, following an unsuccessful uprising against the proprietary government.[4]

Slye, a trader who divided his time between the Chesapeake and England, in 1697 had entered charges against Nicholson at Whitehall, accusations either completely false or distorted half-truths. An additional nineteen charges submitted the following year were simply "ludicrous slanders" of the governor's character.[5] Slye charged Nicholson with having admitted to being an enemy of William III and his government. Among the further crimes and misdemeanors attributed to the governor were that he had made his chaplain walk bareheaded before him to church and that he had often attempted to debauch young women, daughters from gentle families. Moreover, according to Slye, public report in Maryland had it that Nicholson had ravished a Quaker maid in neighboring Pennsylvania. Slye would have sent proof to all of this to London, he explained to James Vernon, a principal secretary of state, but none of the councilors or the justices in Maryland would take depositions while Nicholson remained as governor or until a commission arrived from the king to look into his conduct. Slye's charges received no credence in London. He had failed to make good on his accusations in 1697, and the Lords Justices in Council took no notice of those he submitted the following year. By the end of the summer Slye himself had made his peace with the governor, petitioning for pardon and offering to deliver evidence against his stepfather, John Coode.[6]

By 1698 Nicholson had already shifted his sights to the more lucrative post in Virginia. When he left Annapolis he received a testimonial from the House of Delegates, the judges of the provincial court, the council, and the grand jury of the colony.[7] Although the supporters of Lord Baltimore in Maryland were now hoping for a restoration of proprietary government, the post of governor at Annapolis went to Colonel Nathaniel Blakiston, a nephew of Nehemiah Blakiston, one of the Protestant Associators who had carried out the coup in 1689.

Critical to the political stability of Maryland was the selection of a new provincial council. Coode finally gave up his quest, although his family continued active in local affairs. In the selection of the men named to the council in 1698 Sir Thomas Lawrence, then in London, played a key role. The board was to consist of twelve councilors, with five necessary for a quorum. A hard winter and sickness had reduced the number of incumbents. Three—David Browne, Nicholas Greenberry, and George Robothom—had died, and John Addison was so ill he could not attend meetings. Charles Hutchins and James Frisby lived too far across the Chesapeake Bay to attend regularly. The surviving incumbents returned to the board to join Thomas Bray, commissary of the bishop of London; John Hammond, a provincial justice residing near Annapolis; Richard Hill, a Protestant of Annapolis who had opposed the coup against the proprietary regime; Francis Jenkins of Somerset County; Robert Smith of Talbot, former speaker of the House of Delegates and chief justice of the province; and Thomas Tasker, a planter and merchant residing near the capital.

In drafting instructions for the new governor, Meadows, Pollexfen, Locke, and Abraham Hill at the Plantation Office showed particular concern over a practice common in the colonies: the assembly's occasionally voting monetary presents to a governor, a practice the commissioners for plantation affairs considered subject to "very great inconvenience," for private interest was too apt to sway men from their duty to the crown. The promise of financial reward might induce governors to acquiesce in demands placed upon them by assemblies prejudicial to the king's interest. The commissioners required Blakiston to secure a bill from the House of Deputies granting the governor for the term of his office the revenue from a duty on exported tobacco.[8]

Blakiston arrived on the Chesapeake late in December 1698 to begin what was to be an undistinguished career. Poor health prevented him from exerting himself as governor as bouts of fever left him weak and little able to attend to business. He was little inclined to challenge outspoken men in the assembly for fear of creating an ill impression. He and the councilors who attended him—

Henry Jowles, John Addison, Thomas Brooke, Thomas Tasker, and John Hammond—were loathe to press the House of Delegates for a new law establishing the Church of England. Nor did the governor receive as much support as he could have from London. The Commissioners of Trade allowed months to pass before answering his letters. To compound difficulties, in the first year of Blakiston's administration the home of the proprietor in Maryland was plundered and proprietary account books and papers burned or destroyed, thus throwing the state of revenue into disarray. Baltimore then entered into an agreement with Richard Bennett and James Heath whereby he leased to them all the moneys due him for a term of eight years.[9]

Blakiston served on the Chesapeake for three and a half years before returning to England. For the forty-odd months of Blakiston's administration, he generally deferred to the wishes of the local magnates from Anne Arundel and neighboring counties. Philip Clarke had died, and John Coode had retired from provincial politics. No one pressed to organize a strong royal interest; and no one challenged the local magnates or wielded patronage to build a party to support the claims of the crown. Sir Thomas Lawrence spent his time in London, and his son, also named Thomas, served as deputy secretary in place of his father.

When the first assembly met in the summer of 1699 the delegates refused to give any satisfaction on the act for establishing the Church of England. They simply reenacted the measure already rejected by the crown. As before, the Quakers took their protests to London, with the same result.[10] Such was the state of communications that the royal disallowance of the law was delivered to Blakiston in America by four Quakers. From neighboring Virginia, Francis Nicholson registered his unhappiness over the situation with Archbishop Tenison. The Congregationalists of New England would not fail to insinuate how little interest the Church of England had with the home government. Even then William Penn was making "his brags" of the strength of Quaker influence. Following the arrival of commissary Thomas Bray in the spring of 1700 the assembly of Maryland was prevailed upon to pass a new law, a measure "washed and purged of all the Dreggs," the extraneous clauses and the provision for incorporating the laws of England into the legal code of Maryland.[11]

Following passage of the Act for the Service of Almighty God, the Quakers, speaking through John Feild and other lobbyists, objected at the Plantation Office to the very principle of an established church: the law, enacted for an indefinite period, deprived the Friends of liberty of conscience and required them and other dissenters to pay taxes for a church not of their choosing. In defending the law Thomas Bray belittled the claims of the Quakers and Catholics and noted the failure of the commissioners for plantations affairs to consult with the episcopal bench in England before they had recommended that the crown disallow previous statutes for establishing churches. Moreover, the Friends, the most vociferous among the dissenters, made up merely one-twelfth of the population of Maryland. Bray's arguments notwithstanding, the English law officers sided with the

Friends, for the Act for the Service of Almighty God and the Establishment of Religion According to the Church of England mandated the use of the Book of Common Prayer and the administration of the sacraments and other rites and ceremonies of the Anglican church for every minister and reader in every place of public worship, requirements so general that despite the alleged intention of the framers of the law, they might be construed to apply to meetings of Dissenters and thus prohibit any worship except in the Church of England.[12] At the Plantation Office, Pollexfen, Abraham Hill, and George Stepney proposed to draft a bill agreeable to the principle of religious toleration, but the Quaker lobbyists objected to any law establishing the Church of England in Maryland. Clerics ought to rely on voluntary contributions, not public taxes. This argument the ministers of state would not accept, but they did send off to Maryland a draft of a bill incorporating religious toleration to be enacted by the provincial legislature.[13] This bill for establishing the Church of England but allowing dissenters to hold their own services passed in Maryland, and as expected, the Quakers again complained to the government in London.

Even before the issue of the law for establishing religion had been resolved, and only two years into his administration, Blakiston had determined to give up his post. Ostensibly his health would not allow him to remain in Maryland. The winter of 1701–2 had taken its toll among the councilors also. Four had died: Henry Jowles, Charles Hutchins, Thomas Tasker, and the younger Thomas Lawrence. The council was reduced to eight members, three of them living at a great distance from Annapolis. In the summer of 1702 Blakiston abandoned his post to cross the Atlantic as agent for the colony. To some of the less informed, distant observers, his "humane" treatment of the assembly stood in stark contrast with the behavior of Nicholson in Virginia.[14] Blakiston during his tour on the Chesapeake had done little as the king's governor; at best, his had been a stopgap administration.

Domination by the local magnates continued for almost two years before another governor arrived from London to preside over the government at Annapolis. During the first years of the eighteenth century the inhabitants of Maryland faced several problems. In 1702 war again broke out with France, now joined by Spain, and with it came the disruption of the trade in tobacco, the colony's staple export. War restricted transatlantic shipping, drove up freight and insurance rates, and forced down the prices the planters and traders on the Chesapeake received. These adverse conditions prevailed until the cessation of hostilities in 1713. For more than a decade the provincial economy was depressed.

Tension among various religious denominations continued despite, perhaps because of, the policy of limited toleration allowed in the colony. The Quakers continued to oppose the statute establishing the Anglican church, encouraged by Friends from nearby Pennsylvania. At the yearly Quaker meeting on the West River, Thomas Story, an official of Penn's government and a leading Quaker in Philadelphia, attacked both the doctrine and the discipline of the Anglican church, declaring he held a commission by immediate divine inspiration to convert the people of Maryland to the only truth, that set forth by the Friends.[15] The activities of some Catholics also provoked complaints, particularly the efforts of William Hunter and other Jesuits to convert Protestants. Under the threat of prosecution for violating an act for preventing the further growth of popery, Baltimore promised that for the future the Catholics of Maryland would carry themselves without giving offense and with all due respect to the government.[16]

The warning issued to Catholic priests did not still religious anxieties. A later governor, John Seymour, too complained of a "growing mischief": the great number of Irish papists arriving in Maryland and the encouragement—religious toleration—given them for settling by agents of Lord Baltimore. Hunter and another Jesuit, Robert Brooke, were seeking to convert Protestant servants. In the religious animosities prevailing in Maryland Seymour saw the basis for political unrest, particularly in the House of Delegates, where "some turbulent Spirits were not wanting to create heates and Jealousys." A "restless and pernicious Crew," declared enemies of the Church of England, had instigated opposition to the new administration. While bitter over the behavior of the proprietor, his agents, and their Catholic relations, who maintained the Jesuits, the governor found particularly vexing the pretensions of the local officeholders in the counties.[17]

Even before Seymour left for America it had been brought home to him how limited his authority over appointments to office would be in Maryland. Thomas Bray had presumed to recommend Michael Huitson, the archdeacon of Armgh, as commissary in Maryland and judge in testamentary causes. In England such an ecclesiastical official exercised probate jurisdiction, and Francis Nicholson before leaving Annapolis for Virginia had placed the position at Bray's disposal. At a dinner held in London before the governor-designate set out for Maryland, Seymour became embroiled in a bitter dispute with Bray.[18]

By the time John Seymour had arrived on the Chesapeake in 1704, twenty-one months had passed with no royal governor in Maryland. The interval had served to strengthen a subtle transformation taking place in the colony. A new elite had been emerging, setting the basis for a fresh political order, one the brief administration of Blakiston had done nothing to arrest and perhaps had even encouraged.

Aside from the small circle of close relatives and Catholics associated with proprietary government, the more prominent men in Maryland during the later decades of the seventeenth century were sons and relatives of lesser gentry and merchants in England who had migrated to the Chesapeake in the years following the Restoration. Their sons were now coming to the fore. After the turn of the century the great majority of prominent men were born and reared in the colony. Their fathers, as young men newly arrived in the colony, had staked out the family fortunes in trade, or in land, or by marriage. For the new generation the battles of their fathers were not their battles and the factionalism of the Protestant

Revolution was losing meaning. Nicholson, while governor in the 1690s, had sought to build a party by rewarding men of ability, particularly assemblymen willing to support his administration, with appointments to high office. Under his successor, Blakiston, and during the hiatus following Blakiston's abandoning his office, the local magnates on the council had dominated.

Almost from the outset of his administration, John Seymour demonstrated a marked bias in appointments and a disregard for the sensibilities and claims of the more socially prominent planters and traders of Maryland. John Contee was a factor for a merchant of Plymouth who had come to Maryland in 1699. After he married Seymour's cousin, Mary Townley, the governor appointed Contee commissary general, naval officer, and councilor. Even without the governor's relatives, Maryland possessed too many claimants for the offices available.

Resenting the appointment of outsiders, particularly Sir Thomas Lawrence to the post of provincial secretary, the delegates in the assembly had in 1694 passed an act requiring residence for three years in the colony to hold office and proscribing the practice of officials absenting themselves from Maryland. If enforced, the law would increase the chances for men born in the colony or residing there for some years. The more prominent among the country born were particularly sensitive over appointments to the clerkships of the county courts and the judicial bench.[19] Long intervals during which no royal governor sought to build a party as well as the acquiescence of officials sent out from England to the residency act had markedly lessened the governor's control over patronage and contributed greatly to the ability of the local leaders to influence strongly, if not to control entirely, the structure of government in Maryland.

In the contest for office the "natives" of Maryland were not without influence in England. William Bladen, through the connections of his father, a long-time customs official in the British Isles, secured an appointment as deputy to William Blathwayt, the royal surveyor and auditor of the plantation revenue. A "native," Bladen challenged Sir Thomas Lawrence, the often absent provincial secretary. In Maryland the secretary had the disposal of the clerkship of the counties and maintained the records of the provincial court and the land office. In the latter capacity he was also a probate official for the proprietor and a member of his revenue establishment. In 1693, during his early tenure as secretary, Sir Thomas had become embroiled with the first royal governor, Lionel Copley and Colonel Henry Darnall, the proprietary agent and receiver general, over the fees of his office; and with Charles Carroll, clerk of the land office, over emoluments and custody of records. In ill health and dissatisfied with his financial rewards, Lawrence had departed for England in 1698, leaving his son Thomas to carry out the duties of his office. When the younger Lawrence died in 1701, Sir Thomas had to promise crown officials to return to the colony to best Bladen, the clerk of the council, who had received an interim appointment from Blakiston. Once returned to Annapolis Lawrence again became involved in a dispute with Charles Carroll and Henry Darnall. Pleading ill health, in 1704 he once more departed for

England, leaving as his deputy his friend William Dent. But Dent died within four months. From England Lawrence now contested with Governor Seymour, each naming a deputy as secretary, the governor favoring Bladen, Lawrence backing Philemon Lloyd.

In the House of Deputies resentment ran high against an absentee secretary who appointed clerks of the counties and demanded fees for work done by others. On the council too, sentiment ran against the absentee secretary, as John Hammond, Edward Lloyd, William Holland, Robert Smith, William Coursey, and Thomas Tench also came down against Lawrence. Both houses joined to strip the secretary's office of certain emoluments and applied the money to defray the charges of the provincial government. Although ordered by the crown to secure compensation for Lawrence from the assembly, Seymour procrastinated. By 1710, when the governor died, nothing had been done; by 1714, when a new governor reached the Chesapeake, Lawrence was also dead.[20] Common interest in depriving outsiders or newcomers from the fruits of patronage united the ''natives'' in the provincial House of Delegates as increasingly they sought control over the judicial system, the authority of various courts, and the appointment of justices.

With the provincial leaders determined to exert themselves and with the economy of the colony in a depressed state as a consequence of the war, Seymour had a difficult time convincing the assemblymen to enact a program mandated from London. The crown had required the governor to secure a revision and codification of the laws, a strengthening of the provincial militia, and the enactment of legislation establishing shipping centers—ports with warehouses and facilities for the storing and lading of tobacco. The assemblies of both Chesapeake colonies were also to agree upon a uniform gauge for hogsheads for more efficient loading on merchant vessels. Once in Maryland Seymour also realized the need to settle a long-standing boundary dispute with the proprietor of Pennsylvania and to rectify the provincial system of justice.

Seymour's predecessor had sent to England a collection of laws, including one passed in 1699, an Act for Ascertaining the Laws of the colony, by which the statutes passed at this time together with others were declared as the only laws of Maryland. Others not so designated were thereby repealed. The procedure the legislature thus adopted made the validity of all laws of Maryland dependent on this single act. Officials in England objected to this arrangement: each law ought to have been passed individually so that the crown might judge each on its own merits, whether to allow or disallow. When the crown rejected the Act for Ascertaining the Laws, Seymour had the task of securing a new code.[21]

Given the complexity of the task and the thin number of delegates attending legislative sessions, Seymour was not able to send off a revised code until July 1705. Perhaps he should have paid closer attention to the matter, but he was occupied with the repeated disturbances caused by neighboring Indians and the attempt of a clique headed by Richard Clarke to seize control of the government. Attempts at power by coup d'etat were traditional in Maryland.

Two years passed before officials of the crown acted on the revised legal code. After an examination of the charter granted to the first proprietor of Maryland and the laws enacted since the revolution in the colony, Attorney General Simon Harcourt in 1707 found many of the revised statutes to be unreasonable, others contrary to the laws of England, and still others encroachments on the prerogative of the monarch. Harcourt and his colleague James Montague, the solicitor general, were not as heedful of the claims of the proprietor when Lord Baltimore objected to two statutes—one, an act empowering the farmers of the proprietary rents, Richard Bennett and James Heath, to recover arrears after the expiration of their lease; the other, a law requiring Baltimore's agents to certify to the secretary's office the instructions and conditions for granting lands and a schedule of their fees. While Montague was unhappy with several clauses in these acts, he saw nothing in them prejudicial to the royal government or to the various "Realms" in the British Isles and considered the "Law makers" in Maryland to be the best judges as to the merits of the bills they passed.[22] The proprietor's concerns came to little.

The crown officials would not defer to the judgment of the provincial legislature, however, when the interests of creditors, resident in Britain and on the Chesapeake, were involved. In 1709, they found objectionable an act passed in 1708 setting damages for protested bills of exchange at 10 percent rather than 20 percent, as was the practice in other colonies, and indeed hitherto in Maryland. The Commissioners of Trade also found discriminatory an act for the relief of poor debtors passed that same year. Not until 1709 did the Plantation Office get around to the law enacted in 1694 by the "natives" in the Maryland assembly to exclude outsiders. Under the guise of encouraging learning, the legislature had imposed a residency requirement for holding office. Belatedly the commissioners for plantations affairs concluded that the law had been so penned as to be not easily understood.[23] Seymour himself had long since come to resent this statute, for it served to limit his powers in making appointments and thus molding a party to secure a legislative program.

The Plantation Office also faulted the governor for failing to secure legislation acceptable to the crown for establishing ports for the export of tobacco and imposing a uniform gauge for hogsheads. Hoping to avoid having ocean-going carriers spend too much time plying the waters of the Chesapeake collecting cargo, in 1705 the Plantation Office had instructed the governors of Maryland and Virginia to recommend to the assemblies acts for the building of towns with warehouses, wharves, and quays on the major rivers for the more expeditious collecting of cargo and loading of ships. Seymour had his own version, one designed to prevent abuses in the trade, to eliminate clandestine traffic, and to make more efficient use of seamen. He wanted to limit the loading of tobacco and the discharging of goods to only five ports—Annapolis, Oxford, Somerset, Patuxent, and Saint Marys—where tobacco could be stored in warehouses under the inspection of local officials. The governor doubted that the assemblymen would ever consent to building towns unless compelled by order from England, a threat the Plantation Office seemed willing to use. Should the local assembly not pass an appropriate law, the crown might take the matter to Parliament. But in 1706 the House of Delegates voted a trifling sum to defray the charges of bringing tobacco to loading facilities; it would not, however, designate these as exclusive sites for discharging and taking on cargo. Realizing that without capital the colony could never pretend to develop port towns, Seymour did not press the matter with the assembly; he turned his attention instead to a seemingly more important issue: control of the provincial and county judicial systems.[24]

To reduce expenses, the governor proposed in 1705 to institute a new arrangement, one pitting the authority of the local magnates sitting on the county courts against the jurisdiction of the provincial judges, by issuing a new commission of oyer and terminer to but four judges, men chosen for their knowledge and integrity, who would travel throughout the colony. In addition to saving the taxpayers money the proposal had a further advantage: it would make the royal prerogative shine brighter in a country that had so long been governed by a proprietor. Seymour was particularly unhappy with the view prevalent in the local courts that the statutes of England, unless they specifically mentioned the plantations, did not extend to Maryland. For example, for want of a particular act of the local assembly proscribing rape, bigamy, holding of conventicles, harboring Jesuits, and other felonies, many criminals would escape justice. Unfortunately for the governor, the queen's attorney general, Edward Northey, agreed with the provincial interpretation: the statutes of England, unless they expressly mentioned the colonies, were not in force in the plantations; for the American provinces being governed by their own laws, an act made in England, unless it designated the colonies as other of the monarch's dominions, did not extend to the colonies. Yet such laws of England as were in existence at the time of the founding of a colony by subjects of the English crown, if these laws were received by the inhabitants and put into effect in the colony, became the laws of that community by virtue of the general consent thus evidenced until altered by some act of the local legislature.[25]

Despite any firm support from London and in the face of clear opposition in the assembly, in the spring of 1707 Seymour pressed for reform of the court system. He found the existing arrangement a jest, "tot homines, tot sententiae." As many opinions existed as men, the judges not knowing any rules on which to base their pronouncements. The governor found one hiatus in the legal code especially disconcerting. When he proposed a measure to punish disseminating false news, the "stiff-necked" among the delegates in the assembly—buoyed up by a gainsaying and restless party—refused to agree. Despite encountering opposition on a variety of matters, Seymour pressed on with his plan to reduce the provincial court from twelve to four justices who would travel about the colony holding quarterly sessions. His choices for the bench also caused considerable trouble, as he disregarded seniority, ignored former members of the provincial bench, and promoted lesser judges to the more prestigious tribunal, all in the face of opposition from the local magistrates in the counties.[26]

Other problems plagued the governor, among them ill health and the long-festering dispute with Pennsylvania over the boundary line. The crown must resolve this controversy, Seymour wrote Sunderland in 1707, the "two provinces being ready to cutt throats about their Lymitts."[27] Faced with a hostile majority in the assembly, Seymour in 1708 dissolved the House of Delegates and issued writs for new elections. He hoped the voters would take better care whom they selected to represent them, but the freeholders returned a considerable number of delegates, and when the newly elected house met, it put off the governor's plan to alter the judicial system. Out of patience, he condemned the "turbulent Spirits" in the assembly and the declared enemies of church and state who busied themselves in the counties to get "ignorant and obstinate" men elected. Seymour especially blamed the agents and relatives of the proprietor, but he also took exception to the law restricting officeholders to men who had resided in the colonies for three or more years; it served to promote ignorant, "naturally proud and obstinate" natives, who sat not only as representatives in the assembly but as justices on the county courts. Under the denomination of country-born they distinguished themselves from the rest of the subjects of the queen. Many of the local magistrates had been returned to the assembly, where they voted for laws to confirm their jurisdiction in the counties. They now "almost believe themselves independent of the Queens Governor," Seymour wrote. From the Olympian heights of Whitehall, Secretary Sunderland had little solace to offer the royal governor. The Roman Catholics of Maryland, as elsewhere, although they enjoyed the benefit of the crown's protection, the equity of its laws, and the mildness of its government could not forbear manifesting their dissatisfactions. As to the difficulties with the assemblymen who sat as magistrates on the county courts, the boundary with Pennsylvania, and the allowance for judges on circuit, Seymour would learn the queen's pleasure when she had come to some determination on these matters.[28] Sunderland's cavalier assurances would have been of little comfort to the governor; Seymour died a few days before the secretary sent off this fatuous dispatch.

Five years passed before a successor to Seymour reached Maryland, a hiatus damaging to the cause of government depending directly on the monarchy of Britain. During these years Edward Lloyd and other provincial magnates of the council presided over the affairs of the colony.

Seymour died at the end of July 1709. Word of his demise did not reach England until late in December, when several applicants put in for the post of governor, among them William Byrd II of Virginia and Samuel Vetch, a Scots adventurer with connections in New York and Massachusetts. In July 1710 the ministry came to a decision which should have surprised few: the queen was appointing John Corbett, another of Marlborough's colonels. The duke initially had in mind South Carolina for his protégé, but Anne insisted he go to Maryland. Corbett himself did not want to go to America, preferring to appoint a deputy, as Orkney had for Virginia.[29] Months passed without Corbett's departing for the Chesapeake. Finally in January 1711 the earl of Dartmouth informed the governor-designate that his presence was "very necessary" in Maryland: if he did not depart soon, the queen's service required another to go in his place. Hoping for preferment elsewhere in the army, Corbett surrendered his letters but asked that the queen reimburse him the expense of his equippage.[30] When Marlborough, his duchess, and Godolphin fell from the queen's favor, the duke lost his hold over the provincial governorships.

Competition for the vacant post at Annapolis was open, but in February 1711 the proprietor challenged the right of the crown in taking over the administration: he and his father by patent from Charles I had held this authority until soon after the late revolution, when William III for reasons of state—ostensibly unknown to Baron Baltimore—appointed a governor. Queen Anne, so Baltimore presumed, would not continue in this practice if he could but lay his case before her. If gratified in his wish, Baltimore promised never to presume to appoint any man governor without royal approval; in this he was asking but for the same privilege as that enjoyed by the other proprietors. Baltimore's request went routinely to the Plantation Office, then to William Blathwayt, who had served as clerk of the old committee of the Privy Council for plantation affairs when the crown had assumed the government of Maryland, and finally to the attorney general and solicitor general.

Long opposed to chartered governments, Blathwayt in his recommendation grossly misrepresented the reasons for the crown's taking over two of the proprietary colonies. According to the rationale devised by Lord Chief Justice John Holt, when the crown had taken over the administration of government in Pennsylvania and Maryland, the respective proprietors had failed adequately to protect the king's subjects. This Blathwayt did not emphasize. Rather he cited the Declaration of Grievances submitted by John Coode and the other insurgents who had overthrown the proprietary regime in 1689 and their aversion to popish government under the proprietor. Accordingly, William III on the advice of his council, so Blathwayt reported, had declared that since it was in no way fit to continue Maryland in the hands of papists, he was appointing his own governor. Under this royal administration the people of Maryland were well satisfied and quiet. To Blathwayt it followed that it would be inappropriate to leave to Catholics a colony in the heart of British America, a colony bordering on Virginia, a dominion bringing to the crown more customs revenue than all of the other plantations. After all, the papists acknowledged a "foreign jurisdiction." Only at the conclusion of this narrative did Blathwayt allude to the formal rationale for the crown's action in 1692: the opinion of learned jurists that for exigencies of state and where it tended to the safety of the dominions, the prince might in the fullness of regal authority appoint such governors as would most conduce to the public good and the welfare of the country. The attorney general for the crown, Edward Northey, put the case in a truer perspective, so that when reporting to the queen, the Commissioners of Trade—Winchillsea, Meadows, Turner, Moore, and Gwyn—could cite the commission granted to Lionel Copley for the assumption of government: the failure of the proprietor adequately to provide for the security of the province. Following the suggestion of Northey, the Plantation Office recommended that the monarch continue to appoint a governor to allay the fears of the populace, at least for the duration of the war and until dangers and inconveniences—unspecified—were no longer present.[31]

Months passed without any action. In January 1712 Lord Baltimore again petitioned the queen to allow him to nominate a governor or to annex the colony and grant him, the proprietor, compensation.[32] With Baltimore willing to sell his rights, the crown had an opportunity to put an end to proprietary control in one colony without recourse to parliamentary statute. Still Lord Treasurer Oxford, Bolingbroke, and the other ministers of state would not act. For three years the governorship at Annapolis had lain vacant, and as several merchants trafficking in tobacco had complained, the provincial council had hardly enforced the laws respecting trade. The mercantile community wanted a governor sent over, not a military man, but a person familiar with the country and its trade so that commerce of the colony might be revived. The candidate of the traders was Tobias Bowles, a merchant of Deal, who had spent some time in Maryland and whose son was a rising figure in Saint Marys County. The elder Bowles promised to restore the slumping revenue from customs and shipping. This appeal might have carried additional weight now that Marlborough no longer controlled patronage. The Commissioners of Trade recommended Bowles be appointed, but another candidate then put in a claim, one of the Douglas clan, the queen having promised the late William Douglas, duke of Queensberry, the right of nomination.[33] Throughout, Lord Baltimore continued to press his claim.

To emphasize the urgency of the situation, both the proprietor and the merchants in England involved in the Chesapeake trade raised complaints over legislation enacted in Annapolis. Reacting to the depressed state of the market for tobacco, the assemblymen had pressed on Edward Lloyd and the council the need for a bill staying prosecution of suits at law. Lloyd was prevailed upon to transfer jurisdiction from the provincial to the county courts until the next session following the arrival of a governor from London.[34] More than three years had passed since Seymour had died, and Lloyd had no way of knowing that another governor would not arrive at Annapolis for some time.

The proprietor still held hopes of selling the colony to the crown, but a bitter family dispute among the Calverts intervened. Following the fourth marriage of the eighty-five-year-old Charles Calvert, the proprietor openly quarreled with his son Benedict Leonard. Baltimore warned his heir not to invoke the name of his mother in seeking support against him, for ''many persons in Maryl[an]d know but to[o] well that she and I were Whore and Rogue together long before I play'd the weake Man and Married here [sic],'' a step the elder man had long regretted. Benedict now broke with his father and with his father's faith, for, as he explained to Lord Treasurer Oxford, he had been inclined for some time to embrace the Protestant religion. Apprised of the son's sentiments, the proprietor cut off his yearly allowance of £450. Benedict Leonard was now unable to maintain and educate his own offspring, children brought up by their grandfather in the Catholic faith. Soliciting monetary support for himself from the Treasury the younger Calvert asked the crown not to purchase the proprietorship: whatever Baltimore might receive from the queen for the colony he would bequeath to his new wife. Benedict Calvert suggested that the crown grant him £300 a year for the support of his children and appoint as governor of Maryland his own nominee, Captain John Hart, a nephew of John Vesey, the archbishop of Tuam.[35]

With the backing of the lord treasurer, Hart received a commission from the queen. He arrived in Maryland in 1714, five years after the death of his predecessor. Initially he made a good impression as ''a Civil Gent[leman],'' one resolved ''to endeavor all he can to keep things quiet.''[36] Hart's tenure seemed shortlived, however. With the death of Anne that year and the accession of the Hanoverian elector as George I, the Tories fell from power. Early in 1715 Secretary of State Stanhope announced the appointment of Brigadier Richard Franks as governor in place of Hart. But within a matter of days Benedict Calvert informed the new king that he had renounced the "Romish errors" and had been received into the Church of England. He now asked that Hart continue as governor. Stanhope referred his case to the Plantation Office with the king's commands that all possible encouragement be given for the education of the six Calvert children in the Protestant religion and that Hart receive a fresh commission.[37] A few days later, on 20 February, Charles Calvert died, and Benedict Leonard became the fourth Baron Baltimore and the third proprietor of Maryland—but only for two months. He died in April 1715. His eldest son, Charles, was a minor of but sixteen years. The young Baltimore's guardian was Francis North, second Baron Guilford. Only later did Guilford's Jacobite sentiments come to light. In the fall of 1715, Guilford on behalf of his ward asked that Hart be continued in Maryland. Charles Lowe, a cousin of the proprietor and a merchant in the Chesapeake trade, posted security as required by parliamentary statute to ensure that the governor enforce the acts of trade and navigation.[38]

The involvement of Charles Lowe brought to full circle the comic history of Maryland from proprietary to royal to proprietary colony. As late as August of 1715 the new monarchy was considering purchasing both Pennsylvania and Maryland from their respective proprietors,[39] but with the close of a generation of war and the conversion of Maryland's new proprietor to Anglicanism, local interests and the temptation to gratify place-seekers prevailed. Thomas Beake, a Londoner who had succeeded Sir Thomas Lawrence as secretary of Maryland, agreed to share his office with Lowe. The two men apparently persuaded the administration to recognize Charles Calvert, fifth Baron Baltimore, as proprietor and governor of Maryland with John Hart as his deputy.[40]

Thus came to an end government in Maryland depending directly upon the monarchy. The colony the proprietary Calverts would attempt once more to govern had altered greatly. During the last years of the royal regime the provincial council had achieved a stability and a quality absent during the earlier proprietary period and the initial years following the revolution of 1689. For five years the councilors, with their senior member as president, had ruled. For the first time a majority of the board were native to the province, the leaders of a new generation imbued with a new attitude and presiding over a colony populated increasingly by people without firsthand knowledge of England. These councilors exhibited a more local orientation than had their predecessors on matters of patronage, on the economy, and on measures for defense of the colony; select members of a native interest, they constituted a clan of well-established, interrelated families. Among them, the Lloyds of Talbot County and the Addisons of Prince Georges County were now a recognizable provincial elite.[41]

CHAPTER 7

The Carolinas: Autonomy through Proprietary Negligence

Despite repeated pronouncements by crown officials of the desirability, even the necessity, of exercising direct control over the chartered and proprietary provinces, the ministers of state serving the Hanoverian king in 1715 had returned immediate supervision of Maryland's government to that colony's proprietor. In the same year, when offered an opportunity, they had failed to support pleas to Parliament by colonial spokesmen to assume control of the government of the Carolinas.

Almost from the inception of settlement the southernmost of the English provinces in America had been rent by ethnic and religious animosities. Political instability in the Carolinas and maladministration by a proprietary board seated thousands of miles away in London contributed to political tensions and misrule. Despite internal divisions, however, almost all Carolinians were able for a time to set aside factional disputes and to unite. In 1711 a series of Indian wars began, hostilities threatening the exposed provinces, especially South Carolina, a colony still sparsely populated. To meet the threat from hostile Indians as well as from the Spanish to the south, Carolinians looked to the crown for support. The distant proprietary board in London had appeared almost indifferent to the settlers' concerns and needs.

For many years, in the Carolinas much more so than in Maryland or Pennsylvania, a situation sufficiently precarious existed to justify applying the formula used against William Penn and Lord Baltimore: neglect by the proprietors and a consequent danger to the subjects of the English monarch. But little aid was forthcoming from Whitehall for almost two decades. In the interval leaders of Carolina society appreciated that they must take matters into their own hands.

In the last decade of the seventeenth century, the Carolinas, as yet not distinguished by name, were relatively sparsely settled; the northern district about Albemarle and Pamlico Sounds had about 7,000 souls, only about 300 of them black slaves. The region to be called South Carolina contained about half that number of people, but already the slave population was growing, reflecting the economy of the region about Charles Town and the origin of many of its more influential settlers, immigrant planters from the West Indies. Despite the higher proportion of blacks in the southern settlements, labor was still very short, "negroes being very dear,'' as one plantation resident complained.[1] The great bulk of the settlers in the northern district had come during the second half of the seventeenth century from Virginia. Farmers and small planters for the most part, they engaged in some trade, exporting hides and tobacco. But the commerce of Albemarle and Pamlico, carried on in small vessels of shallow draft, was controlled by New Englanders.

Despite its smaller population, South Carolina by the turn of the century already showed signs of the great export trade in rice and naval stores which was to sustain the colony. In the first decades of the eighteenth century British merchants took up residence, trading on their own accounts or as correspondents of mercantile houses in Britain. As early as 1701 the *George*, a Charles Town–built vessel of about eighty tons, sailed to Terceira in the Azores, to Bilboa, and then to Rotterdam with a cargo of hides and rice.[2] The growing volume of exports stimulated South Carolina's economic development, although the decision of the English government in 1705 to include rice among the enumerated commodities of America and the West Indies, those required to be shipped to some English port before going to European markets, may have injured the trade. The volume of exports of rice continued to grow, however. Planters in the southern district of Carolina for the first time had a staple marketable in England and in Europe and consequently one the proprietors would accept as payment for rents and other dues. In 1699 the arrears in rent alone came to over £12,000. The proprietors had great hopes also for pitch, tar, and other naval stores as well as silk.[3]

The production of commodities suitable for transatlantic markets may also have convinced the proprietors not to part with what had hitherto been for them an unprofitable and troublesome colonial venture. The original proprietary board to whom Charles II in 1663 had granted Carolina had included eight men, some influential in government, others involved in West Indian and American settlement. But changing political fortunes and deaths over time reduced the weight and importance of the proprietary board. By the last years of the seventeenth century its composition had changed drastically. The last of the original proprietors, William, Earl Craven, died in 1697 and was succeeded as palatine, or president of the proprietary board, by John, earl of Bath. Little continuity prevailed on the board in the early eighteenth century, except for Maurice Ashley (1675–1726), son of Anthony Ashley Cooper, second earl of Shaftesbury and younger brother of the third earl, who represented first his incompetent father and later his brother. By purchase, litigation, and expropriation, several shares had passed into the control of two merchants of London, Thomas Amy and William Thornburgh, and a Carolina planter, Joseph Blake. John Archdale of High Wycombe, Bucks, secured two shares; one went to his son Thomas, another to his daughter Mary, wife of John Danson. Thomas Amy assigned his share as a marriage portion to Nicholas Trott, another merchant of London who had a kinsman with the same name residing in Carolina. At least two of the proprietary shares were tied up in litigation. After some years the courts recognized the claim of John Granville, earl of Bath, to the original share of the duke of Albemarle. He was succeeded by his second son, John Granville, Baron Granville (1665–1707), and on the latter's death the title went to his wife and then to her son by a previous marriage, Henry Somerset, later duke of Beaufort. By the turn of the century only three of the proprietors were related by blood to the original patentees: John, Lord Carteret, who did not come of age until 1711 and was represented by his uncle; William, Lord Craven, another minor represented by his guardian, Sir Fulworth Skipworth; and Sir John Colleton, also under age and represented by various individuals at different times at the board.[4] Not until the rise of John Carteret, Baron Granville, to political prominence well into the eighteenth century did the Carolina proprietors have a figure of significant stature and political weight.

For more than three decades following the grant by Charles II, the proprietors had realized little from either Carolina or the Bahama (Somers) Islands. At the end of the century few among them seemed concerned except to insure receipt of their rents. The earl of Bath was inclined to sell Carolina. Thomas Amy, according to his son-in-law, Nicholas Trott, favored surrendering the right of government provided he or Trott obtained a commission as royal governor.[5] The death of Bath in August 1701 may have put to an end, for a while, any idea of giving up Carolina. The proprietary board had held no meeting since 20 December 1699; and it did not meet again until 10 December 1701/2, when Baron Granville succeeded as fifth palatine of Carolina. It now faced several challenges to its control from discontented elements in North and South Carolina, as a compromise worked out by John Archdale in Charles Town a few years before had collapsed. Sent out from London to break an impasse which had paralyzed the provincial government, Archdale had devised a financial and political arrangement to end the stalemate among the contending factions and had secured an agreement for the collection of rents due the proprietors.

The settlements later to be known as North Carolina had a history of political instability and open rebellion against proprietary authority. Early in the eighteenth century religious animosities between Quakers and Anglicans and competition between leaders from the two sections within the northern province rekindled the fires of rebellion. In North Carolina the majority of the farmers and planters were seated in four districts north of Albemarle Sound and east of the Chowan River: Chowan (later Shaftesbury), Perquimans (Berkeley), Pasquotank, and Currituck (later Carteret). Voters in each of these precincts returned five representatives to the assembly. In 1696 the county of Bath was formed for the region south of Albemarle Sound and the Roanoke River to Pamlico Sound. As population increased Bath was divided into three precincts: Archdale, Pamtecough, and Wickham (later Craven, Beaufort, and Hyde). But these new precincts, separated by forty miles of wilderness from those in Albemarle, were each allowed only two or, in rare instances, three assemblymen. With the unofficial seat of government at Little River between Pasquotank and Perquimans, the northern precincts dominated the major political offices. They were also home to the settlers who had accepted the Quaker faith, although most of the farmers and planters adhered to no organized church. As a missionary sent out by the Society for the Propagation of the Gospel (SPG) put it, the majority were "bred up in ignorance and neither knew nor professed any religion at all." The curate at Currituck charged the Friends with seeking to turn out officials simply because they were Anglicans and to replace them with "shoemakers and other mechanics merely because they are Quaker preachers and notorious blasphemers of the Church."[6]

Other issues also aroused the settlers. Assemblymen from Bath complained of the lack of higher courts and the burden of quitrents, higher in Bath than in the Albemarle districts. Prices received for tobacco were low, forced down by the shortage of freighters. The legislature of Virginia did not help matters when it prohibited the transit of tobacco from Carolina. Rumors of threatened Indian raids added to the anxieties of the people and increased tensions.

Above all, men reacted to threats — real or imagined — from innovations in relations between church and state. The first years of the new century saw the rise of an aggressive Anglican missionary movement and attempts by prominent laymen in Charles Town, the residence of the provincial governor, to establish the Church of England. Led by Henderson Walker, the Anglicans in 1701 secured from the provincial assembly in the northern precincts an act creating five parishes and providing for a tax to support ministers and to build churches. This law did not apparently require conformity to the established Anglican church, but Dissenters nonetheless objected to paying the tax for maintaining the clergy of the Church of England. Ironically, the crown disallowed the measure on the ground that the salary allowed the ministers, £30 annually, was inadequate. By another statute, an Act for Oaths, the assembly declared that the ecclesiastical laws of England were in effect in North Carolina. To qualify for office an individual must swear to his belief in the Trinity and subscribe to the Thirty-Nine Articles of the Church of England. Henderson Walker died in 1704, but the men sent from Charles Town to succeed him, first Robert Daniel and then Thomas Cary, insisted that Quakers take the oath in accordance with the law to be eligible for office or to take their seats in the assembly. Cary, a London merchant engaged in the Carolina trade, had become a commercial factor in Charles Town. His father-in-law, the Quaker proprietor John Archdale, had appointed him receiver general. Despite his family connections, he turned a deaf ear to the pleas of the Friends while serving as president of the council in North Carolina. Denied a hearing in Carolina, the Quakers sent John Porter to London to argue their case with the proprietors. Supported by the Quakers on the board, John Danson and Archdale, Porter secured instructions that suspended the law as it related to the taking of oaths, removed Cary from office, and required the selection of a new president of the council. William Glover was chosen to succeed Cary on the assumption that he was sympathetic to the Friends. But Glover too insisted that the Quakers take the oath prescribed by the provincial law.

The division in the northern settlements was not simply between Anglicans and Quakers or a popular versus a proprietary faction. The proprietary board in London itself included both Anglicans and Friends, with the latter, according to SPG missionaries, prevailing.[7] In the colony some Anglicans sided with the Quakers. While the Friends and their allies called themselves the popular party, at times the voters repudiated them. The situation in the northern portion of Carolina was, in fact, confused, with no clear division among the factions as men changed sides. While Thomas Cary had at one time opposed the Quakers, he later emerged as a leader among the Dissenters. Edward Mosely, London born and a recent arrival, was an Anglican but supported the Friends. In contrast to many of the protagonists, who saw the struggle as one between Quakers and Anglicans, one partisan, perhaps with more insight, appreciated another dimension in these contests. Scottish-born Thomas Pollock, after his arrival in the province in 1683, acquired land, slaves, and a seat on the provincial council. To him the causes of the discontent stemmed from the ambition of a small group of men, especially Edward Mosely, who had "not much in such posts of profit and trust in the government as they desired."[8] The struggle pitted an established group in the Albemarle districts against others in the more recently settled districts to the south and west in Bath who sought recognition. Disturbed by the growth of the southern district the more prominent planters of Albemarle aimed to retain power in their own hands. Leaders from Bath County, frustrated by their exclusion from the council and relegated to a minor role in the assembly, sought allies in John Porter and Edward Mosely, men who had broken with Pollock and the Albemarle leadership.[9] When Thomas Cary, a son-in-law of a proprietor and a former deputy of the governor at Charles Town, settled in Bath, the dissidents found a man about whom they could organize. In a contest for power both William Glover and Cary issued writs of election; as a consequence, when the assemblymen gathered in October 1708 two rival sets of delegates claimed to represent the precincts. Professing to fear for his life, Glover withdrew to Virginia, leaving Cary and his faction in power. Pollock, too, fled to the Old Dominion.

Word of the disturbance soon reached England. Edmund Jennings, the provincial secretary of Virginia, blamed the Quakers for the chaotic situation. Having prevailed upon the proprietors to turn out a deputy governor and having received permission to choose their own president, the councilors had turned the president out when he had failed to support them. The Quakers had had "the Cunning to sett all that Country in a flame." All but the Friends were "in arms against one another." The actions of both sides more resembled that of "Madmen" than "men of reason."[10]

Seeking to quiet matters, the proprietors the following spring provided Major Edward Tynte, the newly appointed governor for Charles Town, with ten blank commissions to be filled out with the names of proprietary deputies for

North Carolina. They designated Edward Hyde as lieutenant for the troubled northern precincts. But Tynte died shortly after arriving in America, before he signed Hyde's commission. Did Hyde have any legal claim to the government? En route to Carolina from England Hyde had stopped off in Virginia. William Byrd found him to be "a jolly, good-natured man but no valiant" politician, an assessment Hyde himself confirmed when he confessed to James Adams, an SPG missionary, that he did not think it advisable to cross into North Carolina until he heard from England. Adams himself had little hope from this quarter, fearing the proprietors were unduly influenced by the misrepresentations of the Quakers as advanced through John Danson at the board. Not until the end of 1710 did the proprietors agree to appoint Hyde governor of North Carolina independent of the executive at Charles Town.[11] From the Blackwater River, where he had taken refuge, Thomas Pollock urged Hyde to cross over into North Carolina and settle the religion, liberties, and laws of the inhabitants so that they would never more be "insulted and trodden down by Quakers, atheists, deists, and other evil-disposed persons."[12] Hyde finally screwed up his courage and crossed into North Carolina.

As might have been expected, Cary and his followers challenged his authority. When Alexander Spotswood, deputy governor of Virginia, sought to mediate between the two men, Cary allegedly threatened Hyde with the same fate that had befallen Colonel Daniel Parke, the recently assassinated governor at Antigua. One Cary supporter, Edmund Porter, so rumor had it, had instigated the neighboring Tuscarora Indians to attack planters sympathetic to Hyde. At this point arrived one Richard Roach, a factor sent out by several merchants of London with a cargo of goods. Declaring for Cary he supplied the "mob" with trading guns and ammunition out of his store. Much the same had happened a generation before at the outset of "Culpepper's Rebellion" in Albemarle. At Hyde's request, Spotswood dispatched a contingent of marines from the guard ships of the Royal Navy to put an end to the conflict and had Cary and other insurgent leaders jailed when they fled to Virginia to take passage for England. In a blunt hint to Whitehall Spotswood advised that it would be impossible to reduce the anarchy prevailing in North Carolina without a governor vested with more authority than that the proprietors could confer.[13] Cary, Levi Trewhitt, George Lumley, Collingwood Ward, and Edmund Porter he sent off to England, prisoners charged with raising a rebellion. Hyde, Pollock, Glover, and others on the council of Carolina dispatched a bill of particulars accusing Cary and the Quakers as well with having raised an insurrection.

In London Secretary Dartmouth called on the proprietors for further information and turned over to the law officers of the crown the papers containing the allegations against Cary and the other prisoners. But when the attorney general delayed taking action, the accused men insisted that no just cause existed for retaining them in custody. At a meeting of the proprietary board in December 1711, Beaufort, John Colleton, Carteret, and Danson decided to retain the prisoners until further information arrived from North Carolina. But word then came that the Tuscarora Indians were in open revolt. The proprietors now decided to name a new governor although they confirmed Thomas Pollock and William Glover as proprietary deputies.[14] They also adopted a decidedly Quaker attitude, perhaps at the suggestion of Danson, and chastised Hyde for employing violent measures: the best way to keep the people quiet was to show to those who had been deluded "all gentleness" and as little severity as was consistent with law and justice to those who had been deeply involved in the disorders.[15]

In America officials were concerned with more pressing matters—the Indian war, a direct consequence, they concluded, of Cary's rebellion. Worn out by his burdensome post, Hyde died on 8 September 1712. Pollock took over as president of the council, supported by councilors Thomas Boyd, Nathaniel Chevin, William Reed, and Tobias Knight. Two weeks later he issued a proclamation pardoning all the rebels except Cary, John Porter, and five others proscribed as the chief instigators. The proprietors were more lenient, agreeing to allow the insurgent leaders to return to America because they had been separated from their families for over a year and no accusations had been brought against them; thus did Carteret, Ashley, Colleton, and Danson dismiss the letters of Spotswood and Hyde and an affidavit from Tobias Knight.[16] A generation before, under the first earl of Shaftesbury, the proprietary board had staged a similar charade in dismissing charges against another rebel, John Culpepper. In the spring of 1713 the board named Charles Eden to succeed the deceased Edward Hyde as the best method of restoring the confidence of the inhabitants and administering justice—or so the proprietary secretary, Richard Shelton, explained to Spotswood in Williamsburg.[17] Spotswood would have preferred a royal, rather than proprietary, governor.

The destructive war with the Indians forced the contending factions to set aside their differences for a time. Pollock and the other leaders in the Albemarle district remained secure, their power not to be challenged again until the settlement of the lower Cape Fear River a generation later, when new rivalries arose. Their sense of self-assurance was reflected in the attitude of the councilors and assemblymen when revising the laws relating to proprietary lands, an attitude the board in London resented, but was powerless to combat.

A more immediate threat to proprietary control over Carolina came in 1715, when spokesmen for discontented elements in Charles Town sought at Westminster to have Parliament vacate the proprietary charter.

In South Carolina too religion had been a divisive issue. How a man worshipped mattered, as well as where he came from—England, the West Indies, Scotland, or France—and when he had arrived in South Carolina—early or late. For years the earliest settlers, Anglicans from Barbados, had contested with the proprietors over the disposition of land, payment of rents, control of the Indian trade, and the allocation of governmental offices. These "Goose Creek" men, when elected to the Commons House, the legislative assembly, had fought to dominate the local scene as a faction openly opposed to the proprietors. To offset this Anglican, West Indian party, the proprietors had encouraged religious dissenters from Scotland, England, and France to emigrate to South Carolina. But restricted by the requirement of the charter to make laws for Carolina with the consent of the inhabitants, the proprietors had been unable for a generation to impose their will. Government in Charles Town had been at a stalemate in 1689, when the onset of a protracted war with France and hostilities with neighboring Indians threatened the existence of the sparsely populated colony on the exposed southern frontier of English America. In 1695 the proprietors had sent out one of their own number, the Quaker John Archdale, to restore government and to secure their rights. But once in America Archdale had appreciated that to win legislative support for quitrents and appropriations for governmental officials he would have to make concessions. He did so at the expense of the political rights of the approximately five hundred French Huguenots settled in Craven County. Of the twenty representatives returned to the assembly at Charles Town from the three counties, hitherto Berkeley and Colleton had returned seven each, and Craven six. To obtain approval from the bulk of the members of the Commons House for laws regulating the disposal lands, rents, and salaries, Archdale accepted the exclusion of representatives from Craven. Colleton and Berkeley would return all of the delegates to the assembly. Hereafter the men of Berkeley, and especially Charles Town, resident in the provincial capital, would dominate in the Commons House.

When Archdale left the colony in 1696, he placed executive authority in the lands of Joseph Blake, a Dissenter. Having concluded there was value in having a proprietor resident in the colony as governor, Archdale arranged for the sale of a share in the proprietary board to the newly appointed governor, the son of a prominent Dissenter family and a man related by marrriage to other leading dissenter families, the Axtells, Mortons, and Bellingers. Blake's administration did not prove a happy one, for he and his close associates were concerned with dominating the offices of profit, a situation the proprietary board accepted, as it did the exclusion of the Huguenots of Craven County. Nor did it pursue Robert Daniel's suggestion to modify the structure of government through a revision of the Fundamental Constitutions, one confirmed by the provincial assembly.[18]

The proprietary board was unable to protect or even to control its own officials, men often antagonistic toward each other. When the Commons House took Chief Justice Edmund Bohun to task for charging excessive fees, the board reprimanded him for his too great love of money, a characteristic not worthy in any person, "but particularly unbecoming" in a judge. Blake and the council resisted the claim of the provincial attorney general and naval officer, Nicholas Trott, to the additional post of advocate general of the local admiralty establishment.[19]

The demise of Blake, the last of the Dissenter governors, in 1700 inaugurated a protracted struggle and once more brought into the open pervasive religious animosities. Under the procedures promulgated by the proprietary board the deputies met to choose a successor to Blake. Of the six men present on 11 September 1700, Joseph Morton and Edmund Bellinger held titles of provincial nobility; as landgraves they took precedence over the ordinary proprietary deputies. But when the name of Edward Bellinger was presented, only Morton voted for him. Morton himself received only three votes. Objections were raised against both landgraves: in accepting commissions from the crown as officers of the Court of Vice-Admiralty, they had become ineligible to serve as proprietary officials. With no other landgrave resident in the colony, the other deputies proceeded to elect James Moore, a former governor whose high-handed behavior and imperious manner had earned him the scorn of his opponents and the appellation the "Heating Moor."[20] That he was an Anglican was enough to arouse the Dissenters.

The new governor soon showed where his sympathies lay when he signed a bill passed by the Commons House to restrict the Court of Vice-Admiralty, a popular measure, for as Joseph Morton, the judge of the court, complained, the people in general were averse to the acts of trade and navigation. Moore himself did not bother to seek confirmation as governor from the crown, as the navigation code required. Morton was also incensed at the behavior of Nicholas Trott, who had incited a crowd to violence against Bellinger, a collector of customs: "This is the informer, this is he that will ruin your Country."[21]

Since the Plantation Office was then urging Parliament to pass a bill to take up the provincial charters, the proprietary board acted to remove any grounds of which Parliament could attack the patent for Carolina. In June 1702 it constituted Sir Nathaniel Johnson, a soldier and former member of Parliament, governor of the province. The need for an experienced soldier to head the government received added urgency from the pleas of assemblymen of South Carolina, who were fearful of the consequences of the outbreak of war with France and Spain. As a supporter of James II, Johnson had resigned the governorship of the Leeward Islands and settled in Carolina. Poor health prevented him from taking up his new duties until March 1703. By that time a violent controversy had broken out between the followers of James Moore and the Dissenters, who supported John Ash, a Congregationalist from New England.

The new governor, himself a High Churchman, sided with the Anglicans. When they swept the elections in Berkeley County, Johnson issued a call for an emergency session of the assembly for 26 April, before the Dissenters chosen from Colleton could reach Charles Town. By a narrow margin of one vote the Anglicans pushed through a bill designed to exclude their opponents and insure their own domination, a provincial version of the English law to exclude Catholics and Dissenters. This statute required that men elected to the Commons House before taking their places receive the Sacrament according to the rites of the Church of England sometime within the previous twelve months or take an oath that they had conformed to Anglicanism and had not been in communion with any other church during the past year. Johnson approved this bill as well as another passed later that year establishing the Church of England and the Anglican Book of Common Prayer as the official form of worship. Among other provisions the law did not recognize marriages performed by Dissenter clergymen.

Outraged by this legislation and the tactics employed to obtain control of the Commons House, the Dissenters sent a spokesman, John Ash, to England. Ash died shortly after his arrival in London, but Joseph Boone, a provincial merchant with trading connections in the metropolis, took up the case before the proprietary board. The Quaker Archdale sought to minimize the impact of the laws, however: they did not exclude Dissenter meetings, for example. Moreover, Dissenters should be able to take the Sacrament since the Anglican minister in South Carolina was reputed to be "a pious and moderate" man. Indeed, initially the ecclesiastical laws seemed not to have much political consequence. As Job Howe, speaker of the Commons House, reported to Archdale, the Anglicans had allowed the Dissenters to choose whomever they pleased as assemblymen regardless of religious persuasion. In January 1706 the Dissenters elected to the assembly attended the house, but after only two days every man of them left, seeking, so Howe charged, to "heighten our differences."[22]

Despite Archdale's initial reaction, he voted with Maurice Ashley to disallow the establishment and test laws; but Granville, the palatine, casting three votes (his own and two proxies), with the support of John Colleton, prevailed. Boone then turned to Parliament and hired a polemicist, Daniel Defoe, who turned out a pamphlet on his behalf, *Party-Tyranny; or, An Occasional Bill in Miniature, as now Practised in Carolina,* a piece offered to the legislature at Westminster. On 28 February 1706 Boone and sixteen others calling themselves inhabitants of Carolina and merchants of London—they included David Waterhouse, Thomas Byfield, and Micajah Perry—petitioned the House of Lords, charging that the legislation enacted in Carolina violated the requirements of the charter providing for toleration to all Christians in the free exercise of religion as well as the provision of the Fundamental Constitutions issued by the proprietors that no person be disturbed on account of any "speculative opinion" in religion or excluded from the assembly or any office in civil administration on account of religion. Boone further charged that the elections held in 1703 were "managed with very great partiality and injustice," with "all sorts of people," even servants, Negroes, aliens, Jews, and common sailors admitted to vote. Finally, Governor Nathaniel Johnson and his adherents in passing the bill for the establishment of the Church of England had transgressed on the ecclesiastical jurisdiction of the bishop of London. On this point Boone erred, for the jurisdiction of the see of London over the colonies in North America had never received legal sanction.

The charges leveled by the Dissenters seemed to make an impression. Two days after Boone had presented his petition, Granville asked for a copy to allow the proprietors time to consider; Granville himself was required by the peers to produce a copy of the charter. Archdale testified that he had urged the proprietary board to refer the establishment bill passed by the Carolina Commons House, as an ecclesiastical law, to the bishop of London for examination, but that Granville had told him the prelate had already approved the bill, although he had disliked certain of its provisions. The two Carolina laws, one establishing religious worship and the other preserving church government, were then read. Although some peers already condemned the setting up of a provincial ecclesiastical commission as illegal, Granville and Craven, the two proprietors in the upper house, pleaded for more time to be heard by counsel.

On 9 March two solicitors, Sir Thomas Powys and Sir John Hawles, presented the case for the proprietors: circumstances in the colony justified the ecclesiastical legislation, since no bishop resided in South Carolina to disciple any irregular clergy. If necessary, however, the proprietors were willing to strike the clause establishing the board of twelve laymen to govern the provincial church. The concession was not enough. After debate the Lords in committee voted to declare the act for establishing worship illegal and contrary to royal charter and agreed to an address to the queen condemning the act for preserving the government as repugnant to the laws of England. Three days later the house by a vote of twenty-eight to twelve accepted the report. When the issue came before the crown law officers, Attorney General Edward Northey and Solicitor General Simon Harcourt concluded that enacting such laws constituted an abuse of the powers granted to the proprietors. The queen might proceed against the charter by a *scire facias* in Chancery or by *quo warranto* in the Court of Queen's Bench. By order in council Anne repealed the two acts and ordered the law officers to report on steps to be taken against the charter.[23]

Although Northey and Harcourt were prepared to prosecute the charter, they raised a serious legal point: filing an information against a peer in Parliament might be a breach of privilege. Judging discretion to be the better part of presumption, the Privy Councilors left it to the House of Lords, the peers themselves being the best judges of their own privileges. Nothing came of the matter or of a proposal to have the crown at this time purchase the rights of the proprietors of Carolina.[24] Parliamentary recesses were never long enough to complete legal action against the proprietary peers before the House of Lords again met.

Sufficiently chastised, the Anglicans in the Commons House at Charles Town passed another bill in 1706 establishing the Church of England in little more than name only. The form of church government specified closely resembled that of the Presbyterian model adopted by the Long Parliament in 1641: a corporation of self-perpetuating lay commissioners drawn from among the leading citizens of the colony supervised the church. And in the future neither Anglican orders nor licenses from the bishop of London proved necessary, as the vestries did not examine too closely into the credentials of rectors they employed.[25] This arrangement made it possible for many Dissenters, especially Presbyterians, over the next few years to swallow the established "Anglican"

Church. Religious antagonisms died hard, however. Calling at the home of Joseph Boone in 1707 to gather the assessment for St. Philip's parish, collectors found Mrs. Boone and Thomas and George Smith, two of the leading Dissenters in the colony, present. Landgrave Smith demanded to know how the collectors dared to ask for money. George Smith added that if this was not persecution he desired to know what was: to demand money of him was as good as robbing him. Madame Boone also spoke her mind. Had William Rhett, the proprietary collector, and Nicholas Trott, the attorney general, paid their assessments? Yes, she was told, and they had done so promptly to set a good example. A pity, Madame Boone replied, that Trott had not been hanged years before. Had he not raised a disturbance, there would be no ecclesiastical impositions. Trott still aimed to secure political domination for the Anglicans by legislation to exclude Dissenters from the assembly.[26]

By 1707 other issues divided the partisans: jurisdiction over the Indian trade and authority over the provincial receiver and controller of revenue. Relations with the tribesmen were of particular concern to the inhabitants of Colleton County in the southwest, a region exposed to attacks from hostile warriors aroused by the unscrupulous practices employed by whites in the trade, particularly their employing tribesmen to raid villages in order to acquire captives to be sold for goods. Thomas Naire of Colleton headed a movement for more effective regulation of the traffic with the natives. The key issue was whether Naire and his supporters in the Commons House could wrest control from Governor Nathaniel Johnson and his allies on the council, for the governor feared the loss of perquisites and the potential threat to the commercial interests of his son-in-law, Thomas Broughton.

Naire was able to secure an act appointing him judicial agent to enforce justice among the traders in the Indian towns, but he and Johnson were soon at odds. Two of the traders prosecuted by Naire—one of whom he had formerly committed for buggery—swore that Naire had not only used scandalous words against the governor but had professed Jacobite sentiments. Johnson jailed Naire without benefit of trial. After a confinement of four months Naire managed to get out a letter to a principal secretary of state in Whitehall protesting the governor's illegal proceedings: relief from Johnson's arbitrary behavior was impossible in the colony, for a general rule prevailed in Carolina that no act of the English Parliament was in force in the province until passed by the local legislature.[27] In London Joseph Boone took up Naire's case, urging the removal not only of Johnson, but also of Trott, now chief justice.

The governor's downfall came following an alteration of the proprietary board in 1708. Trott's kinsman, the London merchant, had been unable to persuade the proprietors to accept his right to a share previously held by the late Seth Sothell, and John Danson had replaced the Quaker Archdale. Of greater significance, John, Lord Granville, died and was succeeded as palatine by the more tolerant William, Lord Craven. The newly reorganized board, unhappy with

Johnson, decided to replace him with Major Edward Tynte, an experienced army officer, and to appoint William Sanders and Robert Gibbes as attorney general and chief justice in place of James Moore and Nicholas Trott. Henry Wigginton became provincial secretary. The latter's tenure was short-lived; within a few months the board dismissed him, possibly at the instigation of William Rhett, and appointed Charles Craven, a close relative of the palatine. Both Rhett, then in London pressing the proprietors on the need for greater security for the colony, and Craven would play prominent roles in Carolina politics.

By these alterations the board hoped more effectively to manage affairs in Charles Town. To this end they also ordered their deputies not to allow any law to remain in force for more than two years unless confirmed in London. Reacting to what it considered exorbitant grants of proprietary property, the board also imposed a stringent policy on the disposition of land. Only the proprietary board in London would issue grants, and only a proprietary official would set out land.[28]

The new administration in Charles Town did not long survive. Governor Tynte and several of the gentlemen who had gone out from England with him—lawyers, for the most part—succumbed to disease and illness. Both the provincial attorney general and the governor soon died, Tynte after only nine months in office. Again the councilors and proprietary deputies convened to select a governor. They were soon at each other's throats exchanging charges of bribery. After several of the prominent leaders in the colony—Arthur Middleton, a member of the Commons House and a benefactor of the Anglican Church at Goose Creek; Landgrave Thomas Smith; Trott; and Naire—took the matter to London, the proprietary board acted to end the "confusions" and "disorders" by appointing Charles Craven as governor. Among those named to a new slate of proprietary officials and deputies were Thomas Broughton, Richard Berrisford, Arthur Middleton, Naire, and Rhett, the latter destined to become a highly controversial figure as receiver general of the revenue.[29]

Naire returned to Charles Town in November 1711. Elected to the Commons House, he apparently won over the Dissenters, for thereafter they no longer refused to sit in the assembly and abandoned their opposition to the established church. They may have been able to dominate in the local parishes in their communities under the loose arrangement allowed in the act for the establishment of religion passed a few years before. The waning of the religious issue and the new appointments to office won from the proprietors helped usher in a new political climate, for animosities between Anglicans and Dissenters faded. Although Naire, Middleton, Broughton, and others of the older generation continued to play an important role, the second decade of the eighteenth century saw the rise of new men, such as Samuel Eveleigh, Samuel Wragg, and John Fenwick, merchants and traders who had come to Charles Town as representatives of the London and Bristol mercantile communities. With the expansion of the rice trade, a few Carolinians—among them the Huguenots Benjamin Godin and Benjamin Conseillere—now turned to commerce.

The heads of the older families and the newly arrived merchants won seats in the Commons House but did not hold higher offices, for within a short time control of royal and proprietary patronage fell into the hands of two men, Nicholas Trott and his brother-in-law, William Rhett. Certain changes on the proprietary board had worked to bring about their dominance. When William, Lord Craven, died, the duke of Beaufort succeeded as palatine; but Beaufort seldom attended meetings, being content to have a deputy, John Manley, sit in his place. The other proprietors also evinced little interest in Carolina, allowing their secretary, Richard Shelton, to manage affairs. For several years he controlled correspondence and almost dictated policy. With Shelton as their patron, Trott and Rhett had virtually a free hand in Charles Town. Rhett, for example, treated the new governor with open contempt. Craven suspended him only to be ordered by the proprietors to restore the outspoken receiver general. Rhett had merely to ask for pardon, hardly a sufficient penalty for having said, "This is but a Lords Proprietors government and I would not wipe my arse with the commission."[30]

Little wonder Charles Craven had no stomach for his post. He had been in Charles Town less than a year when he asked for leave to return to England, ostensibly to attend to family business. Robert Johnson, son of the former governor, was named interim governor but without a commission. Although Craven did not leave South Carolina for some time, his commitment lay elsewhere. A firm hand was needed, for even on the governor's council proprietary deputies, in direct violation of orders, failed to oppose a bill for settling inhabitants' titles to their lands and for ascertaining the quitrents due the proprietors. Not Craven, but Trott kept the board in London apprised of the laws enacted in the colony. Once again appointed chief justice in 1713, Trott now consolidated his position. The proprietors required his presence on the council for a quorum and his consent for a bill to become law.[31]

Matters came to a head with the outbreak of the devastating war with the Yamassee Indians, as the Carolinians were hard-pressed to withstand the assaults of the hostile warriors. Whatever differences divided the factions, most leaders could agree that the proprietors had contributed little toward the support of the distressed colony. In the summer of 1715 Abel Kettleby, Joseph Boone, Stephen Godin, and twenty other self-styled planters and merchants trading to Carolina petitioned the king's ministers for relief: in great danger and needing aid, the Carolinians could only throw themselves at the feet of George I. If ever the formula used twenty-three years earlier against William Penn and Baron Baltimore applied, it was now: proprietary neglect endangered the safety of the subjects of the crown. Following several conferences with the proprietors, the Commissioners of Trade concluded that the overlords of Carolina were unwilling to support the province at their own expense or, for that matter, to surrender the government. The plantation board now proposed that the crown take over the colony,[32] a recommendation their predecessors under William and later Anne had made several times before. In support of this proposal, Kettleby, Boone, and the other spokesmen for the Carolinians petitioned the House of Commons. In August a bill for better regulating the chartered governments of America was sent to committee but went no further, as the members seemed at a loss as to how to justify stripping the proprietors of their patent.

Four more years would pass before the Carolinians took matters into their own hands. With war a constant threat on the southern frontier, proprietary officials offered little leadership, and the proprietors themselves no aid. Their policies continued to alienate almost all elements in the colony and induced almost all factions to unite to seize control of the administration of government.

The inconsistency of the proprietors inspired little confidence and served further to undermine their standing in Carolina. Even their own officials had openly showed contempt. Seizing on premature news that some Indians were seeking peace, Carteret and his colleagues in March 1716 predicted to Craven and the councilors at Charles Town that the Yamassee war would soon end, thus relieving the proprietors of any obligation to aid the colony. Even before hostilities terminated the proprietors announced their intention of parcelling out the Yamassee lands in two-hundred-acre tracts to prospective immigrants. Although they appeared ready to accede to the complaints of the assemblymen in the Commons House by revoking the powers granted to Chief Justice Trott, at the same time they sought to chastise the agent for the assembly, Joseph Boone, for his insolent behavior before the proprietary board.[33] Boone and Richard Beresford, the other agent, at the behest of the Commons House, continued to press the crown to take over the administration of government, as did others. The merchant Stephen Godin argued that by approving provincial laws repugnant to the laws of Britain, the proprietors had violated an express condition in their charter, sufficient cause to seek a writ in Chancery or King's Bench. With the precedents established for Maryland and Pennsylvania over twenty years before, the failure of the proprietors to provide adequately for the security of the king's subjects, the crown might well have acted without going through the courts. But Carteret, James Bertie, John Colleton, Fulwar Skipworth, and John Danson continued to insist that Carolina was in no danger and that hostilities with the Indians were at an end.[34]

In Charles Town proprietary officials continued at each other's throats. Governor Charles Craven had departed, leaving Robert Daniel to preside as his deputy. Daniel soon ran afoul of William Rhett over a prize taken by the sloop *Betty,* a privateer commissioned by Daniel. The hot-tempered Rhett, the surveyor of the customs, cursing Daniel as an old rogue, threatened to kill him. Daniel, for his part, actually fired a gun at Rhett and at HMS *Shoreham,* a guard ship in the harbor. Since Charles Craven preferred not to return to South Carolina, in 1717 Carteret, Bertie, Ashley, and Danson named Robert Johnson governor, insisting at the same time that the calls for the crown to take over the province were nothing more than the work of a faction. This charge Thomas Broughton, the speaker, and twenty others in the Commons House, including

Arthur Middleton, Ralph Izard, William Bull, and Benjamin Shenkingh, denied in an address to the king.[35] Seeking to cut their losses, the proprietors in 1717 surrendered their rights of government to the Bahama Islands after leasing the land and royalties of the islands to a group of mariners and merchants of London and Bristol. But to the pleas of the Carolinians they turned deaf ears, even when Daniel and the other proprietary appointees on the provincial council—Thomas Smith, Trott, Francis Yonge, Samuel Eveleigh, and the provincial secretary, Charles Hart—protested that the colony was too poor to bear the burden of defense against the Indians.

In the spring of 1717 Boone and Beresford again turned to Parliament and the ministers of the king, but Carteret, Ashley, Colleton, and Danson made little of the menace from hostile Indians, citing information supplied them by Rhett that the danger from the natives seemed to be over and a general peace concluded. Moreover, they claimed to have expended several hundred pounds on arms and ammunition during the recent war, and to ease the burden on the inhabitants, they offered to apply all arrears in rents owed them to the public use.[36] But they offset this puny gesture with an order that all arrears in salaries owed to proprietary officials in the colony be cleared first. Little would remain to be applied for the defense of the colony. At the same time the proprietors began to apply pressure to settle a rent roll and to secure their control over the disposal of lands. The board may have been reacting to information supplied by Rhett in Charles Town, for he charged that the provincials were not as destitute as they claimed to be. An act of the assembly levying a duty of 10 percent on British manufactured goods was but one of several measures employed to avoid taxing their own estates while discharging debts incurred during the Indian wars. Thus the colonials sought to throw the cost of the conflicts on British merchants. In Carolina resentment over proprietary indifference swelled. In 1718 over five hundred men signed an address from the assembly to the king asking for relief.[37]

The proprietors further alienated the Carolinians by seeming to invite a direct confrontation with the Commons House. In November 1717 the assemblymen had altered the laws on elections by transferring polls for the counties to the parishes and apportioning the thirty seats in the assembly among the parishes, with four each to Charles Town and St. Andrews. Formerly all twenty of the delegates for Berkeley County were returned from Charles Town. According to Francis Yonge, the new arrangement was intended to offset the influence exercised in the capital by Nicholas Trott and William Rhett. The following July, Carteret, Ashley, Colleton, and Danson repealed the law on elections, as well as another act declaring the right of the Commons House to name the public receiver, as prejudicial to the authority of the proprietors. They also disallowed two additional laws, one to appropriate the lands of the Yamassee Indians and another to establish the rights of settlers on lands, as laws encroaching on the property of the proprietors and tending only to the disposal of their estates. To complete the fiasco, Carteret and his colleagues on the board negated an act granting an exclusive right for the conduct of the Indian trade to a single company. On this one day, 10 July 1718, the proprietors swept away the entire program the Commons House had instituted for managing land, finances, and the Indian trade. Still later that year, in September, they prohibited any further granting of land in South Carolina without their prior consent or any further issuance of paper bills of credit, paper money hitherto employed by the provincial government to cover financial deficits. To add insult to injury, on 21 November Ashley, Carteret, and Danson drew lots for over 100,000 acres of land—including Yamasse lands—for themselves and their heirs.

Relations between St. James's, the seat of the proprietary board, and Charles Town were strained to the breaking point. When merchants in London complained of a provincial law levying an additional duty on Negroes imported into the colony, the proprietors were forced to admit they had no knowledge of such a law. They then ordered that any law enacted in the province affecting the trade or shipping of Britain must contain a clause suspending its operation until approved by the proprietors. All laws of the colonial assembly had to be transmitted to London within six months of enactment for approval or disallowance by the proprietors.[38] To Nicholas Trott, the chief justice, fell the hopeless task of defending the authority of the proprietors to void laws enacted by the assembly. He had no success. The Commons House continued to pass and Governor Robert Johnson continued to sign laws previously disallowed by the board at St. James's. Such was the resentment held against the proprietors that Johnson had great difficulty persuading men to accept service on the council.

Matters came to a head in Charles Town in November 1719. When rumors reached the provincial capital of a hostile Spanish naval force at Vera Cruz preparing to attack, leaders of the opposition prevailed on Johnson to call for elections to choose an assembly. The voting was set for 16 November; on the seventeenth the more prominent among the inhabitants formed an association to take over the government, claiming the repeal of the laws by the proprietors was contrary to the charter. First to sign the association was the speaker of the Commons House. Governor Robert Johnson and the councilors took no action. Meeting the next month the assemblymen formed themselves into a convention and offered the government to Johnson. When he declined, James Moore, Jr., took over the post of chief executive. On 24 December the twelve leaders of the insurgent movement addressed a letter to the Plantation Office justifying their assumption of power on the grounds of neglect by the proprietors and the imminent danger to the colony, the same formula used a generation earlier against Baltimore and William Penn. Robert Johnson gave them tacit support, asking that he continue as governor should the crown sanction the takeover and strip the proprietors of their authority.[39]

The royal government accepted the *fait accompli,* falling back on the rationalization employed before for Pennsylvania and Maryland. Because of miscarriage and neglect of government, South Carolina had fallen into disorder, the public peace and administration of justice had been disrupted, and the colony had been left open to invasion. Under these circumstances, the crown must take the government under its own immediate supervision.[40] At first the proprietors attempted to sell their interest to a Quaker syndicate, but the effort fell through, and it was 1729 before they and the authorities in London reached an agreement. Ten years before, in 1719, the Carolinians had done for themselves what the ministers of the crown should have done long before. The long struggle with an irresponsible proprietary board had left the provincial leaders to fend for themselves. Much the same had been the experience with proprietary government of other men in America, along the banks of the Delaware and Schuykill.

CHAPTER 8

Popular Politics and the Delaware Proprietaries

As an astute man well connected in the world of English politics, William Penn, more so than the Calverts and the proprietary overlords of Carolina, was able to fend off efforts by crown officials to assume jurisdiction over his territories in America: the three counties constituting the province of Pennsylvania, settled mainly by Quakers, and the three lower counties on the Delaware River, communities seated first by Swedes and Dutchmen and only later, in 1664, captured by forces of the English king. The Quaker leader had been fortunate in a friendship with Charles II and his brother, the duke of York. From the king Penn had obtained in 1681 a charter for Pennsylvania, and from his royal brother, deeds for the Delaware territories. Penn's connections in English political circles cut across party lines, ranging from Robert Harley, one-time secretary of state, Speaker of the House of Commons, and later lord treasurer, to William Popple, secretary to the Council of Trade and Plantations, and Sir Robert Southwell, the clerk of the Privy Council charged with responsibility during the latter years of the reign of Charles II with drafting reports on the colonies.[1]

Penn's political connections served him well in the arenas of Whitehall and Westminster, but he himself proved no match for the politicians in Philadelphia and Newcastle, those his agent in America, James Logan, called "Menn of Deep Designs or shallow sense."[2] While Penn labored to fend off royal authority, ambitious provincials in his territories effectively hobbled his efforts to check them or to reassert control over the provincial governments. To the Quaker proprietor they owed much, not the least of which was freedom from the administration of a royal governor, Colonel Benjamin Fletcher, an army officer appointed in 1692 by William III to preside over the government of Pennsylvania. Penn's influence brought the restoration two years later of nominal proprietary authority after a very short interval of government directly under the crown. But in the next quarter century Quaker politicians in Pennsylvania and those of other religious persuasions in the lower counties opposed to the domination of the Friends stripped the proprietor of any real authority. In Philadelphia, earlier perhaps than elsewhere in America, an organized party crystalized, and in the contests for control of the provincial assembly, this organization presented the voters with tickets, lists of candidates committed to a goal of local autonomy.[3] Able and at times unscrupulous men led a concerted attack against the proprietors: in Philadelphia, David Lloyd, a Welsh-born lawyer, and in Chester, Jasper Yeates, an English-born merchant. Periodic meetings of the Friends helped to discipline the Quakers and to coordinate their efforts against the proprietor and the officials he appointed.

William Penn's titles to the Delaware and Pennsylvania lands were shaky on three counts. First, failure to provide for the defense of the populace might again provide justification for the crown to take over jurisdiction. Second, careless and gullible in his dealings with his steward in the British Isles, Philip Ford, the proprietor at one time unknowingly signed away his title to Pennsylvania. And third, Penn's right to the government and possibly to the soil of the lower counties—Newcastle, Kent, and Sussex—was clouded. This region, following the English conquest, had been administered by local officials acting under a governor at Manhattan appointed by the royal duke. In 1682 James had executed two deeds to the area about Newcastle and the lower counties. When Penn established his authority, he had but these deeds and orders from the royal duke's governor at New York to local officials to accept Penn's administration. Whether James himself in 1682 was legally possessed of these lands was questionable, but the deeds he gave the Quaker proprietor carried no rights of government although Penn always claimed they did. At the time, James was not the sovereign, and unlike his brother, the king, had no authority to confer powers of government. As James Logan years later confided privately to Penn's wife and son, the duke of York had had no right to the lands west of the Delaware before he received Charles II's patent. Some men on the Delaware who opposed Penn's claims to the lower counties appreciated this.[4]

The proprietor compounded his difficulties by his dealings with Philip Ford. Cavalier in matters of finance, he had left the management of his affairs in the British Isles to his steward. By systematic juggling of finances, Ford brought Penn into his debt for over £10,000. Unwisely, in 1697 the proprietor turned over to Ford his charter, and two years later he confirmed a document he supposed was a mortgage, but in reality was a bill of sale for the province of Pennsylvania. From 1699 Penn unknowingly was renting the province from his own employee.[5] When the arrangement became public, it brought Penn's control over the Delaware communities into jeopardy.

The financial dealings with the Ford family did not surface until 1705, but in the preceding years challenges to proprietary government rose from several other sources. David Lloyd, a persuasive, ambitious Welshman, did not hesitate to employ unscrupulous means to organize opinion in Pennsylvania against the proprietor. As an able lawyer Lloyd loomed large in Philadelphia, for as Penn's man of business observed, "Justices . . . like other Magistrates in these Colonies are known to be no Lawyers."[6] Across the Atlantic at the turn of the century, officials in the Customs House and the Plantation Office pressed a campaign to have Parliament take up the patents of the proprietary and corporate colonies. These bureaucrats received aid and encouragement from a group of royalists in

Pennsylvania, Anglicans of Christ Church and Robert Quary, a ranking customs official in Philadelphia. In his campaign against both the proprietor and the Quakers who dominated in Pennsylvania, Quary had the support of dissidents in Newcastle, Sussex, and Kent. Long before the Friends settled the three northern counties Finns, Swedes, and Dutch had come to the lower Delaware. Englishmen and Scots later arrived. Relations between the northern and the southern counties were strained, marred by differences in national origin, religion, and cultural outlook. "That Frenchified, Scotchified, Dutchified place," one Quaker described Newcastle.[7]

Politics in Penn's proprietary for some years revolved about a patchwork of shifting connections, resulting at times in strange alliances. Pennsylvania and the lower counties did not lack for ambitious, strong-willed men. With the proprietor under a legal cloud shortly after the Revolution because of his association with the deposed Catholic king and his active support of James's policy for religious toleration, Lloyd and other leaders in Pennsylvania had forced Penn's deputy, William Markham, into major concessions in 1696 when he had called the assembly into session to consider the request of the crown to aid the northern colonies against the French and the Indians. Faced with a refusal to vote supplies Markham had won favor with the ruling element among the Friends by submitting to a new "frame" of government, an arrangement by which the men sitting in the assembly exercised power at the expense of proprietary prerogative. Under this frame the council consisted of two members, and the assembly, of four representatives chosen from each county. A revision of voting requirements designed to protect Quakers lowered qualifications from 100 to 50 acres of land. In Philadelphia the franchise was enjoyed no longer by those who paid a local rate, scot and lot, but by men worth fifty pounds. The council became chiefly an advisory rather than a legislative body. Those men who could win the support of the Quaker artisans in the city and the small farmers in the countryside would prevail in the assembly and consequently dominate in the government of the province. The new arrangement was tenuous, for the frame was merely a law enacted in Pennsylvania and not a charter in the sense of a patent granted by the crown specifying the structure and procedures for government. While some substantial Quaker merchants and landowners — John Goodson, Griffith Jones, Francis Rawle, Robert Turner, and Arthur Cooke — would not accept the new frame, others — David Lloyd, Samuel Carpenter, Caleb Pusey, Joseph Growdon, Phineas Pemberton, and Edward Shippen — saw it as fundamental law.

Under a legal cloud and under attack by bureaucrats in London Penn was unable to intercede when the proprietary regime came under fire in Philadelphia. The more immediate threat to control of the proprietor and the Quaker leadership in Pennsylvania came from the charges raised by Robert Quary that Quaker and proprietary officials were ignoring an illicit trade with Scotland and Holland and allowing pirates to dispose of their booty in Pennsylvania. Provincial officials had also failed to provide for a militia in the colony. In defending proprietary officials, Penn accused Quary and his patrons—Francis Nicholson and Robert Snead and John Moore—of collusion, of forming a cabal to disrupt and destroy the proprietary regime. To restore some semblance of proprietary authority, Penn promised the authorities in London to cross the Atlantic and assume control. As the recipient of the king's charter and governor of Pennsylvania and the territories he was legally responsible for any transgressions.[8]

The Anglican communicants of Christ Church in Philadelphia, for their part, condemned Quaker domination of the government as intolerable; they could not call their estates their own, the Friends being so prejudiced and insolent against all men not of their persuasion. Quakers controlled the provincial, county, and municipal governments. In cases tried before them, judges, juries, and evidence were never sworn, so that the Anglicans could not hope to enjoy the property and liberty of subjects of England. Failure to qualify officials and witnesses had long plagued Quaker administrations: from judges to jurymen, down to the meanest official, a solemn promise to perform one's duty was sufficient. In these circumstances and as long as the Friends remained in control, the Anglicans conjectured, unlawful trade would be encouraged. The Quakers, adopting merely the preamble of the parliamentary act of 1696, had passed a bill entitled An Act to Prevent Frauds—a "specious preamble"—with a clause providing that all trials relating to the acts of trade be heard by jury.[9]

Designed to meet the needs of the Quakers, this provincial act removed the obligation of an oath in all matters relating to the navigation code; it became a weapon to be employed against royal officials. In August 1698 Anthony Morris, a justice of the peace in Philadelphia, issued a writ of replevin against Robert Webb, the marshall of the Court of Vice-Admiralty, to force the return of goods illegally brought into the province. The justices in Philadelphia then called in Webb to answer by what authority he continued to hold the cargo in question. Webb produced the royal commission to which was attached the great seal of the High Court of Admiralty. As Quary related the event, his own deputy, David Lloyd, whose duty it was to prosecute offenses against the law, held up the royal seal to ridicule. Acting under a warrant issued by Anthony Morris, the local sheriff had entered the royal storehouse and seized the confiscated goods. At a session held on 9 September at the Court of Common Pleas, John Moore as counsel for Webb produced the marshall's commission. Lloyd, who was also provincial attorney, allegedly asked of Moore: "What hast thou got there, John? Dost think we are afraid of a Baby," pointing to the effigy of the king, and "a Pinn Box?" referring to the Great Seal. Scoffing, Lloyd held up the seal to the view of the laughing spectators. Two or three of the councilors—not Quakers—proposed that the justice of the local court who had ordered the goods taken from Webb's care be turned out of office as an example to others. Lloyd objected: all who encouraged the creation of courts of admiralty were greater enemies to the rights and liberties of the people than those in the time of Charles I who had promoted ship money. The Quakers on the bench threatened that if Anthony Morris were turned out, they would all resign.[10]

The proprietor sought to salvage what he could of the incident by citing the behavior of his deputy: Markham had refused to issue the writ of replevin and had ordered the sheriff to hold the confiscated goods for the king's service. But the case for proprietary government suffered further by a petition from Newcastle signed by Richard Halliwell, Robert French, and twenty-two other inhabitants. After pirates had plundered Lewes, the inhabitants of Newcastle had asked the provincial administration for aid, but the council at Philadelphia had rejected their petition.[11]

Embarrassed by events in America and under pressure from the Customs House in London, Penn was forced to a decision. In 1694 he had promised to return to the Delaware to take charge of the provincial government, but for years he had procrastinated. Now time had run out. In July 1699 the Lords Justices in Council ordered the crown attorney general to consider whether the provincial officials in Philadelphia had not exceeded the powers granted in the charter to Penn. In dire financial straits — in debt to Philip Ford and owing back rent to the crown — Penn now talked of going to Philadelphia in an effort to raise money and bring some order to the provincial regime so as to remove any possible ground for the crown to prosecute a writ against his patent. During the first week in August 1699 the chief business under consideration at the Plantation Office was Pennsylvania. Fortunately for the proprietor, William Blathwayt, the most knowledgeable of the commissioners on plantation affairs and the member most opposed to chartered governments, was then with the king in the Netherlands. Poor attendance at the board as well as at the council also prevented the ministers of state from acting quickly. Before the Commissioners of Trade could report, Penn left for the Delaware aboard the *Canterbury Merchant,* sailing from the Isle of Wight on 3 September 1699.

In his haste Penn allowed himself to be tricked by Philip Ford. The document he signed for his stewart was not a mortgage, but a bill of sale for Pennsylvania. He was now renting the colony from Ford.[12]

Only after Penn had departed did the Lords Justices in Council make known their decision. It could have been worse. The proprietor was to remove his deputy, Markham, as well as David Lloyd and Anthony Morris from public employment. Hereafter the colonists must give obedience to the Court of Vice-Admiralty in Philadelphia and to all officials of the customs establishment. The proprietor must repudiate those turbulent persons who had opposed the Vice-Admiralty Court, and his officials must observe the English acts of trade and navigation and enact proper laws against pirates as well as establish a militia to defend the province and the lower counties.[13] In view of the reference previously made to the attorney general over possible legal action against the charter, Penn had gotten off lightly.

After a "long & sometimes a rude Passage" of three months' duration, Penn arrived at Philadelphia on 3 December 1699. The task before him was a trying one. In addition to his debt to Ford, he owed the crown some £6,000 rent for the three lower counties. He hoped to meet these obligations by closing accounts on sales of land and collecting back rents owed him by the settlers. To this end he established a special agency under James Logan to inspect titles to lands and to ascertain and collect monies due. The young Logan, but twenty-five years old, was the son of a Scottish Quaker schoolmaster of northern Ireland. He and other men who had accompanied the proprietor to assist in the work of rectifying the proprietor's finances and establishing his governmental authority would be greatly resented. These included two Anglicans trained in the law— John Guest and Robert Asheton. Guest became chief justice of the provincial court, and Asheton succeeded David Lloyd as attorney general. Penn's attempt to displace local favorites with outsiders and his effort to extract money hardly endeared him to the populace.

In the Delaware communities Penn faced three hostile groups. To offset the complaints of the "rude factious & troubl[e] some" Anglicans of Christ Church, he sought to undermine their credibility with his political connections in England, Lord Chancellor Somers and the Commissioners of Trade. Although such men as Parson Edward Portlock claimed to love "King and Church," he wrote, they were themselves dealing in booty acquired from pirates. David Lloyd and the residents of the lower counties who opposed the domination of the Friends were not so easily dismissed or their behavior excused. The Welsh lawyer railed against Penn's attempt to reconcile differences, defended his past actions, and threatened to plead his case at Westminster. Resenting his dismissal from office, a dismissal demanded by the ministers of state, Lloyd did not know what it was to bend; fully engaged in a cause, he would stand or fall by it. Penn feared to have the matter taken to London, for he was sensible of the sentiment at Whitehall.[14] And at Newcastle, that "Frenchified, Scotchified, Dutchified" place, other "turbulent spirits" were fomenting differences between the upper and lower counties.

But Penn did have supporters among the wealthier elements in the Quaker community. Robert Turner, Griffith Jones, Francis Rawle, and Joseph Wilcox—men unhappy with the power enjoyed by Lloyd and his allies, who controlled the assembly under the frame passed in 1696—urged Penn to restore the arrangement first established in 1683 when he had founded the colony. Penn decided to return to the practice of appointing councilors, and in the session called for October 1700 he named Edward Shippen, Samuel Carpenter, Turner, Griffith Owen, Caleb Pusey, and Joseph Growdon to the board. The new arrangement made little difference.

After a year on the Delaware, Penn was thoroughly disgusted with "this licentious Wilderness." The continual bickering brought to mind the animosities among the European heads on the division of the territories of the Hapsburg monarch at Madrid. "'Tis our Crown of Spain and we are very full of our

Selves[,] the same passions with less witt being as warmly at work here on our lit[t]le affairs as they are upon greater in Europe.''[15] On one issue the contending Quaker factions could unite against the Anglicans. A law enacted in 1700 specifically permitted Friends to affirm rather than to swear to the truth of their testimony in legal proceedings. Churchmen argued that a mere affirmation was insufficient to bring forth the truth. A defendant not of the Quaker persuasion could bring proceedings to a standstill in a court simply by demanding to be sworn or by insisting that Quaker officials take an oath.

Penn did not remain in America. Informed that royal officials in London were launching a campaign to have Parliament take up the charters, he made plans to return to England. In his haste to get away he capitulated to David Lloyd and other opponents of proprietary and royal authority in their demands for control of government. Penn offered the Quaker leaders a choice of lodging executive authority in the council, as he had done almost twenty years before after his first stay in the colony, or in a single individual. If the latter, he would allow them to name three men. From this slate he would commission one. The provincial leaders opted for the latter alternative, asking the proprietor to name a deputy who would be a good judge of men. Penn suggested Governor Andrew Hamilton of the neighboring Jerseys, a choice gratifying to the assemblymen. The approbation of the crown would not be so easily forthcoming. Hamilton, with other duties in East and West New Jersey, could visit Philadelphia only infrequently. In the absence of the proprietary deputy, the councilors — any five of them — would act as executive.

Capitalizing on Penn's need to return to England, David Lloyd pressed for greater concessions. He inspired a petition presented to the assembly in the name of the inhabitants. Those signing the petition represented an alliance of Quakers now joined in an effort to dismantle the proprietary and to place power in the hands of local men under little, if any, restraint from Penn. A joint committee of the council and assembly then prepared a bill providing for a new frame of government. ''Much grieved, '' a resentful Penn acquiesced, for there was little else he could do. The assembly would do no other business and the ''Philistines be upon us,'' Isaac Norris complained. The Anglicans were ''worse than ever, . . . cock-sure'' that the crown would intercede to take over the government.[16]

On 28 October 1701 William Penn signed a bill known as the Charter of Privileges to the People of Pennsylvania. It was not a charter in the sense of a patent issued by the crown, but merely a provincial statute providing for a frame of government within the limits allowed the proprietor by the royal charter issued twenty years before. The new arrangement provided for an assembly chosen by the freemen, with elections to be held on the first day of October of every year and legislative sessions to commence of the fourteenth. Thus the issuing of writs for elections and the meeting of the assembly would not depend on the executive appointed by the proprietor. The statute confirmed the existing qualifications for the franchise and transferred questions of property to the ordinary courts. The council served merely in an advisory capacity, not as a legislative body. It also lost all judicial functions, as appellate jurisdiction from the county tribunals was now limited to the provincial court. Penn made a further concession: if the representatives from the province and the territories could not agree on legislation within three years, the lower counties might have a separate assembly. Since delegates from these counties had but a few days before protesting the failure of the provincial regime to provide them protection, it should have been a foregone conclusion that they would opt for separation.[17]

Shortly before signing the provincial frame of government, Penn agreed to grant the city of Philadelphia a charter in which he initially named the mayor, recorder, sheriff, clerks, aldermen, and common councilors. Thereafter, elected aldermen and councilors would annually select the mayor. The power to admit freemen to the corporation rested with the municipal officials, but freemen must be twenty-one years of age, have resided within the city for two years, and possess an estate or freehold worth £50. These qualifications gave control for the immediate future to the middle-class Friends, men particularly responsive to the arguments customarily used by David Lloyd.

The final concession the proprietor made related to a charter of property. He received it on 3 November just before boarding the ship *Dolmahoy* for England. While inspecting the document more closely after having signed it, Penn realized that David Lloyd proposed to transfer ultimate authority over land from the proprietor and his agents to men sitting on a court, of whom eight were appointed by the proprietor and thirteen elected by the voters to settle disputes over land. Even before the *Dolmahoy* left the Delaware, Penn instructed Logan, the provincial secretary, not to put this charter on property into effect.

Once gone from America, Penn implored Logan to "give my dear Love to all my friends who I desire may labour to soften angry Spirits and to reduce them to a sense of their Duty."[18] The Quaker proprietor might as well have asked the rain not to fall as to call upon the factious politicians and contentious personalities of Pennsylvania and Delaware to cease their squabbling. Jasper Yeates, the leading merchants of the lower counties, and the Anglicans of Christ Church would have nothing to do with a government dominated by the Quakers. The Friends themselves were divided. One element, led by David Lloyd and calling itself the country, or popular, party, sought to control the government through an elected assembly. The other Quaker clique, representing the well-to-do merchants of the city and led by proprietary appointees, dominated on the council. The men allied with James Logan defended the interests of Penn and the proprietary prerogative; those who followed David Lloyd sought, in the name of the people, to extend the powers of the assembly. Logan, the proprietary men, and the more substantial among the merchants and landowners too could prevail with the voters and, at times, could win a majority of the seats in the assembly. But generally Lloyd and the country faction prevailed, perhaps because they were more assiduous in their political maneuvering and in their appeal to parochial concerns.

In establishing a political base Lloyd appealed to the artisans and shopkeepers of the city and the less substantial farmers in the country side. The self-styled role of enemy of authority—royal or proprietary—and champion of the people made him popular among the rank and file of the Quaker community. Espousing a faith in the common man and appealing to local prejudice against men of means, Lloyd campaigned openly and contemptuously against outside authority and even centralized administration in the colony. He and his followers in the assembly pushed for a decentralized judicial system to circumvent officials acting under the proprietor and to make the county benches virtually independent. Lloyd's posture, his personality, and the tactics he employed all helped to perpetuate divisiveness. Seeking to undermine external control over Pennsylvania, he would further the power of the assembly, whose speaker he was for many years. In this arena, his superior knowledge of law and legislative procedure, his single-minded pursuit of his goal, and his astuteness as a political tactician all gave him an advantage over opponents. In a legislative assembly where the majority of representatives were rustic bumpkins, David Lloyd was a giant.[19] A weak, sick proprietor who had already demonstrated on two occasions a propensity for giving way, a proprietor under constant threat of being stripped of authority by the crown, made an ideal target for an ambitious, willful man such as Lloyd. In accepting a new frame of government when leaving Pennsylvania in 1701, William Penn had provided Lloyd with a legal and institutional instrument to advance the cause of local autonomy.

When Penn left Pennsylvania in 1701, the more immediate threat to his authority lay in the effort to have Parliament assume the patents of the chartered colonies. In the face of this threat some among the Quaker adherents of the proprietor advised Penn to make the best possible terms for them and for himself. His supporters seemed both "Weary & Careless of Gov[ernment]." The proprietor's failure to secure approval from the crown for Andrew Hamilton made the deputy governor uneasy, hesitant to carry out his duties. The proprietors of the neighboring Jerseys resident in the British Isles had already made an accommodation with the crown to secure their claims to the soil in the provinces. Logan and several among the leading Quakers sought to insure their own future should Parliament pass an act to void the charters and send a royal governor to Pennsylvania. The Quaker magnates found Edward Hyde, Lord Cornbury, heir to the earl of Clarendon, attractive. Cousin to Queen Anne, he had just been appointed governor of New York. When the crown assumed the government of New Jersey, he became governor of that colony as well. In the summer of 1702 Cornbury and a retinue of about thirty hangers-on visited Philadelphia, where Edward Shippen gave a dinner in his honor. Cornbury stayed at the proprietor's estate, Pennsbury. On his departure for New York he expressed great satisfaction with Philadelphia and the "decency of his entertainment." Shippen and Samuel Carpenter followed up this approach by sending Cornbury a tun of double beer and a pipe of Madeira wine imported in their own ship. Cornbury promised to be of all possible service whenever he could. As Logan reported, the governor of New York was "exceedingly beloved" in Pennsylvania and much esteemed by the Friends in Philadelphia. Although the proprietor himself was well aware of Cornbury's weaknesses—his luxurious style of living and his "poverty, which is to extremity"—Penn nevertheless concluded that Cornbury had "sense and address."[20] William Penn was not always a good judge of men.

The political scene in London gave Penn hope he might retain the government or at least negotiate favorable terms for its surrender. Despite the rise of what he termed the Church party, the proprietor could boast, following the accession of Anne, of friends in high places, the "wisest men in England, and of the greatest . . . that love me," men of rank who advised him to "be not hasty" in bargaining away the government of his American territories. Yet he was desperate for funds. "Make returns with all speed," he implored his agent in Philadelphia, "or I am undone."[21]

Pending the conclusion of negotiations Penn was able to secure approval for Andrew Hamilton to serve temporarily as his deputy in Pennsylvania and the lower counties with the understanding that the queen's favor was not to be construed as prejudicing the right of the crown to Newcastle, Sussex, and Kent. The proprietor also secured a promise from the Commissioners of Trade that he would have an opportunity to submit a reply before they advised any action: this in the nature of a bill in Chancery so that "nobody may be murder'd in ye Dark." On the recommendation of the Plantation Office the queen in council had allowed a concession to Quaker consciences: all officials in Penn's territories, before entering into office, must take the oath directed by Parliament or submit the affirmation allowed Friends in England by statute. However, judges must allow witnesses, if they so desired, to take an oath in any public proceedings.[22]

Further to strengthen the judiciary in his territories Penn appointed as chief justice Roger Mompesson, an English lawyer recently named by the crown to preside over the Court of Vice-Admiralty for the middle colonies. A moderate Churchman, Mompesson, in Penn's eyes, "knows the world here," that is, in England. Although he had previously served in Parliament, Mompesson "only Steps abroad to ease his forture" of his father's debts. His patron was the earl of Clarendon, father of the recently appointed governor of New York. Offsetting the appointment of Mompesson was the loss of Andrew Hamilton. Discouraged with the situation in Newcastle and Philadephia, Penn's deputy had retired to his home in Perth Amboy, New Jersey, where in April 1703 he died. The government in Philadelphia seemed paralyzed, as the councilors would take little action. When Robert Quary demanded that they submit the required oath or affirmation, Samuel Finney and Joseph Growdon balked. Logan urged the proprietor to send out a deputy immediately. Penn wanted a disinterested man, and he thought he found him in John Evans, the son of an old Welsh friend. The new deputy was a young man, just twenty-six years of age, but sober and sensible, so Penn thought, and entirely in the interest of the proprietor. Penn hoped that the pious Quakers in Philadelphia, and particularly "honest" Griffith Jones, Evans's "countryman," would advise the young proprietary deputy.[23]

Penn sought still to rid himself of the government of the province and the counties if he could obtain good terms. On 11 May 1703 he informed the commissioners for plantation affairs that upon a just regard for the civil rights of the inhabitants according to the laws and constitution of the country and a reasonable compensation for himself, he would resign to the crown the government, saving some few privileges for himself. At this time Penn did not give any particulars, but five weeks later under pressure he submitted specific proposals to the Plantation Office. He asked that the province and territories not be subsequently brought under any other colony; that the laws of Pennsylvania, except such few measures as the proprietor found unacceptable, be confirmed by the queen; and that the crown grant him and his heirs a patent for the counties of Newcastle, Kent, and Sussex. Such a deed would underwrite the rents Penn claimed were due him. He also asked for the sum of £30,000, the amount he claimed to have invested over the years in these American ventures, and further required that all rights and privileges granted him and his heirs as lords of the soil and proprietors, with all incidental offices belonging thereto, in the fullest manner be reserved and confirmed.[24]

Months passed with no decision. In February 1704 Penn indicated that he would content himself with £20,000 and the rights of landlord and lord of the manor of the country. Still the administration took no action. Almost a year later, in January 1705, Penn again took the initiative, informing the Plantation Office that he would be satisfied with his "seignory" and proprietary privileges and an exemption from public taxes in Pennsylvania. But the inhabitants must have entire liberty of conscience and be eligible for any civil employments as hitherto, Quakers especially, because of their numbers, their wealth, and the role they had played in founding the colony. Emphasizing the great effort and expense he himself had incurred for thirty years to foster the unprecedented progress of Pennsylvania, the proprietor pressed the Plantation Office for a quick reply.[25]

To the Commissioners of Trade, Penn's proposals were unclear. What did he mean by seigneurial and proprietary privileges? By entire liberty of conscience did he mean anything more than toleration such as allowed by act of Parliament in England? Did Penn mean to admit Quakers to office without an oath or affirmation as directed by law? Would Friends who held office allow others not of their persuasion to take an oath in any public proceeding? In answering these points Penn stipulated that by seigneurial privileges he meant all of the royalties pertaining to paramount courts, such as fines, forfeitures, and deodands, and jurisdiction of courts leet and baron as well as the erecting of manors, as already specified in his charter. As to liberty of conscience for the inhabitants, he meant not only what related to worship but also to schools, the support of ministers, and service in the militia. Quakers should be eligible for any public office except that of governor by affirmation, as was customary in Pennsylvania, a just and reasonable practice in a country and government made for them, a land where they had never excluded anyone or abridged the privileges of others.[26]

Resisting any unnecessary concessions, the commissioners for plantation affairs expected Penn to surrender his patent for the government with all the powers therein contained, reserving to himself the proprietary of the soil and the quitrents therefrom. But Penn had already suffered the first of several strokes which would eventually incapacitate him and put an end to the negotiations. Even at this early stage, officials at the Plantation Office found his language relating to the Friends vague and imprecise, as was the wording of the laws of Pennyslvania he had recently submitted. The statutory provision against persons with clamourous tongues in the act against scolding was too general and the penalty— standing gagged in some public place or five days' imprisonment—too great. Nonetheless, Penn continued to demand privileges for himself and the Quakers in Pennsylvania: for himself and his male heirs, exemption from paying taxes on their estates; for the Friends, liberty of conscience in faith, worship, and discipline in private and public meetings, freedom to establish their own schools, and exemption from any forced maintenance of clergymen and service in or charge for a militia.[27]

When the Plantation Office balked at Penn's conditions, negotiations were broken off. In 1705 the proprietor's position was already in jeopardy as a result of action taken against him by the Ford family. Ford himself had died in 1702, and his widow and son, now determined to settle accounts, presented the document Penn had signed a few years before. The proprietor did not think he owed the Fords much; to his surprise they presented him with a bill for £14,000. Eventually the matter went to the English courts, but first the Fords took their case to the elders in Philadelphia. On 10 July 1705 Griffith Owen, Edward Shippen, and James Logan, Penn's commissioners for property, received a request to meet with David Lloyd, Isaac Norris, and John Moore on a matter of business. A letter had arrived from the younger Ford informing Norris, Lloyd, and Moore that in March 1697 Philip Ford had purchased from the proprietor the province of Pennsylvania and the territories. Subsequently he had granted Penn a lease for three years at an annual rent of £630. Since that time Penn had been but a tenant at will, yet had paid rent but "very dully." The Fords, now resolved to take over their property, warned the inhabitants not to pay over any quitrents to Penn's agents.[28]

David Lloyd made the most of Penn's embarrassment, for he had not forgiven Penn for removing him from office years before at the demand of the royal government. His attacks on proprietary prerogative and open ridicule of royal government had been intemperate and sustained, but his pose as an enemy to authority made him popular with the rank and file of the Pennsylvania Quakers. A sick, financially embarrassed proprietor, loathe to act against the Friends and threatened by a royal takeover, a man who had always seemed to capitulate to pressure from the Quakers in the colony, was an ideal target for the able, ambitious, and at times, unscrupulous provincial politician.

David Lloyd's power in the assembly had grown considerably as his knowledge of law and legislative procedure gave him an advantage in a society where such knowledge was at a premium. In the corporation of Philadelphia too his allies had been exerting their power, claiming a right for aldermen to act as justices for the county as well as the city. Inasmuch as the proprietor had granted them a charter, no one could interfere with their authority. Executive authority was almost nonexistent. Penn's right to the lower counties was in jeopardy as well, and Richard Hallowell, Jasper Yeates, and five other representatives had balked at acknowledging the charter of privileges signed in 1701. James Logan, under threat of legal action, found it difficult to collect money due Penn. He dared not to meddle in the lower counties, and in the province he found the sheriffs "so remiss that Scarce any thing can be drove forward." David Lloyd had derided Andrew Hamilton during his brief stay in Philadelphia as no more than "a Conservator of ye Peace & no Gov[ernor]." Hamilton had arrived in Philadelphia the day before the assembly convened and departed immediately after the brief five-day session ended, never to return, for he died a few months later in East New Jersey. Executive function had then devolved upon the council. Logan had little faith in the abilities of Griffith Owen, Edward Shippen, Samuel Carpenter, William Clark, Caleb Pusey, and Thomas Story, for some among the Quaker magnates had joined Robert Quary and the vestrymen of Christ Church in attending Lord Cornbury when he published his commission in nearby Burlington as royal governor of New Jersey. The Anglicans had asked Cornbury to request the queen to annex Pennsylvania to his government.[29]

Penn had warded off the threat and sent out a new deputy. To govern the contentious, divided populace would have required the wisdom of a Solomon. Instead Penn sent out John Evans, a young man of little experience and judgment. The new deputy arrived in Philadelphia on 2 February 1704 accompanied by Penn's son, William, "My poor Boy," as his father often referred to him. The heir to the proprietary estate had not followed the path his father would have wished, having been led into youthful follies "when too easily prevailed on."[30] These indiscretions continued as the younger Penn, Evans, and Roger Mompesson set up a bachelor establishment in Philadelphia. Their drinking and carousing greatly distressed the sober Quaker community. Logan found Evans lacking in other respects: for example, the deputy knew nothing of the division between province and the lower counties. In the spring of 1704 when the deputy governor, as required by the crown, called upon the assemblymen to raise money to assist New York against the French, the representatives from the lower counties insisted on exercising the choice offered them in 1701 by Penn and withdrew to sit as a separate body. For their part, the delegates from the province presented Evans with a bill for confirming the charter of privileges wherein the assembly continued from one annual election to another and the governor was excluded from dissolving or proroguing the house. Mompesson soon withdrew to New York in disgust. Hardly more hopeful, Logan urged Penn not to put off accepting any good terms from the crown "one hour after they are offered." The Quakers of Pennsylvania thought "Privileges their Due, and all that Grasped to be their Native Right." Some men's "Brains are as soon intoxicated with Power as the Natives are w[i]th their beloved Liquor and as little to be Trusted w[i]th it." Evans himself had no stomach for the fight, being ill with "the dry belly ache," an affliction many attributed to intemperance. With little money coming in, Evans and the younger Penn looked to Logan for their upkeep.[31]

Matters did not improve when next the assembly met. David Lloyd presented two bills, one for granting additional powers to the corporation of Philadelphia, another for confirming the charter on property. The assemblymen would transact no other business until Evans gave up any pretense of authority to dissolve and prorogue the legislature. Lloyd's professed zeal for the public good had won over the country members, and the follies of young Penn and Evans had alienated the staid Quakers. Although the great majority of the assemblymen elected in 1704 may not have wished ill on the proprietor personally, yet they would not support the cause of his government. Men accepting appointment to the council were looked upon as "ill here as the Court party at home by those that some reckoned the honest men of the Country." Samuel Richardson, Nicholas Waln, and Isaac Norris—the last, known for his sense and probity—might have opposed Lloyd, but they did not always stand for election.[32]

An episode in the fall of 1704, when the rural members were eager to go home and the house was on the verge of breaking up, illustrated the nature of the tactics employed by Lloyd in opposing the proprietor and manipulating the assembly. The members had agreed to send an address to the proprietor, but since time would not permit the entire house to attend to the matter, it was committed to Lloyd, John Wilcox, Isaac Norris, Joseph Wood, Griffith Jones, Anthony Morris, William Biles, and Samuel Richardson. This committee never met. With the aid of Lloyd, Wilcox drew up a paper stuffed with scurrilous and scandalous invectives, some relating to issues not even discussed in the assembly. Showing the address only to Jones and Wood, Lloyd signed the document as speaker of the assembly. To justify his actions he produced an order in the minutes of the assembly, yet on inspection this proved to be an interlineation in Lloyd's own hand entered in different ink between the last of the minutes of the assembly and the notice of adjournment. A letter accompanying the address read as if it were from the body of the Quakers in the house, although actually the work of Lloyd, Jones, and Wood, the last, a nominal Anglican. Norris and five or six other members called on Lloyd for an accounting, but he now professed himself a private man and consequently not concerned in the spurious address.

In England, Penn was outraged over the affair: "There is an Excess of Vanity yt is Apt to Creep in upon ye people" in positions of power in America. He urged Roger Mompesson to take up a commission as chief justice so that the provincials would learn that they were "not to Comand, but to be Comanded, according to the Law & Constitution of English Government." But Mompesson had had enough of Pennsylvania and the Quakers. Not so Logan. He continued optimistic that time would open the minds of the "misled Members" of the assembly to the machinations of that "lurking Snake," David Lloyd, and that the many honest, "tho too careless," assemblymen might yet prevail over the "Menn of Deep Designs or shallow sense."[33]

In the summer of 1705 David Lloyd struck again. On 10 July, accompanied by Isaac Norris and John Moore, he presented to Penn's commissioners of property in Philadelphia the letter from the Ford family relating the elder Ford's dealings with the proprietor. The Fords were now determined to take over the colony. Despite a promise to the contrary, Lloyd made the affair and Penn's plight public. The tactic apparently backfired and the greed of the Fords may have won the proprietor the sympathy of some Pennsylvanians. In the elections held later that year, men sympathetic to Penn won a clear victory. The new assembly was, in Logan's view, one of the best the province had ever had, "but cost no small paines to make it such." Edward Shippen, Samuel Carpenter, Caleb Pusey, and Richard Hill, all of the council, had won seats, as had several other "good heads," Isaac Norris and Lloyd's father-in-law, Joseph Growdon. Having broken with Lloyd, Growdon now succeeded him as speaker. All but one of the representatives were Friends, the generality, honest "pickt" men. Clearly the proprietary supporters had organized for the election. The corporation of Philadelphia by questionable tactics had returned David Lloyd after the county had rejected him. Bucks returned John Swift and a few other "scabbed sheep," but they could do nothing in the face of the proprietary majority. The lower counties were definitely lost, however; their representatives met as a separate assembly under Robert French and Richard Halliwell, leaders opposed both to the province and the proprietary regime.[34]

Whatever goodwill had come to the proprietary cause as a reaction to the greed of the Fords, John Evans, Penn's deputy, lost by an ill-advised tactic in 1706. Attempting to move the Quakers of the province to support measures for defense, he concocted a story that marauding French ships had come up the Delaware and bombarded Lewes. When the hoax was discovered, even some Friends faithful to the proprietor turned against his deputy. Evans further antagonized them when he suported the assembly at Newcastle in taxing all vessels using the river to raise money for the construction of a fort to protect shipping. The old dispute over the exemption for Quaker justices in administering oaths during legal proceedings further set the Friends in the assembly — both proprietary supporters and opponents — at odds with the deputy governor. The electoral victory of the proprietary faction had been short-lived.

David Lloyd once more held the esteem of the bulk of the country people and those who looked upon him as the "Champion of the friend's Cause in Gov[ern]m[en]t." As Logan feared, the elections in 1706 resulted in an assembly "ye worst that Ever I saw." Returned for Philadelphia were Lloyd, John Wilcox, Griffith Jones, Joseph Carpenter, Francis Rawle, John Roberts, Robert Jones, and Samuel Richardson, "all bad, but the last & he very Rough." The representatives from Chester—a county normally inclined to the proprietary side—were of much the same stamp. For some time Bucks had not favored the proprietary cause. What had provoked the voters, Logan concluded, was the tax imposed on shipping and the behavior of Evans. His philandering had alienated the sober Quakers. Another proprietary stalwart had fallen into disgrace. A son had been born to his wife only two months after marriage, to the great scandal and distress of the Friends in Philadelphia. "This place in short runs head Long into Debauchery." In the assembly Lloyd and his followers now pressed "for ye whole Power & leave the Gov[erno]r only a name." Pursuing their advantage, they proposed Logan's impeachment in the house.[35]

The discouraging news from America inclined Penn early in 1707 to close with the crown. Officials in the Plantation Office insisted that the proprietor surrender the government unconditionally, but they would not commit themselves as to the compensation he should receive. Nor would Lord Treasurer Godolphin. When asked for a statement of charges, Penn would not give a specific accounting, but demanded a total of £20,000 (£5,000 to be paid in Pennsylvania and £15,000 in England—£8,000 in money and £7,000 in English copper with a patent for coining it into small money for the colonies).[36] On the political conditions for the transfer of government, no resolution was forthcoming. Early in 1708 the Plantation Office reviewed the opinion given years before that in the event of extraordinary exigency through the default or neglect of a proprietor the monarch might constitute a governor for a colony, but took no further action.

Bridget Ford and her children did, however. Their case against Penn was upheld in the Court of Common Pleas; as a consequence, when Penn left the Quaker meetinghouse in Gracechurch Street on the morning of Sunday, 4 January 1707/8, two bailiffs served him with a writ. Availing himself of a *habeas corpus* the proprietor took refuge within the liberties of the Fleet. Although imprisoned for debt, Penn had comfortable rooms in the Old Bailey, where he received visitors and held meetings. Bridget Ford and her son then petitioned the queen. The Fords had overreached themselves, for Lord Chancellor Cowper ruled that they had no right to the government of the province and territories and must relinquish title to the soil if Penn could raise the money he owed them. The proprietor was able to arrange a loan from a syndicate of prominent Friends in London, who as trustees accepted a mortgage on the province. By the autumn of 1708 he was again free.[37]

Although Penn was now clear of the Fords, his troubles with David Lloyd mounted. Assured of a majority in the assembly, opponents of the proprietary regime had engaged Deputy Governor John Evans in a protracted struggle for control of the provincial court system. After weeks of haggling the assembly adjourned without having agreed on a bill. At a subsequent conference attended by a committee of the assembly, Evans, and the councilors, little was achieved except to demonstrate the pettiness of men on both sides. Lloyd did not rise to his feet when he spoke, leading Evans to rebuke him: it was his duty to stand as did others when addressing the governor. Lloyd refused, and when Evans again spoke to him, Lloyd broke up the meeting: he was affronted and would not stay. "This triffle" cost an entire week in messages sent back and forth. Convinced that Logan was behind the failure to put through the assembly's version of the judiciary bill, Lloyd launched a vendetta against the proprietary secretary, the man he considered the chief obstacle to his achieving power through an expansion of legislative power. Some assemblymen preferred to remain inconspicuous by not opposing Lloyd, or concluded there was little they could do. Left with a free hand, Lloyd and his followers continually abused and insulted the council "under Colour of asserting the People's Privileges."[38]

When organizing his campaigns for the annual elections, Lloyd appealed to a broad constituency: artisans, untutored farmers, malcontents among the Anglicans, and the followers of George Keith, a former Quaker who had turned to the Church of England. The elderly Friends, expecting Penn would give up the government, hesitated to act. Government in Pennsylvania was virtually at a standstill as one unproductive legislative session followed another.[39]

The litany of complaints against John Evans finally told against him with the proprietor. Penn was distressed to learn of his faults and imprudent conduct: his circulating the bogus report of French privateers, his accepting the bill from the assembly at Newcastle imposing a powder tax on all vessels using the Delaware River, his refusal to approve the bill for the judicial establishment in Pennsylvania, his getting a young maid with child and conniving to spirit her out of the province, and finally, his undertaking a "lewd voyage" to the Susquehanna, where he and his retinue debauched the wives and daughters of the Conestoga Indians. Penn now found a new deputy governor, a man of whose morals, experience, and fidelity the proprietor had personal knowledge, one recommended by persons of great rank. Captain Charles Gookin was a forty-six-year-old army officer, highly recommended by senior military officials in Britain and friends of the proprietor. His conduct in Pennsylvania, Penn predicted, would be characterized by sobriety and thriftiness, rather than by luxury and rapaciousness. Penn asked Logan to inform Evans of the decision. The displaced deputy took the news badly. Some time before, he had seemed to have mended his ways, and the dismissal ruined his projected marriage to John Moore's daughter. Logan offered him some sympathy: the assemblymen had indeed treated Evans "most barbarously," as they would all men in the proprietary interest.[40] Gookin might take heed.

The new proprietary deputy arrived in Philadelphia in January 1709 to find the provincial government in a state of paralysis. The last elections had brought no change. To some Philadelphians Gookin seemed a plain, honest man, temperamentally best suited to be a soldier, yet a prudent individual. Penn's deputy was vulnerable: he had already exhausted the £300 he had saved in the army, and the £400 a year promised him by Penn—later reduced to £300—was hardly adequate to maintain him. Gookin had instructions to persuade various factions to accept a legislative union between the lower counties and the province, an impossible task, Logan predicted, for were he blessed with the abilities of a biblical sage he would "meet with enough to try his temper." James Coutts, Richard Halliwell, Robert French, and other assemblymen at Newcastle were eager to set up a port to rival Philadelphia. They not only insisted on sitting as a separate body but called into question Penn's authority to govern the lower counties. They now hoped, through John Evans, to convert the lower counties into a separate royal colony.[41]

With the politicians of the lower counties and Pennsylvania opposed to each other, the Delaware communities were vulnerable. French privateers plundered Whorekill in the spring of 1709. No militia resisted the invaders. In response to a requisition from the crown for 150 men to join in an expedition against Canada, the councilors, after conferring with the leading Friends in the community, gave it as their opinion that the Quakers might without violating their principles vote a sum of money. The assembly, dominated by Lloyd and his friends, voted only £500, however. Gookin was contemptuous of the twenty-odd representatives and their speaker: Lloyd was one of those "cunning" lawyers trained under George Jeffreys, Lord Chancellor under James II, a man who had not adopted the Quaker faith until after he arrived in Philadelphia and married a Friend.[42]

From London, Penn and his advisers undertook a campaign to reconcile differences among the factious provincials. Why must they carry matters on with division and contention? What cause had the proprietor given for opposition? On more than one occasion he had altered the frame of government to meet the colonists' objections and to preserve the Quakers' privileges. Although privileges ought to be tenderly preserved, they should not be asserted to the point of licentiousness, for government served to maintain good order. The Friends must remember that popular turbulence as well as a ruler's excessive power might disrupt the peace of the community.

Penn's remonstrance may have induced the older Friends to take a more active role to win control of the assembly: in the elections held in October 1710, for the first time in several years they won a majority of the seats. Pressure from the Quaker Yearly Meeting may have influenced some voters. They may also have reacted to Lloyd's excesses in his hounding of Logan. Recent immigrants—Scot-Irish Presbyterians and German-speaking Mennonites—may also have tipped the balance against the Quaker extremists.[43] Although Lloyd was returned to the assembly the following year, not until 1715 did he again sit in the speaker's chair.

Isaac Norris, prominent merchant, sometime councilor, and mayor of Philadelphia, played a key role in the campaign against Lloyd. Under the auspices of the Friends' Yearly Meeting he wrote a short tract pointing out the destructive consequences for public affairs of the chronic factionalism in the assembly and calling for constructive change through the election of men of substance, men not concerned solely with opposition. Continued resistance to the proprietary regime might not result in liberty but a royal administration.[44]

Ironically, while Norris argued that a vote for the supporters of the proprietor was a vote against royal government, Penn in 1710 on the advice of James Logan had reopened negotiations with the crown for giving up his right of government. For £20,000 to be paid in seven annual installments he was now apparently willing to surrender all of his powers so that the crown would have the entire administration, the appointment of all officials, and the regulation of all public affairs under its immediate care. As for the Friends in Pennsylvania, Penn now asked for no specific guarantees; he would leave to the queen's favor and royal protection the status of the people called Quakers. But he informed the more prominent Quakers—Edward Shippen, Samuel Carpenter, Richard Hill, Griffith Owen, Isaac Norris, and Caleb Pusey—that if he did surrender the government he would take care of their property and privileges both as *Christians* and Englishmen. Seeking perhaps to intimidate the dissidents, the "malignants," in Pennsylvania, he warned that if they persisted, the "great" men of government in London would put an end to assemblies and leave it to the Parliament of Britain to legislate.[45]

The Plantation Office wanted Penn to renounce his claim not only to the province of Pennsylvania but to the lower counties as well. As Penn's agent in America later explained to the proprietor's family, the Quaker leader had never obtained the right of government for this region. He had received only a grant from the duke of York before James himself had any patent to the territories west of the Delaware from his brother Charles II. Although this circumstance was not generally known, it was appreciated by a few men in the counties who had opposed proprietary rule. The Commissioners of Trade entertained the same views, but the skepticism held at the Plantation Office notwithstanding, Penn's claims received consideration, particularly with the accession to power of Robert Harley, earl of Oxford, as lord treasurer in the Tory administration. "My great friend," Penn addressed him.[46] When Penn dropped his price to £12,000, the negotiations seemed closer to a conclusion. By March 1712 the attorney general, Sir Edward Northey, had prepared drafts of the necessary documents, in which the proprietor humbly prayed the queen to take the inhabitants of his American territories under her protection and expressed his certainty that the Quaker assembly would readily make provision for the financial support of government. On the basis of this tentative agreement Oxford may have authorized an initial payment of £1,000 to Penn.[47] But in April William Penn suffered a stroke—a dangerous illness, so it was reported in Philadelphia, and an alarming forecast of what was to come. Although stricken, Penn was yet able to assure his old Quaker friends on the Delaware—Shippen, Carpenter, and Norris—that while he had agreed to sell the government he had taken "effectual" care that the laws and privileges he had granted as proprietor would be observed by the queen's governor. To induce them to accept the situation, he warned that by act of Parliament the crown would the next winter annex all of the chartered colonies.[48]

A few months later in Bristol William Penn suffered another, more disabling stroke. This "distemper in his head" left him without speech and unable to write. Hannah Penn and the six creditors who held the mortgage on the colony—Henry Gouldney, Joshua Gee, Silvanus Grove, John Woods, Thomas Oade, and John Feilds—were placed in a quandry. Initially they hoped that Penn would recover, but a year later Hannah informed Logan in Philadelphia that while Penn had regained some of his strength, he was still unable to engage in business, the affair of the surrender. Her advisers had recommended she get the matter concluded and confirmed by an act of Parliament, a tactic calculated to circumvent Penn's incapacitation. But during the parliamentary session of 1714 the Penns and their creditors could not come to a full agreement.[49]

There the matter rested.

The unresolved status of the proprietary created uncertainty in Pennsylvania and in the lower counties, as men did not know whether government would continue under Penn's charter and the frame he had accepted in 1701, or with some new arrangement under a commission to a royal governor.

By extraordinary effort Penn's sympathizers had managed to win control of the assembly in 1710 when David Lloyd had overreached himself in his vendetta against Penn and James Logan. Yet the proprietary faction was unable to maintain its position as individual Quaker magnates followed their own interests: Thomas Story left for England; Isaac Norris retired to private life in Chester; and in 1714 Richard Hill declined to serve on the board of property. James Logan too left for England, not to return for more than two years; once back in Philadelphia he devoted himself more to private business ventures than to public affairs. Robert French died in 1713; once a troublesome opponent, in recent years he had served Penn's cause. Even Robert Quary had made his peace with the proprietary men. His behavior illustrated the often transitory, personal nature of political allegiances. With French and Norris as speakers at Newcastle and Philadelphia the proprietary cause had been well served. But with the demise of French and the retirement of Norris the cause of the administration suffered. The proprietary party had difficulty finding suitable candidates to stand for office. Norris himself was not eager to continue the struggle, thinking it best for the proprietor to relinquish the government, as Penn was along in years and his son had shown little desire to succeed him. The best settlement for the Quakers could be obtained through negotiation on such matters as oaths, salaries for ministers, support of a militia, and money for the administration of government.[50]

Control over government appropriations gave the assembly a powerful weapon. In the spring of 1711 the house forced Gookin to accept fourteen laws in exchange for £500 for the deputy governor and payment of the debts of the provincial regime. This was the first such appropriation in five years. Elections for the assembly that autumn were hotly contested. After spending about £2,000, the proprietary supporters had carried their slate in Chester, but lost seats in Bucks. The retirement of older men in favor of younger candidates had cost the party votes.

In 1712 newsletters arriving from New York reported that Penn had actually surrendered the government and that Parliament was about to annex all of the chartered colonies to the crown. Rumor also had it that John Evans — the former proprietary deputy who had so offended Quaker sensibilities — would be the first governor commissioned by the queen, an appointment contrived by James Logan.[51] In the autumn of 1712 proprietary supporters were at a loss how to proceed, not knowing whether any action would stand if Penn had given up the government. In January 1713 word came that the proprietor had died. What was the status of the agreement he had reportedly made with the lord treasurer for continuing the privileges of the Quakers and the charters to the city and the province? What of the confirmation of the lower counties to the Penn family? The inhabitants of Sussex had resolved not to pay rents until the matter was settled. Considering that his days as governor were numbered, Gookin in 1713 was "raking in . . . Money by all means" that his position allowed. Convinced that the proprietary secretary was supporting John Evans, Gookin cut himself off from Logan. In the winter of 1714 the governor failed to call a single session of the council, and the following summer the assembly took it upon itself to appoint a provincial treasurer to succeed the deceased Samuel Carpenter. In the ensuing elections the voters of Chester returned David Lloyd to the assembly. Much to Logan's disgust, "that worthy Patriot" was once more in the speaker's chair and "acting his part again." Gookin now spent much of his time in Newcastle. More willful than ever, he declared himself "a Soldier" who must have "full Satisfaction" from every man who offended him, as became "a Gentleman." In fighting a number of duels he lost several fingers. He rebuffed approaches from the councilors of Pennsylvania, and when the deputies of the lower counties met at Newcastle and chose Jasper Yeates speaker, Gookin charged them with unlawful riot and refused to recognize them as an assembly, a right they claimed by the proprietor's charter — an ironic twist, since for years they had denied Penn's title.[52]

In Philadelphia Gookin had no support, for the country party dominated the assembly and the Quaker councilors repudiated the offensive governor. With the proprietary government seeming extinct, Logan and Isaac Norris suggested that the Friends apply to the crown; perhaps Colonel Robert Hunter, governor of neighboring New Jersey and New York, might be commissioned to preside over the Quaker community according to their laws and constitutions. Hannah Penn could only express her concern over the reciprocal complaints and recriminations and offer solicitous platitudes, but the proprietor being ill, she could do nothing more. Her husband was not inclined to make any changes. The surrender of the government had not been completed, and when it would be consummated, if ever, Hannah Penn could not say.[53]

For a generation Pennsylvania and the lower counties had been nominally under a proprietary regime, under a Quaker proprietor who had neither the means nor, at times, the inclination to impose his will on the strong-minded politicians at Newcastle and Philadelphia. During these years factional opposition, nurtured and encouraged by the tactics and genius of David Lloyd, had become the accepted practice. Political autonomy became the way of life.

CHAPTER 9

New Jersey, 1696–1709: From Proprietary to Royal Government

$\mathbf{D}$AVID LLOYD HAD a political, if not a social, counterpart in Lewis Morris of East New Jersey. Both men sought power, and like the Pennsylvanian, Morris initially saw in popular politics an avenue for personal advancement. But for the New Jerseyan executive not legislative support would ultimately provide him with his greatest opportunities. The nephew of a wealthy Quaker immigrant from the West Indies, the able Morris while still a young man found fertile ground for his ambitions in the chaotic world of East and West New Jersey, communities whose bizarre political structure almost defied rational analysis. Proprietary provinces brought under direct royal government early in the eighteenth century as a unified colony, East and West New Jersey nevertheless proved a disappointment to those who saw in governors responsible to Whitehall the solution to the problem of securing the dependence of the American colonies. Settled by Englishmen, Scots, and immigrants from New England, by Presbyterians, Quakers, Anglicans, and Congregationalists, the Jerseys gave little evidence of social cohesion or political stability.

Government was also fragmented. Initially part of the region taken from the Dutch in 1664 and granted by Charles II to his brother, the duke of York, New Jersey had come into the possession of two members of the royal duke's entourage, although James (who was not then the sovereign) had no right to pass on governmental authority to his two protégés. The two courtiers, Lord John Berkeley and Sir Geroge Carteret, had then divided their territory into an East and a West New Jersey. Within several years they or their heirs had passed on each division to two groups of investors. Title to the soil and allegedly the right to govern then rested in one hundred shares of West New Jersey and twenty-four shares for the eastern division, allotments held by scores of proprietors, some resident in America, others in the British Isles, some with one or more shares, others with but fractions of shares. In 1688 royal officials had merged East and West New Jersey within a larger administrative unit, the Dominion of New England, claiming that certain of the proprietors had surrendered the power of government, a contention other proprietors denied. Following the overthrow of the Dominion in 1689 and after an interlude when only county and town administration existed in the two provinces, the British-based proprietors again commissioned a governor for East and West New Jersey. The Plantation Office under William III would not acknowledge their authority,[1] but did not actively press the issue until the opening years of the eighteenth century, when it sought to have Parliament take up all of the charters and patents.

During the last decade of the seventeenth century, East and West New Jersey continued as distinct provinces, separate from each other and from New York. The status of government remained confused. Most of the twenty-four shares for East Jersey were held by Scots and Englishmen, the latter based in London and led by William Dockwra. These British proprietors attempted to formulate policy for the province. Responsibility for executing proprietary orders rested with the proprietors resident in America, mainly Scots, and with Governor Andrew Hamilton, the proprietary deputy. Hamilton, the resident Scottish proprietors, and the freeholders with titles to land granted by the proprietary regime constituted a proprietary party in East Jersey, one strongly resisted by the settlers who had founded the towns of Elizabeth, Woodbridge, Piscataway, Newark, Middletown, and Shrewsbury in Essex, Middlesex, and Monmouth counties under patents issued in 1664 by the governor of New York, Richard Nicolls, before the ducal governor had learned that James had given the region away. These "Nicolls" patentees and other freeholders who were averse to soliciting new patents from the proprietors for their land or to paying quitrents to a proprietary regime made up an opposition party. East New Jersey politics centered on the rivalry between these two factions.

In West New Jersey, in Burlington and other towns on the left bank of the Delaware, Quakers predominated. A majority among the settlers, the Friends were nonetheless apprehensive over the pretensions of the West Jersey Society, an organization consisting of forty-eight London merchants and English gentry who had purchased two shares of East Jersey and twenty shares in West Jersey from an English courtier and speculator, Dr. Daniel Coxe. Leadership in the West Jersey Society lay with Thomas Lane, alderman and later lord mayor of London, and Paul Docminique, an influential Whig politician. Whatever else may have motivated the Quakers in West Jersey, they feared the society because it was made up of men who did not share their faith. Unfortunately for the cause of the English group, it employed as an agent in America Jeremiah Basse, an erstwhile Baptist preacher. A contentious, unsavory character, Basse antagonized, among others, the council of proprietors resident in West Jersey by refusing to cooperate in disposing of the society's land. He gathered about him several employees of the society and Anglican settlers eager to wrest control of the province from Samuel Jennings and the other Quaker magnates. But while the Friends in the western district opposed Basse, the Quakers in the eastern province supported him, hoping to establish their titles to land against the claims of the proprietors resident in East New Jersey.[2]

The dispute between the proprietors of East Jersey and the settlers claiming their lands under patents from the government of New York came to a head in

1695 in the case of *Fullerton v. Jones,* an action brought by the resident proprietors against Jeffrey Jones, a Nicolls patentee from Elizabeth. The jurymen, themselves patentees, decided for Jones, but Lewis Morris and the other judges appointed by Governor Andrew Hamilton reversed the decision. The young Morris, having succeeded to his uncle's estate and social position, had attached himself to the proprietary government, at that time the apparent path to power and preferment. With the attorney for the townsmen prepared to appeal the judges' actions against Jones in London and the majority in the assembly refusing to support the proprietary governor and council, Hamilton and the resident proprietors sent Thomas Gordon, the proprietary secretary, to England with orders to thwart the efforts of the agent appointed by the town meeting of Elizabeth, William Nicoll, and to urge a resolution of the dispute between New York and East Jersey over a proposed port at Perth Amboy. To prevent a drain on revenue needed to finance the defense of New York, officials at Manhattan wanted ships entering at the East Jersey port to pay the same duties required of vessels using New York.

The passage by Parliament in 1696 of the Act for Preventing Frauds then brought into question the proprietary regime in the two Jerseys. Could an alien, a Scot such as Andrew Hamilton, serve as governor of an English colony? To avoid legal embarrassment—proprietary claim to the government was questionable at best—the London proprietors of both sections petitioned the king in 1697 for approval of Jeremiah Basse as governor of East and West Jersey, but they would not provide sufficient financial surety as required by law. Basse left for America with only a *dedimus potestatem,* a writ ordinarily allowing a private person to act in the place of a judge, under the great seal of England. On the question of a free port—freedom for vessels to use the facility at Perth Amboy set up by the proprietary regime without paying customs to the government at New York—the proprietors suffered defeat when the Plantation Office and the Lords Justices in Council rejected their arguments for a separate facility. The issue would come up again, however.[3]

The new proprietary administration in the Jerseys got off to a weak start following the arrival of Basse late in March 1698. Initially both Basse and the newly appointed governor of New York, Richard Coote, earl of Bellomont, worked together in a campaign to apprehend pirates, but this cooperation, as well as Basse's administration, were shortlived. Almost as soon as Basse arrived he appointed his cronies at Burlington as councilors and judges of the provincial courts. When the local treasurer, Peter Fretwell, refused to surrender the records of his office, Basse had him jailed. Samuel Jennings then organized a secret meeting to petition against the administration, and a pamphlet war followed. Not surprisingly, Thomas Revell, John Jewell, and John Tatham, on behalf of the West Jersey council, supported their patron and condemned the Quakers at Burlington for their "rude perverseness." Those not of the Quaker persuasion, they claimed, had received the governor with "joy." The Quaker-dominated assembly, led by Fretwell, Jennings, and Thomas Gardiner, refused to recognize Basse as governor, citing his failure to secure the approbation of the crown to hold office.[4] Lewis Morris adopted the same argument in East Jersey at the first session of the Court of Common Right at Perth Amboy, when he demanded to know of the judges appointed by Basse by what authority they presided over the court. For his impudence Morris was arrested. Resenting the governor as a social inferior, Morris continued his attack, publicly deriding Basse as a brewer's clerk and a poltroon. But at least three of the councilors of East Jersey had no difficulty in accepting the new governor.

Within a year of the attack by Morris, the new administration was ended. The ambitious Morris, to whom consistency in public affairs meant little, now courted the townsmen of Elizabeth he had previously opposed, arguing that to secure their titles it was necessary to replace proprietary government by having crown annex New Jersey to New York. Excluded from power in Basse's administration but connected by marriage to prominent New York families, Morris may have concluded that the path to preferment was easier in royal New York than in proprietary New Jersey. Abandoning the resident Scottish proprietors, he addressed to the townsmen of Elizabeth a series of what became celebrated as "Red-Hott" letters, wherein he argued that the right of government granted by Charles II to the duke of York could not be transferred by James to others.[5] Authority over the Jerseys remained with officials of New York.

The controversy over the powers of the respective governments and the authority of Basse and Bellomont came to a head in November 1698 when Bellomont had the *Hester*—a vessel owned by Basse and his brother-in-law, John Lofting—and its cargo seized at Perth Amboy and taken off to Manhattan. Basse refused to pay customs at New York.[6] To raise money to carry an appeal to London Basse called a meeting of the assembly, but the Scots on the resident board of proprietors in East Jersey insisted on certain conditions: the governor must not approve any bill unless the assemblymen promised either to pass an act to guarantee the payment of quitrents or to require the townsmen to take out new patents for their lands. Now that Basse had broken with the resident board, Morris decided to throw in with the Scottish proprietors in opposition to the governor. Repudiated by the Shrewsbury voters, he agreed to stand for the seat from Perth Amboy made vacant by the expulsion of the proprietary agent, George Willocks. Morris's opposition notwithstanding, Basse was able to secure legislation from the assembly to finance an appeal of the *Hester*, to exclude the proprietors and their deputies from the assembly, and to reduce the power of the local proprietary board. When Morris publicly attacked the bill levying a tax on unimproved land to provide funds for the appeal, Basse had him jailed, but a mob broke him free. Yet Basse's days as governor were numbered. Word soon arrived that the British proprietors had reappointed Andrew Hamilton, the legal advisers of the crown having decided that Scots were eligible to hold public office in the English colonies. But as Hamilton and Morris both appreciated, the Commissioners of

Trade had refused to approve the new governor, fearing that approbation by the crown might be construed as recognition of the proprietary right to the government of the Jerseys.[7]

The British proprietors, concerned over the chaotic situation in the colonies, apparently appointed Hamilton as a stopgap measure. Unsure of their legal position, some among them were ready to negotiate a surrender to the crown, provided they received acceptable terms. For some months they and the Commissioners of Trade had been at odds over the government of the two colonies. On 14 April 1699 the Plantation Office accepted an offer tendered by one faction among the proprietors for a trial to be held at the bar at Westminster. Accordingly, a case was arranged whereby not only the claim of the proprietors for a port at Perth Amboy but also their right of government might receive judicial determination. But William Dockwra of London, head of an opposing group, objected: the one right did not depend on the other. Later that summer Dockwra made a tentative offer to surrender the right of government on condition that (1) the king confirm the right to the soil and rents, (2) Perth Amboy be established as a port, (3) only the proprietors enjoy the privilege of purchasing lands from the Indians, (4) they name the secretary, register, and surveyor general of the province and (5), as a concession for the Friends, no person be molested or deprived of any civil right because of opinions on religion. In offering to surrender the government, Dockwra was assuming that the Jerseys would not revert back to New York. The Plantation Office was slow to respond, waiting until they could receive advice from the only experienced commissioner of trade, William Blathwayt, then with the king in Holland, could learn the views of the governor of New York and could conduct a long search of the chaotic records relating to the Jerseys.[8]

In East Jersey government seemed to have collapsed, as the assembly failed to conclude any business and armed men broke into jails to free prisoners. Hamilton arrived in America in December 1699 but, like Basse before him, without the royal approbation. Opponents of the proprietary regime in Elizabeth, the men who had broken Morris out of jail, now rose against Hamilton. In March 1700 inhabitants of Piscataway and Elizabeth, disrupting the courts, accused the judges of acting without authority. One irate resident of Elizabeth bid a justice to "kiss his Arse." Mobs continued to harass the magistrates, break into jails, and assault sheriffs. In April 1700 over 200 men petitioned the crown to uphold the patents for land issued by the governor of New York more than thirty years before and asked for the removal of Hamilton. The following month the proprietary governor had to dissolve the assembly when the deputies, incited by John Royce and Andrew Bowne, Basse's cronies on the council, raised embarrassing questions over Hamilton's failure to secure approval from the crown to serve as governor. William Penn, outraged at the behavior of the councilors and rioters and at the attacks on Hamilton, urged the governor to "Clench the Nail[,] for Examples must be made by thee of them that acted so exemplarily."[9]

In London the proprietors of East New Jersey pressed for a legal resolution.

Basse added fuel to the controversies when he presented a petition from a faction in West Jersey complaining of obstructionist tactics by the Quakers of Burlington. He further complicated matters by making a formal complaint before the House of Commons against the earl of Bellomont for seizing the *Hester*. The proceedings before the Court of King's Bench at Westminster during Easter Term of 1700 only added to the confusion. The case seemed feigned, arranged to take the issue out of the House of Commons and into the king's court. Attorneys for Basse, the plaintiff, and Bellomont argued the case on 10 May with Chief Justice Sir John Holt presiding. To Thomas Trevor and Sir John Hawles, the crown lawyers defending Bellomont, the only question was whether East Jersey was dependent on, subject to, the authority of New York. The grant made by the duke of York to Carteret and Berkeley in 1664 was for a tract of land, with not a word of any authority to govern. Consequently, government remained with the duke and passed to the crown when James became king. Now the governor appointed by the king had authority over the entire region, both New York and New Jersey. Holt in his charge to the jury took a narrow view, avoiding the basic issue. In appointing Bellomont William III had intended him to be governor of New York, not the Jerseys. By usage the two proprietaries were distinct from New York.[10]

This setback notwithstanding, by the close of 1700 the evidence of the "distractions and Anarchy" in the Jerseys led the Commissioners of Trade to continue their attack on the proprietors. Dockwra and the other London shareholders made little of the opposition to their administration in America, claiming the protests came from a few mutinous people, men who would not be satisfied with any government and who hoped to deprive the proprietors of their rights to land and rents.[11] By this time the West Jersey Society, the syndicate which had purchased the shares of Dr. Daniel Coxe, had fallen onto hard times; its funds were depleted, its meetings infrequent, and its members flagging in their interest. Its officials were concerned with protecting their only remaining source of profit, the land of the two colonies, a source now threatened by the claim of Colonel Daniel Coxe, whose father, by an indenture, had given his son and heir all of his holdings in New Jersey—including, presumably, the shares he had already sold to the West Jersey Society. The overlords of East New Jersey were themselves divided, for the Scottish proprietors resident in America, led by George Willocks, an ally of Lewis Morris, had repudiated the authority of William Dockwra, secretary of the proprietors in London. Supported by Peter Sonmans, who claimed the largest number of shares of any individual, Dockwra entered into an alliance with Hamilton's opponents in America. Another clique of London proprietors headed by Joseph Ormston, an English merchant who had married a sister of Peter Sonmans and was contesting his brother-in-law's titles, disputed with Dockwra for control. Ormston sided with Hamilton and the Scottish proprietors in East New Jersey. The West Jersey Society, holder of two shares in the sister province, also opposed Dockwra. The erstwhile agent for the society, Jeremiah Basse, spoke for the Anglicans around Burlington, who had long been resentful of the domination of the Quakers in the affairs of West New Jersey.

Following the Board of Trade's initial failure in 1701 to persuade Parliament to assume the proprietary colonies and the decision in the case of the *Hester*, Lewis Morris arrived in London. Once established at Newburgh House in St. James's Park, Morris proved an adept lobbyist in the long months of negotiation for dominance in the government of New Jersey.

In these discussions the key issues to be decided were the terms the proprietary cliques would extract and which among the various factions would prevail in the administration named by the crown. In 1701 Lord Bellomont had died and the succession at Manhattan loomed as a consideration in the political maneuvering, for Morris and others had previously entertained the idea of joining the Jerseys to New York. Ostensibly campaigning on behalf of Andrew Hamilton as royal governor, Morris assumed the role of mediator among the leaders of the various proprietary factions: Thomas Lane, Paul Docminique, and Edward Richier of the West Jersey Society, and Dockwra and Ormston of the London-based East Jersey proprietors. Morris himself represented the Scottish proprietors in America.

In August 1701 Morris opened the campaign at the Plantation Office, advancing proposals for the Ormston faction and the West Jersey Society. To secure their position they requested that assemblymen elected to the New Jersey legislature be freeholders with no less than 1,000 acres of land; voters must have at least 50 acres. Such requirements would secure the Scottish proprietors in America against the Nicolls patentees, of whom few had sufficient land to qualify for office. The aristocratic Morris admitted that the proprietors were among the largest landholders, but, he expostulated, if everyone were eligible for office, including persons of little worth, the men of best estates would be ''at the disposal of ye tag, rag, and rascallity.'' He recommended further that the towns of Perth Amboy and Burlington each return two representatives to the assembly but that the province at large elect the remaining members of the house. By such an arrangement a sheriff amenable to the interests of the proprietors could hold polls at locations inconvenient, if not entirely inaccessible, to their opponents. Morris also wanted to strengthen the control of the proprietors by requiring every freeholder to secure a patent from the overlords for his land.

Although the proprietors insisted on the right to nominate a governor and other officers, they could not agree on a candidate. Morris, on behalf of the proprietors in East Jersey, the Ormston faction, and Thomas Lane and Paul Docminique, nominally supported Andrew Hamilton. Dockwra proposed Andrew Bowne, a councilor to whom he had already sent a commission. But at a meeting of the newly founded Society for the Propagation of the Gospel held in September, Morris contended that none but Anglicans should be appointed as governor or councilors, a proposition hardly flattering to the Scottish proprietors resident in the eastern division or the Friends in West New Jersey. Jeremiah Basse was better attuned to the shifting English political world; he privately suggested to

William Blathwayt Lord Cornbury as governor of New Jersey. Edward Hyde, Lord Cornbury, heir to the earl of Clarendon and cousin to Princess Anne, had already been designated governor of New York.[12] The division over the nomination of the first royal governor reflected the factional alignments in New Jersey. The West Jersey Society, the majority of the proprietors of East New Jersey resident in London, the Scots in America, and the Friends in the western division backed Andrew Hamilton. The faction in London led by William Dockwra, the Nicolls patentees, and the Anglicans around Burlington opposed him. Morris nominally favored Hamilton, but if the Scot could not secure the approval of the crown, Morris himself was available.

The negotiations dragged on for months. Although the various principals— Sir Philip Meadows for the Plantation Office, Dockwra, Docminique, Sonmans, and Morris—occasionally conferred with each other, they were still divided on the governorship when a deed of surrender was signed on 15 April 1702 and presented to Queen Anne.[13] Morris did not remain in England until all of the details for the new government were resolved. He returned to America with a letter from the queen requiring the inhabitants of a unified New Jersey to have due regard for Morris in his task of preserving the peace and quiet of the province.[14] Morris's authority was temporary. Early in July a draft commission was ready for Lord Cornbury, the queen's cousin, to be governor of New Jersey. Inasmuch as the governor of New York also gave him command of the militia of New Jersey, the appointment had some logic, whatever the political influence of his father and his uncle (the earl of Rochester) and William Blathwayt.

Who would serve on the governor's council? Dockwra hoped to pack the board with East Jersey men friendly to his clique among the English proprietors and to exclude Morris and others among the Scots and Quakers, but the administration wanted to balance the contending factions. As finally determined by the Commissioners of Trade and Secretary Nottingham, the council was composed of representatives from the major cliques in both divisions. Not appointed was Jeremiah Basse. Unhappy, he made known his dissatisfaction through the earl of Clarendon, father of the governor designate: Edward Hunlocke he condemned as a patron of pirates, much in the Quaker interest; Samuel Jennings, Francis Davenport, and George Deacon were bigoted Quaker preachers, while William Pinhorne had been turned out from New York by Bellomont for illegal conduct; Samuel Leonard, a man of no estate, was also a zealous stickler for the Friends. But Nottingham, a principal secretary of state in the new administration selected by Anne, chose not to interfere in the appointments, and the Commissioners of Trade discounted Basse's invective against the prominent Friends of the western division. The councilors named in the governor's commission were persons of good estates; the Plantation Office had no evidence that such was the case with Basse or with Colonel Daniel Coxe.[15]

By the instructions issued to Cornbury, the crown united East and West New Jersey into a single province. Its general assembly, meeting alternately at Perth

Amboy and Burlington, was to consist of twenty-four representatives—two chosen by the householders of Perth Amboy, two by those of Burlington, ten by the freeholders of the eastern division, and ten by those of the western section. Representatives must have 1,000 acres of land in freehold; voters, 100 acres of land. The instructions also laid down conditions for the legislature: requirements to enact laws that confirmed the rights of the proprietors to the soil and to quitrents as well as the titles and estates of the inhabitants. Only the proprietors and their agents could purchase lands from the Indians, and only officials appointed by the proprietors could record surveys. Inasmuch as the Friends balked at swearing oaths in courts of justice, the assembly might enact legislation similar to that passed in England providing for affirmations by Quakers as far as might be consistent with good order. On signing a declaration of allegiance comparable to that taken by Friends in England, the Quakers of New Jersey would be eligible to hold office. On the issue of the conscience of Quakers the instructions were also clear. The assembly of New Jersey must provide aid for New York, since the preservation of that colony against the French and hostile Indians was essential for the security of the other provinces and the burden was too great for the New Yorkers alone to bear.[16] Financial support for the defense of the northern colonies was to be a central issue in the politics of both New York and New Jersey during the next dozen years.

If officials in Whitehall had hoped to still the discord in New Jersey by accepting the conditions Lewis Morris and the proprietors in London had demanded, they were badly disappointed. Pending the arrival of Cornbury, Morris, as presiding officer, adopted a vindictive stance toward his opponents in the eastern division. In a direct attack against the Congregationalists he charged that the unsettled conditions not only in New Jersey but also in New York, Pennsylvania, and the Carolinas had their origin in New England. Opposing proprietors, beating sheriffs, challenging judges, assaulting governors and councilors, and imprisoning constituted officials, all—with but few exceptions—were acts committed by the very dregs and rascality of the populace. Crowds of the most necessitous scoundrels, the scum of mankind, were daily insulting the men of best figure and estate. Clearly Morris saw himself and the proprietors in the eastern division as the aristocrats of New Jersey society. The role of leader was not without its rewards. Morris received a new patent for his lands from the resident board and a waiver of quitrents in arrears, allegedly compensation for his service in England. He also strengthened his ties with the West Jersey Society, becoming its agent in America, virtually the overseer of its lands.[17]

The antagonism prevailing during the proprietary regime continued after New Jersey came under the crown. The townsmen in the eastern division holding patents from New York still insisted on the validity of their deeds and refused to apply for confirmation from the proprietors or to pay them quitrents. In the western division the Anglicans, resenting the Quakers, pushed for a militia and for the taking of an oath as a requirement for holding office, proposals anathema to the Friends and threatening their political role.

The creation of a single assembly threw the contending factions into a single political arena. On one side the Scottish proprietors of the eastern division, men who needed a counterweight to offset the Nicolls patentees, aligned themselves with the Friends of the western division. The Nicolls patentees drew close to the Anglicans of Burlington. The antagonisms among the various proprietary cliques in Britain also affected the political alliances in New Jersey. William Dockwra and Peter Sonmans, at the head of a small group opposed to the proprietors resident in America, hoped to offset the power of their colonial rivals, George Willocks and Thomas Gordon, proprietors who had repudiated Dockwra as secretary and register. Colonel Daniel Coxe, claiming shares once owned by his father, placed himself at the head of the Anglicans of Burlington, where he hoped to break the monopoly held by the council over the distribution of land. The spokesman for the proprietors resident in the eastern division and agent for the West Jersey Society was Lewis Morris.

For much of the first two decades of the eighteenth century political life in New Jersey revolved about two loosely knit alliances, one called the proprietary, the other the anti-proprietary party, although after 1703 the latter included the clique in London headed by Dockwra and Sonmans.[18] Following Cornbury's appointment, Morris and his allies—Dr. John Johnston, George Willocks, and Miles Forster—were the first to approach the royal governor seeking support for their titles to the soil and the continuance of their political power. The Scottish proprietors decided to offer Cornbury a bribe, a present of £200.

The first test of the new regime came at Burlington on 14 August 1703, when Morris, Robert Quary, Thomas Revell, and several other councilors were admitted to office but the Quakers Francis Davenport, Samuel Jennings, and George Deacon refused to take the requisite oath, claiming the right to submit an affirmation as provided in England by an act of Parliament. Quary, the Anglican surveyor general of the customs, who had for years been contending with the Quaker politicians in nearby Philadelphia, claimed the statute cited by Davenport and Jennings applied only to Friends when they appeared in courts of law and not when they sought to qualify for civil office. Jennings then cited paragraph 52 of Cornbury's instructions, which allowed the admission of Quakers to office upon their signing a declaration of allegiance; this provision seemed to supersede paragraph 49, which prohibited the governor from admitting to office any person who had not taken an oath. For the moment, Cornbury sided with the Friends and admitted Jennings, Deacon, and Davenport to the council; at the same time, he wrote to the Plantation Office pointing out that without the Quakers the number of men fit to serve in government would be few. As the new governor was at this time also ingratiating himself with the Friends in Philadelphia, some thought he aimed to have Pennsylvania added to his jurisdiction. However, Cornbury's closest confidante at Burlington proved to be Colonel Daniel Coxe, and the Anglican speculator was thought "big against the Quakers."[19]

Undeterred by an initial rebuff, Robert Quary raised another objection to the arrangement for the government of New Jersey when Cornbury issued writs for the election of the first assembly under the royal regime. Quary charged that the property requirements for candidates for the assembly and for voters favored the resident Scottish proprietors of the eastern division, who for several years had been taking up land in order to exclude men from a share in the government. He also attacked the arrangement by which ten representatives were elected in each of the two divisions at large, rather than from the respective counties.[20]

The elections for the assembly late in 1702 illustrated how a faction could manipulate the system for its own benefit. Dr. John Johnston, George Willocks, and Lewis Morris had prevailed on the governor to appoint as sheriff Thomas Gordon, the agent for the resident board of proprietors in the eastern division. To ensure a favorable outcome for the Scottish proprietors, Gordon held the poll at a place thought inconvenient for the opposition voters. Yet over 400 of the opposition voters appeared to declare their preference, as against only 42 of the proprietary supporters—and many of the latter, it was charged, came from New York. At first Gordon attempted to delay the vote, hoping the opposition would tire and go home rather than brave the severe weather. Finally he simply returned the poll contrary to the sentiments of the majority of the voters. In the western division, where the Quakers predominated, diligent organization and astute tactics allowed the Friends at Burlington to prevail. Their leaders had insinuated that unless the freeholders voted for Quakers, the assembly would impose tithes, militia service, and heavy taxes.

The proprietary-Quaker alliance enjoyed a majority in the newly elected assembly, one won at the expense of the Anglicans of the western division and the Nicolls patentees of the eastern section. Gordon and several of the proprietors drew up a bill for securing the rights and titles of the proprietors and the people, commonly called the Long Bill. By this comprehensive measure they held the patents of Elizabeth and Monmouth void, reasserted the claims of East Jersey to Staten Island (then claimed by New York), and denied the obligation of the proprietors to pay the crown arrears in quitrents. Without giving their colleagues in England an opportunity to be heard, they also proscribed the proprietors' holding land in joint tenancy. To establish title to land previously purchased, one must now hold a patent from the resident proprietors. The majority in the assembly then tacked on a money bill to gain the governor's assent to the Long Bill. Cornbury had orders from the crown to secure a long-term appropriation for the expenses of government and to cover expenditures from Hamilton's administration. But the assembly would appropriate only £1,000 and for but one year. Cornbury adjourned the house having assented only to a bill prohibiting the buying of land from Indians without a license. Hitherto he had not sided with one faction or the other, but the tactics adopted by Morris and Gordon in 1703 inclined him against the resident proprietors. The governor now set out to alter the qualifications for holding office and voting and the apportionment of seats as set forth in his instructions. As justification he cited the complaints of the residents of Elizabeth, Woodbridge, and other towns holding patents from Nicolls as well as the failure of the assembly to settle an adequate revenue for the support of government. If the representatives were not in a better humor in the spring of 1704, he proposed calling for new elections.[21]

Lewis Morris, too, was unhappy, but at Cornbury's *volte face*, for the proprietors' surrender of the government had allegedly been conditional upon the terms incorporated into the royal instructions to Cornbury. In failing to accept the Long Bill and questioning the procedures and qualifications for elections, the governor had disobeyed his instructions and violated the terms of the agreement between the crown and the proprietors. But Morris faced opposition as John Bowne and Richard Salter—the latter an agent for William Dockwra—undertook to solicit money for the governor among the townsmen with patents from New York and from other settlers unhappy with the proprietors, money to induce Cornbury to dissolve the assembly. By this "blind tax," as Morris and his cronies called it, Salter and Bowne raised sums variously estimated at £800 to £1,500.[22] In this respect the only difference between the principals for the two factions—Salter and Bowne on the one side and Morris, Gordon, and Dr. John Johnston on the other—was that those opposed to the proprietary clique were more generous in their reward to the governor.

The year 1704 saw an open break between Cornbury and the Scottish proprietors and Quakers of the western division, who by a narrow margin controlled the assembly: thirteen members were adherents of the Quaker-Scottish proprietary party, while the Nicolls patentees of the eastern division and the Anglicans of the western section had returned only eleven delegates. Taking the initiative Cornbury requested a more equitable bill on land titles, another to regulate the provincial militia, and a more generous appropriation for the support of the provincial government. But the Quaker and Scottish-proprietor majority would approve a government appropriation of only £4,500 for a period of three years and determined to take no action on the militia. The governor, they declared, must approve the Long Bill.

The assembly's failure to act on the militia allowed Cornbury to argue that the Quakers must not be allowed to hold public office. In November of 1704 two allies of the governor, Daniel Leeds and Thomas Revell, initiated an attack against the Friends. Employing the tactic Thomas Gordon had successfully utilized the previous year against Richard Hartshore, an opponent of the proprietary regime from Monmouth, the two councilors objected that three Quakers returned from the western division—Thomas Gardiner, Thomas Lambert, and Joshua Wright—were not qualified to sit in the house. For almost a year Cornbury refused to allow them to take their places. With a majority thus ensured them, Richard Salter, Hartshore, and John Bowne put through the assembly a series of measures designed to weaken the Quakers and Scottish proprietors. The house accepted a bill for support of government, voting £4,000 for two years to be raised by a tax of £10 on every hundred acres of unimproved lands, with the burden to fall on the undeveloped land held by the proprietors for speculative purposes. By another measure, a bill to quiet the minds of the queen's subjects, they hoped to prevent prosecutions such as those Morris had urged on the provincial attorney general, Alexander Griffith, against the townsmen of Elizabeth who had opposed the former proprietary governor, Andrew Hamilton. Still another bill, one to regulate elections, was designed to weaken the power of their opponents by electing assemblymen from particular constituencies rather than from two divisions at large and by reallocating seats in the assembly to favor those towns where the Nicolls patentees and the Anglicans were influential. While a proposed bill for settling a militia exempted Quakers from military service, it imposed fines on anyone exercising this privilege. Cornbury accepted these measures, although he was unhappy with the sum voted for the government. However, the leaders in the assembly assured him this was but a trial sum; if the country could bear more, they would vote additional money to meet the public needs.

As might have been expected, Lewis Morris protested against the laws Cornbury had accepted: they violated the terms agreed upon in England as a condition of the proprietors' surrendering the right of government, and consequently, the instructions to the governor. Cornbury evaded the charge—the queen was the best judge of what was proper to instruct her deputy in America— and criticized the imperious Morris; he gave his tongue too great a liberty in telling the inhabitants that they had a right to elect representatives with the same privileges and powers as those who sat in the House of Commons in England. Morris had openly remonstrated with the governor that the colonists were Englishmen, entitled to all of the privileges of Englishmen, and if the queen would not allow them to send members to represent them at Westminster, it was but reasonable that they should have assemblies of their own and be governed by laws of their own making. Such views were not peculiar to Morris, Cornbury found; they were held by others in New Jersey and in New York, particularly in the Long Island towns settled by New Englanders, people generally deemed Commonwealthmen.[23]

Whatever republican rhetoric Morris from time to time chose to espouse, he was an aristocrat seeking power. In later years he achieved this goal by aiding a royal governor to manipulate the elected assemblies in New Jersey and New York. His immediate problem and that of the resident proprietors was the legislation passed by the assembly late in 1704. With the house controlled by his opponents and the governor unsympathetic, Morris took the issue to England, apparently with little success.

In April 1705 the queen in council approved additional instructions for the governor based on Cornbury's recommendations. The number of assemblymen remained at twenty-four, but the householders of Perth Amboy and the freeholders of each of the five counties in the eastern division were to elect two representatives, those of Salem and Burlington and each of the four counties of the western section, two. Representatives must possess at least 1,000 acres of land or a personal estate valued at £500 sterling; voters, 100 acres or personal property worth £50 sterling. But Cornbury lost on his challenge to the three Quaker assemblymen. The Plantation Office advised him to leave the determination of elections to the assembly and not interfere other than to issue writs for election. As to financial support for the charges of government, short-term appropriations were unacceptable. The assembly should vote revenue for twenty-one years, or, a minimum, eleven.[24]

Cornbury had been able to bring about a shift in the balance of the council. On his recommendation Richard Townley, a staunch Anglican long opposed to the resident board of proprietors; Colonel Daniel Coxe; and Roger Mompesson, an Anglican favorite of the governor's father, the earl of Clarendon, all received appointments to the board. But the elected assembly, not the appointed council, was to be the decisive arena, and despite the changes in electoral districts, the Quakers and resident proprietors still dominated in the polls, as Cornbury had orders to restrict his role to issuing writs. The assembly would ascertain if the men elected were qualified to sit. When the three excluded Quakers—Thomas Lambert, Thomas Gardiner, and Joshua Wright—resumed their seats, in 1705, the Friends from the western division and the resident Scots proprietors in the eastern section held a majority of seats in the assembly, although their rivals predominated on the council.

Whatever chance Cornbury may have had to influence the assembly he lost by his injudicious catering to Anglican cronies and his bizarre personal behavior. In the summer of 1705 his wife died after a severe illness. Her death seemed to have affected him strangely. Rumors spread quickly throughout New York and New Jersey of bouts of drunkenness and of the governor's appearing in public in woman's garb. Seizing on these stories, Samuel Jennings and Morris set up a party apparatus complete with platform and candidates and circulated printed satires of Cornbury's eccentricities warning the inhabitants that their liberties and property were threatened. By the list of approved candidates the freeholders would know the men who could be expected not to vote money for the support of government or approve a militia bill.

Voting for the third assembly under a royal government resulted in a smashing victory for the coalition of Quakers and resident Scottish proprietors. The Friends captured eleven of twelve seats in the western division; the Scots and their supporters, six of twelve from the eastern section. Jennings sat in the speaker's chair, and Morris headed the committee to hear grievances. The majority, after voting to expel Richard Slater, set to work collecting evidence that the governor in 1704 had accepted bribes to dissolve the assembly. Even before the session began both sides were on a collision course. Cornbury warned that the queen expected the assembly to renew the law for a provincial militia without delay. The Quakers must acquiesce; if not, they might not be allowed to hold public office, not having taken an oath. Apprehensive for the community of Friends, James Logan came over from Philadelphia to confer with Jennings at Burlington, where he discoursed with him "strongly" but in vain, for "his head Strong temper [would] ne'er admitt a Rein."[25] On 5 May 1707 the assembly approved a petition calling for the replacement of Cornbury after adopting a remonstrance introduced by Morris charging the governor, among other things, with having accepted a bribe to dissolve the assembly from Salter and John Bowne in 1704. Three days later Jennings read the remonstrance aloud and to Cornbury's face in an openly insulting manner. The governor replied on 12 May, attributing the dissatisfaction of the assembly to the malicious influence of Morris and Jennings, and on 16 May he adjourned the house. As expected, the council, dominated by opponents of the Quakers and Scottish proprietors, Coxe, Revell, and Leeds, supported the governor by condemning the remonstrance as "a most scandalous Libell."[26]

News of the confrontation spread quickly. Outsiders not directly involved in the acrimonious dispute differed in their estimates. After much reflection James Logan concluded that whether the assemblymen had been right or wrong, their treatment of the governor was "certainly scurrilous." New Yorkers, concerned with securing support for the English effort against the French, found the situation in New Jersey lamentable. Some wished that Cornbury were not so closely related to the Queen, but nevertheless "hope[d] yt God in his due time will send a Deliverance." Not Providence directly, but two Anglican missionaries disgusted with the behavior of Cornbury, came to the aid of the Friends. Throwgood Moore, the priest at St. Mary's in Burlington, publicly declared the governor should be excommunicated for wearing women's clothes. In response, Cornbury had Moore arrested and jailed in Manhattan. Morris was to use this episode with his correspondents in the Society for the Propagation of the Gospel.[27]

Provincial government in New Jersey was at a stalemate. Jennings openly proclaimed that since the crown had taken over jurisdiction from the proprietors, the queen might send whom she pleased as governor but the inhabitants would keep him poor enough. Cornbury had alienated almost all elements. When the assembly voted on 27 October, *nemine contradicente* to raise no money until the governor consented to redress the grievances of the colony, Cornbury adjourned the house until the next April. Even if the governor should comply with their demands, the assembly had pledged to vote but £1,500 for a single year. Quary saw the matter in wider perspective: the Quakers of neighboring Pennsylvania having balked at voting money for the support of government and establishing a militia, the Friends in New Jersey were playing the same game, resolving to allow no prerogative to the crown, no power to its governor. They would lodge all power in themselves. If not checked quickly, this growing evil would spread over the entire American continent.[28]

Lewis Morris told a much different story. No democrat, a man contemptuous of the mob although not loathe to employ demagoguery, he spoke for gentlemen of means when in 1708 he set out for the secretary of state in London a long analysis of the situation in New Jersey. He condemned the governor and his cronies—Jeremiah Basse (agent for William Dockwra), Richard Salter, John Bowne, Revell, and Leeds—for graft and corruption. Because of misapplication of funds, the assemblymen were utterly averse to voting money for more than a single year. Cornbury's behavior both in New York and New Jersey made it impossible to trust such a man. Not content to excoriate Cornbury, Morris extended his condemnation generally to all governors sent out from England. The injustices they imposed, their sordid and mercenary dealings, the measures to which they stooped, the trash of mankind they raised as favorites to posts of honor and whom they employed as their tools—all had prejudiced the royal service in America. Here Morris resorted to classical history with an implied threat. Cornbury's administration was nowhere so exactly matched as by that of Gessius Florus, governor of Judaea during the reign of Nero, when the province was entrusted to a governor of procuratorial rank. In A.D. 166 an onslaught against the Hebrews, one the procurator allowed to take its course, had led to a retaliatory uprising in Jerusalem.

But Morris, the one man more than any other who had worked to bring royal government to New Jersey, was yet unwilling to abandon this source of power. Cornbury must go, but Morris had his own candidate to succeed Cornbury as the queen's deputy, his neighbor in Westchester, New York, Colonel Caleb Heathcote, brother of the wealthy merchant and prominent politician of London Sir Gilbert Heathcote. No man understood the province and the people better or was more capable of doing the queen real service. Heathcote was an honest man, the reverse of Cornbury, of whom Morris could not resist adding one more observation, a point others would not think it worth their while to make: every day Cornbury appeared in public dressed in woman's clothes.[29]

Morris's denunciation of Cornbury was superfluous; the ministers of state had already decided to remove the errant governor: he had become too great an embarrassment. On 28 March 1708 Secretary Sunderland informed the Plantation Office that the queen was pleased to appoint Colonel Lord Lovelace governor of New York and New Jersey. One of Cornbury's most bitter opponents did not live to enjoy the news of his disgrace. Debilitated by long illness, Samuel Jennings died the same month. Cornbury lingered in Manhattan for some time, hounded by creditors. He finally took ship for England, where, following the death of his father, he succeeded as third earl of Clarendon. Yet dissident politicians on the New Jersey council still saw him as a potential source of influence and power.

In addition to the title Baron Lovelace of Hurley, John Lovelace had inherited a sheaf of debts from a cousin overly addicted to gambling. This condition may have made him susceptible to the blandishments of Paul Docminique and

other proprietors of New Jersey resident in Britain. Lovelace's appointment sig-
nified victory by Marlborough and Godolphin over the duke of Newcastle for
control of royal governors in the colonies, in a contest between those who wished
to reward officers for their service in the army as against politicians who wanted
to use colonial patronage to reward followers in the House of Commons. Neither
side, however, paid much attention to the qualities and conditions necessary for a
governor effectively to render the colonies dependent upon the crown.

Another battle was waged in Whitehall. When the Plantation Office drafted
the commission and instructions for the new governor, the English proprietors
and the West Jersey Society had an opportunity to strike at the Anglican ring
Cornbury had favored in America. Before the new governor left for his post, he
and Docminique presented nominations for the council. Under Cornbury the
provincial board had obstructed Morris and the resident proprietors in issuing
patents for land. This point was critical for Morris, who was locked in a struggle
with Colonel Daniel Coxe for control of the provincial board of proprietors and
the rights to thousands of acres of land. For the Quakers of the western division of
New Jersey, it was essential that their agent, Morris, sit on the governor's council. Protesting strongly against Coxe and his allies, Docminique charged that
Revell owned no land in the colony and had abetted felons in escaping justice. On
behalf of the West Jersey Society, Docminique offered a list of men with sufficient estate and integrity: Miles Forster, Hugh Hoddy, William Hall, John Harrison, and John Hamilton. William Penn, by virtue of his shares in New Jersey,
also joined in the attack on Cornbury's Anglican ''ring.'' Dropping Revell and
Leeds from the council would promote public quiet and satisfaction. At the behest of various proprietors in England, the Plantation Office restored Morris to
the council, dropped Revell and Leeds, but hesitated to displace Coxe and Peter
Sonmans.[30]

In sending out the new governor the Plantation Office saddled him with
instructions to secure modifications of the legislation enacted during the previous
administration. The act for settling the militia that had been passed by the temporary anti-proprietor, anti-Quaker majority provided that money voted by the
house be paid to the receiver general, the provincial secretary, or any person
appointed by the governor for such public use as the governor designated, a
provision the commissioners for plantation affairs thought too vague. Money
ought to be paid to the receiver general and spent for purposes expressly specified. Also needing modification was the act for quieting the minds of the
residents, the law enacted to clear men who had assaulted officials during the
proprietary regime by allowing the queen through her governor to pardon trans-
gressors. The law for regulating elections also needed clarification, for it did not
specify the number of acres necessary to qualify a person to vote or to sit in the
assembly. If Lovelace found the requirements specified in the royal instructions—100 acres of land or a personal estate of £50 for voting, 1,000 acres or

£500 to sit in the assembly—too high, he might seek another provincial law lowering these qualifications. Responding to complaints from proprietors in the western division, the Commissioners of Trade further directed that all records to proprietary titles remain with their agents. Cornbury had ordered them turned over to Basse, his provincial secretary.[31]

In Burlington Colonel Daniel Coxe, although thankful that he had escaped the fate of Revell and Leeds, concluded that Lewis Morris and his "Tools," Sir Thomas Lane and other principals of the West Jersey Society, had prevailed at the Plantation Office. As president of the council Morris was second only to the governor. Next in precedence was George Deacon, a Quaker miller, a "poor wretch" who could "scarce say bo[o] to a Goose," a man fit only to be manipulated by others, as Morris had well known, Coxe contended, in recommending him for the council. In November 1708, before Lovelace arrived and called for an assembly, Morris and his "Gang" had procured indictments at Perth Amboy against their opponents. A "packt" grand jury, one that "hell itself could almost have Spued out," brought in indictments against Peter Sonmans and Jeremiah Basse.[32]

In the assembly held in March 1709 Morris's influence was evident when his ally Thomas Gordon was elected speaker and Miles Forster, another colleague, replaced Peter Fauconnier, Cornbury's premier minister—so Morris called him—as provincial treasurer. The new governor proved compliant. For his cooperation he received a bill for the support of government. The assembly also passed a bill in effect lowering the requirements for voting and standing for election by evaluating personal estates in local currency rather than in sterling. (One hundred pounds New Jersey money brought only £60 sterling.) Lowering the qualifications might have been an effort to win support for the resident proprietors from the Quakers in the eastern division and the Nicolls patentees. In an effort to proscribe their opponents, the assembly majority censured Jeremiah Basse and branded Richard Ingoldsby, the deputy governor under Cornbury, and the councilors who had criticized opposition to the former governor as men unfit to hold office under the crown.[33]

With Morris, Thomas Gordon, and their followers seemingly well in command, fate intervened. Lovelace died on 6 May 1709. Major Richard Ingoldsby, as lieutenant governor, headed the administration when, the following month, Colonel Francis Nicholson and Samuel Vetch, a Scottish promoter, appeared with orders from the crown for New Jersey to furnish men and money for a proposed expedition against Canada. The house rejected a bill for raising £3,000. Thomas Gardiner, the Quaker who had succeeded to the leadership of the Friends in the western division on the death of Samuel Jennings, asked leave to enter a statement on behalf of the Quakers. To raise money for the support of soldiers was against their religious principle; for conscience' sake they could not agree to the request of the crown. Some observers charged that the defeat was contrived by Ingoldsby and Coxe to embarrass the Quakers by having two members from Monmouth, Elisha Lawrence and Gershom Mott, vote against the bill; others held the Friends in Philadelphia responsible.[34]

Nicholson, Vetch, Ingoldsby, and the Anglicans then raised a cry: men who would not take an oath must be excluded from public office. Taking the threat seriously, the assembly majority at a subsequent legislative session in Burlington voted to support the expedition. Not intimidated, however, Lewis Morris pressed the attack against Ingoldsby at Whitehall, as a man unfit for office. Again he urged the appointment of his neighbor at Westchester, Caleb Heathcote, as governor.[35] Heathcote had little chance, as the duke of Marlborough and Godolphin still dominated in the administration; the choice to succeed Lovelace went to another of the duke's army favorites, Colonel Robert Hunter. Lewis Morris would not regret the appointment, for more than any other man Hunter would promote the career of the ambitious colonial aristocrat.

The appointment of Robert Hunter led to a reorientation in the career of Lewis Morris and the course of New Jersey provincial politics. Hitherto Morris had been involved almost exclusively in New Jersey, but with the arrival of Hunter, Morris devoted himself mainly to affairs in New York. For a generation the course of New Jersey politics would be strongly influenced by events in Manhattan as Morris became the legislative manager for the royal governor in both colonies. Hereafter Morris sought not to bend the governor to the will of the assembly but to utilize the power of the executive to secure a compliant legislature.

PART III

Royal Government in the North: The Limitations of War, 1696–1715

The northern colonies of America were critical to the efforts of the crown of England to marshal support in an extended conflict against Bourbon France and her allies in the Western Hemisphere while at the same time seeking to exercise direct control over their governments. The two southernmost of these five colonies — Connecticut and Rhode Island — were virtually autonomous provinces enjoying corporate privileges by royal charters. Their connection with the government of England was nominal, and the English monarch was but their titular ruler. On the northern colonies of New Hampshire, Massachusetts, and New York fell the great burden of the war against French Canada. But in these colonies, regarded as the bulwark for English America, royal officials were particularly vulnerable to pressure from the elected representatives in the assemblies, men representing local interests and a populace not yet imbued with a sense of identity with the larger English community, one parochial in outlook and resentful of any financial burden imposed by government. As one New Yorker observed, the appeal by candidates standing for election most likely to prevail with the people "is the saving of their money."[1] By allowing the crown's representative to depend on the elected assemblies for financing the civil and military establishments, the ministers of state created a situation conducive to the growth in power of the local legislatures.

CHAPTER 10

New York, Massachusetts, and the Captain-Generalcy of the Earl of Bellomont, 1696–1701

AT THE CLOSE OF the seventeenth century New York and Massachusetts offered observers a contrast: one weak, thinly populated, ethnically diverse with a history of social and political instability, the other populous, stable, and cohesive. The two diverse colonies were administratively linked by a single governor, the earl of Bellomont, an arrangement ostensibly adopted better to coordinate the common English effort against the French and Indians. A more immediate and personal motive had also prevailed: the need to provide an adequate salary for the impecunious governor over and above what the elected representatives of the legislature in Boston would consent annually to grant him. Appointed governor of the Bay colony following the death of Sir William Phips, Bellomont had resisted crossing the Atlantic to take up his duties until he received a commission to preside over the government at Manhattan as well. The government of Boston still continued without the king's deputy for some time after Bellomont arrived in America, for it was to affairs in New York that he was required by officials in London to attend first.

The history of New York during the reigns of the last three Stuart monarchs more than that of any other colony in America illustrated the difficulties besetting the English communities in America, problems ranging from an economy made stagnant by war to slave insurrection, ethnic animosities, the vulnerability of the thinly populated frontier, and intense factionalism verging on civil war as ambitious men claimed prerogatives as servants of the crown or liberties as elected representatives of the people.

In the last decade of the seventeenth century New York still suffered from the effects of the civil conflict following the overthrow of James II in 1688, the collapse of the Dominion of New England, and the assumption of power in Manhattan by a clique in the name of the new Protestant monarchy in England. In seizing power, the insurgents, under the nominal leadership of Jacob Leisler, claimed to be frustrating a plot by papists, French, and Indians to destroy the Protestants and to hold New York for the deposed Catholic king. The Leislerians intimidated any who might question them, confiscated property, and incarcerated innocent men. The insurgents had the support of many of the Dutch residents of Manhattan, although not necessarily elsewhere in the province, and among those they attacked were the heads of prominent Flemish and Dutch families—Van Cortlandt, Philipse, and Bayard—men who enjoyed high appointive office.

Through the negligence of the newly established Protestant monarchy, the Leislerians ruled the province for almost two years before royal troops and loyalists in New York and neighboring Connecticut, under a governor appointed by William III, took control at Manhattan. Jacob Leisler and his chief lieutenant, Jacob Milbourne, refused to recognize the authority of Major Richard Ingoldsby, commander of the royal troops, or of the new governor, Henry Sloughter, and had their men fire on the soldiers. Although Leisler and Milbourne refused to plead and thus denied the jurisdiction of the court, they were convicted and executed for treason. Several of their lieutenants—Abraham Gouverneur, Gerardus Beekman, Abraham Brazier, Myndert Courteen, Johannes Vermillie, and Thomas Williams—were also convicted, but their sentences were stayed. To justify their actions and cause, the Leislerians, when the Whigs became dominant in the royal administration and in the House of Commons, appealed to London with partisan rhetoric. Inaccurately they branded their opponents as Tories, even Jacobites: Governor Henry Sloughter, who served only a few months before he died, referred to them more accurately as "loyalists." While the Whigs were in the ascendancy in London, lobbyists for the Leislerians secured from Parliament an act reversing the attainder of their two martyrs and pardon for the convicted lesser lights of the party.

The two factions, implacable in their hatred for each other, continued opposed as the century drew to a close. The groups were called, inaccurately, Dutch and English parties. National origin did not always determine a man's political allegiance. Family ties were important, for marriage bound the members of the ruling elite—of the "English" party—whom the Leislerians had sought to displace, the Van Renssaelaers, the Van Cortlandts, Philipses, and Schuylers. Scottish-born Robert Livingston had married Alida Schuyler, the widow of Nicholas Van Renssaelaer. Another Schuyler daughter was wife to Stephen Van Cortlandt, and his sister had married a Van Renssaelaer. In the ranks of the opposition, four of the insurgent Leislerian leaders had married into the family of Samuel Edsall. Neither partisan politics in London nor the royal governors sent out to New York had initiated party strife in Manhattan; rather, the leaders of the provincial factions—particularly those of the Leislerians, of the Dutch faction—sought to capitalize on party sentiment in Whitehall and Westminster in order to discredit their rivals in New York.

Bitter animosities—the legacy of the seizure of power by the Leislerians and retribution by the loyalists for the wrongs they had inflicted—jeopardized political stability in New York, as did the bickering and the unscrupulous behavior of royal officials charged with enforcing the orders of the crown. Among the royal appointees, few were individuals of stature; many were petty men squabbling with each other for monetary gain. Nor was the level of the men elected to the provincial assembly high. Few were "men of substance, sense and moderation,'' as a later governor put it, a sentiment shared by at least one veteran of the political wars in New York.[1]

Representative government had come relatively late to New York, the first elected assembly having met for a short session at the end of the proprietary regime of the duke of York before the province was amalgamated into a larger administrative unit in 1688, one governed by an appointed governor, his deputy, and several councilors. Following the restoration of regular government in 1691 royal governors had instructions to issue writs for the election of representatives for a legislative assembly, but the ensuing contests appeared to be easily manipulated by sheriffs or aldermen, members of one contending faction or another. As for the voters, what most prevailed with them in choosing a representative, as one observer put it, was his pledge, once elected, not to spend their money.[2] At times, the sentiments of the electorate were not allowed to stand as partisanship in the assembly led to the unseating of candidates who had won at the polls. In 1701 the Leislerians, aided by a governor favorable to their cause, took twelve of the twenty-four seats in the house, and to increase their power, expelled four of their opponents. The voters of Queens and Westchester—mostly of English descent and bent on defending their rights—returned another slate of Englishmen, but to no avail. Both sides tended to employ the same rhetoric and to articulate the same concepts.

These contests were not between Jacobites and Williamites, between papists and Protestants, for both sides, Dutch and English, Leislerian and loyalist, accepted the Revolution of 1688.[3] Nor was the struggle necessarily between those of great and those of moderate or no means. Although the Leislerians often assumed the pose of plebeians, the ranking members, including Leisler himself, were men of some wealth; Abraham DePeyster, one of the foremost among the "Dutch" party, by 1698 was perhaps second in wealth only to Frederick Philipse. Factional lines were not consistently held. A party, once it achieved dominance and no longer needed to close ranks to gain power, might be rent by the clash of personalities. During the upheaval of 1689 Robert Livingston and Stephen Van Cortlandt strongly opposed the Leislerian insurgency, but they later found it expedient to moderate their position. In Livingston's case he needed support to collect from the crown money he had loaned the government to maintain the provincial administration and to defend the colony against the incursions of the French.

Successive governors could not remain aloof from these party animosities. Earlier governors of New York, dependent on private loans, had issued generous, indeed extravagant, patents for manors; one went to Livingston, another for Staten Island to John Palmer. In the later years of his administration, when he was under attack by the Dutch faction in New York and the Whig ministry in London, Colonel Benjamin Fletcher granted several extensive tracts of land to his political intimates, including Lewis Morris, his father-in-law; James Graham; and Frederick Philipse. But the governor had antagonized the Leislerian ringleaders by refusing to allow them to hold office or to sit in the assembly despite Parliament's reversal of their convictions for their roles in the insurgency. Jacob Leisler the younger, Abraham Gouverneur, and Peter Delanoy undertook a campaign in London to have Fletcher removed, accusing him of violating his instructions, coercing voters, extorting money, misapplying funds, and with the leaders of the "Jacobite" party, engaging in illegal trade with pirates.[4]

Robert Livingston also wanted Fletcher removed, but for different reasons: the governor had blocked payment of money claimed by the New Yorker. Livingston had survived a hazardous crossing of the Atlantic and a shipwreck to appear at the Plantation Office, where, with other witnesses he supported the charges against Fletcher. The partisan nature of the witnesses and the *ex parte* evidence presented made it difficult to get at the truth of the allegations. Certainly the Whig ministers had little, if any, cause to excuse Fletcher's behavior. Had the charges had much substance, they would have acted. As to the accusation of abetting pirates, Fletcher later pleaded that he could not be blamed if men whom he commissioned as privateers against the French turned pirate once they left port. Fletcher's downfall was the result not so much of the proven case against him as the political influence and financial needs of Richard Coote, earl of Bellomont.

An impecunious, outspoken peer of the Irish establishment, Bellomont had friends in high places once the lords of the Whig junto forced themselves upon the king and assumed office. The time was propitious for his political aspirations, for the royal governor of Massachusetts and neighboring New Hampshire had died. Bellomont's political connections — he had the backing of Lord Somers and the duke of Shrewsbury — were much weightier than those of Joseph Dudley, a native of Massachusetts and a protégé of John, Lord Cutts, the governor of the Isle of Wight, then living in England. Bellomont's pretensions as well as his financial needs were great. For him the income from the governorship of Massachusetts and the few small, poor towns of New Hampshire was inadequate and uncertain, since under the charter granted by the crown in 1691 the governor depended for his salary on funds voted from time to time by the assembly. Belloment wanted not only the governorship of the Bay and New Hampshire but that of New York as well. To this end, Fletcher must be discredited and the king, then in Europe, persuaded to recall him.

Ostensibly to coordinate the military forces of the northern colonies under a single command, the Whigs urged that Bellomont be made governor of the three colonies. William III was reluctant to remove Fletcher, an experienced officer familiar with the situation on the northern frontier, and he saw difficulties in one governor's attempting to administer such diverse and separate colonies as New York and Massachusetts Bay. But Shrewsbury, the senior of the principal secretaries of state, and the other Whigs among the lords justices in council persisted on behalf of their favorite; Bellomont won out. By his appointment the military resources of the English in the northern colonies would be united. Shrewsbury notified the Commissioners of Trade on 16 March 1696/7 that the king was appointing Bellomont governor of New York, Massachusetts, and New Hampshire and captain-general *during the course of the war* of the king's forces in these colonies as well as of the militia of Rhode Island, Connecticut, and the two Jerseys.[5] Inasmuch as the Treaty of Ryswick concluded hostilities among the European powers later that same year, Bellomont's command over the militia of the corporate and proprietary colonies was of little significance.

Since the cavalier governor-designate delayed leaving the British Isles Fletcher remained in office until the spring of 1698. Realizing that his days in office were numbered, he may have extended his protection to privateers and merchants in the city engaged in illicit trade.

Months before the governor-designate left for America, Bellomont and Robert Livingston undertook a venture calculated to bring them great profit; it almost brought them disaster. Among the protégés Livingston had brought with him from New York to London was Captain William Kidd. Livingston proposed to Bellomont that Kidd receive a commission from the crown to hunt down pirates. After Bellomont took the proposition to his patron, Shrewsbury, a syndicate was formed, consisting of Bellomont, the London merchant Edmund Harrison (who evidently put up much of the money), and four of the leading Whig lords in the administration: Shrewsbury, Somers, the earl of Romney, and Sir Edward Russell, earl of Orford. Unknown to the other officials in the administration, Shrewsbury had prevailed upon the king to sign a warrant giving the syndicate the proceeds of any prizes Kidd might take.

Armed with the king's commission, William Kidd left England in the *Adventure Galley,* a ship of 287 tons and thirty-four guns, for New York, where, short-handed, he was forced to take on additional crewmen. After conferring with Robert Livingston, he sailed for the Cape of Good Hope and the Indian Ocean. Livingston was apprehensive over Kidd's ability to control his crew and with good reason: even as Bellomont made ready to depart for America, word came that the *Adventure Galley* was preying on the trade of the East India Company from the Red Sea to the Malabar Coast. The political repercussions in England and, consequently, in America would be great, particularly in view of the association of the Whig ministers of state with the new East India Company. Their opponents in the old corporation would make political capital of the affair. Later, Charles Lodowyck, formerly a merchant of Manhattan who had opposed the Leislerians and a supporter of Fletcher, would reveal to Robert Harley the private articles of agreement linking Kidd with Bellomont and the Whig lords.[6] When later apprehended and tried, Kidd claimed he had been forced into the project by Bellomont and Livingston.[7]

The Kidd episode was potentially damaging to the careers of the Whig lords in London, Livingston, Bellomont, and those in New York who associated with them. Livingston was already in difficulty when he returned to New York in the summer of 1696 with the crown's commission as secretary for Indian affairs and warrants for payment of the money he had expended to supply the companies of royal soldiers in the colony and the Iroquois Indians. Informed by friends in London of Livingston's role in the campaign against him, Fletcher was incensed. Until Bellomont arrived, Fletcher was in a position to punish his enemies and reward his supporters, among them Caleb Heathcote, who advanced his private fortune for the administration when the provincial treasury was low. In the time remaining to him, Fletcher rewarded his friends with grants for vast tracts of land. Aware that Livingston had testified against him and had procured witnesses to appear before the Board of Trade, he held him responsible for his troubles. Many on the council—Nicholas Bayard, William Pinhorne, Gabriel Minvielle, William Smith, John Lawrence, Frederick Philipse, even Livingston's relative Stephen Van Cortlandt—sided with the governor in his refusal to allow Livingston to assume his office and placed obstacles in the way of his monetary claims. Fletcher dismissed him as a "little book-keeper" who had "screwed himself into one of the most considerable estates" in the province. A man of no morality, Livingston had but one ambition, to enrich himself by any means. Allegedly he preferred to be called "knave" Livingston rather than "poor" Livingston.[8]

Months passed, and despite repeated urging and a subsidy from the crown, Bellomont remained in the British Isles. Not until the second week in November 1697 did the ship bearing Bellomont leave the Isle of Wight. In crossing the Atlantic she was forced by contrary winds to put in at Barbados. Bellomont did not reach Manhattan until 2 April 1698.

For the new governor it was essential that Fletcher not clear himself of the charges against him and so possibly return once more to preside over the administration of government at New York. If he did, Bellomont would be left only with administration of Massachusetts and the few poor towns of New Hampshire. William III had been reluctant enough to recall an experienced army officer he himself had selected for New York. To make leaving Manhattan difficult for Fletcher, Bellomont required that he give security for whatever public money officials in England should determine he had diverted to his own use. Captain John Evans of HMS *Richmond* (a frigate assigned to New York), along with eight merchants—Miles Forster, Robert Lurting, Ebenezar Willson, Thomas Wenham, Caleb Heathcote, John Morris, and William and Jeremiah Tothill—joined by five officials—Nicholas Bayard, William Nicoll, James Emott, William Merrit, and Matthew Clarkson—pledged £10,000 sterling. These merchants and officials constituted almost the entire leadership of the English party. For these "loyalists" who had opposed the Leislerians, the guilt or innocence of Fletcher as decided in England would determine their future status in provincial politics, whether or not they would continue to enjoy power and favor under a royal administration.

The subsequent hearings at the Plantation Office did not go well for Fletcher, as might have been expected given the political complexion of the administration. The council, with Bellomont's friends in control, denied Fletcher's request to have the bond posted in his name discharged and ordered the commissioners for plantation affairs to examine any evidence Bellomont could collect in New York. Appealing to intimates in London Fletcher reminded William Blathwayt and Robert Southwell of his thirty-five years of service to the crown, years without reproach, nine of them in Ireland and America. But Fletcher's reputation was beyond saving in a partisan administration. Secretary Vernon, Shrewsbury's protégé, wrote Bellomont in Manhattan to "give the first precedent there of what a good governor ought to do, In a faithful discharge of his trust in keeping clean hands & partaking with no man in his unjust gains."[9] On the basis of information that the governor and two Leislerians presented in the provincial council, the Whig Commissioners of Trade submitted a damaging report against Fletcher; the Lords Justices in Council—they included Somers, Romney, and Orford—then sanctioned the sweep Bellomont had carried out in New York when he had removed from the council William Nicoll, William Pinhorne, and the royal collector, Chidley Brooke. Also dismissed were Bayard for allegedly procuring Fletcher's protection for suspected pirates and Frederick Philipse for illegal trade. Abraham DePeyster, James Graham, Staats, Robert Livingston, and Dr. John Corbile replaced them.[10]

Benjamin Fletcher denied all wrongdoing, charging that the evidence presented against him was hearsay and, in some instances, coerced. All arose from the enmity of two of his mortal enemies in New York, two Scots—Livingston and James Graham. Of the men who had given security for Fletcher, Captain John Evans of the *Richmond* and Nicholas Bayard also offered testimony that the evidence given before Bellomont and the provincial council linking Fletcher with pirates was false, extorted by threats and promises of favor by Bellomont. It was of little use; even Blathwayt, who had once supported the former governor, now seemed to draw back: the colonel was upon the "Anvill" at the Plantation Office. When informed of the proceedings before the Commissioners of Trade, James Graham drew the proper conclusion: "My lord [Bellomont] has great friends."[11]

The governor's great friends, the Whig lords, were already losing their grip, however. In July 1699 Kidd and his crew appeared off the coast of Massachusetts. In a rush of zeal so that he might not be held responsible for whatever depredations Kidd had committed, Bellomont had the unfortunate seaman taken into custody and sent back to England along with booty valued at £14,000. When the news reached London, officials of the old East India Company again set up a clamor; clearly they intended "to make all the bustle about it they can," Vernon ruefully reported.[12] The agreement between Kidd and the Whig lords and Bellomont would be an embarrassment; the junto's days in office were numbered, and Bellomont's position in New York was in jeopardy.

Bellomont was already under attack by the merchants in Manhattan and their correspondents in the English mercantile community for encouraging the insolent Leislerians, men who had endangered the trade of New York. Moreover, the governor had treated the accomplices of the executed traitor as if their illegal seizure of the government merited reward; he had swallowed completely the charge that Bayard and other heads of the loyalist party were papist Jacobites, and had dismissed most of the councilors, sheriffs, and justices of the peace, replacing them with ignorant men, mostly Leislerians. He had also attempted to pack the assembly, but failing this, had dissolved the house. Further, he had acted arbitrarily, granting judicial commissions without consent of the council and altering minutes of the board without the consent of its members. The governor had abetted a faction in the Dutch church while publicly affronting William Vesey, a minister of the Church of England, by calling him a sycophant, a hypocrite, and a dissembler of God Almighty.[13]

If Bellomont, a hot-tempered Whig ever quick to make partisan judgments, had intended to remain neutral when he first arrived in New York in the spring of 1698, he very quickly committed himself to the cause of the Leislerians and joined them in labelling Stephen Van Cortlandt, Nicholas Bayard, William Smith, Gabriel Minvielle, William Nicoll, and William Pinhorne as Tories and Jacobites. A partisan Whig, even before leaving the British Isles Bellomont had had his views of the political world of New England and New York influenced by Fitzjohn Winthrop of Connecticut, Sir Henry Ashurst, a violent Dissenter politician of London, and Robert Livingston. Having opposed Fletcher and supplied evidence against him, Livingston had broken with the loyalists. He and a few relatives—James Graham, Colonel Peter Schuyler, and Stephen Van Cortlandt—made up a small group of trimmers. Livingston and Bellomont were tied together by the role they had played against Fletcher, their involvement in Kidd's expedition, and the governor's dependence for credit to supply the soldiers stationed on the northern frontier.

The earl of Bellomont was a victim of his own prejudices and weaknesses. Long-winded, self-righteous, and self-serving, he attempted to justify his conduct in New York by appealing to the partisan sentiments of the Whig lords in London. Bellomont had no love for the lower orders; he was contemptuous of plebeians. His political prejudices matched his social biases; to him, keeping a public-house was not an honest calling. He had the landed gentleman's disdain for "marchands," men engaged in commerce. He even held it against John Evans, captain of HMS *Richmond,* that his father had once been a shoemaker and grazier. These prejudices Bellomont made clear in the many long, tiresome letters he sent off to London.

Immediately on arriving in Manhattan Bellomont found cause for complaint against Fletcher: he had placed "vermin"—mean, pitiful men—in employments of trust. He had even retained a tailor as sheriff of Queens County for five years because the tailor would return such members for the assembly as Fletcher directed. The new governor promptly devoted himself to compiling evidence against Fletcher for condoning piratical trade and granting large tracts of land to favorites on the council—the "Tories" and "Jacobites," as Bellomont called them. Within five weeks Bellomont had accepted the opposition's views: Leisler's execution he condemned as "barbarous" and the proscription of his followers as oppression. The "English" of New York were, for the most part, as "profligate" as one would expect from the "offspring of Newgate," for they were made up of broken merchants, tradesmen, and persons transported from English jails. By contrast, the Dutch "have all the virtue and sobriety and most of the wealth too."[14]

To justify the removal of Fletcher and his supporters on the council, Bellomont, aided by Livingston, James Graham, and Dr. Samuel Staats, gathered— some said coerced and fabricated—evidence implicating the former governor, William Nicoll, Nicolas Bayard, William Pinhorne, and others in illicit trade. Chidley Brooke, the collector, also was dismissed. Without knowing any particulars, Bellomont concluded that Brooke must be corrupt, since the customs receipts for the port had declined while trade had supposedly increased.[15]

The loyalists protested, but in vain. Two of Bellomont's witnesses—Edward Earle and his wife, Hanna—claimed to have overheard William Pinhorne some years before say contemptuously of William III, "[Was] it not a pitty yt such a humped backed, crooked dog (or rogue) or both should rule the kingdom of England?" Moreover, Bellomont claimed, Pinhorne was a man of most scandalous character, having misappropriated merchandise for his own use while employed as a factor of a London woolen draper. Nicholl and Brooke—indeed all the men disaffected with Fletcher's administration—were papists and Jacobites; all had been intimates of Fletcher, employed by him in corruptly electing assemblymen.[16]

Bellomont now openly committed himself to the cause of the Leislerians— the Dutch he called them. For the council he proposed a slate of Leislerians and trimmers—James Graham, Samuel Staats, Robert Livingston, Dr. John Corbile, and Robert Walters—and as colonel of the militia of the city he named Abraham DePeyster. Through the provincial attorney general, James Graham, he also launched an attack on the extensive grants Fletcher had made to Nicholas Bayard, William Smith, and Caleb Heathcote, and most controversial of all, on a grant in the Mohawk country engineered by Peter Schuyler and the Dutch minister at Albany, Godfrey Dellius. As if publicly to flaunt his sentiments, Bellomont acquiesced in the requests of Staats, Walters, and DePeyster to have the bodies of Leisler and Milborne taken up from their graves near the gallows where they had died. The exhumations took place to the sound of trumpets and drums; after lying in state for some days, the corpses were given Christian burial in the Dutch church, contrary to the wishes of the officials of the congregation, so the loyalists charged. To demonstrate the wickedness of those who disturbed his administration, Bellomont noted that few of them and none of the leaders of their party attended church services when the governor had proclaimed a day of fasting to end partisan animosities. But then the men responsible for the executions of Leisler and Milborne were Jacobites.[17]

With the aid of the Leislerians, men more "obedient" than their opponents, Bellomont undertook a campaign to control elections and returns to the assembly. Since the Huguenots previously had sided with the "Jacobites" and had been so insolent as to boast that they were able to tip the scales in elections toward one side or the other, Bellomont refused to allow thirty-three Frenchmen to be included in an Act of Denizenation without paying fees: some French who during the war passed for Protestants he had since discerned were papists. Until the fall of 1698 Bellomont had removed only one of the sheriffs, the official who supervised elections. Ebenezar Willson, a merchant and sea captain, appointed sheriff by Fletcher, had brought a legal action against Thomas Weaver, the governor's protégé, for saying that Willson had submitted false returns. Much to Bellomont's disgust the jury returned a verdict in favor of Willson, awarding him £500 in damages. Bellomont now determined through a "little management" to rectify the situation and by means "fair and square" to allow the Leislerians a share in the government. Some two dozen Manhattan loyalists had organized a Saturday Night Club under the leadership of Bayard, Minvielle, Willson, and Nicoll to synchronize plans to oppose Bellomont in London and to offer a slate of candidates in the elections. Nicoll and David Jamison went about the colony promising voters to reduce taxes if elected. In response, the Leislerians also organized; they were known as "the Mayor of New York and Company"; their opponents, as "Wenham and Company." William Nicoll preferred the name "English party," although the ticket he and his colleagues put up in Manhattan listed three Dutchmen and but one Englishman. Bellomont did his part by revising the list of sheriffs and granting two extra seats, one for Albany and another for Orange county. The loyalists charged that in most of the counties, the sheriffs did not allow sufficient time for polling, admitted some men not qualified to vote, and turned away some freeholders. On protesting, would-be voters were told: "If you are aggrieved, complain to my Lord Bellomont."

Of the twenty-one men returned to the assembly, seven were English, fourteen Dutch—men of the meanest sort, half of whom, the loyalists charged, could not understand the English language. But Bellomont made the same complaint of the three Dutchmen who ran on the Wenham ticket in the city. With only five seats the loyalists challenged the returns in Manhattan and Orange and Richmond counties, but were rebuffed. When the assembly met in March 1699 the Leislerians were in control.[18] After electing Abraham Gouverneur speaker, they voted salaries for the governor and his deputy, Captain John Nanfan, and passed bills to satisfy the monetary claims of the Leisler family, to reverse the attainder of the leaders of the insurrection in 1689, and to outlaw all suits stemming from actions committed during the rebellion. But Bellomont could not prevail upon them to vote money for the repair of the decrepit forts at Albany, Schnectady, and Manhattan or to pay the debts of the government.

Bellomont also encountered resistance on the council. Although he had succeeded in breaking a deadlock among the members of the board on vacating land grants to Heathcote and Bayard, he feared opposition if he pressed against those to William Smith, Peter Schuyler, and Robert Livingston. Smith, the chief justice, and James Graham, the provincial attorney general, he did not trust. Both had challenged his right as governor to constitute courts of judicature without the consent of the council. Bellomont held provincial lawyers in low esteem; one was a fencing master, another a glover by trade, and a third, Jamison, an outlaw from Scotland. He viewed Nicoll and several others as enemies to his administration, men ignorant of the law who infected the populace with ill principles. Could not his patron, Lord Chancellor Somers, send out a good judge and a ''smart, active'' attorney general?[19]

On 16 May 1699 after fourteen months in New York Bellomont prorogued the assembly and took ship for Boston to initiate his administration in Massachusetts. While he had brought about a shift in political power in Manhattan and installed the Leislerians in a dominant position in the assembly, he had done little to increase the authority of the crown or to provide for the defense of the colony.

In contrast to New York, a weak underpopulated colony, Massachusetts was the most prosperous, the most powerful, and with the exception of Virginia, the most populous of the English provinces in America. In the last years of the seventeenth century the colony numbered about 50,000 white inhabitants with an economy oriented toward trade with distant lands: an extensive traffic in lumber, grain, bread, flour, beef, and pork to the West Indies, masts and spars to England, and fish to the Iberian ports of Europe. Boston and the lesser ports of the Bay colony boasted about 200 ships in the carrying trade, ranging from vessels of about 100 tons burden to small craft of less than 50 tons plying the coastal and West Indian waters.

For over half a century Massachusetts had functioned as a virtually independent commonwealth under the control of Puritan saints supported by full members of the Congregationalist churches, who qualified as freemen of the corporation under a charter granted by Charles I in 1629. After a score of years during which the Restoration monarchy had attempted to force some recognition of the crown and a more tolerant stance by the saints toward Protestants dissenting from the Puritan ecclesiastical system, the courts at Westminster vacated the patent. There followed a short interval of government by appointed governor and council until the ouster of James II.

Massachusetts had figured prominently in the thinking of the ministers of state who served William III. They wanted to insure the aid of the Bay colony in the struggle against France in America. Consequently they had acquiesced in the request of the Puritan divine, Increase Mather, and named one of Mather's parishoners, Sir William Phips, as first royal governor of the Bay colony. In the new charter issued in 1691 the names of Mather's nominees appeared as the first councilors appointed by the crown. With the support of the Dissenter community of London, Mather had won a further concession: after one year the deputies elected by the townsmen annually would select the council, subject only to the veto of the governor. Although the Puritan divine had asked that the vote for assembly representatives be given, as before, to freemen, members of the corporation—thus continuing the role of the members of the churches in full communion—the ministers of state granted the franchise to freeholders, owners of property. The requirement was sufficiently low to allow widespread voting.

The tradition of an independent commonwealth remained strong in the Bay colony. Phips had served only three years in Boston before he was called to London. Almost five years had passed since the departure of Phips for England when Bellomont arrived in 1699. He found the inhabitants "seem here to hate those that are English-born" as if they were foreigners.[20] As ever, the earl exaggerated, but a numerous element in Massachusetts had never forgiven Increase Mather for compromising—unnecessarily, to their minds—with the ministers of the crown and accepting a new charter rather than insisting on the restoration of the original patent by which the rulers of the Bay colony claimed the status of a self-governing commonwealth of saints appointed by God, with the monarch as but a titular head. For almost three years—from the overthrow of the Dominion of New England in April 1689, until Sir William Phips, a rustic shipwright and merchant seaman from Maine who had been knighted for recovering a rich treasure trove, had returned as a royal governor—Massachusetts had been governed by a coalition representing the factions which had seized power in Boston. The coalition included William Stoughton, Waitstill Winthrop, and Bartholomew Gedney, moderates willing to accept some accommodation with the crown to preserve the Congregationalist churches. Others in the coalition—Samuel Sewall, John Richards, and Nathaniel Saltonstall—represented the old orthodox commonwealth element who had resisted acknowledging the crown, certain that Providence would save the godly elect as (within the memory of some) it had seemingly done before with the overthrow of the tyrannical kings Charles I and his son James II. Peter Sergeant, a cousin of Sir Henry Ashurst, represented a new element seeking power.

The choice of Sir William Phips as governor had proved an unhappy one. His behavior, including his moderate stance on the men and women condemned for witchcraft in Salem, had antagonized many, even William Stoughton. As the implacable enemy of Phips, Stoughton maneuvered to have Phips replaced by Joseph Dudley, a native of Massachusetts of impeccable Puritan background who had nonetheless served the crown by accepting office in the royal administration following the loss of the first charter. Phips, an uneducated, hot-tempered man from the lower orders, had made many enemies, among them Nathaniel Byfield, English-born brother to a London merchant engaged in the New England trade and, following his emigration to Massachusetts, an influential member of the House of Representatives. He too sought to have Dudley replace Phips. Also opposed to Phips, but also to any royal governor, was Elisha Cooke. He and Increase Mather had once served as agents in London commissioned by the colony's ruling coalition to secure a restoration of the charter. Cooke and Dr. Thomas Oakes had remained true to this trust, blindly committed to the impossible; Mather, more flexible and realistic, seeing the need to compromise, had negotiated a new patent with the ministers of state. He had had the satisfaction of having his nominees confirmed as governor and councilors for the first royal administration.

Elisha Cooke had never accepted the loss of the commonwealth status. From his base among the voters of south Boston he and his brother-in-law, Samuel Willard of the Old South Church, and James Allen of the First Church led the adherents of the old charter party against Mather, his son Cotton (the Puritan pope, some called him), and their protégé, Sir William Phips. Cooke consolidated his position with Boston voters after the assembly required property to be rated at full value rather than at annual income in determining eligibility for voting. In Boston the tax commissioner rather than the selectmen assessed property, and during the first decade of royal government, the only elective office Cooke held in the town was that of tax commissioner. During his tenure the number of voters doubled. The town tended to return the same men to office; none held any appointed post under Phips; and none supported the governor's administration. At the level of provincial politics no clear pattern existed. Only eight of the twenty-eight men named by Mather and appointed to the first council won election by the House of Representatives in 1693. But a majority of the deputies, by a vote of twenty-six to twenty-four, had supported Phips in his contest with Byfield, the speaker, by passing a law requiring representatives to be residents of the towns electing them.[21]

Accused of abandoning the heritage of the independent saintly commonwealth, the Mathers assumed the mantle of defenders of the traditional rights of Englishmen, a role adopted a decade earlier by John Wise when protesting the Dominion regime under Sir Edmund Andros. Before 1686, however, the Puritan leaders had shown little concern over the rights of Englishmen, claiming for themselves divine sanction. Now the Mathers put forth the idea that the charter Increase Mather had helped draft in 1691 encapsulated the traditional rights of Magna Carta. Further to defend themselves from the attacks of those who resented the loss of the first patent, the Mathers and their allies in the legislature sought to define more explicitly the privileges and immunities contained in the recent charter. By law the provincial assembly set forth general privileges, reiterating the principles of Magna Carta and including additional guarantees relating to the security of titles to land and the right to bail. Yet as long as their man, Sir William Phips, presided over the administration of government, the Mathers did not claim privileges and immunities against the governor; they exercised power from behind the governor's chair, unlike dissidents like Nathaniel Byfield, who countered the pretensions of the executive by claiming for the House of Representatives what were held to be the accustomed privileges of an English assembly.[22]

With the demise of Phips in 1695 after he had been called to London to answer complaints against him, the immediate supervision of government in the colony resided with Deputy Governor Stoughton and the council. Sentiment was divided on a successor. Stoughton and Byfield placed their hopes on the appointment of Joseph Dudley, a man both the Mathers and Cooke, for different reasons, found anathema. Wait Winthrop, for the time being, kept his own ambitions in check.[23]

Over four years passed before another governor from England appeared in Boston. The orthodox commonwealthmen, in association with the Leislerians of New York, feared the appointment of Dudley: he had participated in a government in Massachusetts operating without benefit of elected assemblies and had taken part in the trial at Manhattan which had condemned the Leislerian martyrs. At this time, however, his patrons, William Blathwayt and John, Lord Cutts, did not have sufficient influence in higher ministerial circles to offset the support Shrewsbury, Somers, and the other Whig lords brought to bear in favor of the Whig partisan, the earl of Bellomont. The issue was not whether Bellomont or Dudley would receive the post at Boston—the exaggerated accounts of the arch-Whig, Sir Henry Ashurst, on his strenuous efforts to block the appointment of Dudley notwithstanding—but whether Bellomont would preside at Boston only or over the governments of Massachusetts and New York. Bellomont considered the salary for the governor of Massachusetts and the few poor towns comprising New Hampshire inadequate and wanted the revenue from New York as well. After he arrived in America he set his sights on a project to provide naval stores to the Admiralty further to fatten his slim purse.

Other men had a material interest in the government of the Bay colony: a coterie of New England investors initially organized by Richard Wharton but now grown into an Anglo-colonial syndicate headed by Sir Matthew Dudley sought from the crown a charter with exclusive privileges in exploiting the timber and mining resources of New England. Sir Henry Ashurst and his associate, another New England–born financier of London, Sir Stephen Evance, as well as independent operators both in England and in America, had hotly contested the projected monopoly. The patent to Matthew Dudley and Associates was still pending when, in the summer of 1695, the announcement of Bellomont as governor-designate for the Bay colony and New Hampshire was made.

The year 1696 passed, and the earl still had not left for America. From Dublin he wrote one of the principal secretaries of state for the additional appointment as governor of New York, a request supported at the Plantation Office by Ashurst and Edmund Harrison, a London merchant involved in financing Bellomont's share in the Kidd venture, on the grounds that the defense of the northern provinces required a single commander of the forces in time of war. Over a score of New Englanders involved in the timber trade reinforced this argument.[24] By March 1697 Shrewsbury was able to announce to the Plantation Office that the king was appointing Bellomont governor of New York, Massachusetts, and New

Hampshire and, *for the duration of the war,* captain general of the militia of Connecticut, Rhode Island, and the Jerseys. But on the question of salary, Bellomont suffered disappointment. Bellomont then argued that the honor of the king and the interest of the monarchy and the people all required that the governor's salary be sufficient to keep him from growing rich by oppressing the populace or accepting bribes; an ample salary should be provided from the royal revenue, not from funds granted by the assemblies.[25]

With the king absent the six Lords Justices in Council met in July 1697; three—Somers, Shrewsbury, and Romney—were supporters of the governor-designate. They decided that if the assembly of the Bay colony did not settle an annual salary upon him, they would intercede with the king on his behalf for a salary to be allowed from England. The impecunious earl was still unhappy; he wanted the lords justices to write to Massachusetts for a salary to be settled on the governor, but the board drew the line: it would be best for Bellomont to waive this, for upon so nice a subject one could hardly avoid saying either too much or too little. To ease the debt-ridden governor on his way they agreed to grant him £1,200 sterling to meet the expenses of his journey. Weeks passed, and still Bellomont did not leave. In August 1697 he again pressed the lords justices to write to Boston for the assembly to provide for his salary. Again the ministers of state demurred: the subject was too delicate. When William Stoughton wrote from Boston asking for instructions on several urgent matters, the Commissioners of Trade assured him that there was no need for them to reply, as Bellomont was near leaving for America. They neglected to inform Stoughton that the governor was under orders to take up his duties first at New York.[26] Bellomont did not arrive in Manhattan until April 1698, and more than another year passed before he put in an appearance at Boston.

Since the departure of Sir William Phips late in 1694 Stoughton had presided over the government in Massachusetts but not to the satisfaction of some in the Bay colony or in the Plantation Office. The Commissioners of Trade had found unacceptable many of the bills passed by the House of Representatives to which he had given his assent. During the decade about one in six of the statutes enacted in the Bay colony, including fifteen of the fifty-two passed in the first General Court meeting under the charter of 1691, later suffered disallowance. Indeed, the Privy Council struck down many laws intended to reestablish the old charter procedures as contrary to English law or infringements on the royal prerogative. In many instances, however, the enforced accommodation to the ways of Whitehall and Westminster required "somewhat cosmetic," rather than substantive, changes. The proportion of laws disallowed to those passed steadily decreased so that after 1701 officials in Whitehall struck down but one in fifteen statutes enacted in Massachusetts.[27]

Among the laws the commissioners for plantation affairs found unacceptable during Stoughton's tenure were two acts, one establishing a court of chancery and another incorporating Harvard College. The first was contrary to the new charter in that it seemed to restrict appeals to the king in council; the other involved the governance of the school at Cambridge, then a bone of contention between strong-willed men. Elisha Cooke and William Brattle—tutor at Harvard and brother of Thomas Brattle, the wealthiest resident of Boston—were opposed to the nomination of Increase Mather as president of the college. Their candidate was Cooke's brother-in-law, Samuel Willard of the Old South Church. The ministers in London had objected to any provincial law incorporating the school which did not reserve a power for the monarch (through his governor) to appoint official visitors to inspect the college.[28] Also found objectionable in London was a judiciary act requiring that all issues be tried by jury. The measure seemed directly contrary to the recent parliamentary act for the prevention of frauds which provided for violations of the navigation code to be tried in vice-admiralty courts. The Parliamentary statute of 1696 was ambiguously worded, however. Over the protests of Jahleel Brenton, the collector of customs, Stoughton and his council had looked to the local common law courts to try alleged violations of the navigation code, and when decisions by juries went against customs officers, the provincial officials had denied their right to appeal to England. By charter they had the authority to establish courts, and appeals from these tribunals extended only where the suit involved property in excess of £300. Should these claims be allowed and the parliamentary act to prevent frauds be interpreted as allowing trial by jury, many small vessels and cargoes run by illegal traders would escape forfeiture. To the commissioners at the Plantation Office and to the law officers of the crown, the value of ships and cargoes notwithstanding, appeals from the provincial courts in cases relating to illegal trade lay with the king in council.[29]

Despite the unhappiness of the ministers of state over the situation in Boston, their first concern had been with New York; consequently they had ordered Bellomont to make Manhattan his initial stop. After a prolonged journey by way of the West Indies, he arrived in New York in the spring of 1698. Ambitious contenders for office in the Bay colony could hardly await the arrival of the new governor. In London Henry Ashurst had paved the way for Waitstill Winthrop, suggesting to Bellomont even before the governor had departed that Winthrop was more worthy than his rival, Nathaniel Byfield, for the office of judge of the Court of Vice-Admiralty. At Manhattan Winthrop pressed his claim with the governor, but Bellomont was more concerned over William Stoughton. Ever the Whig, Bellomont accused the lieutenant governor of corresponding with Jacobites, Dudley and his friends in England. Not until the following year did Ashurst secure for Winthrop the coveted post. This, Winthrop crowed, "breakes the measure[e]s of the Jacobites," Byfield and Stoughton.[30] Waitstill's prejudices made him a fitting companion in politics for Bellomont.

After fourteen months in New York, in May 1699 Bellomont finally set out for Massachusetts. Almost five years had passed since his predecessor had left Boston. Bellomont would spend but fourteen months in Massachusetts, and his tour was interrupted by visits to the Piscataqua and Narragansett Bay. Hostile to the aged deputy governor, Stoughton, whom he associated with the attempts of the "Jacobites" to place Dudley in the governor's chair, Bellomont was inclined toward Wait Winthrop and Elisha Cooke and their friends. Nathaniel Byfield and Stoughton now drew closer, having common political enemies. In addition, the lieutenant governor's nephew, Edward Lyle, had married Byfield's daughter, Deborah. Wait Winthrop complained bitterly of the deputy governor: "I never knew a minister but left preaching for the sake of worldly interest ever good for any thing after." [31] As Winthrop well knew, Joseph Dudley too had left the Puritan ministry for the more mundane calling of politics.

Even as Bellomont arrived in Boston, men were actively working to have a local man, at least a man of New England birth, supersede him. While Stoughton and Byfield placed their hopes on Dudley, others, among the irreconcilables, looked elsewhere. Samuel Sewall, a Puritan who pined for the days of autonomy under the ancient charter, wrote to a native son of the Bay colony, Nathaniel Higginson, to persuade him to return to New England, hopefully as governor of Massachusetts. The son of the Reverend John Higginson of Salem and a graduate of Harvard College, Nathaniel Higginson had lived for a time in England, where he had accepted employment as steward for Philip, Baron Wharton, a leading Dissenter peer, and tutor to his children. Subsequently he had become a merchant at Fort St. George (later Madras) in India, where he succeeded Elihu Yale as governor of the factory established by the East India Company. As Bellomont complained, in the Bay colony they seemed to "hate those that are English-born as if they were foreigners." [32]

In the summer of 1699 Bellomont faced more immediate problems than the threat of a rival halfway around the world: among others, a troublesome attack of gout and the arrival of William Kidd off the shores of New England. The governor had the suspected pirate apprehended and packed off to England in chains. Kidd's trial proved embarrassing. Less easily disposed of were challenges to royal authority as provincial officials, refusing to allow appeal from local tribunals, insisted that their courts were competent to hear cases of alleged violations of the parliamentary navigation code. When Bellomont met his first assembly, the representatives presented him with a bill for the college at Cambridge; it did not provide for the appointment of visitors by the king's governor and excluded all adherents of the Anglican church from the governance of the institution. Nor was the governor's council especially cooperative. When Bellomont suggested a bill for punishing pirates, the majority on the board demurred, objecting to the clause making piracy a felony, punishable by death. In Massachusetts piracy was not a capital offense, but Bellomont argued that provincial laws must conform to the statutes of England. At this several councilors jumped to their feet, demanding with some warmth to know what the laws of England had to do with them. Commonwealth sentiment died hard. One councilor declaimed that the Bay colonists were already too cramped in their liberties: they must be great fools should they abridge those left them by a law the governor suggested they themselves pass. Others—Waitstill Winthrop, for example, who had just accepted a commission as judge of admiralty—evidently had no difficulty accepting the laws of England or recognizing the authority of royal courts. The same councilors who disputed with Bellomont over a bill for punishing piracy also contended with him over the right to name provincial officials, citing the clause in the charter that the governor was to name judges and other officers with the advice and consent of the council. Phips and Stoughton had been so weak as to yield to them on this point, but Bellomont would only acknowledge the right of the councilors to veto any nomination. After some debate the councilors acquiesced to the governor's interpretation.

On the issue of the governor's salary—Bellomont wanted a permanent appropriation of £1,200 sterling annually—the majority among the councilors and representatives remained firm. The assembly voted him only £1,000 in local currency—equivalent to £700 sterling—as a present. In the months left to Bellomont in Boston nothing would induce them to change. His successor would do no better. The assembly was equally tight-fisted with other salaries. So low was the stipend of £40 a year for naval officers—officials appointed to record vessels' entering and clearing ports—that Bellomont could find few men willing to accept the office.

Matters did not improve appreciably when the assembly met the following spring, at a time when the trade of Boston had slumped. On 25 June 1700 an unsigned paper appeared on the council table, a document urging the legislature to consider measures to revive commerce. Taking up the issue, some councilors expressed great discontent with the acts of trade and navigation, laws they claimed were attempts by London merchants to force the colonists to buy from them alone and restraining the provincials from a free, open trade everywhere. The residents of the colonies were as much English as those of England, with the same privileges as those of inhabitants within the realm.[33]

After fourteen months in Massachusetts Bellomont had little to show for his stay as the king's representative. Faced with the seemingly implacable determination of the Congregationalists to exclude Anglicans from the governance of Harvard College, Bellomont allowed the council a voice in appointing visitors for the school. Despairing of securing a long-term appropriation for the salary of the governor, Bellomont fell back on the ministers of the crown: the king must support his deputies in America with salaries so as to allow men of quality and honor from England to preside over the provincial governments. As matters then stood, Bellomont was but the pensioner of the assemblymen for as long as they pleased. His plea received little sympathy in London. Remarking on the sum already voted him by the House of Representatives, £1,000 in local currency, one secretary of state noted cynically that this was more than he thought the deputies would give him, "they never having yet allowed a Governor above [£]100 p.a."[34] However, the councilors and assemblymen did not think it amiss that while denying the authority of the crown they should still address the king for aid against the encroachments of the French.

In the summer of 1700, on learning that the Canadians were tampering with the Iroquois—hitherto the bulwark shielding the English of New York from the Canadians and their Indian allies—Bellomont left Massachusetts, never to return.

The earl of Bellomont met with little success during his second tour as governor of New York in the few months remaining to him. When he arrived in Manhattan in the summer of 1700, the situation was not what it had been two years before. His Whig supporters in London were now losing power, and the Tories regarded him with hostility, as the loyalist, or English, party in Manhattan appreciated. At the Plantation Office William Blathwayt had predicted that Bellomont would lay New York desolate by driving out men of substance and installing "Massaniellos" (Leislerians). The reference was to the Neopolitan fisherman Thomas Aniello, who earlier in the century had led a revolt of the lower orders against Spanish rule. Merchants in Manhattan had already aroused their correspondents in London's mercantile community to protest against the governor. Nicholas Bayard and Godfrey Dellius were then in London to register their complaints. Fearing prosecution by an assembly dominated by vengeful Leislerians, Bayard had sought protection from the crown. Once he secured assurances from the earl of Bridgewater at the Plantation Office and the earl of Portland, a confidant of the king, Bayard returned to America. His fears proved well founded.[35]

Bayard arrived in Manhattan with copies of Bellomont's letters to various English officials, documents in which the governor had indiscriminately charged the loyalist leaders and merchants of the city with crimes. Party animosities again flared up, as the Leislerians tried and convicted Bayard for stirring up hatred against the government, under the same statute employed against Jacob Leisler. Ironically, both Bellomont and Bayard appealed to the same man in London, the earl of Bridgewater, the accused maintaining "I am as innocent as the Child unborn." Bellomont painted Bayard in different colors, as a malicious, violent man, highly disaffected to government, a man who by corrupt means had risen from the status of a beggar boy to an estate of several thousand pounds; Bayard, James Graham (now estranged from the governor), William Nicoll, and Major Richard Ingoldsby had been responsible for the deaths of Leisler and Milborne.

Manhattan was in turmoil. As James Graham reported, "All things looking dark and cloudy, and the town more full of murmurrings and discontents than ever and I see no likelihood of their removal." To some, Bellomont's connections in London still seemed strong, so that despite the attacks upon him, the governor appeared "too powerful against all his enemies."[36] But the loyalists— "Jacobites," Bellomont insisted on calling them—were sanguine, laying wagers that the governor would soon be replaced. According to information that Robert Livingston received, Edward Hyde, the well-connected Lord Cornbury (he was heir to the earl of Clarendon and cousin to Princess Anne), had put in for the post at Manhattan.[37]

The governor had indeed been under heavy attack at Westminster. He, Shrewsbury, and Somers had been charged in the House of Commons with obtaining a commission for William Kidd contrary to law. Word then arrived in London that Bellomont had secured the capture of the alleged pirate and had shipped him off to England secured by sixteen-pound irons, a light enough burden, Bellomont had noted, remembering that "poor" Dr. Titus Oates had had a hundredweight of iron on him when imprisoned by Charles II. (The reference was to the psychopathic liar whose fanciful testimony years before had sent several Catholics to their death during the hysteria over the Catholic Plot.)[38] Bellomont could never resist the temptation to evoke Whig prejudices. With the arrival in London both of the prisoner Kidd and the capture booty taken from his ship, for the time being the governor was saved. Bellomont supporters won a decisive vote in the House of Commons, 189–133. News of this victory was not long in reaching Boston and New York. Undeterred, Nicoll, Bayard, Philip French, Charles Lodowyck, Stephen DeLancey, and twenty-seven other loyalists, calling themselves merchants of New York, petitioned for a new governor, charging Bellomont with damaging the trade of the city and burdening them with heavy taxes. Five or six hundred men allegedly signed the document.

Bellomont, too, was unhappy with his post in New York, but for different reasons. Although Somers and Secretary Vernon had supported his request for £2,500 a year from his three governments, little had been forthcoming. "I shall be undone for want of a sufficient salary," he complained. If money was not paid him, he threatened to return to England before another year passed.[39]

Without funds from England and with only token support from the provincial assemblies, Bellomont found himself dependent on men such as Robert Livingston and Peter Schuyler to maintain the English interest with the Five Nations of the Iroquois confederation, Indians who were now inclined to adopt a neutral stance in view of the inability of the governments of New York and New England to act decisively. With fewer than 200 of the 400 soldiers of the four companies stationed on the frontiers available for service, the Five Nations were the only real barrier between the French in Canada and New York. When Bellomont had returned to Manhattan from Boston in the summer of 1700, he had found disheartening news from London: a reduction in the military support for the colony. Twenty-seven months' pay and subsistence for the four companies were cut off, and each unit was reduced from 100 to 50 men. Sir William Ashurst, the fiscal agent for the troops, had quit his post. Bellomont blamed Blathwayt (the commissioner of trade and secretary of war) for the reduction.[40]

Equally disturbing for the governor was the news that the English solicitor general, Sir John Hawles, had cast doubt on the legality of the law Bellomont had secured from the provincial assembly to vacate the huge grants of land made by Fletcher. John Montague, a solicitor engaged by Bayard and Caleb Heathcote, had questioned whether the governor and the Leislerians in the assembly had followed proper procedure. Moreover, the provincial act established a dangerous precedent, one rendering uncertain all property in land and subjecting it to the will of the governor and fourteen men sitting in the provincial assembly. The act was disallowed and Bellomont ordered not to vacate the grants to Livingston, Peter Schuyler, William Smith, and Van Cortlandt.[41]

Bellomont hardly needed this additional setback. He was now having difficulty in persuading the assemblymen to finance the construction of a fort in the Iroquois country. Voting but a meager sum of money, to be raised by impost, they took it upon themselves to appoint commissioners to direct the building of the fortification and to examine the state of public accounts. During Bellomont's stay in Boston the assembly of New York had undergone a change. Bellomont attributed the shift in sentiment to the defection of two of the Leislerians, men frightened by rumors circulated by Robert Wenham that Fletcher would soon return to govern the colony; the crown's refusal to accept the act vacating extravagant grants of land they took as a sign that Bellomont was in disgrace. To compound the governor's difficulties, the records of the provincial revenue had become jumbled under the aged and infirm collector, Stephen Van Cortlandt. The arrears due the victualers for the royal troops, according to Robert Livingston, came to about £10,000. Despite his diminishing support Bellomont proceeded to alienate the moderates on the council by stripping James Graham and his son of their offices and appointing Abraham Gouverneur, the Leislerian speaker of the assembly, recorder of the city. Peter Schuyler also came into disfavor, as did Livingston for having opposed the construction of a fort in the Onondaga country. By the close of 1700 Stephen Van Cortlandt was beyond the governor's displeasure; he died on 16 November. His widow — who was related to Nicholas Bayard — refused to surrender her husband's accounts to Bellomont's agent, Thomas Weaver. In this the governor was quick to see a villainous design to "imbezell" the royal revenue. When Weaver produced a warrant issued by the commissioners for public accounts, officials named under the authority of the assembly, the widow Van Cortlandt, after some hesitation, finally complied.[42]

The surrender was significant for the status of the assembly. Concerned with the immediate advantage of forcing Bayard's relations to back down, Bellomont helped to create a precedent for the authority of the commissioners of public accounts, officials authorized by and responsible to the assembly. Power in the house had passed to the members elected from the outlying counties, as one episode relating to taxes demonstrated. As recorder of the city James Graham had advised the mayor to pay the cost of patching up the municipal works by a tax on flour brought in from the countryside. The rural members in the assembly, who outnumbered the delegates from the city four to one, warned that no money bill would pass until this city ordinance was rescinded. The municipal officials remained obstinate until Bellomont prevailed on them to revoke the tax. Reflecting this shift in the assembly, leadership would soon pass to William Nicoll, a representative from Suffolk, and his supporters. In 1702 he would win the speaker's chair, a post he would not relinquish until his retirement seventeen years later. Under his leadership the assemblymen further increased their authority against governors sent out from London.

At the outset of 1701 government in New York was near a standstill, with many of the councilors hardly attending a meeting, living too far off or put out by the governor's behavior. No one in Manhattan, Bellomont complained, understood how to draw up an act of the assembly. Since the chief justice and attorney general he had requested from the home government had not arrived, he put off calling the assembly and adjourned the supreme court until the first week in April. By that time the two lawyers from London should have appeared.[43] Bellomont never lived to see them. At six o'clock on the morning of 5 March 1701 he departed this life. His widow did not have enough money to bury him.

Thus ended the captain-generalcy, the effort to unite under a single executive the forces of the northern colonies against France.

CHAPTER 11

War, Imperial Authority, and the Corporations of Southern New England

T HE ROYAL GOVERNORS of New York and Massachusetts viewed the chartered provinces of Connecticut and Rhode Island as hindrances to their efforts to integrate the resources of the disparate English colonies against the French. The governors appointed to preside at Manhattan and Boston looked upon these corporations as nests for illicit traders and pirates, as havens for deserters from military service, and as colonies whose inhabitants generally shirked their responsibilities to the common English cause. These royal appointees sought to cut down Connecticut and Rhode Island by challenging their boundaries and, in the case of Joseph Dudley, the New Englander who succeeded the earl of Bellomont as governor of Massachusetts, to attack the charters on which their separate governments rested. For years wars had threatened the northern frontiers, and when hostilities again broke out in 1702 between England and the Bourbon powers, the governor of Massachusetts received command of the militia of Rhode Island in order to coordinate the military resources of the English colonies for the duration of the conflict.

Dissident elements within Connecticut and Rhode Island welcomed the exercise of authority by royal officials, if only to add weight to their own criticisms of the established order in the two corporate provinces. For some time Connecticut had been a beleaguered colony, contending with its neighbors— New York, Rhode Island, and Massachusetts—over boundaries and resisting the demands of outsiders to control its militia and the claims of distant speculators to the soil of the province. The local magistrates had also to withstand the efforts of dissidents within the colony to challenge their authority by carrying appeals to the crown from decisions of the local courts as well as the efforts of officials in London to review laws enacted by the provincial legislature.

The charter granted by Charles II in 1662 created a corporation of the governor and freemen of Connecticut. By this patent the General Court of the colony consisted of the governor, his deputy, assistants, and representatives of the several towns. They met twice yearly to enact laws. By one contemporary account about half of the estimated 4,000 heads of households had been admitted to the status of freemen of the corporation and were thus entitled to vote for provincial officials.[1] Although the patent provided that the statutes of the province could not conflict with the laws of England, the charter contained no specific mechanism to insure this requirement nor an explicit reservation to the crown of the right to hear appeals from the decisions of Connecticut courts.

In protecting the interests of the provincial regime against attack from within and without, the ruling families in the colony had been fortunate in having the Winthrops of New and the Ashursts of Old England to act as agents in London. Two generations of Winthrops served as governors in the colony and as agents in London. John Winthrop, Jr., son of a founder of Massachusetts, had secured the charter from Charles II in 1662; a generation later his son as agent had fended off attacks against the patent and the provincial regime. In this effort Fitzjohn Winthrop had enjoyed the help of Sir Henry Ashurst, a member of an influential Dissenter family of London who had sat in Parliament. Ashurst was now old and at times unclear in mind, but his violent Whig prejudices served the Congregational ruling order of Connecticut well.

The threat potentially most dangerous to the inhabitants of Connecticut—indeed to all the settlers of southern New England—was the claim of a noble Scottish family, the Hamiltons, to the soil of the entire region. The Hamiltons based their claim on a grant allegedly made in the 1630s by the defunct Council of Plymouth, a syndicate to whom James I in 1620 had bestowed the region later called New England. Before relinquishing its rights, the Council of Plymouth had made several grants of much of the soil in the area to certain of its members: Maine to Sir Ferdinando Gorges; New Hampshire (Laconia) and a portion of Massachusetts to John Mason; a part of what later became Connecticut to the earl of Warwick; and the "County" of New Cambridge, encompassing Rhode Island and a portion of Connecticut, to James, marquis of Hamilton. Not all of the recipients of these grants secured their titles. Massachusetts bought out the claim of the Gorges family. The crown confirmed the right of the heirs of John Mason to the soil, but not the government, of New Hampshire. The authorities representing the families who had settled Connecticut had never been able to validate the title of the grant from the earl of Warwick on which they had based their government, but subsequently, the younger John Winthrop secured for them a patent directly from the crown, the charter of 1662. At that time the Hamiltons failed to have the crown confirm their title.

In 1697 the earl of Arran, on behalf of his mother, Anne, duchess of Hamilton, resurrected the claim to the county of New Cambridge, a jurisdiction encompassing Rhode Island, the eastern portion of Connecticut, a section of Massachusetts, and the "King's Province"—the mainland of Rhode Island west of the Narragansett Bay, a region disputed for more than thirty years between the two corporations of Connecticut and Rhode Island themselves. Henry Ashurst, then agent for the Bay colony, immediately entered a protest against the Hamilton claim on the grounds that it jeopardized the estates of hundreds of families in what had once been the colony of New Plymouth, a province annexed to Massachusetts by the charter granted to the Bay in 1691. In rebuttal the Hamiltons contended that the outbreak of the Civil War in England had prevented them from pursuing their claim until after the Restoration. Moreover, the charters granted by Charles II for the region unjustly ignored any former right. The Hamiltons simply dismissed the contention of Connecticut that the colony had won the disputed region from the Pequot Indians in 1637. Fitzjohn Winthrop asked for time to contact the settlers since a great number of New Englanders threatened by the Hamilton claims had not received notice. His counterpart as agent for Rhode Island, Jahleel Brenton, simply pleaded ignorance of the matter, having received no authority from Rhode Island to act. The more astute Winthrop, working quietly behind the scenes, secured a report from Lord Chief Justice Pemberton against the Hamiltons and through some intimates of Arran made it clear that it was not in his best interest to pursue the matter.[2] Thereafter rumors occasionally circulated that speculators might attempt to resurrect the Hamilton claim, but nothing came of them.

Challenges from within Connecticut were not as easily rebuffed. When Fitzjohn Winthrop returned from his agency in England to be rewarded with the governorship of Connecticut, he found a province still unsettled from the attempt under James II to amalgamate the northern colonies into a single administrative unit and the subsequent revolution against this Dominion of New England: acting on the assumption that Connecticut and Rhode Island officials were voluntarily submitting to royal authority—actually they were under pressure—James's ministers of state had, without taking action in court against the charters, placed these corporate colonies under the jurisdiction of Edmund Andros, governor of the Dominion of New England. Following the collapse of the dominion, those government officials in the two provinces who had formerly exercised authority under the charters, after some hesitation, again took up the reins of government.

A small group of royalists, led by Gershom Buckeley of Wethersfield, challenged the resumption of authority under the charter. These dissidents had encouraged London to place the militia under a single command for the common defense, a move Fitzjohn Winthrop as agent had resisted, claiming the charter expressly gave power over the militia to officials of the corporation. Also challenging Winthrop and the leading families were other men: the ambitious James Fitch, Edward Palmes, and the Hallam brothers of New London. To the heads of the prominent families, the men who had advanced to power in an almost settled order of succession, the appeal made by Fitch to the lower classes was threatening. Men of no estate or little means ought not to be eligible for office; this was the prerogative of persons of good parentage, education, ability, and integrity. Narrow private interests were also at stake. Fitch challenged Fitzjohn and Waitstill Winthrop over the ownership of a large tract of land in eastern Connecticut, the Quinebaug lands, while Palmes, their brother-in-law, contested with them for their deceased sister's estate. When the Hallams and Palmes appealed their causes from the provincial courts to the crown, private disputes became public issues.

Fitzjohn Winthrop's successful defense in London of the right of the provincial government to control the militia of the colony established him and his allies with the freemen of the corporation as the champions of the charter. Elected governor, Winthrop and his supporters in the General Court acted quickly to establish control over the local judiciary. By legislation enacted in 1698 judges named by the provincial governor rather than elected assistants would henceforth preside over the county courts. Despite the considerable support James Fitch commanded among his neighbors, he would no longer rule over the bench in New London County. With the threat from domestic opponents blunted, Governor Winthrop kept up a correspondence with royal officials to fend off interference from London: the colony was not backward in aiding the defense of the frontiers; there was "noe cry of oppression or Complaints" against the execution of the laws in matters civil or ecclesiastical "Unless by bold and incorrigible offenders whom noe indulgence would reclaime."[3]

Winthrop sought further to gratify local concerns and to reward men of substance and influence—in the western section of the colony, Robert Treat (once governor and now deputy governor), and in the eastern portion, the Reverend Gurdon Saltonstall, his New London paster, business agent, secretary, and confidant. During the decade Winthrop served as governor the assistants constituted a stable group of men united by a heritage of long-held power and family ties; they included Andrew Leete and Samuel Wyllys, both sons of former governors; Samuel Mason, the son of a founder of the colony; Nathan Gold (Gould), one of the wealthiest men in the province; and Gold's brother-in-law, John Selleck. James Fitch, although elected as an assistant, could do little harm faced with a solid phalanx of votes against him on the board of assistants. In October 1698 Winthrop had induced the General Court to abandon the unicameral arrangement. Henceforth, the assistants, with the governor and the deputy governor, sat as a body separate from the deputies elected from the towns. No act could be passed or repealed without the consent of both houses. The Winthrop administration also cultivated the Congregational clergy of the colony by providing them more generous financial support.

In each town three or four leading families constituted a pool from which the freemen elected representatives to the provincial assembly. Generally, the deputies supported the administration as long as it was able to defend the charter and function with reasonable efficiency and a minimum of expense. No organized bloc could muster sufficient strength to offer an alternative to the standing order of leading families. Only three towns regularly returned deputies hostile to the Winthrop administration. In the eastern section Norwich was under Fitch's influence. Fitch's father had served there as pastor. Stonington was the seat of the Masons, a family who had fallen out with the ruling assistants over ownership of lands of the Mohegan Indians. New London was home not only to Fitzjohn Winthrop and the Reverend Saltonstall, but also to their opponents Edward Palmes and John and Nicholas Hallam.[4] Fitch, the Hallams, and Palmes all had grievances against the leading families and the Winthrop administration; Fitch was unhappy with the limited role allowed him and the disposition of the Quinebaug lands, the Hallams over the disposition of their uncle's estate by the local court and the confiscation of their ship, *Liveen,* at New London by order of the General Court, and Palmes with the administration of the will of his dead wife, Anne Winthrop.

Fitch was a dangerous opponent as the leader of those men in eastern Connecticut with titles to land based on purchase from the Indians, townsmen who resented the requirement that the legislature must pass on all such purchases. While the magnate of Norwich posed as the champion of the charter, the danger from the Hallams came from their appeal to authorities in London after local officials had seized their ship. When the court of assistants refused them redress they asked the king in council for an order to the provincial government to admit their appeal with the right of a further appeal to the crown should the judgment in Connecticut go against them. This challenge to the authority of the colonial government came at a time when the commissioners at the Plantation Office were asking for copies of the provincial laws to be sent to London for inspection and review. Palmes expanded the attack in a remonstrance charging the government with irregularities. He claimed that several of the laws, orders, and procedures of Connecticut were unwarranted by the charter and grievous to the king's subjects. The patent from the crown empowered provincial officials only to make by-laws in the manner of a municipal corporation in England, not to assume unlimited power over the lives and liberties of the subjects. Palmes also accused the General Court of assuming an unwarranted authority over ecclesiastical matters so as to determine and punish heresies. Under Connecticut law, no shipmaster could bring in and no resident could entertain Quakers, Ranters, or Adamites. Winthrop and the assistants were in no hurry to answer, but the well-organized lobby of Quakers in London would make much of this last charge.[5]

In 1700, before the court of assistants at Hartford, the Hallams protested unsuccessfully a decision of the court at New London. When they sought to appeal to a higher authority, Governor Winthrop ruled that no appeals would be allowed to the king in council. Nicholas Hallam then crossed the Atlantic, and in London presented affidavits to corroborate his claim that the provincial authorities had refused the right of the subject to appeal to the monarch. Officials at the Plantation Office seemed sympathetic to Hallam's cause: although the charter granted by Charles II had not expressly reserved to the king the right to receive appeals, did not the monarch have an inherent right to decide appeals from his subjects in all of the colonies?[6] Months passed with no resolution of the question, as the Plantation Office pressed in Parliament for a bill revoking the charters of the corporate and proprietary colonies. But the threat might have led some men in Connecticut to consider the need for concessions. Samuel Wyllys of Stonington recalled for Winthrop that one article held against the commonwealthmen of Massachusetts was that they had publicly declared their ''avers[e]ness to the

Laws of England.'' Wyllys feared continued complaints against the government if Connecticut's commonwealthmen, Fitch and his allies, grew too strong. So adept was Fitch in the art of flattery that he made many people believe that he, rather than Winthrop, was the chief patron of the charter privileges enjoyed by the freemen.[7] Wyllys misjudged the political situation, for in 1703 the freemen dropped Fitch and Samuel Mason from the board of assistants. The controversy over appeals from the provincial courts to the Privy Council in London dragged on, with Fitzjohn Winthrop ignoring orders Edward Palmes received from England concerning litigation he had brought in the courts of Connecticut. After Winthrop died in 1707, his brother-in-law apparently lost interest in the appeals. Palmes himself died in 1715 at the age of seventy-eight.

Another issue had come up in 1703, a dispute over title to lands in the southeastern section of the colony. In 1659 the Mohegan sachem, Uncas, had conveyed title to all of the lands of his tribe not actually planted by Mohegans to Major John Mason, the principal Indian agent for the province. The next year Mason made an informal surrender to the colony of the right to these lands, about 800 square miles in all, covering sections of the towns of Lyme and New London and all of Colchester. The provincial government thus claimed these lands on the basis of the deed from Mason and by virtue of conquest from the Pequot Indians. Subsequently settlers had moved in, and both Fitzjohn Winthrop and Gurdon Saltonstall had obtained tracts from the legislature. In 1703, however, Owaneco, son of Uncas, complained to Daniel Mason, whose father had received the initial Indian title, of encroachments by whites and deprivation of hunting grounds. Daniel Mason now contended that his father's deed of 1660 had vested the provincial regime only with jurisdiction—that is, governmental authority—not with the right of property in the soil; the latter remained with the Mason family as guardians for the Mohegans. Various opponents of the Winthrop administration—Nicholas Hallam, Governor Joseph Dudley of Massachusetts, Edward Palmes and Fitch ("Black-James[,] ye Sagamore of Piggscomscutt," the Winthrops called him)—encouraged the Indians. The Masons of Stonington were related by marriage to Fitch and, through him, connected with Palmes and Hallam.[8] Dudley, since his appointment as royal governor of Massachusetts, had been campaigning in London against the corporate colonies. Hallam carried the complaint of the Mohegans to London, where, according to Robert Livingston, it raised a great noise. The ministers of state appointed a commission to investigate, one weighted with opponents of the Winthrop administration, including Dudley, Lieutenant Governor Thomas Povey of Massachusetts, Palmes, Francis Brinley of Newport in Rhode Island, Giles Silvester, Jahleel Brenton, Nathaniel Byfield of Bristol, and five men from Connecticut.[9]

Joseph Dudley and the commissioners gathered on 23 August 1705 at Stonington, where they encountered a delegation from Connecticut. William Whiting, John Chester, and Gurdon Saltonstall of the Connecticut group challenged Dudley and his associates and read a letter from Governor Winthrop denying the authority of the commission. Local men called upon as witnesses refused to testify, as did Saltonstall; he could not, being forbidden by proclamation of the governor of Connecticut. As might have been expected, Dudley, Palmes, and the other commissioners reported back to the crown in favor of the Indians, a view the Plantation Office accepted, but it had not counted on Sir Henry Ashurst, who waged a persistent legal battle before the Privy Council. Ashurst also prevailed on two peers whose families had been involved in the early settlement of New England, the dukes of Bedford and Somerset, to attend meetings of the council, and although he had no specific authority, he employed at his own expense his cousin, Spencer Cowper (brother of the lord keeper), John Hollis, and Peter King to contest the findings of the commission of inquiry. These efforts were rewarded. After Ashurst agreed to post bond of £400 as security, the Lords of the Council decided to appoint a new board of inquiry. In the end the new commission was never sent from London because Ashurst managed to have the matter put off. In America the authorities of Connecticut may have taken matters into their own hands: rumor had it that Captain John Livingston, Fitzjohn Winthrop's son-in-law, had threatened to bring the dreaded Mohawks down on the hapless Mohegans.[10]

Years passed before the Mohegan case again came up in London, but one immediate consequence of the attack by Palmes, Hallam, and their allies against the government of Connecticut was the entrance of the Quakers, an influential Dissenter group in the metropolis, into the campaign against the corporation and against the laws enacted by Connecticut against inhabitants who dissented from the Congregational church in the colony. The government of Connecticut stood accused of prohibiting by law Christians from meeting to worship or employing a minister without license from the General Assembly. Allegedly when John Rogers of New Haven had appealed to the crown against a sentence imposed on him for refusal to worship in the established church, his children had been taken away. Families were taxed for the support of the Congregationalist clergy and fined when they attempted to call in ministers of their own persuasion. Supporting these dissidents, a committee of London Quakers headed by Joseph Wyeth and John Feild objected to the harsh laws passed in Connecticut against Friends, especially the statute against heretics. In defense of the colony Sir Henry Ashurst protested that the law in question had been passed over thirty years before and had been directed chiefly against Ranters and Adamites. The provincial authorities now regarded the statute as obsolete. Moreover, the Quakers of London had not complained that the Friends in Connecticut had suffered any penalties; they were able to live there as Quakers did in any other colony. This last contention Wyeth and Feild denied.[11] Ashurst then asked for time better to inform himself of the situation in Connecticut.

Ashurst as well as Robert Livingston, who was then in London, saw in the complaints of the Quakers the work of Dudley at Boston: the governor of the Bay colony and his counterpart at Manhattan had orchestrated a chorus of complaints

and charges, among them, enacting oppressive laws on religion, condoning illicit trade, refusing to provide men for the common war effort, and depriving the
queen's subjects of the benefit of laws, all actions not justified under the charter.
To Ashurst these charges were but "Cunning Artifices," put forth by Dudley to
oppress the men of Connecticut and to disturb the quiet of the colony. Such was
the argument in rebuttal Ashurst employed with Lord Henry Paget, his wife's
brother-in-law and a leading member of the Dissenter interest in Parliament, and
with Robert Harley, speaker of the House of Commons. A change in office in
New York later brought some relief, although Dudley continued at Boston.
Ashurst remained rigid in his condemnation of Dudley, a man of "such in-
sinuation . . . that only Satan himself hath greater."[12] In time Dudley too grew
tired of attacking Connecticut and Rhode Island.

Much of the success of the provincial regime of Connecticut in putting off
the ministers in Whitehall had stemmed from the astute work of Fitzjohn Winthrop and his connections in London. But on 27 November 1707 the able governor died. Pressed into service, the superannuated deputy governor, Robert
Treat, called a special session of the General Court (General Assembly) to meet at
New Haven. As the law of the colony then stood, a governor must be selected
from the list of men nominated the previous year for the office of assistant, but the
legislature now altered the arrangement to provide for the freemen of the towns to
elect the governor and deputy from the members of the corporation. An easy
transition followed with the election of Gurdon Saltonstall, friend and confidant
of Winthrop for many years. An able, astute politician, Saltonstall continued in
office for sixteen years until his death. So adept was he too in fending off the
British government that officials in London at times were ignorant of what was
happening in Connecticut.[13]

Under Saltonstall the standing order maintained its control and circum-
vented any opposition capable of provoking the British government to intervene
in the affairs of the colony. During the early years of his administration the Anglicans of the southwestern corner of the province, particularly those in Stratford,
complained bitterly of harassment and of having to support the established Congregational clergy. Under Saltonstall the provincial regime allowed sober persons who dissented from the Congregationalist way to register at the county
courts, but they were exempt from attending an established church only if their
ministers obtained licenses from the provincial government. By existing law,
authority to call and settle a minister rested with those inhabitants of a town
allowed to vote in local elections or in full communion with the church. The
minister's salary came from local rates collected by the constable. Yet no person
was exempt from paying rates to the minister of the Congregational church in the
town in which he resided. The Anglicans persisted with their complaints: they
were maligned, imprisoned, and had their estates distrained when they refused to
pay taxes for the support of Timothy Cutler, the Congregational minister at Stratford. The General Assembly could not officially recognize the problem. To the

east, in New London County, Baptists were fined for not attending the established church. More objectionable were the Rogerenes, members of a sect who, seeking to restore early, primitive Christianity, disrupted services in the orthodox churches. Rogerenes, Baptists, and others who disturbed church services or maligned a minister were liable to fine of £20 and other punishment.

The hostility raised by these Dissenters perhaps reflected a nagging fear that all was not well with Congregationalism, a concern over declining piety, and an anxiety which may have led the clergy to exaggerate the threat from within the established order to the power of the pulpit as against the authority of the brethren, to church discipline and institutional purity. Gurdon Saltonstall in his first year in office sponsored an effort to resolve various problems. He persuaded the legislature to issue a call for a synod to draw up a code of ecclesiastical discipline for the approval of the General Assembly. At sessions subsequently held at Saybrook the clergy promulgated the doctrinal base of Connecticut Congregationalism, its ecclesiastical organization, and the administrative machinery for maintaining discipline. They called for a general association of clergymen meeting annually to report on the state of the church and to recommend policy to the congregations. The assistants to the governor later added a qualification: only churches accepting the Saybrook platform would be recognized by the provincial government as established churches; those refusing lost the support of the state. Most congregations accepted.[14]

The ruling order in Connecticut had closed ranks, moving to impose uniformity and cohesion within the province and at the same time preserving the autonomy of the corporation against the calls by royal officials that the provincial regime conform to legal and administrative standards set at Whitehall.

While the established families in Connecticut sought to preserve the province free of restraint from England, they did not scruple to appeal to London to further the claims of the colony in a long-standing dispute with neighboring Rhode Island. Since 1660 the Winthrops and other Connecticut families had joined with speculators, a few from Rhode Island but most from Massachusetts, in an effort to secure title to the region stretching west from Narragansett Bay. At stake was almost the entire mainland of Rhode Island. The Atherton Associates, as they initially had styled themselves, claimed the Narragansett country on the basis of forfeited mortgages from the local Indians. Initially the region came within the boundaries of Connecticut as delineated by the charter John Winthrop, Jr., had obtained from Charles II in 1662. The government of Rhode Island was seeking a patent at the same time. Due to a confusion of Narragansett Bay with the Pawtucket River, the region west of the bay was included within Connecticut in the provisions of the charter although in an agreement made subsequent to the issuance of the patent to Connecticut, an agreement negotiated between an agent for Rhode Island and Winthrop, the boundary between the two colonies was set at the Pawtucket River. Officials of Connecticut did not acknowledge the agreement Winthrop had signed even after he returned to New England and became governor of the province. Subsequent efforts by commissioners appointed by the crown to settle the controversy failed as both Connecticut and Rhode Island continued to claim jurisdiction over the region, sometimes called the King's Province. Since Rhode Island rejected the validity of the mortgage held by the Atherton Associates for the soil of the region, the speculators supported Connecticut jurisdiction. The discovery of lead ore in the disputed area intensified interest.

In 1697 when Fitzjohn Winthrop as major general of Connecticut was in London to defend the right of the government to command its own militia, he took the opportunity to reopen the matter of the King's province with the ministers of state. Ignoring the agreement made by the elder Winthrop, Connecticut officials claimed the Narragansett country as territory falling within their charter boundaries. If Fitzjohn's brother, Waitstill, then living in Boston, had had his way, Rhode Island would have gone out of existence. As he saw it, under the grants made early in the century, no territory existed between Connecticut and New Plymouth, the latter colony having become part of Massachusetts in 1691.[15] What the younger Winthrop ignored was that New Plymouth itself had never had a charter from the crown, merely a patent to hold land from the defunct Council of Plymouth, much the same as that of the duke of Hamilton for New Cambridge and John Mason for New Hampshire (or Laconia).

Officials in England had urged an amicable settlement, but neither side would compromise. Apprehensive that Rhode Island would impose taxes on settlers in the region, the Atherton Associates urged officials of Connecticut to issue a proclamation placing the disputed area under the protection of Connecticut. Governor Fitzjohn Winthrop warned the authorities at Providence not to levy taxes, and when sheriffs appointed by Rhode Island demanded rates from the settlers, they were seized by George Dennison, a magistrate of Connecticut. Five residents of Westerly, a town set up under Rhode Island authority, were also arrested and carried off as prisoners to Connecticut. Despite pleas for aid from Providence, the crown did not intervene. Rhode Island then proceeded to exert its authority. A full decade later Wait Winthrop and Elisha Hutchinson of the Bay colony again asked the crown to confirm to them title to their lands; the queen in council merely referred the matter to the Plantation Office and the law officers for study.[16]

The challenge from Connecticut and the Atherton Associates was but one of several problems faced by the regime at Providence as Rhode Island authorities were confronted with challenges from within the colony as well as from without. The presence of Francis Brinley—an Atherton Associate, a merchant of Anglican persuasion, and a royalist—was symptomatic of significant changes which had occurred in Rhode Island society during the last years of the seventeenth century.

The towns composing the confederation of Rhode Island had been founded two generations before by strong-minded, highly individualistic sectarians fleeing from state-imposed religious orthodoxy in Massachusetts. Refusing to allow government a role in ecclesiastical affairs, they had made Rhode Island a refuge for Quakers, Baptists, and other pietists. For over half a century strong-willed individuals had clashed in conflicts pitting town against town and local communities against the provincial regime. Distracted by internecine strife, schemed against by neighboring Massachusetts, Connecticut, and New Plymouth, Rhode Island officials had not resisted amalgamation into the Dominion of New England in 1688. With the collapse of the royal regime following the overthrow of the Catholic king, the officials who had presided over the confederation had hesitated but then resumed control as Rhode Islanders entered into the last decade of the seventeenth century.

The passage of time had seen change, as old quarrels cooled and death came to several of the original founders. Some of the leading antinomian families—the Hutchinsons, Brentons, Sanfords, and Coddingtons—drew together. Peleg Sanford, a grandson of Anne Hutchinson, became a royalist and an intimate of Francis Brinley. English born, Brinley had come to New England with his aunt, the third wife of William Coddington. Regarding themselves as socially superior, these families, with the exception of the Sanfords, gravitated toward the Church of England and inclined toward royalism; they resented the sectarians as base men from the lower orders. Nonetheless, Quakers and Baptists prevailed, electing such men as Walter Clarke and Samuel Cranston rather than Brentons, Brinleys, and Coddingtons to preside over the provincial regime. Unhappy with what they considered their inadequate role in the management of the affairs of the province, the royalists, like their counterparts in Boston and Manhattan, branded Newport and Providence as havens for pirates and illegal traders. Privateers who preyed indiscriminately on vessels off the New England coast had little to fear from the Rhode Island authorities, they claimed. Doubtless the officials who granted privateering commissions had reason to suspect they might be abused, but for an aggressive trading community such as Newport "the advantages of plunder on the high seas, legal or illegal, were so great as to mute scruples." Reports reaching England made it clear that Thomas Tew and other pirates were outfitting their ships in Rhode Island ports.[17]

By the terms of the Act to Prevent Frauds, Parliament in 1696 required governors in the plantations to swear an oath to enforce the navigation code, and in reaction to the discovery of a plot to assassinate William III, Parliament had also enjoined officials to subscribe to an association to support the Protestant monarch. No royal officials qualified to administer the requisite oaths resided in Rhode Island until Jahleel Brenton returned from London early in December 1697 with commissions for himself as collector of customs, Peleg Sanford as judge, and Nathaniel Coddington as register of a court of vice-admiralty. Walter Clarke, the Quaker elected governor in May 1696, refused to take the oath or to sign the association prescribed by Parliament. Early in January 1698 Sanford appeared before the General Assembly, where, presenting Clarke with the commission Brenton had brought over from London, he asked the governor to publish it and to swear him into office. Clarke put him off: he would consider the matter and refer it to the assembly. But in the lower house the governor denounced the commission as an infringement of the charter rights: if the deputies elected from the towns allowed the royal commission, he, Clarke, would take his leave of them, for there would be no election of officials according to the patent. The lower house took no action, and Clarke refused to return the commission to Sanford.[18] To avoid any further legal responsibility, Walter Clarke resigned his office, and in May the assembly chose his nephew, Samuel Cranston, to succeed him. Cranston would remain in power for almost three decades, reelected each year until his death in 1727. Clarke had not removed himself entirely from the scene, however. In 1700 he succeeded John Greene as deputy governor and served in that post until the end of his life.

The new governor was the son of John Cranston, a Scots physician who had migrated to Rhode Island and married Clarke's sister. Samuel Cranston had gone to sea, become a merchant, and then turned to public life. Regarded by some as a Quaker, he did not associate completely with any church. He was to prove himself a master of obfuscation and evasion when dealing with the government in London, of seeming to give in and yet avoiding compliance with orders from Whitehall. Immediately following his election as governor, Cranston signed an address from the colony to the king in response to a complaint from London over illicit trade. Officials of the provincial regime begged the king's pardon for any offense but said nothing of their refusal to honor the royal commissions to Sanford and Coddington. The charge that Rhode Islanders outfitted pirates was a misrepresentation, officials of the colony claimed, as were the complaints of their not complying with requests to aid in the defense of New York.[19]

Initially these evasive tactics seemed not to work. The crown issued a commission for the earl of Bellomont, governor of neighboring Massachusetts and New York, to investigate the irregularities in Rhode Island, possibly as grounds for a writ of *quo warranto* to vacate the charter. Jahleel Brenton gave Bellomont a list of questions to be put to Clarke and Cranston, as well as the names of men, royalists all—Francis Brinley, Peleg Sanford, Nathaniel Coddington, Caleb Arnold, and Josiah Arnold—who could provide information. Brinley himself complained directly to the Plantation Office of the refusal of the Rhode Island courts to allow appeals to London, thus denying the prerogative of the crown and encroaching upon the liberties of the king's subjects.[20]

The provincial authorities apparently did not apprehend any danger. Cranston apologized to the Commissioners of Trade for not maintaining a regular correspondence, pleading lack of shipping to England. The Rhode Islanders—a plain and mean sort of people—were loyal, and if they had erred, it was only from innocent ignorance. Seeing in Cranston's letters only "some frivolous vindications," the commissioners resolved to return him "a very sharp Answer."

Particularly distressing to them was the chaotic collection of provincial laws the governor had sent to the Plantation Office, some pages stitched together, blotted in some places, blank in others, with some statutes lacking sense, other laws with no titles, and no order or system to the lot. Cranston must correct "all such shuffling" in his correspondence and the Rhode Islanders reform their ways, else they could expect drastic action by the crown.[21]

That the records of the provincial government of Rhode Island were in a chaotic state would have surprised no one familiar with the situation in the colony, for as Bellomont discovered during a brief inspection tour in September 1699, the judges and other officials who conducted public business were uninformed, untrained, and often without experience. Although Bellomont's acquaintance with the American colonies was limited to New York, Massachusetts, and New Hampshire, a week in Rhode Island was sufficient to prove to him that the government there was the most irregular and illegal of any in the English provinces. Cranston's address to the assembly he found unique for insolence and nonsense. Bellomont did not tarry long in Rhode Island; he returned to Boston after Cranston had promised to call the legislature into session to bring the laws of the colony into some semblance of order. Sanford, Coddington, and Brenton, as representatives of the royal government, were to receive the revised laws and the journal of the house of deputies. These three found little support, however, being looked upon as men who infringed on charter privileges, as enemies of a free state.

Cranston himself had remonstrated with Bellomont that it was an imposition upon the government of Rhode Island that royal officials in London should require copies of provincial laws to be sent to Whitehall. Imposition or not, in December 1699 the governor sent over an alleged transcript, but a version of the laws, according to Sanford, not as they stood in the records. Some had never been passed. Isaac Addington, secretary of the Bay colony, described them as incoherent and nonsensical, jumbled together.[22] If the officials of Rhode Island themselves did not know what was in the laws, how could the people of the colony?

Cranston's performance prompted the Commissioners of Trade and Plantations to call for the attorney general and solicitor general to review the evidence for possible legal action. Although the Privy Council concurred, the administration took no action specifically against Rhode Island. In 1701 the Plantation Office proposed that Parliament take up the patents of all the chartered colonies, but a bill to this end failed to win sufficient votes that year or the next.

Playing the innocents, Cranston and the deputies of Rhode Island sent over to London a prayer for the continuation of their privileges according to the charter. A poor, distressed, and persecuted people, they had been wonderfully preserved for more than sixty years despite the endeavors of their neighbors—a reference to the Atherton Associates, Massachusetts, and Connecticut—to dismember Rhode Island. To finance the defense of the colony in London the provincial regime imposed a special tax. Some townsmen in Westerly, uncertain as to whether their community fell within Connecticut or Rhode Island, protested at a local town meeting. Rhode Island authorities jailed them. Although a grand jury twice in March 1700 returned a verdict of "Ignoranmus" to the charges against Joseph Pemberton, John Lewis, and Edward Blening, the judges— Cranston, John Greene, Walter Clarke, Robert Carr, James Barker, Giles Slocum, Joseph Sheffield, and Joseph Hull—proceeded to name additional members to the grand jury. After some hours, twelve of the twenty jurymen agreed to bring in a "Billa Vera" because the court would accept no other. In later reporting on the judicial system to London, Cranston again begged pardon for any "irregularities" committed through the weakness of any individual.[23]

By the spring of 1701 Bellomont was dead, and the administration in London had given up hope of uniting the forces of all the northern colonies under the command of a single captain general. Another year passed before Bellomont's successor as governor of Massachusetts appeared with a commission to command the militia of Rhode Island. In August 1702 Joseph Dudley, accompanied by members of the council of the Bay colony, arrived in Rhode Island. There, in the presence of Cranston, the assistants, and several notables, he made public his authorization from the queen to command the forces of Rhode Island in time of war and his commission as vice admiral. Over the protests of the outraged Quakers of the colony, Dudley proceeded to take the requisite oaths and to order the muster of two companies of militia at Newport. The following month he confronted the provincial authorities, pointing out to Cranston and the assistants that by act of Parliament, command of the militia was vested in the crown; the queen might dispose of it as she thought fit and no one might controvert the commands of the monarch issued under the broad seal of England.

Cranston did just that. The governor and the assistants designated Isaac Martindale, major of militia, to put their case to Dudley. Well primed, Martindale cited a clause of the charter to the effect that authority over the militia was inherent in the authority of the civil government as established by the patent. Cranston would not give in to Dudley's demand without first consulting with the assembly, scheduled to meet that October. Martindale, for his part, would not accept a warrant from Dudley, claiming that by his orders he was sworn to obey the government of Rhode Island. At Rochester—a town in the Narragansett country which Dudley, sixteen years before as president of the Council of New England, had named—the situation was quite different. There, Captain Daniel Eldridge and his company of militia took the oath of allegiance Dudley tendered them. The next day the governor and his entourage left for the Bay colony, the dispute with the provincial regime at Providence unresolved.[24]

This confrontation between Dudley and the authorities of Rhode Island gave the Commissioners of Trade a reason to contend that the safety of the queen's subjects in the colony was endangered by the failure of the provincial authorities, acting under the charter, adequately to provide for the defense of the province. Such a rationalization had received legal sanction some years before, allowing the crown to appoint governors for proprietary Maryland and Pennsylvania. Indeed, a royal appointee still presided over the government of Maryland. The Plantation Office now asked the queen to appoint Dudley governor of Rhode Island.[25] Aware of the potential danger, in February 1703 the provincial authorities prepared to send over a special agent, Captain Joseph Sheffield, a member of the council, who, according to one report, "kept a little blind rum-house," an establishment frequented for the most part by Indians, since hardly any Englishmen would go near it. But several of the deputies in the assembly protested against the tax ordered to defray the agent's expenses in London. Cranston and his colleagues dropped the idea of a mission, sending over instead another vague, pious apology for their behavior: the ministers of state must not harbor or give credit to any complaints made against the Rhode Islanders until they could be heard in lawful defense.[26]

Fortunately for Cranston and the Quaker regime, the Plantation Office had coupled complaints against Rhode Island with charges against Connecticut, and Fitzjohn Winthrop and his colleagues of the sister corporate province had employed Sir Henry Ashurst to work in their behalf in London. Twice before in a campaign against the chartered colonies, the independent governments in America, the Plantation Office had suffered disappointment in Parliament. Nonetheless, at the close of 1703 the Board of Trade—now under the presidency of the earl of Weymouth—hit upon a new argument. Did not the passing of an act establishing the General Court of Rhode Island as a court of admiralty constitute cause for vacating the charter? Edward Northey, the attorney general for the crown, was not inclined to support such a prosecution, for the law in question, enacted almost a decade before, had been only provisional. The Plantation Office now fell back on the opinion given the previous decade, that in case of extraordinary exigency arising from the neglect of a proprietor to defend a colony and its inhabitants, the crown might constitute a governor. Northey and the solicitor general, Simon Harcourt, agreed, but with one significant qualification as to the civil administration: a governor appointed by the crown was not to alter any of the rules relating to property or the methods of proceeding in civil causes established pursuant to charters.[27]

Sir Henry Ashurst as agent for Connecticut made good use of the constraints the law officers had raised. On 12 February 1704/5 he and William Wharton, a New England–born lawyer recommended by William Penn, were given a further six months to submit their case. Ashurst then also won postponements before the Privy Council. The regime in Rhode Island, for its part, denied most of the charges and cited opinion of counsel that it was not required by law to furnish any colony with a quota of men for military operations, since by charter the provincial government had command of the militia. Moreover, the patent expressly empowered the provincial authorities to try all crimes and to make all manner of good laws.[28] The briefs drawn up by Ashurst's lawyers and Ashurst's own delaying tactics and political influence saved the Dissenter regime of Rhode Island.

In Parliament the Commissioners of Trade and Plantations achieved little in their attacks on the charters of Rhode Island and Connecticut.

The royalist attack on the provincial government did have a decided effect in the colony, nonetheless, as Samuel Cranston undertook over the course of a decade to bring about a transformation in the colony. While preserving *de facto* autonomy, he effected a major change in the governmental structure of Rhode Island in response to pressure from London as power passed from the towns to the provincial government.

To alleviate pressure on the colony while he carried out his program of internal change, Cranston prevailed on Connecticut to accept a compromise over the disputed Narragansett country. The settlement did not endure, but it gave the shrewd Cranston time. The administration of Fitzjohn Winthrop, itself challenged by James Fitch and other dissidents in Connecticut, in May 1703 agreed to a compromise on the boundary line with Rhode Island. Both sides agreed to accept claims to private property. The vague language employed in this agreement led the Atherton Associates to conclude that they had won; not until later did they learn otherwise. Yet the agreement made possible the imposition of Rhode Island authority in the disputed region. No longer would Connecticut undermine the authority of the towns of Westerly and Kingston.

In the first years of the new century, Cranston and his colleagues — Isaac Martindale, Joseph and Nathaniel Sheffield, Giles Slocum, and Walter Clarke — brought about a transformation in the colony by strengthening the central government. During this time Newport began to fulfill the hopes that it would become a major trading center as the provincial government, reorganized under Cranston, supported the town's commercial ambitions. With the rise of Newport, the towns in the interior also prospered and grew. During Cranston's tenure as governor, laws were overhauled and the scope of control by the provincial government extended. Without this reconstruction of the machinery of government, retaining the privileges claimed under the charter might have been neither possible nor worthwhile. To achieve this reorganization, the General Assembly had first to gain the authority assigned to it in the charter; its power to tax had to be established, its laws compiled, additional statutes passed to remove any defects, and old laws reenacted to render them acceptable to technical English standards. In the process, the provincial regime had to assume the powers exercised by the independent towns and local associations of landowners, since hitherto, many aspects of public affairs had been only nominally within the purview of the General Assembly.[29] The process of bringing order to Rhode Island and centralizing the functions of government stemmed directly from the pressure of the crown and the tour of inspection conducted in the last year of the seventeenth century by the earl of Bellomont. Ironically, as a result of the complaints of Bellomont, his successor, Joseph Dudley, and the royalist coterie in the colony, the autonomy of Rhode Island vis-à-vis the crown in time became greater than ever.

During the last fifteen years of the reign of the Stuart monarchs royal officials in Whitehall had accomplished little to bring the corporate colonies of Connecticut and Rhode Island under closer supervision. Over a decade after Samuel Cranston had promised the earl of Bellomont to present a coherent body of provincial laws, the wily governor wrote to the Plantation Office to apologize for the delay. Nor had the royal government interfered to resolve the dispute over the Narragansett country. In the summer of 1711 a petition by Wait Winthrop of Massachusetts in behalf of the Atherton Associates had been referred to the crown law officers; more than four years later, the attorney general had not responded, leading the Commissioners of Trade to reproach Sir Edward Northey: it was a disservice to the crown to let plantation business lay so long undetermined.[30]

CHAPTER 12

Northern New England under a Governor "of Our Nation"

In NORTHERN NEW ENGLAND, as in southern New England, the pretensions of outside speculators threatened communities and disrupted governments; in addition, a generation of English colonists lived under the threat of raids by the French and their Indian allies from the north. Reacting to the inability of successive governments in the English provinces to take effective action, the tribes of the Iroquois confederation had succumbed to the arguments of the French and had adopted a neutral stance during the interval, 1697–1702, between the wars waged by the Europeans. When hostilities resumed in 1702, the northern frontiers—Massachusetts with the outlying district of Maine and the handful of small townships composing New Hampshire—bore the heaviest burden, as the French and hostile Indians were free to concentrate their forces against the villages of northern New England in sudden, destructive forays.

Wedged between the Merrimack and Piscataqua rivers, the small, exposed settlements of Hampton, Portsmouth, Exeter, and Dover (Newcastle and Kingston were founded later) had once been included within Massachusetts; the bulk of their inhabitants had been content to live within the governmental and social system the ruling Puritan element in the Congregationalist commonwealth had imposed. But in 1677 the king's judges in Westminster had ruled that title to the soil of New Hampshire belonged to the heirs of John Mason on the basis of a grant made in 1635 from the Council of Plymouth (or Council of New England). Since the English corporation had no authority to confer powers of government, political jurisdiction reverted back to the crown after the company became extinct. In 1679 the crown took over New Hampshire as a colony separate from Massachusetts and appointed a governor and council with authority to convene elected representatives from the towns to sit as a legislative assembly. After a brief hiatus within the Dominion of New England, New Hampshire had continued as a separate royal province, and in 1691 the heirs of John Mason had sold their holdings for £2,750 to Samuel Allen, a London merchant seeking to exploit the rich timber resources of the Piscataqua and Maine towns. Allen faced stiff opposition not only from London merchants seeking contracts with the navy and their correspondents in Boston and Portsmouth, but also from the townsmen of New Hampshire. A lawsuit initiated in 1683 by the Masons against one of the leading settlers, Richard Waldron of Dover, to force the townsmen to accept the proprietary claims had dragged on for years in the provincial courts. Allen renewed the suit, but with no success despite the support he received from John Usher, a Boston bookseller turned merchant who had been appointed by the crown as deputy governor.

As the executive official responsible for governing the roughly 800 families residing in the small New Hampshire towns, Usher had little success. Residing for the most part in Boston, he found himself frustrated on his occasional ventures to the Piscataqua. Richard Waldron, John Hinckes, and William Vaughan, councilors and ranking officers of the militia, openly mocked his authority. On one visit when the local militia failed to support Usher, he retired to Boston claiming his life was not safe and calling on the royal government to send over a hundred soldiers to discipline the unruly townsmen. Usher was still fighting the old battles, still seeing the old bugbears as he linked the resistance he encountered to the old commonwealth supporters in the Bay colony, the men who longed for the old charter. "That is their onions and garlic."[1] So Usher, a son of Massachusetts, condemned the Puritans as ungrateful as the ancient Hebrews delivered from bondage in Egypt. In a moment of pique Usher had offered to resign. To his chagrin his resignation was accepted, and at the request of Sir Henry Ashurst the post of lieutenant governor went to William Partridge, a Piscataqua shipwright then visiting London. Samuel Allen, the proprietor, also supported Partridge for the position, much to his later regret.

Rather than merging the colony with Massachusetts, as geography, military necessity, and history suggested, the ministers of the crown appointed the earl of Bellomont governor of the two distinct but adjoining provinces, with Partridge to preside over public affairs in the absence of the governor. But several years passed before Bellomont, occupied with his personal finances and faced with more pressing duties in Manhattan and Boston, put in an appearance in New Hampshire. To compound the difficulties, Allen, as proprietor, thought of himself as governor. Matters were even more confused because Partridge when he arrived on the Piscataqua failed to take the requisite oath of office to enforce the navigation code or to publish his commission; he may have been unable to find someone to post the necessary bond or may have been merely waiting until several of his ships returned from voyages of questionable legality. When he did assume control of the government, he placed several of his followers in office, displacing William Redford and Charles Story, recently arrived immigrants from England. At a public meeting in Exeter, Story, the displaced provincial secretary, denounced the proceedings of Partridge, Vaughan, Waldron, and the other councilors as illegal. Usher, still claiming the deputy governorship, tried to intervene but was forced to withdraw on learning that Vaughan and John Pickering, at the head of the militia of Portsmouth, were about to seize him.[2]

On hearing that Samuel Allen was to arrive in the colony with still another commission as governor, the councilors and Henry Penny, the newly appointed secretary, sent Ichobod Plaisted to Manhattan to enlist the aid of the earl of Bellomont. Both sides, adherents and opponents of the proprietor traduced the loyalty of their opponents. The majority of the assemblymen, Joseph Smith, Marshall of the New England admiralty court, charged, were men of antimonarchial principles, elected by questionable means—not more than six men had voted in Exeter, not above twenty in Hampton—and the speaker of the house, John Pickering, was a common drunkard and a notorious felon.[3]

In the summer of 1698 confusion mounted on the Piscataqua. As the councilors and assemblymen had feared, Samuel Allen, the putative proprietor, arrived with a commission as governor procured for him by William Blathwayt at the Plantation Office. With good reason Allen anticipated strong opposition. Partridge, Hinckes, Vaughan, and Waldron all taunted him: when Bellomont arrived, they would strip him of his government.[4] Joined by Pickering and eight other assemblymen, they wrote to Bellomont in New York that they could hardly wait for the happy day of his coming. Allen, in the meantime, turned out the officeholders who had opposed Usher and appointed Nathaniel Fryer, Joseph Smith, Kingley Hall, Sampson Sheafe, Thomas Packer, and Peter Weare.

Not until the end of July 1699 did Bellomont put in an appearance. But his stay in New Hampshire was brief, for affairs at Boston required that he return soon to the Bay colony. Usher pressed charges against Partridge, Hinckes, Vaughan, and Waldron for taking up arms against the king's deputy governor, but when Bellomont asked for proof, Usher fled back to Boston, pleading his wife's illness. Dismissing the charges, Bellomont canceled the commissions issued by Allen and brought to a halt the trial the proprietor had initiated over lands occupied by the townsmen. In contesting the claims of the proprietor Vaughan and Waldron had appealed to the townsmen, arguing that they were not bound to observe any grants, commands, or laws from the king or Parliament. They now raised money to defend the union with Puritan Massachusetts, as they put it, "the good old cause." Allen, to curry favor with Bellomont, then informed the governor that several of the governor's appointees—Hinckes, John Plaisted, Waldron, and Partridge—were engaged in questionable trade: exporting large quantities of timber to Portugal. This traffic, much of it carried on by men on the Piscataqua acting as factors for merchants in London, was not illegal; but Bellomont, who hoped to win approval for his own grandiose scheme for supplying naval stores, acted as if it were, or ought to be.[5]

Bellomont's short stay in New Hampshire confirmed for him his prejudices against provincials' holding high office. Appointing men of low quality—William Phips, for example, a carpenter, a mere mechanic who once worked for day wages in Boston—as governor debased the king's authority. William Partridge, whose appointment as lieutenant governor of New Hampshire Sir Henry Ashurst had secured, was also a carpenter and a weak man.[6] The ministers of state did not accept Bellomont's distaste for provincials in high office when they later named as his successor a New England man, Joseph Dudley.

As distressing to Bellomont as the plebeian origins of some New England officials was the corrupt management of plantation affairs in Whitehall, specifically a bargain allegedly concluded between Samuel Allen and William Blathwayt, the governor's nemesis at the Plantation Office, a bargain reported to Bellomont by Robert Armstrong, a secretary whom he had appointed naval officer for New Hampshire. Armstrong claimed to have seen evidence in England proving that Blathwayt had a direct financial interest in Allen's claim to New Hampshire. Three peers—the duke of Leeds, Lord Lonsdale, and the duke of Leinster—had once been associated with Allen in his claim, but had sold out to Blathwayt. The commissioner of trade was to retain half of Allen's claim to the province if the proprietor did not repay a debt of £3,000, but only one-third if the money was repayed in time. Thus involved financially, Blathwayt had allegedly secured a mandamus to force the inhabitants of the New Hampshire towns to a trial with Allen. Bellomont now offered evidence he felt confirmed this story. Before leaving for America the governor had met Thomas Osborne, Marquess of Carmarten and later duke of Leeds at the Treasury. Carmarthen had asked that Bellomont be particularly kind to Allen's concerns, for Leeds purportedly admitted that he himself held a large tract of land in that country. Bellomont advanced still more proof: Allen had offered him a bribe! If the governor would but favor the proprietor's cause against the townsmen, Allen would match his daughter to Bellomont's younger son, bestow on the girl a dowry of £10,000, and divide the province with Bellomont. With righteous indignation Bellomont reported he had spurned the offer: he would not sell justice, even if he gained the entire world by so doing. Parliament must vacate all excessive or extravagant grants, including Allen's "pretended" title to New Hampshire.[7] Bellomont may have been misinformed, or merely confused. Allen was certainly short of money, but it was John Usher with whom the proprietor became financially involved. In 1699 the Boston bookseller and erstwhile deputy governor of New Hampshire had married Elizabeth Allen and accepted a mortgage from his father-in-law for half of the province for the sum of £1,500.

Bellomont did not tarry long in New England. By the fall of 1700 he was back in New York, and by the following spring he was dead. William Partridge then presided over the government of New Hampshire. His archrival, Usher, pressed the attack against the deputy governor, employing the same charge used by Bellomont—that Partridge was shipping timber to Portugal—and adding another: the deputy governor and his colleagues on the provincial council did not believe in kingly government or that acts of Parliament could apply to America unless the colonists had representatives in the English House of Commons.[8] At the behest of Allen, Usher returned to London to reclaim the deputy governorship while the proprietor himself, pressing his suit against Richard Waldron, brought an action in ejectment in the Superior Court of New Hampshire. Since all of the judges and jurymen would be his tenants if he won the case, the decision went against him. He then entered an appeal to the king in council.

Disturbing news now reached the New England towns. Despite the efforts of the brothers Ashurst, Joseph Dudley, the former Congregationalist minister who had left his calling and introduced royal administration fifteen years before, would now return to his native New England as governor of Massachusetts and New Hampshire. With eyes lifted up to Heaven, some among the old common-wealthmen cried out: "Poor New England hath seen its best days; now Popery will be brought into this land of uprightness." Hitherto the Puritan element, men opposed to the proprietor and to royal government, had dominated public affairs in New Hampshire. Any deputy returned from the towns who was not of their persuasion they turned out of the House of Representatives. With the assembly purged of dissidents the speaker, Samuel Penhallow, appointed the provincial treasurer.[9]

In the administration of Joseph Dudley, the townsmen of New Hampshire were to be much surprised and gratified, as Dudley proved to be a bulwark in defense of local interests against Allen and John Usher after the Boston merchant returned from England with a commission as lieutenant governor of New Hampshire. When Usher arrived in the Piscataqua towns at the end of 1703 he found his old enemies ensconced in office, Richard Waldron sitting on the inferior court at Newcastle and John Hinckes presiding over the superior court of the colony. Despite the fears of the former commonwealthmen, Dudley's sentiments were with the inhabitants rather than with the Allens, Samuel and his son, Thomas, John Usher, and William Blathwayt. When appointing officials, including coun-cilors, Dudley favored men from the leading families opposed to the proprietor's claims. He also held the key to the outcome of the dispute between the Allens and the townsmen of New Hampshire over lands. Early in his administration Dudley signed two bills passed by the assembly, one for confirming town grants and another against trespassing on town commons, laws Allen charged were de-signed to prevent him from proceeding with his legal claims. The assembly also voted Dudley a gift, first of £250 and then another £160, the first salary voted a royal governor in New Hampshire.[10]

Despite adverse opinion Allen persisted in pressing his suit of ejectment against Waldron in the local courts. Dudley did not favor a judicial resolution, however. On 23 March 1705 a trial was held at Newcastle. Dudley did not attend, but as ordered by London, he directed John Hinckes to secure a special verdict; the jurymen were to determine certain facts at issue as established by evidence, leaving it to the court to apply the law. When the jury brought in a verdict for Waldron, Allen's attorney asked the judges to direct them merely to find a special verdict as ordered by the crown. This the judges would not do, refusing also to read the order from the queen in council. Instead they commanded that the verdict for Waldron be recorded.

Dudley then intervened to arrange a nonjudicial compromise. At a meeting held on 3 May the assemblymen and two of the principal freeholders from each town decided to allow the proprietor 800 square miles of waste lands; 500 acres each in Portsmouth and Newcastle; 1,500 acres each in Hampton, Dover, Exeter, and Kingston; and £2,000 in New England currency. In return Allen would waive his claim to back rent. Dudley urged Allen to accept, but the proprietor hesitated. A few days later, on 8 May, Samuel Allen died. His son and heir, Thomas Allen, refused the offer on the advice of John Usher and petitioned the queen to be allowed to revive his father's appeal in his own name.[11] To finance this appeal Thomas Allen sold half of his interest in the colony to Sir Charles Hobby, a London merchant with connections in Boston. Those Bay colonists opposed to Dudley later used Hobby as a stalking horse in their efforts to unseat the governor.

At stake in New Hampshire and the region beyond the Piscataqua were rich timber lands where no fewer than seventy saw mills were in operation. In 1708 Robert Armstrong returned to England with the mast fleet as solicitor for Thomas Allen. In London George Vaughan, William's son and an agent appointed and paid by the assembly, spoke for the inhabitants. Dudley supported the townsmen, settlers who had lived on these lands and defended them with their lives, blood, and money. The queen ought not to eject her subjects or "put them to a rack rent." Years passed without Allen obtaining satisfaction. In 1715 Usher urged the crown to buy out the Allen claim, one in which he himself had a share.[12] Thomas Allen died that year, and his claim, such as it was, passed to Sir Matthew Dudley, the head of an Anglo-colonial syndicate which had sought unsuccessfully to obtain a monopoly from the crown to exploit the timber resources of northern New England. For years aggressive English competitors and their associates on the Piscataqua had blocked the efforts of Dudley's syndicate to obtain a charter. Several decades later a clique of New Hampshire land speculators finally settled the dispute by purchasing the Allen estate.

With the Allen family unable to obtain sanction for its claim and the Dudley Associates unable to secure a charter, the forests of New Hampshire and Maine were open to exploitation by rival gangs of local merchants and lumberers, some associated with contractors in London. Efforts by John Bridger, the surveyor of the woods, and his deputies, employed to protect trees suitable for masts for the royal navy, counted for little. When Bridger protested over the destruction wrought by the brothers John and Ichobod Plaisted and by John Mico, who were agents for the London contractors Francis Collins and John Taylor, Governor Dudley found excuses for the lumbermen: while they were careful not to waste trees, there was no knowing the soundness of a tree until it was felled; some might then be found defective, not worth a penny as a mast.[13]

Despite the fears of the New Hampshire townsmen, many of them nurtured in the tradition of the Puritan commonwealth of the seventeenth century, Joseph Dudley had supported the Piscataqua communities against the crown surveyor of the woods, the Allens, and the deputy governor serving the would-be proprietor. Dudley had sought to confine John Usher to Boston, for the deputy need only be in New Hampshire a week and "he puts all there into a flame[,] sometimes beyond my capacity to mend." Through patronage Dudley won over some of Usher's potential adherents. Joseph Smith proved an embarrassment to Dudley, however, when a young woman accused him of fathering her bastard child. A local justice ordered Smith to pay for the support of the infant, although many persons, including Dudley, thought him innocent. The governor still found him acceptable for the council. Not so Thomas Packer, for he kept a tavern: it would be difficult to have him at the board while he was so employed.[14] John Usher was reduced to grasping at straws. Objecting that warrants for the appointment of Richard Waldron and Mark Hunking to the council were not in order, he suspended them. The ministry in London overruled him and restored the two councilors to their places.

Usher lost all sense of proportion; at one time he urged that Massachusetts and Rhode Island be annexed to New Hampshire. And when Colonel Francis Nicholson appeared in Boston to organize an expedition against the French at Port Royal, Usher urged that he be made governor of New England, an appointment desired by all of the queen's true and loyal subjects. As evidenced by the response of councilors, assemblymen, officers of the militia, and many of the ministers and merchants of the towns of New Hampshire when the incumbent governor came under attack in England, this was not the case. With good reason New Hampshiremen supported Joseph Dudley. He spent almost all of his time in Boston, stripped the deputy governor of any real authority, and left the leading men of the province to manage affairs themselves. As Usher complained on one of his infrequent visits, the councilors generally conducted matters, with sessions of the assembly held only infrequently. William Vaughan contemptuously dismissed Usher in 1708: they had no need for a lieutenant governor, for the council could act without him.[15]

In neighboring Massachusetts by the turn of the century the pattern of political life if not government was changing. While there were vestiges of the old animosities between commonwealthmen, moderates, and royalists, between die-hard Puritans and those who were willing to accept an accommodation with a crown that was insisting on toleration for all peaceable Protestants, other divisions were becoming manifest between men willing to cast their lot in a court faction, to accept administrative office under the crown, and a country faction. The provincial minded, men residing mainly in the small towns in the rural districts with their vision limited to the immediate horizon, had few aspirations and little ambition for themselves; they evinced a pervasive suspicion of the outside world and of the ways of executive government. And during these years the main concern and constant preoccupation of provincial government was with administration. Distinct from this country bloc were two fluid, unstable groups made up of men willing to accept, perhaps even actively seeking, office, distinguished from each other more by their success or failure in winning places and influence than by their commitment to ideology. They were less fearful than their parochial-minded neighbors of the allegedly corrupting influence of the outside world, especially across the Atlantic; they preached the virtues of order and leadership. By contrast, the representatives from the country assumed the mantle of defenders of the people and argued the necessity of vigilence to protect an overly powerful and inherently suspect administration, both imperial and provincial, from stiffling liberty and corrupting a virtuous people.

Professed ideologies alone did not explain the workings of politics in the Bay colony, as men responding to various pressures and needs at times shifted sides. Early in the last decade of the seventeenth century Samuel Willard condemned Governor William Phips on his failure to rule the people responsibly, but Willard moderated his dissatisfaction once his brother-in-law, Joseph Dudley, sat in the governor's chair. Increase Mather and his son Cotton had apologized for the behavior of their parishioner, Phips, the man the elder Mather had persuaded William III to appoint as governor, but they violently condemned the same behavior when exhibited by Joseph Dudley.

Among the concessions Increase Mather had won from the crown, one distinguishing Massachusetts from the other provinces where the monarch appointed the governor, was the right of the assembly, beginning in 1693, annually to choose the council, subject only to the veto of the governor. By the close of the first decade under the new charter, the proportion of residents from Boston and the other coastal towns elected to the council had grown considerably. With a majority of them connected by blood and marriage, they predominated on the board. This clique constituted an extended political family, a "cousinage."

Despite the much larger size of the lower house, among the representatives elected from the towns to the assembly a small group was also in control. Between 1692 and 1715 the rate of turnover was great, for more than half of the representatives elected had not served in the previous house. The average length of service was less than three terms. Four of every ten members served only a single term. A small number served for many years, however, averaging ten terms each; these men occupied the speaker's chair, sat on the important committees, and dominated the proceedings of the House of Representatives. James Converse of Woburn, John Burrill of Lynn, Nehemiah Jewett of Ipswich, and Thomas Olive of Cambridge fell into this select group. Boston's four representatives were also influential, often sitting in the speaker's chair, and, with their allies from the outlying towns, by the close of the seventeenth century running the House of Representatives. Under the charter the governors appointed from England depended upon this body to finance the civil and military establishments of Massachusetts.[16]

In the summer of 1700, learning that the French from Canada were tampering with the Iroquois in New York, Governor Bellomont had left Boston for Manhattan. Late in the following winter, on 5 March, he died — so poor as not to leave enough money for the support of his family or even to pay for his funeral. Even before word arrived in London of the death of the governor, some officials were voicing concern over the inadequate arrangements for the command of the

English military forces. A prudent gentleman well skilled in military affairs should be sent from England with the king's commission to preside at Boston in place of Lieutenant Governor William Stoughton, now nearly seventy years of age and in ill health. Some men in the Bay colony agreed on the need for another executive, but for different reasons. Wait Winthrop aspired to replace Stoughton through the influence of Sir Henry Ashurst, perhaps to become governor, but the majority in the House of Representatives, apparently following the lead of Speaker John Leverett, refused to ratify Ashurst as agent. Wait's older brother, the governor of Connecticut, obligingly then secured for Ashurst an appointment as agent for the neighboring colony. The younger Winthrop, aware that Stoughton had long supported Joseph Dudley, recommended that the councilors and assemblymen petition the king for a restoration of the privileges held under the ancient charter of choosing the governor, deputy, and any officials the General Court thought fit. The representatives in the assembly settled merely for an address to the crown to promote Stoughton. The lieutenant governor failed to oblige them; he died on 7 July 1701. As president of the council, Wait Winthrop took over the administration of the government. His colleagues on the board as a show of support promptly elected him to the post of chief justice of the Superior Court.

The decision had already gone against Winthrop in London, even before the death of Stoughton was known in England. Despite the heated opposition of Sir Henry Ashurst, Joseph Dudley would return to his native Massachusetts with a commission from the crown as governor. One English bureaucrat, unfamiliar with the convolutions and complexities of Massachusetts politics, thought Ashurst's opposition to Dudley "strange because they are lookt upon to be of a Feather." Dudley had once been an "Independent preacher" before taking up the more worldly avocation of politics.[17] On 5 July 1701, Ashurst had entered an objection with the Lords Justices in Council against Dudley: he had been one of the judges at the trial of Jacob Leisler almost a decade before. Admitting that he had served at the trial, Dudley contended that he had done his best to prevent the execution of the insurgent, a point Colonel Richard Ingoldsby, a witness at the trial, confirmed. Dudley also produced a letter from the speaker of the House of Representatives in Massachusetts confirming that Ashurst no longer spoke for the colony, having been dismissed as agent. But Ashurst explained—at least to Winthrop—that as a private man he was moved to stop the appointment to prevent the ruin of the Protestant cause should Dudley become governor.[18]

Ashurst did not speak for all men in the Bay colony; Dudley presented a letter from Nathaniel Byfield charging that the erstwhile agent represented only a few ill-tempered malcontents, among them Wait Winthrop, Elisha Cooke, John Saffin, and Elisha Hutchinson. Deputies in the assembly had voted against sending Winthrop over to London as special agent, ostensibly to obtain a restoration of the ancient privileges but actually to solicit his appointment as governor. Dudley had also been able to offset Ashurst's religious bias by prevailing on nine prominent Dissenter clergymen of London to write to Increase Mather and Samuel Willard in Boston in behalf of Dudley's candidacy: under his governorship they would be secure in their holy religion as well as in their civil rights and privileges.[19] Even the Mathers, stung by the criticism of Elisha Cooke that Increase had betrayed the Puritan heritage by agreeing to a restrictive charter, came to accept Dudley's appointment. The younger Mather now informed Dudley that "the most considerable" in New England saw in his appointment "a blessing." Cooke had abused the inhabitants with false representations that they might have their old patent. The Mathers appreciated the threat to the charters of all of the provincial corporations and proprietaries by an act of Parliament. Under Dudley the government would be in the hands of a gentleman, one of their own countrymen who "perfectly understands how to serve the King, as well as how to ease the people." This manifestation of support as well as the representation of the Presbyterian divines of London came to the hands of William Blathwayt, to be used with William III and the ministers of state. Merchants engaged in the Anglo–New England trade were divided in their views: David Waterhouse favored, Stephen Mason (an ally of Ashurst) opposed Dudley—for religion's sake, he assured Elisha Cooke.[20] Nothing if not partisan in his religious and political sentiments, Sir Henry Ashurst had his brother enter a caveat that no commission for Dudley pass until Ashurst received notice. But Dudley assured Robert Harley—and his influence would be decisive—that he would keep the people of New England "to a steady dependence" if he had the honor to do the king's service in the Bay colony.[21]

The appointments of Dudley as governor and Captain Thomas Povey, a cousin of Blathwayt with nine years' service in Flanders, as his deputy, reflected an alteration in the English political world, one underway even before the death of William III: a shift away from the Whig lords upon whom Ashurst had depended. The aged Dissenter attempted to salvage something of his reputation in New England: he would have secured an appointment for Winthrop as lieutenant governor if Dudley, who favored Nathaniel Byfield, had not produced evidence indicating that Wait had moved in the council to have the assistants take up the old charter. Denying the charge, Wait hinted that it had been Byfield who had made this suggestion. Byfield and the Mathers, supporters of Dudley, "deserved to be hang'd for their pains." Common talk had it that several men had been marked out beforehand "for displeasure, at least, if not to be *Leislerized,* as they call it."[22] Waitstill Winthrop had indeed been marked out, but not for extinction. In November 1701 William Atwood arrived in Boston with a commission as judge of admiralty. Although Winthrop remained on the provincial council for the next dozen years, he never recovered the power he had exercised all too briefly after the death of Stoughton.

In March 1702, as a crisis with France developed, Joseph Dudley hurried out to his post. He was still a vigorous man of fifty-seven years when he returned to his native province, a colony threatened by war and unsettled by competition for power and influence and conflicts over authority.

A decade under the charter of 1691 had done little to bring Massachusetts directly under the crown of England, as the ministers of state had hoped when in following the recommendation of Increase Mather they had appointed two other natives of the Bay colony, Sir William Phips and William Stoughton, as governor and deputy. Many bills passed by the House of Representatives and the council and signed by the king's governor had been found unacceptable in London. The Plantation Office, the Customs House, and the crown law officers had raised objections to provincial laws for regulating the colonial courts, for appointing judges by the authority of the local legislature rather than by that of the crown, and for designating ports for entering and clearing vessels. George Larkin, a customs officials conducting a survey of the American provinces, concluded that the Bay colonists abhored the laws of England and hated the thought of royal government. If not checked, they would set up a state of their own.

However much the provincials who espoused country sentiments would have welcomed reestablishing the Puritan commonwealth, they needed—as almost all of them realized—the support of England. Elisha Cooke, Nathaniel Byfield, and Samuel Sewall were among the councilors and elected deputies from the towns who had addressed the crown in the summer of 1701 for military assistance. Although the representatives had voted funds for fortifications on the eastern frontier, they would not approve money for maintaining forts in New Hampshire and for men to assist New York, pleading the need to defend the five hundred miles of frontier in Massachusetts Bay. In the instructions given to Governor Dudley the crown stressed the need for Massachusetts to aid its neighbors with men and money, to the extent that the safety of the Bay colony would allow. The ministers of state were much less forgiving on the subject of the financial responsibility of the provincial assembly for the civil establishment of the Bay colony, particularly for a permanent fund to pay the salaries of the governor and judges.[23]

As governor of the Bay colony Joseph Dudley was caught between the need to fulfill the demands of the crown and the desire to satisfy the representatives of the local populace within a system of government providing for an elected assembly and council. He had also to protect his political base in London from attack by provincial opponents, for it was a base none too secure, as he soon learned from John Chamberlain, secretary of the Anglican Society for the Propagation of the Gospel. Hardly had Dudley arrived in Boston when rumors began circulating in London that the governor-designate of New York, Edward Hyde, was seeking to have Massachusetts added to his commission.[24] As had been evident in the appointment of Sir William Phips and Dudley himself, the ministers of state had been sensitive to the need to placate the provincials and their allies at Westminister. Dudley had to fear potential rivals such as Nathaniel Higginson and Sir

Charles Hobby, an English merchant and sometime resident of Boston, men with reputations beyond the confines of the Bay colony. Fortunately for Dudley, those in the colony who opposed him and commanded support locally, such as Elisha Cooke, hesitated to appeal to London to rid themselves of the governor: by so doing they would acknowledge the right of royal authorities to intervene. Nathaniel Higginson and Hobby might not hesitate to call on Whitehall, but they did not have a strong enough appeal with the local populace. To secure his base in London, Dudley played on the cherished sentiments of the ministers of state. When informing Sidney Godolphin of his arrival in Boston, he assured the lord treasurer of the warm welcome accorded him by those who loved the Anglican church and the dependence of the plantations on England.[25]

Many men in Massachusetts apparently did not hold dear either the Church or the government of England, as William Atwood, judge of Admiralty, had discovered when he clashed with members of the council and the judges of the Superior Court of Massachusetts. Some local clergymen even maintained that the people of the Bay colony were not bound in conscience to obey the laws of England, having no representatives there of their own choosing.[26] Discouraged, Atwood left Boston, giving Dudley an opportunity to recommend the appointment of Nathaniel Byfield to the post Wait Winthrop coveted.

Although Dudley and his family found social acceptance with several of the leading families of the Bay colony—one daughter, Rebecca, married a son of Samuel Sewall; another, Ann, later married a son of Wait Winthrop—these connections did little to lessen the hostility against the governor of strong-willed men ambitious for influence and power. Promoting Byfield earned Dudley the emnity of the Mathers. Shortly after Dudley arrived in Boston, Cotton Mather visited him to warn against coming under the influence of Byfield and John Leverett, with whom Increase Mather had been contending for the presidency of Harvard College. The younger Mather himself had been at odds with the founders of the Brattle Street Church, a congregation formed in 1699, whom he accused of imitating the Episcopalians.[27]

The founders of the new church had been as much concerned to establish new rules for church membership and worship as they were to exclude the Mathers from control of the college. William Brattle, now pastor of the church, and John Leverett while tutors at Harvard had opposed some of the elder Mather's ideas when the president had been absent in England. Abandoning the traditional relation of religious experience by prospective members before admitting them to communion, the new church was willing to give to all baptized adult males who contributed to the support of the minister a voice in his selection. If widely followed, this innovation might erode the power of the visible saints, the members in full communion who had hitherto controlled the Congregational churches. For some time in Northampton Solomon Stoddard had been admitting to full communion any person who had behaved without offense and had a competent knowledge of Christian belief. He had not required a narration of the experience of saving grace. The church in Charleston had also gone against convention in allowing all residents to vote on the call to a new minister, Benjamin Colman, a graduate of Harvard who had received his theological training in England and had been ordained by the London Presbytery. On his return to America Colman had published a *Manifesto,* which raised the ire of the Mathers. Admission to full church membership of the visible saints only after satisfactorily recounting a religious experience of saving grace had been critical to the control of the churches and of the government of the Bay colony under old charter since the first decade of settlement, when the General Court had by law made full membership in a Congregational church a requirement for freemanship; only freemen had had the right to vote in the annual election of officials of the corporation, governor, deputy governor, assistants, and deputies from the towns. Increase Mather while agent in London had been unable to persuade the crown to restrict voting to freemen. Under the charter issued in 1691, the franchise was based on a property qualification rather than on a religious test. The visible saints had thus lost their exclusive hold on the vote and provincial office, and the doctrine put forth by Stoddard, Colman, and the Brattles now threatened their control of the churches.

Cotton Mather did not take it kindly when his father was eased out of the presidency of Harvard College in 1700, after the General Assembly had voted that the president must reside in Cambridge. At the same time the council voted to appoint Samuel Willard vice-president without the burdensome residency requirement. Among the councilors so voting was Samuel Sewall, who earlier that year has published his *Selling of Joseph,* an antislavery tract. Two days after the upper house had voted to appoint Willard, Cotton Mather openly berated Sewall when the two met in Richard Wilkin's bookstore for the blatant personal insult to the elder Mather. As Sewall related, Cotton Mather ''talkt very sharply against me as if I had used his father worse than a Neger; spake so loud that people in the street might hear him.'' Mather later complained to Sewall's son, alluding to the antislavery tract, that ''one pleaded much for Negro[e]s, and he had used his father worse than a Negro.''[28]

Both of the Mathers carried their self-esteem high, but despite Cotton Mather's warning, Dudley at first opportunity moved to eliminate from office men who had opposed his coming and to reward others with civil and military commissions. Several of those he appointed—Francis Foxcroft, Nicholas Paige, John Nelson, Benjamin David, Giles Dyer, John and Samuel Legg, Nathaniel Byfield, and Jahleel and Thomas Brenton—had first entered government during the time of the Dominion or had stood out as ''Tories,'' according to their opponents, after the fall of the Andros administration. But Dudley, a dexterous politician, did not limit his appointments to Anglicans, former officials of the Dominion, or men labeled, however erroneously, as Tories, as his rewarding Isaac Addington, John Appleton, and John Leverett illustrated. To chastise his opponents Dudley exercised his veto when the House of Representatives elected the governor's council in 1703. On the ground that they were too poor or superannuated, he refused to accept five men chosen by the assembly: John Saffin, John Bradford, Elisha Cooke (a leader among the adherents of the old charter), Thomas Oakes (Cooke's colleague in England in the attempt to retain the former patent), and Peter Sargeant (a cousin of Sir Henry Ashurst now married to the widow of Sir William Phips). Although the representatives in this first test did not insist that the governor accept all of their choices, Dudley was unhappy with the provision of the charter allowing the deputies from the towns annually to elect the councilors subject merely to the veto of the queen's governor. Under this arrangement, the "best" men in the province could have no share in the civil government. He preferred to have the governor recommend and the monarch appoint members of the upper house. Even before Dudley had exercised his veto on the selection of the councilors, rumor had it in Dissenter circles in London that he had broken in on the "Constitution" of Massachusetts, had violated the charter, and had turned out all of the old justices, especially those he suspected were not well inclined to Episcopacy.[29]

To offset any impression that dissatisfaction with the governor was based on religion, the Mathers undertook a campaign with officials in England on behalf of Sir Charles Hobby, formerly a resident of Jamaica and now a merchant in Boston. In contrast to Dudley, who had now allegedly rendered himself universally unacceptable, Hobby—a vestryman of King's Chapel and a candidate supported by its rector, Samuel Myles—was nonetheless acceptable to the best friends of New England, Cotton Mather assured the earl of Nottingham, an Anglican stalwart. While the Mathers were promoting Hobby's candidacy, Samuel Sewall and his friends were seeking the appointment of Nathaniel Higginson, and Sir Henry Ashurst was pushing for Waitstill Winthrop as governor, or at least deputy governor, in his continued effort to remove "that wicked Hamon," as he referred to Dudley, "from that good people." Ironically, both Dudley and his nemesis appealed to the same officials in England, Robert Harley. Dudley particularly appreciated what ministers of the crown wanted to read. No one, he assured Harley, more than he favored the interest of the Anglican church or loved the government of England and the strict dependence of the colonies. Those who opposed the governor and supported Hobby desired to keep the monarch's administration in Massachusetts indigent and precarious; they would thus govern themselves. The elected councilors on the governor's board of assistants took care to please their master, the people, and forgot their sovereign, the queen.[30] Yet Dudley, a former minister of the Bay colony, was still prepared to defend the Congregational religious establishment from attacks by Quakers in London and in New England.

Although Dudley could veto the selection of councilors—he continued to exclude Elisha Cooke—he had no control over the election of deputies from the towns and the choice of a speaker of the House of Representatives. Excluded from the council, Cooke was elected to the assembly from Boston in 1704, the first time since 1690. He declined to serve but may have played a role from behind the scenes, outside the house. Leadership of the old charter party passed to younger men, among them Cooke's son, also named Elisha, a graduate of Harvard, a physician, landlord, a man generous to the needy and a drinking man without peer—in short, a perfect ward boss. For a time Dr. Thomas Oakes served as Boston's leading deputy in the assembly, along with two other adherents of the elder Cooke. Initially Dudley opposed the choice of Oakes as speaker, but acquiesced in the contention of the deputies that they had the right to choose their own presiding officer and to judge of the election of members of the house. He also accepted their choices for the council, ostensibly because of the need to carry on public business during time of war.[31]

The imperatives imposed by international conflict had great consequences in Massachusetts Bay. To Dudley's misfortune, hardly had he arrived in Boston when war broke out between England and France, and he received orders to have the assembly raise men for the defense of the colony, finance the construction of fortifications on the northern and eastern frontiers, and make a settlement for the salaries of the governor and other officials. His predecessor, the earl of Bellomont, having accepted but occasional presents from the deputies, had left the government without a penny. When pressed to vote a permanent appropriation, the assemblymen refused; they would not even set an annual appropriation for the governor and judges. At the end of each year they voted the justices a mere £50 each. The deputies also begged off voting money to rebuild the fort at Pemaquid on the far eastern frontier. Nonetheless, as French and Indian raids mounted, in 1704 they joined the councilors in asking the crown for aid, stores of war, and funds to cover the expenses incurred by Dudley in raising men, in arming friendly Indians to patrol the frontiers, and in hiring frigates to guard the coasts. Not until rumor came of a massive threat by a thousand French and hostile Indians against New Hampshire and Massachusetts did the deputies vote £23,000 for the defense of the colony, but they still refused to make permanent provision for the governor.[32]

The justices of the superior court of the colony were unhappy with their meager salaries, having complained to the assembly with no success. Isaac Addington resigned, and the others threatened to follow suit; in the meantime, the council refused to consent to Dudley's nominee to fill the vacancy. In 1705, while Dudley was forced to give in on the choice of speaker in order to save the £23,000 appropriation, the deputies again refused to settle fixed salaries or to provide funds for additional fortifications, claiming that the fort on the Piscataqua was not their concern and that the post at Pemaquid beyond the means of the province. As to salaries, it was the native right and privilege of every English subject by consent of Parliament to raise money from time to time and dispose of such sums as the exigencies of their affairs might require. As Dudley saw the situation, the deputies were determined that he must depend on them; they would decide what to give the governor in the last hour of any legislative session, so that he could not prorogue or dissolve the house before they were pleased to rise.[33]

Checked by the deputies in the House of Representatives Dudley still faced the threat of a rival appointed from London. In the spring of 1706 a rumor circulated that Sir Charles Hobby would return to Boston with a commission as governor, "purely on the Whiggish interest," but apparently the supporters of Nathaniel Higginson were induced to sign a petition against Hobby in an effort to keep the position open for their candidate.[34] Dudley himself was not without supporters in the Bay colony, given the patronage at the disposal of a governor and his power to award military contracts to merchants. To support the administration might prove disadvantageous, however—indeed, dangerous; it might raise the suspicion of the parochial-minded country members in the House of Representatives. In 1703 three judges of probate appointed by Dudley had failed to win reelection to the council, and five years later three more of the governor's supporters lost their seats in the wake of a trading scandal. Andrew Belcher and Samuel Appleton narrowly retained their places.

Dudley's alliance with certain merchants provided the grounds for an attack on the governor, as anger mounted at the seeming inability of the administration to deal with the menace of the French and Indians. In the spring of 1706 hostile parties ravaged exposed communities along two hundred miles of frontier from Wells in the east to Deerfield in the west. Not knowing where the raiders would strike, Dudley had assigned 1,500 men to garrison the vulnerable towns. This static, passive defense was both costly and futile; a large, well-coordinated campaign against Port Royal and Quebec would have eliminated the seat of French power. Responding to the trading community whose shipping the French privateers at Port Royal threatened, early in 1707 Dudley organized an expedition from New England of about a thousand men and several vessels to capture the Acadian base. It proved a total failure, as from first to last, the ill-disciplined common soldiers would not obey their officers. The New England force returned to Boston, where the officers and men were met at Scarlet's wharf by a crowd of jeering women who heaped scorn and ridicule on them as they passed along the streets. "Is yor piss-pot charg'd, neighbo^r? So-ho, souse ye cowards, Salute Port-Royal."

Frustrated by the failure to cope with the enemy, the populace also took out its ire on several merchants—John Borland, Samuel Vetch, William Rouse, and Robert Lawson—men accused of trafficking with the enemy under the guise of exchanging prisoners. Some among the opposition to the administration thought Dudley himself had traded with the enemy and accused him of manipulating the trial of the merchants, but the commissioners for plantation affairs dismissed the charges against him as frivolous. Vetch, Borland, and Lawson, convicted of misdemeanors and heavily fined, complained to the crown that the assembly had acted illegally and violated their rights as English subjects by imprisoning them without bail and assuming an excessive power not warranted by the charter, a view the English attorney general shared.[35]

The strongest, most concerted attack against Dudley came that same year when opponents calling themselves inhabitants of New England asked the queen in council to remove him for maladministration. Among those in New and Old England signing the petition were Nathaniel Higginson (Samuel Sewall's candidate for governor), William Partridge (the former deputy governor of New Hampshire), and Thomas Allen (the putative proprietor of New Hampshire). Sir Henry Ashurst probably orchestrated the affair in London. In the summer of 1707 the Plantation Office received a printed piece, *A Memorial of the Present Deplorable State of New England, with the many Disadvantages it lyes under the Male-Administration of . . . Joseph Dudley. . . .* In this tract—put together by Cotton Mather—Dudley and his son, Paul, the provincial attorney general, stood accused of countenancing trade with the French and corrupting justice.[36]

Apparently this "clamour" against Dudley provided an excuse in higher administrative circles to replace him, as the duke of Marlborough and the Earl Godolphin were then contemplating several changes. What Dudley's opponents in the Bay colony did not appreciate was that the removal of Dudley would not mean the appointment of their candidate, whether Higginson or Hobby, for Marlborough had in mind only deserving army officers: Colonel Robert Hunter for New York and Colonel Richard Sutton for Boston. Fortunately for Dudley, Sutton preferred to remain in England and stand for Parliament under the patronage of the duke of Newcastle.[37]

Dudley aggressively aided his own cause, marshaling almost the entire political community in New Hampshire—the council, assembly, militia officers, and the clergy—in support of an address to the queen repudiating the petition presented in London. Some of the signatures on the petition against Dudley—those of Thomas Allen and Stephen Mason—may have been forged. Higginson was in no position to know first-hand the situation in New England, for although a native, he had not lived in Massachusetts for more than a quarter century. In contrast, his brother, others on the council, the clergy of Hampshire County (among them Solomon Stoddard), and the members of the Brattle Street Church all supported the governor.[38] Samuel Sewall had not the courage to stand alone on the council when the board voted the charges leveled against the governor as scandalous. Wait Winthrop seemingly came to terms with Dudley when his son John revealed that he and Anne Dudley were in love. In December 1707 the two were married, and several weeks later the governor restored Winthrop as chief justice.[39] Behind the scenes Wait still encouraged Ashurst to work against the governor, but to no avail as Dudley's friends in London pressed for a quick resolution of the charges against him. Early in 1708 Dudley won a public vindication as the queen in council dismissed the complaints as frivolous.

While an address signed the next month in Boston in support of Dudley by forty prominent men—including Benjamin Colman and William Brattle—did not affect the outcome, it confirmed the support the governor enjoyed among those in public life who did not shun the executive branch and illustrated the factional nature of Massachusetts politics.[40] Later that year Higginson died in

London of smallpox, and Hobby soon came to appreciate that he stood little chance against Dudley. But Sir Henry Ashurst and the Mathers remained implacable in their opposition. When Dudley secured the appointment of John Leverett as president of Harvard College, the Mathers could not contain themselves. Personal animosities and the craving for recognition made for transitory, but strange alliances; the Mathers were joined in opposition by Nathaniel Byfield. Passed over for Wait Winthrop, he had broken with the governor. But Sir Charles Hobby, within a year after he returned to Boston, became reconciled with Dudley and along with Samuel Vetch was named to command regiments being raised for an expedition against Port Royal.

Family alliances, personal animosities, and the rewards and gratification of office may have influenced potential adherents of a court party, ambitious men willing to accept office in the administration, but for the parochial-minded deputies from the outlying towns little changed. In 1708 the House of Representatives voted but £200 for the governor and insisted on naming the provincial treasurer. Nor would they allow any money to issue from the treasury for military expenditures or for the support of government without their permission. They also refused to establish a salary for William Taylor, the deputy governor. A connection of the deceased William Stoughton and an officer who served in an expedition against Port Royal, Taylor had secured the post following the fall of the Whigs in London. Cotton Mather refused to believe the news of Taylor's appointment as lieutenant governor of the Bay colony: ''Twas impossble,'' he exclaimed.[41]

The expanded campaigns undertaken by General Francis Nicholson in 1710 against Port Royal and by General John Hill and Admiral Hovenden Walker the following year against Quebec heightened the need for supplies, men, and money from a provincial government already heavily in debt. To finance the hundreds of men needed to maintain a static defense against French and Indian marauders, the provincial authorities had voted nearly £40,000 by the spring of 1705. By 1711 the colonial treasury was some £120,000 in arrears. Dudley, Nicholson, and other officers commanding the royal forces had to rely on the credit of merchants in New England and in London to launch their offensive operations. In Massachusetts Samuel Vetch, John Borland, and Jonathan Belcher were among the merchants the administration called on to provide supplies. When success crowned the British effort against Port Royal, Vetch became provisional governor and Borland victualer of the garrison there. But the expedition against Quebec ended in disaster, a venture handicapped and delayed through mismanagement in procuring stores for the thousands of troops and seamen and aborted by blundering in navigating the waters of the Gulf of St. Lawrence. Seeking to shift blame, British officers looked to the provincials at Boston. Colonel Richard Hill, brother of the commanding general, condemned the ill disposition, the ''sourness,'' of the people; he found their political doctrines, their hypocrisy and cant, intolerable. While appreciating the need for liberty of conscience he warned the home government that they would grow even more stiff and disobedient, more burdensome and less advantageous to Britain unless their charters were taken up. Those Tories in the ministry who had argued for a greater military effort against the French in America rather than continuing with the Whig strategy of campaigning in Europe needed a scapegoat. They found it in the Bay colony. The failure of the expedition against Canada "is all owing to the avarice or treachery of the godly at New England: the same party are doing all they can in Old England." Dudley sought to correct the impression created by Hill and other British officers: nothing had been commanded in Boston but what was obeyed with all readiness, and the pilots selected to guide the queen's ships had all been experienced men.[42]

With the failure of the offensive to take the seat of French power in North America, Dudley fell back on a static defense for northern New England. Along 200 miles from Wells to Deerfield sixteen towns were fortified and garrisoned, each with forty to fifty men. Roving patrols hoped to intercept any hostile raiders.

Ironically the long-drawn-out conflict with the French had weakened the authority of the royal governor and enhanced the power of the assembly, where men ever suspicious of executive authority and loathe to spend money had allied themselves with dissatisfied aspirants for office to make the House of Representatives a dominant force in government. They circumscribed the executive by limiting the terms of laws, and they authorized taxes and sanctioned Dudley's powers in military affairs only for brief periods, sometimes for a year only, renewing such authority from time to time as they saw the need. They refused him a regular salary, holding him on a short leash and allowing him but a small sum of money voted biennially, sums not even sufficient to meet his incidental expenses. War and the appetite for money it generated led to the consolidation of the powers of the House of Representatives. Employing high-minded rhetoric, denying the claims of the executive as arbitrary, as illegal, or as violating English or charter rights, the deputies erected a comprehensive system of detailed appropriations when framing money bills. Military necessity compelled the governor to accept this development.[43]

The same development occurred in New York, as the home authorities failed to offer the crown's deputy any financial support. The two provincial assemblies during this conflict of 1702–13 were following the path marked out a generation before by the House of Commons during the Third Dutch War under Charles II.

The end of hostilities and the signing of a formal peace treaty in 1713 brought some relief in Massachusetts, but the war had left a heavy financial burden. To ease the strain both on the government and on the trading community, various proposals were put forth. In 1712 the assembly passed and Dudley signed a bill to make paper bills of credit issued by the provincial treasury currency. But with specie in short supply and the bills issued during the war scheduled to be called in and retired, trade would suffer from want of a medium of exchange.

About two hundred traders and merchants—Nathaniel Byfield, the younger Elisha Cooke, Oliver Noyes, and Thomas Lechmere among them—proposed to establish a bank of credit with a charter from the crown to issue up to £300,000 in bills secured by land. Opposed to the scheme, Dudley hoped to have London block it, but his influence in the metropolis was at a low point. Harley (the earl of Oxford) and the Tories were out of power following the death of Anne and the accession of the Hanoverian elector. Dudley's influence was almost nil, and his days in office seemed numbered. Now almost seventy years of age, he had little stomach for a fight.

The prospect of a new administration in the Bay colony as a result of the accession of the Whigs raised the specter of an outsider's presiding over the government of the Bay colony. The Mathers now appreciated that they might do worse than Dudley; Whitehall might impose on them some disbanded colonel, some terrible "Flanderkin"; better a man like Dudley, "a Gentleman of fine Accomplishments," than a boisterous, worldly army officer, "a stranger among us or not of our nation." But Nathaniel Byfield, then in London to promote a charter for the land bank, thought otherwise. Jeremiah Dummer, the provincial agent who had married Dudley's daughter, found Byfield adamant: "He is so excessively hot against Col. Dudley, that he cannot use any body civily that is for him." Byfield put himself up for the post, citing his long residence in New England of more than a quarter of a century and his service as a judge.[44]

The worst fears of the Mathers seemed realized with the announcement that any army officer would replace Dudley. Elizeus Burges was a mercenary office-seeker who had once served as aide to General James Stanhope, now a principal secretary of state in the Whig administration. Hardbitten and profane, Burges was the embodiment of what the Mathers had feared. But Burges wanted money, and he appreciated Dummer's argument that, like Dudley before him, he would find little financial reward as the king's governor of Massachusetts. For a thousand pounds sterling—money put up by the agent and Jonathan Belcher, another New England timber merchant and contractor—Burges resigned the governorship. His successor was another army officer, but one of a different reputation and background. Colonel Samuel Shute was descended from a renowned dissenting family.[45]

The townsmen of New Hampshire, however, had as a deputy governor one of their own. For more than a dozen years under Dudley, the leading families had controlled affairs in the province and had dominated the executive board, the courts, and the militia. John Usher had long been excluded from any real power. To fill vacancies on the council, John Wentworth and Samuel Penhallow in 1714 had recommended three assemblymen; of the trio, two had had the honor of having fathers who had served and died on the board. In view of the virtually autonomous position of the councilors in New Hampshire for over a decade, it was fitting that under the Hanoverian king the post of lieutenant governor went to

George Vaughan, son of William Vaughan. The Commissioners of Trade at the Plantation Office first learned of the appointment of the younger Vaughan on reading the *Gazette*. Protesting, they voiced the same objection Bellomont had raised almost twenty years before against William Partridge: the deputy governor was a millwright by trade, a carpenter of sorts, and "to set a carpenter to preserve the woods, is like setting a wolf to keep sheep." Vaughan had made no attempt to conceal his origins. At the Plantation Office he introduced himself: "I am of ye country of North America in New England."[46] His phrasing was confused but his sentiment clear.

John Usher joined Dudley in retirement, the former governor to his seat in Roxbury, where he died in 1720 at the age of seventy-three, Usher to his estate at Medford, where he passed away four years later at the age of seventy-eight. Shifting factional loyalties and the conflict of personalities had allowed Dudley, once a hated man in Massachusetts, to preside over the government of his native province for a dozen years. But his tenure as the representative of the monarch had been a failure in that during his administration financial control over the civil, judicial, and military establishment had remained in the hands of local leaders entrenched in the House of Representatives. In Connecticut and Rhode Island executive administrations continued strong, but these administrations were divorced from Britain, and succession politics remained entirely a local matter since the inhabitants continued to choose their governor and other officials, provincial officers who successfully put off attempts from Whitehall to supervise the administration of justice and to review local legislation.

Whatever success Dudley enjoyed had resulted from his support of local interests in Massachusetts and New Hampshire and his dexterity as a politician, an ability not shared by his counterpart in New York, Edward Hyde, Lord Cornbury.

CHAPTER 13

New York under Cornbury and Hunter: The Growth of Assembly Power, 1702–15

F OR THE PEOPLE of Massachusetts Bay, the burden of the brutal war against the French and Indians weighed all the more heavily because of the seeming unwillingness of neighboring New Yorkers to assume their share in the common cause. Beset by bitter factional rivalries and mutual suspicions, some men at Manhattan also opted for neutrality.[1] The death of the earl of Bellomont in 1701 had ended the crown's attempt to unite the military forces of the northern colonies under the command of a single official. The English were further weakened when the ineptitude of the various provincial governments led the Iroquois tribes, hitherto a mainstay against the French, to adopt a neutral stance once war broke out between the English and the French in 1702.

Bellomont's administration had not seen the end of the internecine strife which had threatened to bring civil war to New York. Indeed, the early, and open, commitment of the Whig governor to the side of the Leislerian faction had prolonged animosities, as the contests among the councilors who presided over the administration following his death testified. In confirming members of the governor's board of assistants the ministers of state in London preferred men of means, councilors financially secure enough to resist bribes. Unfortunately, in appointing governors to preside at Manhattan—men such as Bellomont and his successor—they selected persons in dire financial straits and left them to depend for support on the provincial assembly.

More than a decade of strife and disorder had embittered the leading men of New York, with the supporters of the dead Jacob Leisler of the so-called Dutch party on the one hand, and on the other, those who had suffered by his assumption of power in 1689, the English or loyalist party or, as they were erroneously labeled by their rivals, the Jacobites. Each side claimed to represent the Protestant cause and to defend the rights of Englishmen. The contest was actually a struggle for power and status. A trimmer such as Robert Livingston, who hoped to follow a moderate course, found that the extremists would allow him little choice. The loyalists had been weakened by the loss of office and seats in the assembly under Bellomont and by the deaths of Stephanus Van Cortlandt and James Graham. At the time Bellomont died in March 1701, the Leislerians held a majority on the council, and the lieutenant governor, John Nanfan, a relative of

Bellomont by marriage, was then absent in Barbados. Over the protests of William Smith (the senior councilor), Robert Livingston, and Peter Schuyler (Livingston's brother-in-law), the four Leislerians—Abraham DePeyster, Dr. Samuel Staats, Robert Walters, and Thomas Weaver (the last, appointed collector of customs by the governor shortly before his death)—took control of the government. With the minority on the board again protesting, they called into session the assembly—a house in which their followers, because of the favors of the governor, predominated—in order to lend credibility to their assumption of power.[2] When Nanfan returned to Manhattan on 19 May, he threw his weight to the Leislerians. Unknown to Nanfan, the ministers of state had decided to send out a new governor, Edward Hyde, Lord Cornbury, the heir to the earl of Clarendon and cousin to Princess Anne.

The dispute between William Smith, the council president, and the Leislerians on the council had convinced the Lords Justices in Council that matters in New York were in such disarray as to make it imperative to hasten the new governor off to his post. However, Cornbury had a "rub put in his Way" which prevented his leaving for his government. In London a mercer had him arrested for failing to pay a debt of £600. Claiming immunity from arrest as a member of Parliament, Cornbury threatened to sue the hapless merchant and asked the lord keeper for a writ of supersedeas. But as the protection the governor-designate claimed was understood by law to extend only during the sitting of Parliament, the lord keeper and the judges all ruled that the matter of privilege for a member was not within their cognizance but was for Parliament to decide.[3] Almost a full year passed before the new governor arrived in Manhattan, and during that interval the Leislerians on the council, with the support of Nanfan, consolidated their position. Two other royal officials appointed earlier in response to a request by Bellomont did arrive in New York in the summer of 1701: Samuel Shelton Broughton as attorney general to succeed James Graham, and William Atwood in place of William Smith as chief justice. Almost immediately Atwood joined the Leislerians, but Broughton was more hesitant, puzzled, it seemed, by the opposing factions, parties distinguishing themselves by national origin, as English and Dutch.[4]

In the assembly that met in August 1701 the Leislerians had held a narrow margin, eleven seats to ten. They elected Abraham Gouverneur speaker over the protests of William Nicoll that as an alien Gouverneur was not eligible for office. For this presumption Nicoll, a member from Suffolk, and Dirck Vessels, a representative from Albany, were expelled. In protest other loyalists from Albany, Westchester, Queens, and Suffolk demanded a dissolution and left the assembly. The Leislerians then expelled them for nonattendance, but the freeholders in several counties persisted in returning delegates opposed to the Dutch party. The rump assembly expelled these newly elected representatives and ordered the provincial attorney general to prosecute them. The sheriff of Suffolk in certifying the return for Nicoll reported that some voters had declared that they were Englishmen and that no alien—that is, a Dutchman—was qualified to represent them.[5] In the reconstituted assembly at least twelve men were Dutch. The Leislerians then proceeded to pass several bills, one to pay the salaries of Nanfan and Atwood, and another to increase the representation of those counties under the control of the Dutch party. With the hold of the faction seemingly secure, on 18 October Nanfan prorogued the house until the following spring. In the interval between sessions the loyalist leaders—Nicholas Bayard, William Nicoll, Rip Van Dam, Philip French, Thomas Wenham, and John Hutchins—organized a campaign through petitions and addresses to the king protesting the actions of the Leislerians as violations of their rights as English subjects. Nanfan and the Leislerians on the council now charged Bayard, Alderman Hutchins, and the others of the ''Jacobite'' party, as they called the loyalists, with a conspiracy to raise sedition and mutiny. They dismissed those in Manhattan who had signed the remonstrances as mainly soldiers inveigled by false information, common seamen, sojourners, boys, and aliens; they, the Leislerians, were the true Protestant subjects, the party supporting the king.[6] In fact, however, among the men signing the protests were prominent, well-to-do merchants and landowners, Dutch and Huguenot as well as English.

To eliminate the opposition's leadership, Nanfan and the Leislerian councilors had Bayard and Hutchins committed for treason under the act for quieting disorders, the very law used in 1691 to condemn Jacob Leisler. When Attorney General Broughton objected that the evidence to sustain the charge was insufficient, Nanfan dismissed him. Legal authorities in England later upheld the provincial attorney: the *form* of the indictments against Bayard and Hutchins was proper, but the evidence against them had not warranted their arraignment. But early in 1702 Atwood, the Leislerian supporter whose appointment as chief justice Bellomont had secured, played a key role when Weaver undertook to prosecute the two loyalists. Atwood and Weaver were openly partisan. Weaver insisted that, as prosecutor, he had a right to sit with the grand jury and that it examine no witnesses but those he thought proper. When four of the jury objected, Atwood dismissed them, notwithstanding that they had already been sworn, and appointed four others. Only eleven of the nineteen men who served on the panel, including the foreman, John DePeyster, brother of Abraham DePeyster, endorsed the return, *Billa Vera*. When counsel for the accused insisted that the prisoners could not be put on trial because the indictment had not been duly found, Atwood rejected the argument: in this instance the grand jury was but an inquest of office, and although the bill was found by fewer than twelve jurors, it was sufficient to try the accused. Weaver obtained convictions against Bayard and Hutchins, and Atwood sentenced both men to death. Several other loyalist leaders fled to New Jersey when a grand jury consisting entirely of Dutchmen brought in four more indictments, including one against Broughton for neglecting his duty as attorney general in not prosecuting Bayard and Hutchins, and another against Robert Wenham for signing a petition stating that Lord Cornbury was to succeed Nanfan.

In April 1702 the rump assembly met. Nanfan accepted several bills to strengthen partisan control, to weaken the opposition by limiting the commercial privileges hitherto enjoyed by New York City, and to pay the expenses incurred by the Leislerians during their tenure in power a dozen years before.[7]

The arrival of Cornbury on 3 May put a stop to the farce.

That very day, coincidently, a principal secretary of state signed a royal letter suspending the execution of the sentences against Bayard and Hutchins: the grounds on which they had been indicted had been insufficient, and the Leislerians on the council had attempted to force Hutchins to accuse himself.[8]

Edward Hyde, Lord Cornbury, was not quite what some men in New York had wanted, despite the favorable assessment of William Penn, several of the Quakers in Pennsylvania, and even the inveterate Whig Sir Henry Ashurst. Robert Livingston had long played the uncertain game of politics and finance in New York. With the threat of war imminent in 1701, he had laid down for the Plantation Office the qualities needed in a governor to provide for the defense of the province: he must be a soldier, a man who feared God and hated covetousness, one who would administer impartially without taking sides.[9] Never did a man meet these qualifications less well than Lord Cornbury, as events would show. Officials in Whitehall in addition to Livingston had been concerned to end the disruptive factionalism in New York and to provide for the security of the colony. Through contractors in London and their correspondents in Manhattan they provided £1,250 sterling for the subsistence of the depleted four companies of troops stationed to protect the colony as well as additional arms. They also ordered Cornbury to put an end to the animosities that had so long divided the people and weakened the province and to treat all men impartially. Partisans of both factions were to be included on the council.[10]

The old animosities would fade, but slowly. As was appreciated in Manhattan even before Cornbury left England, the ''knott of Lords whereof'' the earl of Bellomont had been one was now gone, dismissed from office, or dead. The Tories at the helm in London would now hear all complaints, one loyalist confidently expected, and ''do equal justice.'' Within a week after Cornbury arrived in the province, he had declared himself in favor of the English party; he then moved quickly against the ''troublesome spirits'' to bolster the English merchants and the more prominent among the Dutch residents. The governor turned out Gouverneur as recorder of the city and appointed Ebenezar Willson sheriff. As a majority on the common council, the loyalists were able to admit soldiers of the garrison to the freedom of the town as voters. Striking at the leadership of the Leislerian faction, Cornbury suspended from the council without hearing Atwood, Thomas Weaver, DePeyster, Staats, and Robert Walters. The collector, Weaver, forced to post bond of £4,000 while his accounts were being inspected, fled with Atwood to Philadelphia, where both took ship for England. To carry out the duties of receiver and collector of the customs Cornbury appointed Caleb Heathcote and Robert Wenham.[11] He also restored William Smith as chief justice, but later that year a warrant signed by Nottingham arrived from London appointing Dr. John Bridges. Bridges died shortly after, and to fill the vacancy Cornbury named Roger Mompesson, a lawyer of Lincoln's Inn and sometime member of Parliament for Southampton who had been persuaded by William Penn to go to America. Cornbury's father, the earl of Clarendon, then obtained for Mompesson a commission as judge of admiralty. To the Leislerians Abraham and John DePeyster, brothers who still communicated with each other in Dutch, the appointment of an official from London, "a stranger," was ominous; it was even more so when Thomas Byerly became collector and receiver of the revenue and George Clark provincial secretary and deputy auditor, a post Abraham De-Peyster had once held.[12] In recommending men for the provincial council Cornbury supported the younger members of the English party: Kiliaen Van Renssaeler, Philip French, Stephen DeLancey, William Lawrence, John Barbarie, and Adolph Philipse.

The new governor was aware of his predecessor's efforts to manipulate the legislature—of his appointments of sheriffs and justices of the peace, officials essential to controlling returns to the assembly.[13] Nonetheless Cornbury's greatest political blunder was to allow the leaders of the assembly to develop the lower house as an institutional center of resistance to the royal governor. Ironically, William Nicoll—the veteran from Suffolk, one of the loyalists whom Bellomont had dismissed from the council, and the man the Leislerians had ejected from the assembly in 1701—was to lead the struggle against Cornbury. Returned to the assembly the next year, he was elected speaker, a post he held for the next fifteen years.

Cornbury faced two long-standing, related problems at the outset of his administration: public finances and the defense of the colony. In providing for the needs of the province his predecessors had incurred debts amounting to more than £12,000. The royal government in London itself had compromised governors and those who had advanced them funds. Robert Livingston had to wait for years to be reimbursed for the money he had advanced to several governors and expended on provisions for the soldiers and the Five Nations. Early in Cornbury's administration, Livingston undertook another voyage to England seeking relief. Nanfan himself had been under heavy pressure from creditors in New York for nonpayment of bills he had drawn on the Treasury in London for money borrowed to subsist the soldiers.

Sources for public funds were limited in New York. In 1703 Thomas Byerly attempted to compile a roll for the collection of quitrents on land—two shillings, six pence per one hundred acres—owed the crown. Most of the landowners had not paid this tax since they had taken up their holdings.[14] Revenue from rates levied on real property by the provincial assembly depended on the willingness of the elected representatives to tax land, a risky business since the bulk of the voters were landholders. The base for revenue from duties on imported commodities shrank as trade languished, a consequence of the perils of wartime commerce, for French privateers were preying on vessels carrying flour and grain to the West Indies as well as on transatlantic trade. Boston merchants willing to offer more for specie also took away trade from Manhattan.[15]

When Cornbury arrived in the colony, he found the forts at Albany and Schenectady in ruinous condition, Albany and Manhattan with few stores, and the four companies of royal troops stationed in the province each considerably below their full complement of officers and men. Not having been called out or exercised for many years, the militia was also in a deplorable state. Cornbury instituted training for the units in Ulster and Albany, the two frontier counties, as well as for the militia of the city. The neighboring provinces had been less than enthusiastic in support. Maryland had furnished but £300 of its quota of £650, while the Quaker-dominated assembly of Pennyslvania refused any contribution; officials of Connecticut and Rhode Island consistently put off the governor of New York, referring the matter to authorities in London. In Manhattan the assemblymen initially voted £1,800 for the maintenance of about 180 men, but only for a limited time, and coupled that grant with the demand that they have the same powers as those of the English House of Commons. As the governor saw it (and injudiciously warned the house in 1704), holding assemblies was not one of the privileges of the inhabitants of New York, but merely a favor granted by the crown. When the assemblymen persisted in coupling financial grants with other legislation Cornbury found offensive to the prerogative of the monarch or to the authority of the governor, he adjourned the house. The assemblymen persisted, even refusing to allow the council to amend money bills. Cornbury pointedly reminded the ministers of state that James, duke of York, as proprietor and later as king, had appointed governors to administer the public affairs of the colony without elected assemblies. The crown might do so again, as was the queen's right, especially when the assembly proved refractory.[16]

In November 1704 Cornbury dissolved the assembly and issued writs for elections, but for the most part the freeholders returned the same men. Again William Nicoll of Suffolk sat in the speaker's chair. When voting to raise £1,700 for the defense of the frontiers, the assemblymen insisted on nominating a public treasurer, one responsible to the house and not to the officers of the queen, a provision directly contrary to the governor's instructions from Whitehall. Moreover, they voted money for a limited time to be expended as they specified in the appropriation bill. Certificates by officers of the militia or by officials of New York City or Albany would be sufficient authority to the treasurer, Richard Willett, to pay out money. This procedure bypassed the governor and receiver general. Cornbury's instructions specifically required him not to suffer any public funds to be issued other than by warrant under his hand and with the advice of the council. The assemblymen responsible for the tactic to circumvent the governor were Robert French, a man who had often declared that he would prefer no government at all; Nicoll, the speaker; and Thomas Codrington and Thomas Garton, the last two notorious for opposing any measure originating with the executive. Both the Dutch and the English were obstreperous, particularly the townsmen of Long Island, Independents in religion who had originally come from Massachusetts and Connecticut.[17]

The Independents in the Long Island communities were especially sensitive to the stance taken by Cornbury when an itinerant Presbyterian divine, Francis Makemie, published a narrative of the harrassment he had experienced for preaching without first obtaining a license. What exactly passed between Cornbury and Makemie is not entirely clear. In a published pamphlet the cleric claimed that the governor and the acting provincial attorney general contended that the English Act of Toleration of 1689 did not extend to the colonies. Nonetheless, toleration as it was then understood and practiced did not exempt dissenting ministers from obtaining a license from the authorities to preach. But the impression created by Makemie's tract among the Congregationalists and other Dissenters in New York and New England was that Cornbury was striking at freedom of religious conscience—no crime, according to such Puritans as Cotton Mather, as long as Congregational orthodoxy was upheld. In his pamphlet Makemie printed several pages of conversation verbatim.[18] His must have been a prodigious memory. Cornbury left only a summary of his talk with the Presbyterian divine in which he and the attorney general claimed that *if*, as Makemie contended, the English Act of Conformity did not extend to America, neither did the Act of Toleration.[19] Makemie could not have it both ways, claiming that the Act of Uniformity did not extend to America but that the Act of Toleration did even though there was no explicit declaration to this effect.

Almost any governor would have had a difficult time in New York in the face of the limitations imposed by the crown, the mounting public debt, and economic distress. The death and retirement of the leaders of the two contending factions, Leislerian and loyalist, eased tensions between the two parties somewhat. The English faction no longer needed to close ranks against their opponents, now reduced in power and no longer able to mount an effective threat. With each group fragmented, neither was able to put through a positive program other than to fulfill campaign promises to lower taxes and to strip executive officials of control over expenditures. But Cornbury by his personal behavior contributed to the executive's loss of influence and to the determination of the assemblymen to oppose him. When Robert Livingston returned to America from England in 1707, he was shocked by the governor's conduct. Relying on a few sycophants, Cornbury was wholly addicted to his own pleasures and to enriching himself. Evenings were spent with the bottle. So swollen was the public debt that a decade of appropriations, even if voted, would not clear it. Complaints were frequent that Cornbury had converted public money to his own use and that he browbeat the councilors and would not allow them freedom of debate.[20]

Matters between the assemblymen and the governor remained at an impasse as the leaders in the house refused to allow Cornbury or any official responsible to him any control over expenditures. In 1706 the Plantation Office had been willing to compromise: when the assembly voted extraordinary supplies for particular purposes, such as military operations, these appropriations would not be considered part of the monarch's standing and constant revenue. Hence the representatives might be permitted to name their own treasurer, and for such expenditures he might be accountable to the house as well as to the governor. [21] This proposed formula remained a bone of contention in New York for years to come.

In London ministerial opinion was running against Cornbury, but with party strife between Whigs and Tories intense, some ministers of state were averse to calling him home. Yet as against the claims of the candidates sponsored by the duke of Newcastle and Marlborough's colonels for patronage, Cornbury had little to offer. In 1707 the commissioners for plantation affairs rebuked him for unfairly prosecuting a vessel he had charged with violations of the acts of trade and for interfering with royal customs officials. By 1708 Cornbury's blatant disregard of orders became too much for the Whigs, then in power. In March the earl of Sunderland informed the Plantation Office that the queen was appointing John, Lord Lovelace, governor of New York, and in June the secretary of state notified Cornbury of his recall.

Cornbury ended his career as governor of New York as he had begun it: a man hounded by creditors. On 18 May 1708 an act passed early in his administration for supporting government by revenue from import duties had expired. Even before the expiration of the law, such was the reduced state of trade that the Customs House in Manhattan did not have sufficient money when William Anderson, sheriff of New York, presented two warrants from the governor for £50: not more than £32 had been taken in since the previous Christmas. As to quitrents, the receiver general had never collected more than £20 a year since taking office. [22] Cornbury owed £10,333 to ten merchants of the town, among them Rip Van Dam, John Cruger, and Stephen DeLancey. On 12 January 1708/9, after the arrival of Lovelace, DeLancey initiated legal action to have Cornbury jailed for not paying his debts. Other creditors immediately followed suit. That evening Peter Fauconnier, a crony of the former governor, called on the irate Huguenot merchant to dissuade him from prosecuting, but with no success. When DeLancey, who had extended Cornbury credit for over three years without the governor's ever repaying him a farthing, had learned that Cornbury had had the timerity to order goods from another merchant, promising cash, he had taken legal action. Certain royal officials who were also unhappy with Cornbury— Mompesson, George Clark, the deputy auditor, and John Johnson—had urged DeLancey to this step. In despair, the displaced governor wrote to his father, the earl of Clarendon, to have the queen send for him. She might also grant him the wherewithal to live, for Cornbury did not have £200 in the world. "A Porter in the streets of London is a happier man than a Governour in America." [23]

Cornbury's enemies in London saw in his successor a man of decidedly different qualities. Both William Penn and Sir Henry Ashurst thought Lovelace sober, good-tempered, honest, and honorable. Let the men of New York and New Jersey use him well, Penn counseled, and let the Friends be among the first to congratulate the new governor on his arrival and to recommend themselves by a just regard for his good qualities.[24] Lovelace soon gave promise of fulfilling the expectations of Penn and Ashurst. In the spring of 1709 he secured from the assembly a grant of £6,000 to defray the charges of an intended expedition against Canada, although the money was to be paid to and issued by the provincial treasurer, an official responsible to the assembly. The rapprochement between legislature and administration was short-lived. A few days later, on 6 May, Lovelace died, much to the regret of Lewis Morris, the imperious political manipulator of New Jersey and Westchester. No better man had ever come to preside over the government of the colony, he confided to Secretary Sunderland. In the future a governor the equal of Lovelace must demonstrate to the colonists that the queen's prerogative was not inconsistent with the liberties of the people, but was rather absolutely necessary for the preservation of their freedoms and their property. Seeking to capitalize on the situation Morris recommended as a successor his neighbor in Westchester, Caleb Heathcote, should the ministers be willing to appoint a local man.[25]

But Marlborough's influence was yet too strong for a local candidate to be considered; he had prevailed on Anne to reserve all appointments of governors in the royal colonies to officers of the army. In September 1709 the choice fell on Colonel Robert Hunter. Initially selected to preside over the administration in Virginia, Hunter had fallen captive to French privateers, but had recently been exchanged. With Lovelace's death Marlborough had decided that Hunter was needed in New York. "He is an honest man, and is a good officer." But something more was involved in the selection. Pressed by the mercantile community of London, Halifax and Somers had proposed a massive campaign against the Spanish in the West Indies with several thousand men to be raised in Jamaica, Massachusetts, and New York, where Hunter, as governor of the two North American provinces, would provide the necessary number of volunteers. Fortunately for Hunter, Marlborough did not agree to the harebrained scheme.[26] The governor would have trouble securing men and money for more immediate military objectives.

The appointment of a new governor presented a potential opportunity for New Yorkers out of office to recoup their political fortunes through the favor of royal patronage. William Atwood, dismissed as chief justice by Cornbury, now submitted a long memorial on behalf of the old Leislerian stalwarts who had suffered under the former governor: Abraham DePeyster, Robert Walters, and Samuel Staats. In bitter, violent language he attacked the chiefs of the English party: Kiliaen Van Rensselaer, Robert Wenham, John Barbarie, and Rip Van Dam were united in illegal trade; old William Peartree was a nonentity managed

by the others. But only two of the five Leislerians Atwood recommended—
Staats and Walters—were named to the council in Hunter's commission.[27] By
1709 the assembly, not the council, was the crucial arena and the feud between
the Leislerians and the loyalists had been overshadowed by the campaign William Nicoll, Robert French, Thomas Codrington, and Thomas Garton waged to
establish the power of the house they now led. Here the new governor would meet
his most serious challenge.

Colonel Robert Hunter was perhaps the best qualified man ever sent out to
govern in English America. A soldier, but a cultured man and a companion of
prominent literary figures such as Swift and Addison, Hunter enjoyed good relations with men in both party camps in London. He had served as Marlborough's
aide-de-camp and was on good terms with Robert Harley, the man who would
replace Godolphin at the Treasury and Marlborough in the affections of the
queen. Of particular significance for Hunter's career in America, he enjoyed
some measure of financial independence; he had married a wealthy heiress.[28]
Better than other governors he might hold out against parsimonious assemblymen in America.

By 1709 William Nicoll and his colleagues among the younger loyalists
who had come to dominate the New York assembly had already laid down the key
elements in their program. The previous May the law providing revenue for the
administration had expired, and no provision as yet had been made to pay the
debts of the government. Indeed, four years after the death of the former governor, Charlotte, Lady Lovelace, was still importuning the crown for the payment of warrants chargeable to the revenue of New York.[29] At the time of Hunter's appointment little money had actually come into the provincial treasury from
quitrents, the only standing source for crown revenue in the colony. Only a law
enacted by the local legislature would make it feasible to compile an accurate rent
roll. On the issue of taxes voted by the assembly, rural landowners and city
merchants were at odds: traders such as Jacobus Van Cortlandt and Stephen
DeLancey sought to avoid duties on goods they imported; leaders from the rural
counties such as Samuel Mulford and William Nicoll, who represented the farmers on Long Island, sought to avoid taxes on land. Although each side differed on
taxes, they agreed on the need to limit and control public expenditures. Despite a
fairly high turnover in the assembly—at least twelve of the twenty-two representatives chosen in 1709 and nine of those returned the next year were newly
elected—the house remained committed to spending as little as possible. When
campaigning for election, assembly leaders promised to vote no new taxes and to
vest control of public expenditures in the house rather than in appointed officials.
The trend discernible during the administration of Cornbury—in part, a reaction
to his obnoxious behavior—continued. At the same time the old animosities
based on personal antagonisms, ethnic loyalties, and party labels were fading.
New alignments were emerging as the merchants of New York City and the
descendants of the farmers who had migrated to New York from New England

contested for control in the assembly to limit the power of the administration, to achieve economy in government, and to reduce restrictions on trade.[30]

The problems facing Robert Hunter when he arrived in America in June 1710 were numerous. In addition to administering the affairs of New Jersey, with its recalcitrant Anglican councilors, he had to manage the assembly of New York, placate the disgruntled Iroquois, raise forces for a campaign against Canada, and settle some hundreds of German Palatines on the frontier in an ambitious scheme to provide naval stores. The demands on his time and energy, his patience and skill, would be great. Almost immediately he was fortunate to find in Lewis Morris an able, ambitious man whose aristocratic demeanor and cultivated tastes matched his own and who saw in the governor the road to power and influence.

That summer Hunter met with the assembly in Manhattan and recommended bills for settling a revenue, defending the frontiers, regulating the militia, and restoring the credit of the government. Initially he found the assemblymen in an ''indifferent humour,'' but after a time they sent for an estimate of the yearly expenses of the provincial government and then passed two bills, one for taxing lands and another for laying an excise for one year on liquors sold at retail, a duty on ships' tonnage, and a tax on chimneys, the money so raised to be paid to the provincial treasurer and applied to such uses as the assembly stipulated. No arguments by the governor would dissuade them on this last point. As to the ordinary expenses of government, the leaders in the assembly now began to strike off items. When Lewis Morris asked them to give the governor's views some credence, they expelled him for scandalously vilifying the honor of the house. Moreover, the sums they voted fell far short of the amount needed by the administration. Discounting Hunter's pleas, the leaders cited the poverty of the inhabitants, a consequence of financing earlier unsuccessful campaigns and the misuse of funds by Cornbury. They treated the governor with open contempt.

Hunter prorogued the assembly and urged the home government to have Parliament provide for revenue. Such a step, if followed, might well have basically altered the course of political development in America, but the Plantation Office was not ready to go that far at that time, content merely to recommend that the governor warn the assemblymen that if they continued to encroach on the prerogatives of the crown when settling salaries for royal officials and in neglecting to provide for necessary public expenditures, an act of Parliament would follow. To this end the commissioners for plantation affairs drafted an Act for granting Revenue to Her Majesty to arise within the Province of New York in America for the support of that Government by a duty on imports, a measure Attorney General Edward Northey and Solicitor General Robert Raymond approved.[31]

The threat, if it was that, had little effect. During March and April of 1711 weeks passed with no quorum in the assembly as the representatives straggled into Manhattan. At last fourteen of the twenty-two deputies were present, but at that point Nicoll became involved in a dispute with the governor over procedural matters. Finally Hunter went off to conduct business in New Jersey. The assemblymen at Manhattan then claimed he had thereby dissolved the house. In Hunter's view they were now assuming to themselves another power belonging to the queen's governor, and on the advice of the council, he dissolved the assembly rather than suffer the house to do so itself. As a consequence, government officials were without funds, the forts on the frontier in a ruinous state; but the French and their Indian allies yet remained a threat. Hunter appeared at a loss as to what to do; to secure a quiet government in New Jersey was a relatively easy task — remove a few obstreperous councilors — but matters with the assembly at Manhattan were "past all possible remedey on this Side" of the Atlantic. Hunter regretted the dearth of men of substance, sense, and moderation who might offer themselves for election to the assembly. "Here is the finest air to live upon in the Universe," he later confided to Jonathan Swift, "and if our trees and birds could speake and our assembly men be silent the finest conversation too."[32]

But from London the governor received nothing but platitudes and orders to procure three months' provisions for an overland expedition under General Francis Nicholson to be carried out in conjunction with a seaborne attack on Canada. The governors of New York, Rhode Island, Connecticut, and Pennsylvania were to raise 2,000 men for Nicholson's attempt against Montreal. Hunter had no confidence in his ability to persuade assemblymen who stood for office on no other pledge than to save public money or to oppose the administration. He was overly pessimistic. In July 1711 the house voted to support the expedition, although some grumbled that the quota of 600 men allotted to New York was too high. Of the contingent raised in the colony, 350 men were "Christians," 150 were Indians from Long Island, and 100 were recently arrived Palatines. To help defray the cost of the campaign Hunter drew bills on the British Treasury for over £24,000. Getting the expedition underway depended on procuring provisions, some from distant Virginia, but the only vessel immediately available was the *Feversham*, and she was left almost unmanned by death, sickness, and desertion among her crew. The local populace not only encouraged but also protected deserting sailors. When rioters who freed deserters from the custody of the constables were prosecuted, juries would not convict them, further evidence, coupled with the claim of the assembly to all of the privileges of the House of Commons and more, of the erosion of the powers of the crown.

To Hunter it was clear that time had come for the queen by royal letter — the word of a governor passed for nothing — to put the representatives in mind that all such privileges as they claimed, they held by her special grace and for no longer than they used them in the interest of the crown and the support of its government. Should the elected element grow dominant in the colonies, the provinces would become independent national states, Hunter warned. He found the situation distressing even after the war was winding down following the disaster which struck the Walker expedition in the Gulf of St. Lawrence and the aborting of the overland campaign against Montreal under Nicholson. The provincial administration was still without means of support, and the extraordinary expenses now fell on the governor as the frontiers were still exposed and the once friendly Indians, now neglected by the English, were growing "saucy." The assemblymen were resolved to give only what they pleased and when. "They may starve me but never *oblidge* me to compliment them with her Maj[es]ty[']s rights or transgress her Instructions."[33] So Hunter pledged. On two points the assemblymen remained adament—settling salaries and the custody of public money—thus reducing the governor and council to ciphers.

In response to the provincial assembly's long-standing refusal to make adequate provision for the support of government, the Plantation Office in November 1711 brought the matter to the attention of the higher ministers of state. But with no success. With no promise of aid from Britain, Hunter took the initiative and attempted to piece together a coalition in New York, to duplicate an apparently successful tactic used before in New Jersey. He saw the task as difficult, for in his view the provinces were blessed with few men of substance and ability; Lewis Morris was one of the few exceptions. In both New York and New Jersey Morris and the governor sought to form a party committed to satisfying the immediate needs of the administration.

The task was easier in New Jersey than in Manhattan, for in the former proprietary Morris and his friends were well entrenched and the opposition limited for the most part to an Anglican ring, a clique which had supported the discredited former governor, Lord Cornbury. But by building a court faction within the assembly, both in New York and New Jersey, Morris and Hunter were pursuing a potentially dangerous course. Unwittingly, perhaps, they were laying the foundations for the further rise in power of the elected element in the provincial governments. Morris was eager to purge the New Jersey council of the men who had opposed the proprietors, to invest the Scottish landlords with authority over sales of land and the collection of rents, and to protect the Quakers of the western division, mainstays in the assembly bloc he hoped to forge and to control. Hunter played his part by appointing new magistrates and sheriffs so as to elect at least one-half of the representatives to the house. In London Paul Docminique of the West Jersey Society and Joseph Ormston, also eager to be rid of their rivals, Colonel Daniel Coxe and Peter Sonmans, backed Hunter and Morris. William Dockwra was now suffering from a fatal illness, and Cornbury (now earl of Clarendon) was out of favor at court. The tenuous alliance in New Jersey between the Nicolls patentees and the clique of London proprietors headed by Dockwra, strained by Sonmam's attempt to enforce proprietary rights in the eastern division, then dissolved. The West Jersey Society, having decided to divest itself of its holdings in America, instructed its agent to sell its lands to the highest bidders. Morris used the opportunity to enrich himself and to reward local farmers.[34]

In New Jersey Hunter played an active role in favor of the Quakers and Scottish proprietors against the Anglicans. In 1711 the coalition put through the assembly resolutions condemning an address to the queen promoted a few years before by the Anglicans on the council as a false and scandalous representation on the assembly, expelled some members for having signed the document, and voted others who had supported it as incapable of holding office until they recanted. These resolutions had been concerted by Hunter with his advisers, initially drawn up by George Willocks, revised by Morris and John Johnston, and engrossed by John Barclay before being brought into the assembly. The house then passed them *pro forma*. At meetings of the council Morris, Thomas Gordon, Thomas Gardiner, and Hunter would brook no opposition, often interrupting and silencing the Anglican dissidents on the board.[35] The rewards for Hunter and Morris were immediate: an appropriation of £5,000 and 200 men for the expedition against Canada. And in 1713 the assembly voted a bill for the support of government for two years, but the price was the governor's approval of another measure to secure the right of Quakers to hold office and to serve on juries.[36] In acquiescing to the demands of the assembly, Hunter and Morris were thus acknowledging its authority, power other men with different objectives might later use against an administration.

Robert Hunter and Lewis Morris would employ in New York the same tactics they had used with apparent success in New Jersey to build a political bloc in the assembly—a court faction—by juggling commissions for justices of the peace, sheriffs, and the slate of officials dealing with Indian tribes. But in deferring to the leaders in the assembly over matters of patronage, the governor was making it possible for them to take control into their own hands and further to weaken the power of the deputy of the monarch. Nonetheless, Morris, the governor's chief lieutenant, with the assistance of Caleb Heathcote, Dr. John Johnson, David Jamison, and even two of the old Leislerians who had received Hunter's favors, Robert Walters and Samuel Staats, began to cultivate a party among the representatives in the lower house.

In March 1713 the governor dissolved the assembly, and in the ensuing elections he and Morris set out to influence the voters directly. In a tract, *An Address to the Inhabitants and Freeholders of Westchester County,* Morris appealed to the landowners to support taxes on trade, thus shifting the burden to consumers who purchased imported goods rather than contenting themselves with using locally made commodities. Hunter joined in the campaign with *To All Whom These Presents May Concern,* a printed piece in which, after offering to share with the assembly control of the royal receiver of customs, he warned that the ministry in London was considering appealing to Parliament to impose a financial settlement on the New Yorkers.[37] Indeed, in May of that year the queen in council approved a representation from the Plantation Office recommending that a bill be brought into Parliament for granting a revenue in New York for the crown for the support of government. But little time remained in the parliamentary session; it was to end on 1 July and not meet again until 16 February 1714. With partisan feelings running high, the conduct of business at Westminster was hampered. As Samuel Vetch reported from London to one New Yorker, the "violence of partys taking up almost every body's time here." In Manhattan Hunter was active to promote the election of delegates favorable to his administration, but only five of the twenty-two members returned were new to the assembly. The leaders of the opposition had all won reelection; the men inclined toward the governor had been rejected merely for supporting him. Disappointed, Hunter could only look forward to another speedy dissolution and a general alteration of the commissions of peace and militia, so that ill-disposed men might not use the authority of the queen against her.[38]

As before, the issue of control of financial appropriations was critical. In his address at the opening session on 27 May 1713 Hunter warned the assemblymen that they could not lodge money appropriated for the support of government in the hands of any other officials than the officers appointed by the queen or divert payments to any other channel than that prescribed in the queen's instructions, a warrant issued by the governor with the consent of the council. Hunter now renewed the offer to have the royal receiver general be responsible jointly with the treasurer appointed by the assembly, but he refused to allow the representatives to determine salaries of officials appointed by the crown: the queen was the sole judge of the rewards of her servants.[39] News arriving from London gave Hunter some assurance against opponents who had claimed that his position was weak, that he had little support in the ministry, for the home government had approved his nominees for the council in neighboring New Jersey. More significant was the news that Parliament might intercede to impose taxes for New York. In the provincial assembly the majority now seemed inclined to make a token concession: not a long-term appropriation, but a measure for the support of government for one year with part of the money voted to be lodged with the receiver appointed by the crown and the remainder with the treasurer named by the assembly, to be paid out as it designated.

With the harvest season approaching, the governor granted a request for an adjournment.

By the spring of 1714, when the assembly again took up an appropriations bill, it was evident that the measure enacted the previous year had brought in only about £1,800 in local currency. No funds were available to retire the long-standing public debt.[40] Claims on the provincial government went back many years to the Protestant insurgency in 1689; Leislerians sought payment for an expedition initiated some years before against Canada, loyalists demanded compensation for property confiscated by the insurgents, workmen and militiamen sought their wages, and various creditors demanded payment for money advanced to various governors. The legislative session proved a lengthy one, beginning in March and not ending until September. Morris took the lead in putting together a bill for discharging the public debt. The measure set the colony's financial arrears at £27,680 and provided for payment in bills of credit to be retired periodically over twenty years by an excise on liquor sold at retail.

Another critical issue remained unsettled. On 2 April Samuel Mulford, an ally of the speaker and also a representative from Suffolk, to prevent misappropriation of money as allegedly had occurred in the past proposed to place all funds voted with the treasurer chosen by the assembly. The treasurer would disburse money as the elected representatives stipulated. In the final draft of the bill Morris worked out what seemed on the surface to be a compromise: the assembly would dispose of the money it voted and lodged with the provincial treasurer, while the governor and council would determine how money held by the royal receiver would be spent. Compromise this was not; by denying any funds to the official of the crown, the assembly could reduce his office to a nullity, diminish any discretionary power by the governor and his board, and enhance its own authority over finances by entrusting the money it raised to the provincial treasurer.

Later that session the house passed a bill for supporting the government for the coming year, almost the same measure as it enacted in 1713 for imposing duties on wine, rum, and other goods imported into the colony from Europe — but the new bill left out the duty on rum, the only commodity Hunter thought worthwhile, since the province was already overstocked with wine and other European imports. He expected to have to return begging to the assembly to make good an anticipated shortfall.[41]

Hunter assented to the bill for paying the public debt; although it carried a clause suspending its operation until approved by the crown, the governor had capitulated. Why?

Queen Anne had died early in August, about four weeks before Hunter accepted the bill for funding the public debt, but her health had been precarious and her demise expected, so that the tenure of the Tory ministers who had hitherto sustained Hunter had not been expected to survive the accession of the Hanoverian elector as king of Great Britain. Hunter's London friends had kept him apprised of the situation. For some time he had borne resentment against the ministry for relegating him to an inferior role. While Frances Nicholson, a man who had never commanded troops in the field, had received command of the overland campaign against Montreal, Hunter, a brigadier with a distinguished record in battle, had been relegated to the drudgery of collecting provisions for the force Nicholson would lead. To make his humiliation all the greater, the bills he had drawn for the service were returned from London protested. They remained unpaid, a threat to his financial position. To make matters still worse, Nicholson, a man Hunter regarded as mad, had arrived at Manhattan with a commission to inspect the governor's accounts. Until these were settled he was left to beg his bread from a hard-hearted assembly. So Hunter described his situation. Although the queen on a representation from the Plantation Office — a representation Hunter himself had inspired — had ordered a bill to be laid before Parliament for settling a revenue in New York for the life of the monarch, Hunter's friends had warned him that it might be better for him if Parliament did not pass such a measure. A financially secure office might tempt the ministers of state to reward a favorite placeman with Hunter's post. To the governor it seemed the Tory ministry had betrayed him: it had consistently refused his pleas for help. He remonstrated with the long-time secretary at the Plantation Office: William Popple knew well that the parliamentary bill for revenue in New York was never intended to be passed.[42]

The Whig administration under George I, a ministry and a monarch occupied with the problems of the royal succession and heavily oriented toward European affairs, also capitulated in accepting a representation from the Plantation Office on the bill passed in New York for public revenue. The Commissioners of Trade saw no reason not to confirm, as Hunter had asked, the act of the assembly for the public debt. Did the governor, they wrote, see any prospect that the assembly would settle a fixed revenue for the support of government?[43]

The death of Anne and the succession of George I had required the dissolution of the old assembly in New York. When a newly elected house met in 1715, its members were roughly divided for and against a long-term revenue for the support of the provincial government. Initially the members devoted their attention to bills to confirm citizenship on residents of New York of foreign birth and to appoint an agent in London. They allowed Hunter no voice in the selection. If the governor insisted upon playing a role, they would drop the excise voted for his salary. As it was, the tax had brought in but half of the sum anticipated.[44]

A resolution of the dispute over the agency and the impasse on long-term appropriations came when Morris engineered the expulsion of Samuel Mulford on technical grounds: the representative from Suffolk had committed a breach of privilege by publishing a speech he had made in the assembly the previous year. Mulford's expulsion gave Morris's faction a narrow majority, twelve of twenty-three seats. The "court" party then proceeded to appoint John Champante, a London merchant employed some years before by the earl of Bellomont, as agent and to pass a bill naturalizing Protestant aliens in the colony. Hunter gave this last bill a favorable cast: it would have a good effect by reconciling the majority of the people, the Dutch inhabitants. In exchange for signing the naturalization and agency bill, the governor received a five-year support measure, a bill imposing duties on imports and on ships entering the port of New York. Moreover, the assemblymen would determine in what ways the money would be spent. Hunter had agreed to a similar restriction voted by the assembly of New Jersey. The money raised from imports and ship tonnage was to be lodged with the provincial treasurer, an official appointed by and responsible to the elected assembly. Even the royal receiver general had agreed to this procedure.

Ignoring, or perhaps forced to accept, the long-range implications of the arrangement, Hunter gave credit to Morris, whom he nominated to be chief justice of New York, along with others he recommended for preferment to the council—Augustine Graham, Stephen DeLancey, Robert Lurting, Robert Watts, and John Johnson—all men of credit, good sense, and well affected to the government, as Hunter described them. Morris came in for special attention; to him the governor particularly owed the financial settlement.[45] The Plantation Office concurred in the nominations; men in the provinces who distinguished themselves in the interest of the monarch and for the good of the government should be rewarded with the offices at the disposal of the governor. Bestowing such rewards would encourage gentlemen in America to exert themselves for the public good and to strengthen the monarch's deputies in carrying out their duties in the colonies.[46]

It was not always to be. Ministers of state expected that the rewards of office under the crown would gratify the aspirations of men of means among the Americans, but as the earl of Chesterfield was to observe of the task confronting ministers managing parliamentary politics in Westminster, the problem was "to find pasture enough for the beasts they must feed."[47] And in America an expanding, dynamic economy and a more fluid society produced many more aspirants for office and recognition than the patronage of the crown could satisfy.

Conclusion

Events in America during 1714–15 were in marked contrast to those of 1688–89. The news of the accession of William and Mary had triggered in politically unstable America a series of revolutions. But a quarter of a century later George I was proclaimed "from Boston to Virg[in]ia w[ith]out any other ord[er]s than Gazette & Authentick Prints."[1] The peaceful transition in the colonies masked on ongoing, fundamental change, one in which power was shifting from governors dependent on the crown to cliques of prominent provincials sitting in locally elected assemblies or, in some cases, on the councils.

Who had won in New York during the political struggle of 1714–15—the assemblymen or Robert Hunter and his ally Lewis Morris? Unlike Joseph Dudley, who failed to retain the governorship of Massachusetts, Hunter continued as the monarch's deputy, but the years remaining to him in that office were not happy or even tranquil ones. In 1715 he had secured a bill providing him with a salary for the next five years, but the measure fell far short of the standing appropriation desired by London. The court party created to secure this bill was a personal creation, a transitory bloc which later governors would not be able to rely on. Hunter had given in on a critical issue: he had accepted the assembly's control of the treasury and the civil list. In the future assemblymen would put this power to good use to circumscribe the authority of governors. Hunter too would suffer. Left in a precarious position by successive administrations in Whitehall who sought to control the overseas possession with as little expense to the royal treasury as possible, Hunter had capitulated. Governors of extraordinary skill and personal charm would be needed successfully to manipulate the factious politicians sitting in the assemblies. Few men sent out to represent the British crown in the half century remaining to the first British empire in North America possessed the requisite temperment, skills, and judgement.

By the summer of 1719 Hunter had had his fill of the politicians of New York. He was now suffering from rheumatism; his wife Elizabeth had died three years before, and her family estate now needed his attention. He left New York in July 1719, never to return, exchanging his office as governor with William Burnet, the comptroller of the customs in London. On Hunter's departure from Manhattan the assemblymen voted the departing governor a vote of thanks. Years later a veteran of the political wars in the colony, Cadwallader Colden, reported what William Smith had heard of the governor's privately expressed views on that occasion. Colden himself had a poor opinion of the men elected to the American assemblies in this own day, at mid-eighteenth-century: generally they were of the "low rank of people who had no generous principles. But it had been much worse" in Hunter's day. With indignation Hunter had exclaimed in 1719: "People think it is a fine thing to be a governor. A governor by —— a Tom Turdman's a better office than to rake in the dunghill of these people[']s affections."[2]

Among the few New Yorkers, men of substance and sense, the Plantation Office deemed worthy for reward and preferment for their support of the king's government was Lewis Morris's friend, political ally, and Westchester County neighbor, Caleb Heathcote. For his service to Hunter's administration Heathcote in 1715 received a deputation as surveyor general for the Northern District in America. As a customs official of the crown, Heathcote welcomed a report current in Manhattan that Parliament was about to pass an act to rescind the charters of the proprietary and corporate colonies and vest their governments directly in the monarch. He also looked forward to the time when the crown would settle a revenue through customs and excise for the entire continent of America. Such a measure would produce sufficient revenue to defray all necessary expenses of the various provincial governments, for nothing could be more reasonable than that the plantations abroad should, as far as they were able, bear the expense for the support of their own governments and for their own defense.[3] Half a century later, George Grenville as first lord of the Treasury and chancellor of the Exchequer would express virtually the same sentiments when promoting a bill to have the imperial legislature at Westminster tax the overseas plantations to raise revenue in America. By that time, however, the opportunity had long since passed. Caleb Heathcote's assessment illustrated the contrast between what some thought was long needed and what had been done.

The history of imperial administration of the English colonies in North America during the seventeenth century had been a story of missed opportunities, lack of will, and miscalculation. For a century the English government had been generally ill prepared and little capable of the task of governing overseas possessions, distracted by civil wars, internal dissension, and financial and administrative weakness. Only on rare occasions—the interregnum under Cromwell being one—had the national government been in a position to impose its will in America. In 1660 monarchy had returned to England by default through the inability of the various factions to agree. Although the government of Charles II had formally enunciated the goal of bringing the American colonies under more direct and immediate control, it had also furthered the cause of localism and diversity by sanctioning the creation of half a dozen new colonies, each enjoying charter privileges. The attempt by James II to consolidate the provinces and impose greater control was misconceived, if only because little, if any, financial and military resources were committed from London. James's scheme collapsed with the Revolution of 1688, which brought in the Protestant monarchy, a generation of European conflicts, and uprisings in America to restore the dozen or so parochial colonial jurisdictions. Rigid control was neither intended nor possible. Even limited goals had proved unreachable because of localism, poor communications, and limited resources and particularly because of political, economic, and personal interests that complicated, compromised, and stifled most initiatives. The power of imperial government was limited by political and religious factionalism, faulty administration, military and fiscal deficiencies, conflicting interests, and endemic localism. In reviewing the experience of the previous decades well might William Blathwayt at the turn of the century anticipate the complaint of Caleb Heathcote: ''Ye Security of our colonies & rend[e]ring them more usefull to England etc. are common places that have entertain'd us these many years but the means which are very plain have always been opposed or not prosecuted.''[4]

Neglect—salutary or otherwise—was no innovation devised only later in the eighteenth century by British administrations when Sir Robert Walpole and the duke of Newcastle presided over the Treasury and the Secretariat. It characterized almost the entire imperial experience in the administration of the American colonies. This chronic condition allowed men in America over the course of several generations to prevail and to apply in local governmental institutions—especially the elected assemblies—the rhetoric and ideas so successfully utilized in England during the seventeenth century.

Inconstancy and neglect, parsimony and concerns with private rather than public interest, had characterized the administration of the overseas colonies by ministers of state in London. In contrast to 1689 no coup, no insurgency in the American colonies, had been necessary from 1696 to 1715 for ambitious men to gratify their ambitions and their need for recognition and status. The situation in South Carolina was exceptional. Neglect and ineptness by the imperial government were allowing prominent men to advance through local institutions and to set themselves upon the road to autonomy, if not in theory then to a significant degree in practice. As Hunter had predicted in 1711 and Robert Quary in Pennsylvania before him, should the provincial assemblies grow dominant the colonies would become independent national states. In contrast to the situation prevailing in the generation following the Restoration, more and more of the men coming to power in America were ''natives,'' born in the colonies or long-term residents.

In some colonies nominally under the immediate direction of the crown—Virginia and Maryland, for example—several years passed at a time without a governor from England making an appearance. Cliques consisting of prominent provincials sitting on the council held sway. In New Hampshire too, although a crown-appointed governor resided in nearby Boston, a small group of the more affluent Hampshiremen controlled the government. For years Whitehall had allowed the farcical wrangling by John Usher, William Partridge, and Samuel Allen to continue. The ministers of state had allowed Pennsylvania, the Delaware counties, and the Carolinas to drift without direction either from the proprietors or the crown. They had failed to support governors sent out to the Old Dominion against attacks by provincial magnates, James Blair, the Burwells, and the Ludwells. Edmund Andros, Nicholson, and after them, Spotswood had not been adequately supported. To neighboring Maryland the crown sent out weak men—Lionel Copley and Nathaniel Blakiston—and after Blakiston left the province, they allowed almost two years to pass before dispatching a replacement. Another hiatus of four years passed before Hart succeeded Seymour at Annapolis. By 1715, with the restoration of Maryland's government to the Calverts, the province had experienced almost a quarter century of government independent of proprietary control under lax imperial supervision. Four years later the local magnates in Charles Town, not the ministers of the crown, took matters into their own hands to end the rule of the distant proprietary board. At best the crown merely sanctioned a coup carried out by the merchants and planters of South Carolina. Fortified by years of bitter struggle against an irresponsible proprietary board in London the leaders of Carolina society continued strong in defense of local prerogatives when governors appointed by the crown finally succeeded executives commissioned by the proprietors. The pattern was set long before 1719.

At an even earlier date the Friends in Pennsylvania had conducted themselves as a virtually independent society. For years they had held off the representatives of the crown and of the proprietor, treating both with open contempt. A weak, sick proprietor, prone to uttering empty threats, but also inclined to give way, had allowed power to pass to a faction headed by the able, ambitious David Lloyd and had acquiesced in the Frame of 1701 to advance the power and authority of Pennsylvania's assembly. In failing to take over the government, in not coming to terms quickly, the crown had allowed Lloyd and his followers to become entrenched and to advance the cause of local autonomy against distant prerogative. Ironically it was William Penn early in the century who through his connections in England saved the Quakers and the inhabitants of the other chartered colonies from Parliamentary legislation which would have brought their governments under the direct control of the monarch and the ministers of state. For a generation after the collapse of the Dominion of New England, officials of the corporations of Connecticut and Rhode Island had successfully cited their patents to ward off demands from London to review legislation enacted in the provinces and the decisions of the provincial courts.

The ruling handed down by lawyers of the crown that laws enacted by Parliament did not extend to the colonies unless they so expressly stated, and that the plantations were governed by laws enacted there, further aided the growth of local autonomy. Efforts to provide imperial control by requiring the consent of governors to any bills were often ineffective, as the executives were left financially dependent on the assemblies to carry out their duties.

In the northern colonies, where the need to mobilize the resources of the

English against the French during the quarter century of international conflict was chronic and where the burden of war fell most heavily, the assemblies were able to coerce significant concessions from the governors. With the ministers of state unwilling to have England bear the financial responsibility of the civil establishment and military expenses, the locally elected men possessed an effective lever. In Virginia, where the king's governor enjoyed a salary from a long-term appropriation, Robert Spotswood did have some success, but he too could not ignore the growing power of the Burgesses, whom he attempted to win over by patronage. But as Lewis Namier once remarked of the later English political scene, the offering of political bribes was a sign not of strength but of weakness: he who can bully, need not bribe. In contrast to executives elsewhere, the governors in Rhode Island and Connecticut remained strong, but they represented not the distant crown or proprietors but the local hierarchy, and they depended on local support.

The duke of Shrewsbury, the earl of Nottingham, and other ministers of state appreciated the impact, direct and indirect, of North America on Anglo-colonial trade and the revenue in customs duties the crown reaped from this trade, yet they would not accept the financial burden of securing the financial independence of royal officials in America and the protection of the mainland colonies from the menace of various hostile forces. Instead they left governors and other royal officials vulnerable to the demands of the parochial assemblies. And the locally elected assemblies — notably those in New York and Massachusetts, in their confrontations with Cornbury, Hunter, and Dudley — had adopted the same stance as had the House of Commons against Charles II during the Third Dutch War by insisting on greater control over monetary appropriations. To gratify local interests, at times Whitehall appointed provincials to head the administration in Massachusetts, but as the Lords Justices in Council had appreciated only later, Sir William Phips had never really been the king's governor, and they had allowed five years to pass after his death before another governor from England appeared in Boston. Even then they had shied away from requiring the Massachusetts House of Representatives to make permanent provision for the earl of Bellomont's salary. It was too delicate a matter. Bellomont's successor was an American, and however much some New Englanders disliked Joseph Dudley, he was, after all, one of their own, a man who for the dozen years he presided over the government protected the interests of northern New England and never pressed hard to gain the concessions demanded by the imperial prerogative.

Dudley's counterpart in New York had recommended in 1710 that the home government have Parliament impose taxes to finance the colonial civil establishment. Had this suggestion been implemented at that early date, the subsequent course of provincial political and constitutional development might well have been different. With no support forthcoming from London, Hunter and Lewis Morris resorted to an immediately effective but potentially damaging tactic to raise finances for the provincial regimes in New Jersey and New York: building a court party, a faction in the assembly willing to vote money, but on conditions. Tacitly they were conceding to and furthering the growth of the authority of the assemblies.

Another significant phenomenon had its origins in the politics of the last years of the seventeenth century and first decade of the eighteenth, as men of ambition and genius introduced innovations in electioneering. David Lloyd in Pennsylvania, Robert Wenham and Lewis Morris in New York and New Jersey, Arthur Middleton in South Carolina, and the Cookes in the Bay colony introduced a popular element in politics, and not only with traditional but empty rhetorical references to the ''people,'' but also by appealing to the rank and file directly, by organizing parties, coining slogans, campaigning on platforms, and running tickets—practices which later came more fully to characterize the American way of politics.

Abbreviations

Add. MSS	Additional Manuscripts, British (Museum) Library, London
BL	British (Museum) Library, London
Bodl.	Bodleian Library, Oxford
CO	Colonial Office, Public Record Office, London
CW	Colonial Williamsburg, Williamsburg, Virginia
FDRL	Franklin D. Roosevelt Library, Hyde Park, New York
HL	Henry E. Huntington Library, San Marino, California
HMC	(Royal) Historical Manuscripts Commission, London
HSP	Historical Society of Pennsylvania, Philadelphia
LPL	Lambeth Palace Library, London
MHS	Massachusetts Historical Society, Boston
MHSC	*Massachusetts Historical Society Collections,* 9 series, 79 vols. (Boston: Massachusetts Historical Society, 1792–)
NUL	Nottingham University Library, Manuscripts Department, Nottingham
PC	Privy Council, Public Record Office, London
PRO	Public Record Office, London
SP	State Papers, Public Record Office, London
SPG	Society for the Propagation of the Gospel, London
T	Treasury, Public Record Office, London
VMHB	*Virginia Magazine of History and Biography*
WMQ	*William and Mary Quarterly*

Notes

Preface

1. John Putnam Demos, *Entertaining Satan: Witchcraft and the Culture of Early New England* (New York and Oxford: Oxford University Press, 1982), p. 275.
2. J. P. Greene, *The Quest For Power: The Lower Houses of Assembly in the Southern Royal Colonies, 1689–1776* (Chapel Hill: University of North Carolina Press, 1963).
3. James Henretta, *"Salutary Neglect" : Colonial Administration under the Duke of Newcastle* (Princeton: Princeton University Press, 1972), p. 104; Thomas C. Barrow, *Trade and Empire: The British Customs Service in Colonial America, 1660–1775* (Cambridge: Harvard University Press, 1967), pp. 116, 255. In thus writing "political" history concerned with the location and use of power and in utilizing conventional written sources, I would not go as far as G. R. Elton, *Political History: Principles and Practice* (New York: Basic Books, 1970), in claiming primacy for such history.

Introduction

1. Blackwell to Penn, 13 Jan., 25 Feb. 1689/90, HSP, Blackwell Letters to Penn.
2. Blathwayt to Sir Robert Southwell, 5 May 1688, NUL, Portland MSS, PwV53; Blathwayt to Edward Randolph, 10 March 1687/8, *Memoir of Edward Randolph, Including His Letters and Official Papers with Other Documents*, ed. Robert Noxon Toppan and Alfred T. Goodrich, 7 vols. (Boston: Prince Society, 1898–1909), 4:216.
3. Randolph to Southwell, 1 Aug. 1685, Randolph, *Memoir of Edward Randolph*, 4:29–30; John Povey to Southwell, 1 April, 26 May 1686, NUL, Portland MSS, PwV60; Lords of Trade to the Lord President, 26 Aug. 1685, CO 5/904/p. 251; and Gertrude A. Jacobsen, *William Blathwayt, a Late-Seventeenth-Century Administrator* (New Haven: Yale University Press, 1932), pp. 134–35.
4. Representation of the Commissioners of trade and plantations, 29 April 1701, CO 324/7/pp. 454–55; minute of the king in council, 30 April 1701, CO 323/3/f. 278.

Chapter 1

1. There has been the temptation on the basis of estimates of voting to place all members of the House of Commons with either the Whigs or the Tories and to see consistency in voting. Yet as the assessments of such knowledgeable contemporary managers as Harley and Sidney Godolphin make clear, the key lay with the mass of country gentry,

members considered by some to be Tories but actually unattached. For Harley's assessment see Geoffrey Holmes, *British Politics in the Age of Anne* (New York: St. Martin's Press, 1967), p. 322. Also valuable is Henry L. Snyder, "The Third Earl of Sunderland and the Office of Secretary of State under Queen Anne" (Ph.D. diss., University of California, Berkeley, 1963), pp. 47–50.

2. Stephen B. Baxter, *William III and the Defense of European Liberty, 1650–1702* (New York: Harcourt, Brace & World, 1966), pp. 338–44, 360–61, 377; Geoffrey Holmes, *The Trial of Doctor Sacheverall* (London: Eyre Methuen, 1973), pp. 79, 94.

3. Peter G. M. Dickson, *The Financial Revolution: A Study in the Development of Public Credit, 1688–1756* (New York: St. Martin's Press, 1967), pp. 64–66; and Thomas S. Ashton, *Economic Fluctuations in England, 1700–1800* (Oxford: Clarendon Press, 1959), pp. 116–17.

4. Daniel Defoe, *Party-Tyrany; or, An Occasional Bill in Miniature; as now Practised in Carolina. Humbly offered to the Consideration of both Houses of Parliament* (London, 1705).

5. See Talbot to John Chamberlain, 1 Sept. 1703, LPL, Fulham Palace Papers, vol. 36, ff. 35–36; also entry for 19 Sept. 1701, SPG Journals, vol. 1; the memorial of Lewis Morris and the account of Joseph Dudley, in appendix to the SPG Journals, nos. 2, 3; and Francis Nicholson to the bishop of London, 15 Oct. 1703, CW, Archives Department, Nicholson Papers.

6. Memorial of Evan Evans of Philadelphia, 18 Sept. 1707, BL, MS Rawlinson, C. 933, ff. 50–51; Swift to Robert Hunter, 12 Jan., 22 March 1708/9, *The Correspondence of Jonathan Swift*, ed. Sir Harold Herbert Williams, 5 vols. (Oxford: Oxford University Press, 1963–65), 1:120, 134, 139 n.3; and Jordan D. Fiori, "Jonathan Swift and the American Episcopate," *WMQ*, 3d ser., 9 (July 1954): 425–33.

7. Nicholson to Thomas Tenison, 22 May 1710, LPL, Lambeth Palace MSS, vol. 941, no. 24; Compton to Dartmouth, 5 Oct. 1710, HMC, *Eleventh Report*, app., pt. 5 (London, 1887), p. 298; petition of the missionaries of New Jersey, 12 April 1711, SP 34/33/p. 397; and abstract of the proceedings of the SPG, LPL, Fulham Palace Papers, vol. 36, ff. 42–43.

8. Entry for 27 Feb. 1711/12, *The Diary of Samuel Sewall*, ed. M. Halsey Thomas, 2 vols. (New York: Farrar, Straus, Giroux, 1973), 2:681; paper sent by Compton to Lord Treasurer Oxford, 27 March 1713, BL, Portland Papers, Loan 29/131/0/78; and address of the Newbury dissenters, CO 5/751/f. 203.

9. See the representation of the SPG, 28 Oct. 1714, T 1/181/f. 164, and abstract of the proceedings of the SPG, LPL, Fulham Palace Papers, vol. 36, f. 42; and Sharp to Jonathan Swift, 4 June 1713, Williams, *Correspondence of Swift*, 1:362.

10. Edward F. Carpenter, *Thomas Tenison, Archbishop of Canterbury: His Life and Times* (London: Society for the Promotion of Christian Knowledge, 1948), p. 119; and G. V. Bennett, "Conflict in the Church," in *Britain after the Glorious Revolution*, ed. Geoffrey S. Holmes (New York: St. Martin's Press, 1969), pp. 167–74.

11. J. H. Plumb, "The Organization of the Cabinet in the Reign of Queen Anne," *Transactions of the Royal Historical Society*, 5th ser. 8 (1957): 137–57; and Edward R. Turner, *The Privy Council of England in the Seventeenth and Eighteenth Centuries, 1603–1784*, 2 vols. (Baltimore: Johns Hopkins Press, 1930–32), 2:111.

12. Snyder, "The Third Earl of Sunderland," pp. 69–70.

13. See, for example, the newsletters sent by Robin Yard (an undersecretary) to Sir Joseph Williamson, SP 32/2/nos. 118, 119, ff. 237, 238–39.

14. Sunderland to the Council of Trade, 3 Jan. 1706/7, CO 324/9/pp. 133–34.

15. See, for example, Shrewsbury to William Blathwayt, 23 June 1697, *Report on the Manuscripts of the Duke of Buccleuch Preserved at Montague House*, 3 vols. in 4 (London: HMC, 1899–1926), 4, pt. 2:483–85; Blathwayt to Shrewsbury, 25 July (n.s.) 1697, ibid., p. 494; James Vernon to Shrewsbury, 26 June 1697, *Letters Illustrative of the Reign of William III from 1696 to 1708 Addressed to the Duke of Shrewsbury by J[ames] Vernon, Secretary of State*, ed. G. P. R. James, 3 vols. (London, 1841), 1:289; and Vernon to Blathwayt, 27 Aug. 1697, BL, Add. MSS 3427, f. 70. When Sunderland was dismissed in 1710, Thomas Hopkins, who had come in with Joseph Addison, also went. Addison in turn had replaced John Ellis. With the Tories in power, in 1710 George Tilson became undersecretary to St. John, and Erasmus Lewis to Dartmouth. At the Hanoverian succession James Stanhope brought in his relation, Charles Stanhope, while Horatio Walpole served under Townshend. Tilson managed to survive as joint undersecretary in the northern department.

16. William Lowndes (secretary to the Treasury) to William Popple, 6 Nov. 1702, CO 323/5/f. 70. See also the memorandum in T 1/64/pp. 126–28 on the appointments for William Bladen and George Larkin as auditors in Maryland and the Leeward Islands.

17. Godolphin to Marlborough, 16 June 1707, *The Marlborough-Godolphin Correspondence*, ed. Henry L. Snyder, 3 vols. (Oxford: Clarendon Press, 1975), 2:823. See also Marlborough to Godolphin, 19 May 1710 (n.s.), and Godolphin to Marlborough, 16 May 1710, 18 Oct. 1709, ibid., 3:1486, 1498, 1400.

18. Stepney to Blathwayt, 25 June 1701, BL, Add. MSS 9712, f. 23; Blathwayt to Stepney, 18 Feb. 1697/8, SP 105/51/no folio; Stepney to John Ellis, 24 June 1697 (n.s.), and Stepney to Charles Montagu, 23 May 1697, SP 105/57; and Shrewsbury to Blathwayt, 23 June 1696, HMC, *Manuscripts of the Duke of Buccleuch and Queensbury, Montagu House*, 2, pt. 1:354.

19. Ian K. Steele, *Politics of Colonial Policy: The Board of Trade in Colonial Administration, 1697–1720* (New York: Oxford University Press, 1968), pp. 85–92; Weymouth to Nottingham, 5 June 1702, Hatton-Finch Papers, BL, Add. MSS 29,588, f. 47.

20. Byrd to Blathwayt, 12 Nov. 1707, CW, Blathwayt Papers, vol. 13.

21. Sunderland to William Popple, Jr., 19 Oct. 1709, SP 44/108/ff. 156, 157; Steele, *Politics of Colonial Policy*, pp. 113–14.

22. Winchilsea to [Oxford], 18 June 1711, *Report on the Manuscripts of His Grace the Duke of Portland Preserved at Welbeck Abbey*, 10 vols. (London: HMC, 1891–1931), 5:12; Steele, *Politics of Colonial Policy*, pp. 123–33.

23. Townshend to Hunter, 30 Nov. 1714, CO 5/190/f. 11.

Chapter 2

1. See the complaints of John Sanders to the Board of Trade, 14,17 Feb. 1700/1, CO 388/8, pt. 2/f. 292; and the memorial of the merchants of Whitehaven and Penrith, 18 Jan. 1709/10, CO 388/12/f. 303.

2. Orders in council, 18 July 1700, 31 July 1701, PC 2/78/pp. 72, 241–42.

242 Notes (pp. 25–29)

3. Report of the Commissioners of Customs, 12 Oct. 1698, CO 323/2/f. 411; draft instructions to the governors, T 1/57/f. 98; order in council, 18 Dec. 1701, CO 323/ 3/no. 108; Commissioners of Trade to Quary, 18 Feb. 1703/4, CO 5/1290/f. 221; Commissioners of Trade to Nottingham, 22 Oct. 1703, CO 5/1290/f. 193; and secretary to the Board of Trade to Josiah Burchett of the Admiralty, 22 Oct. 1703, CO 5/1290/ff. 192/93.

4. Circular from the Commissioners of Trade, 19 Jan. 1709/10, CO 324/9/p. 422; memorial to the Commissioners of Trade from Samuel Brise, n.d., but read 31 Jan. 1709/ 10, CO 388/12/f. 299; representation of the Commissioners of Trade, 9 Feb. 1713/14, CO 5/913/pp. 469–71; and Archibald Cummings (surveyor general of the customs for the northern district) to the Commissioners of Trade, 2 Aug. 1716, CO 5/866/f. 304.

5. William III to Penn, 22 April 1697, CO 5/1287/ff. 35–36.

6. See Ian K. Steele, "The Board of Trade, the Quakers, and the Resumption of Colonial Charters, 1699–1702," WMQ, 3d ser. 23 (Oct. 1966): 596–619; Steele, Politics of Colonial Policy: The Board of Trade in Colonial Administration, 1697–1720 (New York: Oxford University Press, 1968), pp. 76–77; and J. M. Sosin, English America and the Revolution of 1688: Royal Administration and the Structure of Provincial Government (Lincoln: University of Nebraska Press, 1982), pp. 249–52.

7. Reply of the Board of Trade, 27 March 1701, to the request of the House of Commons of 12 March 1700/01, CO 389/17/pp. 159–80, esp. pp. 170–73 on the chartered colonies.

8. Blathwayt to Marlborough, 12 Oct. 1703, BL, Add. MSS 9722, f. 147. Penn served as Godolphin's agent in the negotiations over the prosecution of Daniel Defoe for seditious libel. Godolphin to Nottingham, 17 July 1703, Hatton-Finch Papers, BL, Add. MSS 29, 589, f. 28. See also Penn to [Nottingham], 5 July 1703, enclosing a letter from Godolphin, SP 34/3/no. 2, f. 4. The duke of Shrewsbury thought Penn a man to be reckoned with on matters of church and state. See Shrewsbury to James Vernon, 1 Feb. 1706/7, Vernon papers, BL, Add. MSS 40,776, f. 31.

9. See, for example, William Wharton to Fitzjohn Winthrop, 11 Aug. 1702, MHS, Winthrop Family Papers.

10. Northey to the Commissioners of Trade, 24 Dec. 1703, CO 5/1262/f. 213.

11. Penn to [Robert Harley], 9 Feb. 1703/4, HMC, Report on the Manuscripts of His Grace the Duke of Portland Preserved at Welbeck Abbey, Fifteenth Report, app. pt. 4 (London 1897), pp. 79–80.

12. Representation of the Board of Trade, 10 July 1704, CO 5/911/pp. 358–64; orders in council, 16 Nov. 1704, 12 Feb. 1704/5, PC 2/80/pp. 197, 269; Robert Livingston to Fitzjohn Winthrop, 7 April, 7 May 1705, MHSC, 6th ser. 3:285–87, 291; Penn to [Harley], 9 Feb. 1703/4, HMC, Fifteenth Report, app., pt. 4, p. 79.

13. Draft bill, CO 5/3/ff. 74–83; Hedges to the attorney general, 16 Feb. 1705/6; and Hedges to the Commissioners of Trade, 18 Feb. 1705/6, SP 44/105, pt. 2/pp. 7, 8.

14. Report of the Commissioners of Trade, 19 Nov. 1707, CO 389/19/p. 259; opinion of Northey and Harcourt, 10 July 1704, CO 5/1264/f. 30; and order of the House of Lords, 6 Jan. 1707/8, CO 5/1264/f. 30.

15. Northey to the Board of Trade, 22 July 1714, CO 323/7/f. 78.

16. Heathcote to Oxford, 8 July 1712, HMC, Fifteenth Report, app., pt. 4, p. 199.

17. Leo Francis Stock, ed., Proceedings and Debates of the British Parliament

Respecting North America, 5 vols. (Washington, D.C.: Carnegie Institution of Washington, 1924–41), 3:360–64.

18. Order in council, 16 Feb. 1698/9, CO 5/324/7/pp. 30–31; circular from the Commissioners of Trade to the governors, 26 June 1699, CO 324/7/pp. 53–55. One man appointed secretary of Barbados refused to reside on the island, claiming his affairs would not permit him to leave England, and through the lord steward appealed for dispensation. Edward Villars, earl of Jersey, to William Blathwayt, 1 Aug. 1699, Boston Public Library, Villars-Blathwayt Papers.

19. Entry for 31 March 1710, *The Secret Diary of William Byrd of Westover, 1709–1712,* ed. Louis B. Wright and Lois B. Tinling (Richmond, Va.: Dietz Press, 1941), p. 159.

20. See the Lords of Trade to Lord President Sunderland, 26 Aug. 1685, CO 5/904/p. 251.

21. Representation of the Council of Trade, 18 Oct. 1709, CO 5/995/p. 20; order in council, 24 Oct. 1709, CO 5/970/f. 257; and Board of Trade to the president of the New Jersey Council, 1 Nov. 1709, CO 5/995/p. 24.

22. Commissioners of Trade to the Lord Justices in Council, 26 Aug. 1697, CO 324/6/pp. 176–78; Secretary Hedges to the Commissioners of Trade, 6 Nov. 1706, SP 44/105, pt. 2/p. 128; order of the Lords of the Committee of the Privy Council, 4 June 1714, CO 323/7/f. 66; Commissioners of Trade to Secretary Hedges, 1 Nov. 1706, CO 5/3/f. 103; and Attorney General Northey to the Board of Trade, CO 323/4/f. 78.

23. Proposal by Jeffreys, 9 Feb. 1702/3, SP 32/2/no. 41, f. 80.

24. Commissioners of Trade to Edward Northey, 22 Oct. 1703, CO 324/8/pp. 261–62.

25. See the assessment of John Pollexfen of the Board of Trade on the state of justice in the American plantations and Barbados, 4 Sept. 1700, CO 324/7/pp. 311–31; order of the Lords Justices in Council, 18 July 1700, CO 323/3/no. 75; and Secretary Dartmouth to the Board of Trade, 21 Aug. 1712, SP 44/113/p. 164.

26. Livingston to Fitzjohn Winthrop, 7 May 1705, *MHSC,* 6th ser. 3:293.

27. Bellomont to the earl of Bridgewater, 22 June 1700, HL, Bridgewater Americana, 9782; report of the Board of Trade on Bellomont's complaints, 4 Oct. 1700, CO 5/1117/pp. 406–7; Caleb Heathcote to the earl of Oxford, 21 June 1712, HMC, *Manuscripts of the Duke of Portland, Welbeck Abbey,* 5:189.

28. Report of the Commissioners of Trade on Bellomont's commission, 8 April 1697, CO 5/907/p. 152; Penn's plan of union, read at the Plantation Office on 8 Feb. 1696/7, CO 323/2/f. 130.

29. Secretary Manchester to the Commissioners of Trade, 27 April 1702, SP 44/101/f. 205; Board of Trade to Cornbury, 29 July 1702, CO 5/1120/p. 9.

30. Winthrop to Cornbury, 22 April 1704, MHS, Winthrop Family Papers.

31. Blathwayt to the Treasury, 22 Jan. 1704/5, T 1/93/f. 58; Secretary Hedges to Dudley, 1 Feb. 1705/6, CO 324/30/pp. 62–64; and Robert Quary to Godolphin, 20 April 1708, T 1/107/f. 23.

32. Richard Hill to Secretary St. John, 25 July 1711, CO 5/898/f. 67; report of Auditor Edward Harley, 6 Aug. 1712, T 1/150/f. 148.

33. See, for example, the minute of the king in council, 30 April 1701, CO 323/3/f. 278.

34. Blathwayt's accounts, 26 Aug. 1701, T 64/88/pp. 44–53; Blathwayt to Godolphin, 22 March 1702/3, T 1/85/ff. 69–74; the account of the so-called "dead tax" in the West Indies in the Matthew Prior Papers, Portland Papers, BL, Loan 29/169/misc. 5; order in council, 10 April 1703, PC 2/79/pp. 353–56.

35. Byerly to Godolphin, 20 May 1703, T 1/87/f. 553; Blathwayt to Godolphin, 2 Aug. 1703, T 1/87/ff. 6–7; Blathwayt's state of the revenue in Virginia, T 1/90/f. 116.

36. Quary to the Commissioners of Trade, 10 Jan. 1707/8, CO 323/6/ff. 142–43; Quary to Pulteney 2 Dec. 1709, CO 323/7/ff. 1–2; report by Montagu and Raymond to Secretary Dartmouth, 8 Sept. 1710, SP 44/110/p. 91.

37. Blathwayt to Oxford, 15 Dec. 1713, T 64/90/p. 91; draft act for revenue in New York with notations by Northey and Raymond, 13 March 1710/11, CO 5/1084/f. 222; Commissioners of Trade to the queen, 13 Nov. 1711, CO 5/1084/ff. 254–55; Commissioners of Trade to Secretary St. John, 23 April 1712, CO 5/1223/pp. 489–90; paper headed "North America, received on 27 Aug. 1712," Portland Papers, BL, Loan 29/289/no. 17; Hunter to Oxford, 31 Oct. 1712, ibid., Loan 29/289/no number, page, or folio; and order in council, 4 May 1713, CO 5/1050/f. 461.

38. Blathwayt to Secretary Vernon, 17 Sept. 1700 (n.s.), Vernon Papers, BL, Add. MSS 40,744, f. 305; Blathwayt to Oxford, 13 Dec. 1713, T. 64/90/p. 91.

39. Hunter to William Popple, Jr., 8 Nov. 1714, CO 5/1123/pp. 289–90.

Chapter 3

1. Commissioners of Trade to Godolphin, 12 Nov. 1707, CO 389/36/pp. 341–42; Narcissus Luttrell, *The Parliamentary Diary of Narcissus Luttrell, 1691–1693,* ed. Henry Horwitz (Oxford: Clarendon Press, 1972), p. 383.

2. See the general estimate of the state of trade among the papers of Abraham Hill, a commissioner of trade, 14 Jan. 1697/8, BL, Sloane MSS 2920, f. 115. For the importance to the revenue of channelling trade through England see the Commissioners of Trade to Secretary Charles Hedges, 1 July 1702, SP 34/1/no. 54 and the Commissioners of Trade to the Lord Justices in Council, 15 Sept. 1699, CO 389/16/p. 366.

3. See, for example, the Commissioners of Trade to Sunderland, 18 Oct. 1709, CO 324/9/p. 410; the heads of instructions for negotiating a treaty with Portugal proposed by the Board of Trade, 8 Oct. 1709, CO 389/25/p. 73; and Rowland Tryon to William Popple, 8 Oct. 1709, CO 323/6/f. 210. In advancing proposals for settlements to be made by the South Sea Company, the lord mayor of London suggested agents be sent to Boston to buy provisions and lumber. Such settlements could be supplied sooner from New than from Old England. Lord Mayor to Harley, 23 July 1711, BL, Loan 29/45c/no. 18, f. 189.

4. See the case of the iron master Ambrose Crowley, Portland Papers, BL, Loan 29/293; Crowley to Paul Foley, 30 Nov. 1708, BL, Loan 29/284/no. 108 and the printed case for British manufactures, ibid., no. 111. See also the position of the British merchants dealing in ironware with the colonies, "Reasons for Continuing the Drawback on foreign iron & steel imported to the Plantations," ibid., no. 112. For a general account see Phyllis Deane, *The First Industrial Revolution* (Cambridge: Cambridge University Press, 1965), pp. 103–5.

5. Thomas S. Ashton, *Economic Fluctuations in England, 1700–1800* (Oxford: Clarendon Press, 1959), p. 140; P. J. Bowden, "Wool Supply and the Woollen Industry," *Economic History Review,* 2d ser. 9 (Aug. 1956): 44–58.

6. See John Cary to Edward Long, 19 Aug. 1696, BL, Add. MSS 5540, f. 76; the complaints of the clothiers of Leeds and Colchester; the testimony presented in the House of Commons in CO 388/5/passim; and report of the Commissioners of Trade, CO 389/16/pp. 148–49 (also BL, Harliean MSS 1324, ff. 5–6 and the draft act, CO 389/16/p. 158). See also Francis G. James, "The Irish Lobby in the Early Eighteenth Century," *English Historical Review* 81 (July 1966): 543–57, and H. F. Kearney, "The Political Background to English Mercantilism, 1695–1700," *Economic History Review*, 2d ser. 9 (April 1959): 495.

7. As is claimed in Curtis P. Nettels, "The Menace of Colonial Manufactures, 1690–1720," *New England Quarterly* 4 (April 1931): 231, and in Oliver M. Dickerson, *American Colonial Government, 1696–1765: A Study of the British Board of Trade in Its Relation to the American Colonies, Political, Industrial, Administrative* (Cleveland: Arthur Clark Co., 1912), p. 303.

8. Stock, *Proceedings of Parliament Respecting North America*, 2:287, 365.

9. For the reactions of the Lords Justices in Council see Undersecretary Robert Yard to Blathwayt, 27 Sept. 1700, Boston Public Library, Manuscripts Department, Blathwayt Papers, no. 73.

10. Report of the Board of Trade on woolen manufacture, 28 Oct. 1702, CO 389/17/pp. 462–64; the assessments of Jahleel Brenton, 30 March 1703, CO 5/863A. pt. i/f. 80, and John Bridger, 5 March 1705/6, CO 5/864, pt. i/f. 77; and report of the Board of Trade to the House of Commons, 24 Nov. 1696, CO 389/6/p. 15.

11. Commissioners of Trade to Secretary Charles Hedges, 18 May 1704, CO 5/3/ff. 31, 33–35; the evaluation of John Pollexfen, 19 May 1704, CO 5/3/ff. 38–39; and Hedges to the Commissioners of Trade, 2 June 1704, SP 44/105/p.79.

12. Gilbert Heathcote to William Popple, 30 Sept. 1700, CO 388/8, pt. ii/f. 274; report of the English envoy, John Robinson, to Hedges, 4 Aug. 1703 (n.s.), CO 388/9, pt. ii/f. 295; the later representation of the Commissioners of Trade, 14 Feb. 1709/10, CO 389/21; and Joseph J. Malone, "England and the Baltic Naval Stores Trade in the Seventeenth and Eighteenth Centuries," *Mariners Mirror* 58 (Nov. 1972): 380–85.

13. William Lowndes to Hedges, 21 Feb. 1703/4, with memorandum, SP 34/3/nos. 103–4; proposal by Mason, CO 5/863A, pt. ii/f. 196; proposal by Bridger, SP 34/4/no. 4; Josiah Burchett to the Admiralty, 15 Sept. 1703, SP 42/118/f.120; order in council, 14 Dec. 1704, CO 5/1262/f. 320 and Stock, *Proceedings of Parliament Respecting North America*, 3:87, 88.

14. Secretary Hedges to Governors Francis Nicholson and John Seymour, 20 April 1705, CO 324/30/p. 29.

15. William Popple to William Lowndes, 22 Feb. 1705/6, CO 5/1120/pp. 414–16, and Heathcote's proposals to Harley, n.d., Portland Papers, BL, Loan 29/289.

16. Navy Board to Josiah Burchett, 1 Feb. 1716/17, with enclosed account of contractors and imports, CO 5/4/ff. 51–52, 53.

17. Dudley to Godolphin, 17 Feb. 1707/8, T 1/105/f. 180; Bridger to the Commissioners of Trade, 17 Aug. 1709, CO 5/865/f. 125; and John Phillips to the Commissioners of Trade, n.d., CO 5/865/f. 239.

18. Eyre to the Commissioners of Trade, 12 May 1710, CO 5/865/f. 234; Commissioners of Trade to Secretary Dartmouth, 10 Nov. 1710, CO 5/3/ff. 134, 136; and Stock, *Proceedings of Parliament Respecting North America*, 3:241–42, 262–63. Jeremiah Dummer, agent for Massachusetts, protested against the measure as injurious to the lum-

ber trade with the West Indies. See his proposals in the Portland Papers, BL, Loan 29/289/no. 6.

19. Bridger to Dartmouth, 2 Feb. 1711/12, CO 5/1091/f. 284; Bridger to Bolingbroke, 7 Dec. 1713, CO 5/751/f. 199; and the evidence presented at the Plantation Office against Bridger, CO 5/866/ff. 135, 137, 139.

20. See the estimate on shipping by Sir Philip Meadows, 7 April 1697, CO 388/6/n.p.; Patrick Crowhurst, *The Defense of British Trade, 1689–1815* (Folkestone, Eng.: William Dawson and Sons, 1977); R. D. Merriman, ed., *Queen Anne's Navy: Documents Concerning the Administration of the Navy of Queen Anne, 1702–14* (London: Navy Records Society, 1961), pp. 338–39; J. S. Bromley, "The French Privateering War, 1702–13," in *Historical Essays, 1600–1750, Presented to David Ogg*, ed. Henry E. Bell and R. L. Ollard (New York: Barnes and Noble, 1963), p. 227; and John H. Owen, *War at Sea under Queen Anne, 1702–1708* (Cambridge: Cambridge University Press, 1938), p. 56.

21. See the representation of the Commissioners of Trade, enclosed in their letter to Nottingham, 29 Oct. 1703, CO 324/8/pp. 262–67; merchants trading to New York to the Commissioners of Trade, 14 Dec. 1703, CO 5/1048A/f. 199; and William Popple to Josiah Burchett, secretary to the Admiralty, with a report of the escort vessels needed for the plantation trades, 15 Dec. 1703, CO 324/8/pp. 295–308.

22. See, for example, the account of duties and drawbacks by debentures on tobacco, dated 1 May 1706, CO 389/19/p. 52.

23. Byrd to Perry and Lane, 21 July 1690, *The Correspondence of the Three William Byrds of Westover, Virginia, 1684–1776*, ed. Marion Tinling, 2 vols. (Charlottesville: University Press of Virginia, 1977), 1:118–19; Anderson to Cuthbert Jones, 16 June 1700, University of Virginia, Charlottesville, Alderman Library, Robert Anderson Letterbook, 1699–1717.

24. The fleet from the Chesapeake in 1697 consisted of nearly 150 vessels, about 50 of them between 400 and 500 tons, loaded with over 70,000 hogsheads of tobacco. The yield in customs was estimated at about £200,000. The fleet sailing from Bristol that same year consisted of only 23 ships. See the Commissioners of Trade to Shrewsbury, 8 April 1697, CO 5/1359/p. 33 and ——— to John Ellis, 25 March 1697, John Ellis Papers, BL, Add. MSS 28,881, f. 160.

25. Board of Trade to the lord admiral, 22 Dec. 1702, CO 5/1360/pp. 347–50; order in council on a memorial from the lord admiral, 31 Dec. 1702, CO 5/1313/f. 30.

26. Petition read at the Treasury on 30 May 1704, and endorsed notation, T 1/90/f. 331.

27. Quary to the Treasury, enclosed in Secretary Hedges to the Commissioners of Trade, 22 Feb. 1705/6, CO 5/1315, pt. i/ff. 14, 16–18; Quary to the Commissioners of Trade, 2 April 1706, CO 5/1315, pt. i/f. 66; and Commissioners of Trade to the queen, 26 April 1706, CO 5/3/ff. 96–102.

Chapter 4

1. See the contemporary analysis in George Tollet to Robert Harley, 17 Jan. 1701/2, Portland Papers, BL, Loan 29/284/f. 102.

2. Arthur Pierce Middleton, *Tobacco Coast: A Maritime History of Chesapeake Bay in the Colonial Era* (Newport News, Va.: Mariners' Museum, 1953), pp. 97–99.

3. Jacob M. Price, *France and the Chesapeake: A History of the French Tobacco Monopoly, 1674–1791, and of its Relationship to the British and American Tobacco Trades,* 2 vols. (Ann Arbor: University of Michigan Press, 1973), 1:509 and 93.

4. James Vernon to William Popple, 6 Aug. 1697, BL, Add. MSS 40,777, f. 224; Sir William Trumbull to Blathwayt, 6 Aug. 1697, *Report on the Manuscripts of the Marquess of Downshire Preserved at Easthampstead Park, Berkshire,* 4 vols. in 5 pts. (London: HMC, 1924–40), 1, pt. 2: 755–56; minutes of the proceedings of the Lords Justices in Council, 7 Aug. 1697, SP 44/275/pp. 170, 174; Commissioners of Trade to the Lords Justices, 10 Aug. 1697, SP 32/7/no. 15, ff. 289–91; Matthew Prior to the marquis of Winchster, 13 Sept. 1697 (n.s.), *Report on the Manuscripts of the Marquis of Bath, Preserved at Longleat, Wiltshire,* 3 vols. (London: HMC, 1904–8), 3:161; two memorials of the merchants and traders to Virginia, ibid., p. 149, and CO 5/1309/f. 130; and Stock, *Proceedings of Parliament Respecting North America,* 2:217.

5. Jacob M. Price, *The Tobacco Adventure to Russia: Enterprise, Politics, and Diplomacy in the Quest for a Northern Market for English Colonial Tobacco, 1676–1722,* Transactions of the American Philosophical Society, 51, pt. 1 (Philadelphia, 1961), pp. 3, 24, 27–32, 81–83; case of the contractors, CO 388/7/f. 20; and the testimony before the House of Lords, *The Manuscripts of the House of Lords,* n.s., 10 vols. to date (London: HMC, 1877–), 3:293–97.

6. Petition and memorial of the free traders, CO 5/1314, pt. iii/ff. 343–44, 346; the case of the contractors, 23 May 1705, CO 5/1314, pt. iii/ff. 235–51; report of the Commissioners of Trade, 26 May 1705, CO 5/1361/pp. 226–36; and order in council, 31 May 1705, PC 2/80/pp. 370–72.

7. Nathaniel Gould, Samuel Heathcote, William Dawsonne, and Edward Haistwell to the Commissioners of Trade, 5 March 1705/6, CO 5/1315, pt. i/f. 52; and Robert Harley to the Tobacco Contractors, 3 Sept. 1706, enclosing an extract of a letter from the queen's envoy to the czar, Sir Charles Whitworth, Portland Papers, BL, Loan 29/168. For information on Aleksei Kurbatov I am indebted to Professor Ann Kleimola.

8. Price, *France and the Chesapeake,* 1:93, 181.

9. William Popple, Jr., to Sir John Cook, 19 March 1705/6, CO 5/1362/pp. 19–20; Quary to Godolphin, 2 April 1706, with memorandum, CO 5/3/ff. 86, 87; and report of the Commissioners of Trade, 26 April 1706, CO 5/1362/pp. 44–53.

10. Representation of the Commissioners of Trade, 1 July 1707, CO 5/1315, pt. ii/ff. 315–16; order in council, 20 Feb. 1707/8, CO 5/1316/f. 3; and Price, *France and the Chesapeake,* 1:515–16.

11. Linton to John Ward, 25 Nov. 1707, Portland Papers, BL, Loan 29/289; Customs Board to the Treasury, 20 July 1708, T 1/108/f. 170.

12. Customs Commissioners to the Treasury, 27 Nov. 1708, with the printed Reasons of the Virginia merchants, T 1/110/ff. 111, 113; Customs to the Treasury, 20 Jan. 1708/9, T 1/111/f. 53; and Customs to Godolphin, 5 Oct. 1705, Portland Papers, BL, Loan 29/285.

13. Price, *France and the Chesapeake,* 1:520–22.

14. Commissioners of Trade to Secretary Sunderland, 18 Oct. 1709, CO 389/20/p. 411; Price, *France and the Chesapeake,* 1:523–25.

15. Jacob M. Price, "The Tobacco Trade and the Treasury, 1685–1733," 2 vols. (Ph.D. diss., Harvard University, 1954), 2:897.

16. George Tyrer to Richard Norris, 6 June 1703, Liverpool Record Office, Norris

Papers, 920 Nor 2/309; Peter Hall to Norris, 20 Oct. 1702, and Thomas Johnson to Norris, 22 Dec., 29 Dec. 1702, in *The Norris Papers,* ed. T. Heywood (Manchester, Eng.: Cheltham Society, 1846), pp. 99–100, 110, 112; John Ellis to Sir Joseph Williamson, 29 June 1697, SP 32/7/no. 86, f. 115. For an excellent study of the problem of credit for the tobacco trade see Jacob M. Price, *Capital and Credit in British Overseas Trade: The View from the Chesapeake, 1700–1776* (Cambridge: Harvard University Press, 1980).

17. Price, "Tobacco Trade and the Treasury," 1:276, 2:858, 876–80.

18. Commissioners of Customs to the Lord Treasurer, 26 March 1711, T 1/132/f. 193.

19. Commissioners of Customs to the Lord Treasurer, 9 Sept. 1713, and the petition of Micajah Perry and eight other merchants, T 1/164/ff. 21, 23.

20. On the act to encourage the tobacco trade see Price, "The Tobacco Trade and the Treasury," 2:736–46, 891–98; HMC, *Manuscripts of the House of Lords,* n.s. 10:211–15, 347–49; and Stock, *Proceedings of Parliament Respecting North America,* 3:298–99, 320–21, 324, 325, 330–41.

21. Cole to the Lord Treasurer, 7 Nov., 25 Nov. 1704, and Commissioners of Customs to the Lord Treasurer, 7 Dec. 1704, T 1/92/ff. 296, 298, 299; Stock, *Proceedings of Parliament Respecting North America,* 3:96; and the additional instructions to the colonial governors, CO 5/210/ff. 51–53.

22. Representation of the British merchants at Lisbon, 1 Oct. 1711, CO 388/15/nos. 14, 20; representation of the British factor at Oporto, 30 Aug. 1711, memorial of the British merchants at Lisbon, 1 Aug. 1711, and British merchants at Leghorn to the earl of Dartmouth, 20 July 1711, CO 388/22/pp. 300, 311, 370; and Converse D. Clowse, *Economic Beginnings in Colonial South Carolina: 1670–1730* (Columbia: University of South Carolina Press, 1970), pp. 139, 168–69.

23. For the arguments of the merchants trading to Carolina, Portugal, and Spain before the House of Commons and the Treasury, see their petition and annexed reasons, CO 5/385/ff. 146, 147–48; and Stock, *Proceedings in Parliament Respecting North America,* 3:456.

Part II

1. Penn to Charlewood Lawton, 21 Dec. 1700, HSP, William Penn Letterbook, 1699–1703; Penn to his commissioners of state, 12 Aug. 1689, HSP, Dreer Collection, Letters and Papers of William Penn; Samuel Mac. Janney, *The Life of William Penn: With Selections from His Correspondence and Autobiography,* 4th ed. (Philadelphia, 1876), p. 277; and Bonomy Dobrée, *William Penn, Quaker and Pioneer* (Boston: Houghton Mifflin, 1934), p. 203.

Chapter 5

1. Wormeley to William Blathwayt, 16 July 1697, CW, Blathwayt Papers, vol. 15.

2. Bradford Spangenberg, "Vestrymen in the House of Burgesses: Protection of Local Vestry Authority during James Blair's Term as Commissary (1690–1743)," *Historical Magazine of the Protestant Episcopal Church* 32 (June 1963): 79–89.

3. Nicholson to Archbishop Tenison, 13 Feb. 1696/7, LPL, Fulham Palace Papers, American Colonial Section, vol. 2, ff. 79–80.

4. Commissioners of Trade to Andros, 1 Feb. 1696/7, CO 5/1359/pp. 27–28.

5. Andros to Shrewsbury, 27 April 1697, CO 5/1309/ff. 52–53; Nicholson to [Locke], 30 March 1697, Bodl., MS Locke, c. 16, f. 157; Nicholson to Tenison, 30 April 1697, LPL, Fulham Palace Papers, vol. 11, f. 32.

6. Slye to Godolphin, 23 June 1697, SP 32/7/no. 79; and minutes of the Lords Justices in Council, 29 June 1697, SP 44/275/pp. 91, 96.

7. "Cheif Grievances," Bodl., MS Locke, p. 9, ff. 1–71.

8. Hartwell to William Popple, 13 Sept. 1697, enclosing thirty-seven queries and answers, CO 5/1359/pp. 90–109; Popple to Hartwell, Blair, and Chilton, 8 Oct. 1697, CO 5/1359/pp. 124–25.

9. A copy of the account of Virginia, CO 5/1309/ff. 84–122. The account by Hartwell, Blair, and Chilton was edited by Hunter Dickinson Farish as *The Present State of Virginia, and the College* (Williamsburg, Va.: Colonial Williamsburg, 1940).

10. The memorial on Andros and the short character of his conduct are in LPL, Fulham Palace Papers, vol. 11, ff. 34–51.

11. The account of the conference at Lambeth Palace, 27 Dec. 1697, ibid., ff. 55–78; Blathwayt to Andros, 14 Jan., 1697/8, and Andros to Blathwayt, 17 March 1697/8, CW, Blathwayt Papers, vol. 3.

12. Tenison to Somers, 21 May 1698, LPL, Fulham Palace Papers, vol. 11, ff. 80–81; Blair to Locke, 20 Jan. 1697/8, Bodl. Library, MS Locke, c. 4, f. 8; Nicholson to [Locke], 26 May 1698, Bodl., MS Locke, c. 16, f. 159; Secretary Vernon to the Commissioners of Trade, 31 May 1698, SP 44/99/p. 516; and Blathwayt to George Stepney, 31 May 1698, SP 105/51.

13. Bishop Compton to Sir Philip Meadows, 9 Aug. 1698, CO 5/1309/f. 171.

14. Commissioners of Trade to the Lords Justices in Council, 28 Aug. 1698; instructions to Nicholson, 13 Sept. 1698, CO 5/1359/pp. 216, 252–59.

15. Harrison to Nicholson, 1 Sept. 1698, CW, Archives Department, Nicholson Papers.

16. Locke to Nicholson, 10 Oct. 1699, CW, Nicholson Papers. Emphasis added.

17. Nicholson to the Commissioners of Trade, 2 Dec. 1701, CO 5/1312/ff. 200–202. For a recent treatment of the native-born English in Virginia, or "Creoles," see Carole Shammas, "English-Born and Creole Elite in Turn-of-the-Century Virginia," in *The Chesapeake in the Seventeenth Century: Essays on Anglo-American Society,* ed. Thad W. Tate and David Ammerman (Chapel Hill: University of North Carolina Press, 1979), pp. 274–96.

18. David Alan Williams, "Political Alignments in Colonial Virginia, 1698–1750" (Ph.D. diss., Northwestern University, 1959), pp. 5–8, 38–39, 40–44, 49–51.

19. Byrd to Philip Ludwell, Jr., 6 July 1702, Tinling, *Correspondence of the William Byrds,* 1:186.

20. Robert Beverley, *The History and Present State of Virginia,* ed. Louis B. Wright (Chapel Hill: University of North Carolina Press, 1947), p. 106.

21. Blair to Tenison, 13 July 1702, and clergy of Virginia to Bishop Compton, 25 Aug. 1703, LPL, Fulham Palace Papers, vol. 11, ff. 123, 170.

22. See, for example, the letter from an unknown supporter, a clergyman, to Nichol-

son, 8 Dec. 1702, CW, Nicholson Papers, printed in *Historical Collections Relating to the American Colonial Church*, ed. William Stevens Perry, 5 vols. (Hartford, Conn., 1870–75), 1:69–74.

23. The best treatment is Williams, "Political Alignments in Colonial Virginia," pp. 53–60.

24. Depositions and letters submitted in April 1704, CO 5/1314, pt. i/ff. 20–25, 39–75; Blair's deposition, 1 May 1704, ibid., ff. 34–35; William Byrd II to the Commissioners of Trade, 30 May 1704, ibid., f. 104; and Thrale's answer to the charges, 4 May 1704, ibid., ff. 80–85.

25. Marlborough to the duchess of Marlborough, 8/19 May 1704, Snyder, *Marlborough-Godolphin Correspondence*, 1:297; entry for 24 Aug. 1704, Narcissus Luttrell, *A Brief Historical Relation of State Affairs from September 1678 to April 1714*, 6 vols. (Oxford, 1857), 5:458.

26. Nicholson to the Commissioners of Trade, 30 Oct. 1704; extract of Beverley to David Gwyn, 12 Feb. 1703/4; Beverley's "Narrative"; proceedings of the Virginia council, 28 Sept. 1704; justices of King and Queen County to Nicholson, n.d., CO 5/1314, pt. ii/ff. 195, 198, 198–99, 199, 200.

27. Nicholson to the Commissioners of Trade, 1 March 1704/5, 6 March 1704/5, CO 5/1314, pt. ii/ff. 223–28, 252–62, 305–12; memoranda by Nicholson, "Papers Relating to the Administration of Nicholson," *VMHB* 8 (Jan. 1900): 55–56; and Nicholson to Undersecretary John Ellis, 8 March 1704/5, John Ellis Papers, BL, Add. MSS 28,893, f. 72.

28. Blair to Ludwell, 6 Jan. 1704/5, *VMHB* 5 (July 1897): 52; entries for 8 March, 29 March 1705, Luttrell, *Historical Relation of State Affairs*, 5:528, 535; and Blakiston to Ludwell, 20 April 1705, *VMHB* 23 (Oct. 1915): 355.

29. Proceedings of the House of Burgesses, 4 May 1705, and the statement by the four councilors, 12 May 1705, *VMHB* 8 (Jan. 1900): 133–34, 142–44; Parke Rouse, *James Blair of Virginia* (Chapel Hill: University of North Carolina Press, 1971), pp. 168–73; and Williams, "Political Alignments in Colonial Virginia," pp. 70–74.

30. Nott to the Commissioners of Trade, 22 Sept. 1705, CO 5/1314, pt. iii/ff. 993–94; Byrd to William Lowndes, 9 May 1705, HL, Blathwayt Papers, BL95; Blathwayt to Godolphin, 12 July 1705, T 64/89/pp. 264–65; and memorandum by Blathwayt, 16 Oct. 1705, T 64/89/p. 281.

31. Nott to the Commissioners of Trade, 24 Dec. 1705, CO 5/1315, pt. i/f. 45.

32. Simon Harcourt and James Montague to the Commissioners of Trade, 23 Dec. 1707, CO 5/1315, pt. ii/ff. 354–55.

33. Jennings to the Commissioners of Trade, 24 June 1708, 20 Sept. 1709, CO 5/1316/ff. 19–21, 33–34; James LaVerne Anderson, "The Governors' Council of Colonial America: A Study of Pennsylvania and Virginia, 1660–1776" (Ph.D. diss., University of Virginia, 1967), p. 23.

34. Godolphin to Marlborough, 18 Aug. 1709, *Private Correspondence of Sarah, Duchess of Marlborough . . . and the Select Correspondence of . . . John, Duke of Marlborough*, 2 vols. (London, 1838), 2:370; entry for 31 March 1710, Byrd, *Secret Diary*, p. 159; warrant signed by Sunderland, 18 Feb. 1709/10, CO 5/210/f. 101; and Blakiston to the president and council of Virginia, 20 Feb. 1709/10, *VMHB* 19 (Jan. 1911):21.

35. Alexander Spotswood to John Spotswood, 17 Aug. 1710, "Correspondence of

Alexander Spotswood with John Spotswood of Edinburgh,'' ed. Lester J. Cappon, *VMHB* 60 (April 1952): 227.

36. Pierre Marambaud, *William Byrd of Virginia, 1674–1744* (Charlottesville: University Press of Virginia, 1971), pp. 30–31; Rouse, *James Blair,* pp. 194–95; Williams, "Political Alignments in Colonial Virginia,'' pp. 124–25, 130, 137.

37. Spotswood to Blathwayt, 6 March 1710/11, *The Official Letters of Alexander Spotswood, Lieutenant Governor of the Colony of Virginia, 1710–1722,* ed. Robert A. Brock, 2 vols. (Richmond: Virginia Historical Society, 1882–85), 1:69.

38. Nathaniel Blakiston to Philip Ludwell II, 18 Jan. 1711/12, *VMHB* 4 (July 1896): 21.

39. Spotswood to Blakiston, 21 Oct. 1713, Brock, *Official Letters of Spotswood,* 2:39; Basset to Ludwell, 22 Sept. 1713, *VMHB* 23 (Oct. 1915): 359; Spotswood to the Commissioners of Trade, 15 Oct. 1711, CO 5/1316/ff. 295–97.

40. Spotswood to Blakiston, 1 Dec. 1714, Brock, *Official Letters of Spotswood,* 2:79; John Melville Jennings, ed., "The Lamentations of John Grymes in Four Letters Addressed to William Blathwayt,'' *VMHB* 58 (July 1950): 389, 391n; Blakiston to Philip Ludwell II, 18 July 1714, *VMHB* 4 (July 1896): 22–23.

41. Spotswood to the Board of Trade, 6 March 1710/11, CO 5/1316/ff. 203–4, 218–19; and Dartmouth to Spotswood, 14 April 1712, CO 324/32/pp. 80–82.

42. Spotswood to the Commissioners of Trade, 8 Feb. 1711/12, 26 July 1712, 15 Oct. 1712, 11 Feb. 1712/13, CO 5/1316/ff. 341, 363–64, 384, 391–93; 9 Aug. 1715, CO 5/1317/f. 35A.

43. Spotswood to the Commissioners of Trade, 27 Jan. 1714/15, 4 June 1715, CO 5/1317/ff. 118–19, 140; address of the councilors and burgesses, CO 5/1317/f. 12.

44. Spotswood to the Commissioners of Trade, 16 June, 29 Dec. 1713, CO 5/1317/ff. 92–93, 68–71; Williams, "Political Alignments in Colonial Virginia,'' p. 150; and Anderson to Micajah Perry and Company, 10 Aug. 1714, University of Virginia, Alderman Library, Robert Anderson Letter Book, 1698–1717.

45. Leonidas Dodson, *Alexander Spotswood, Governor of Colonial Virginia, 1710–1722* (Philadelphia: University of Pennsylvania Press, 1932), pp. 55–57, 117, 118–19, Williams, "Political Alignments in Colonial Virginia,'' pp. 159, 161.

46. Spotswood to Secretary Stanhope, 24 Oct. 1715, CO 5/1342/ff. 6–7; Spotswood to the Commissioners of Trade, 24 Oct. 1715, CO 5/1317/ff. 142–44; and Commissioners of Trade to the king, 12 Sept. 1715, CO 5/1364/pp. 240–41.

47. Ludwell to Blathwayt, 22 Sept. 1715, CW, Blathwayt Papers, vol. 15.

48. Spotswood to the Commissioners of Trade, 24 May 1716, CO 5/1317/ff. 211–14; Spotswood to the Treasury, 23 May 1716, T 1/199/f. 76.

Chapter 6

1. Snyder, *Marlborough-Godolphin Correspondence,* 1:255 n. 3.

2. Nicholson to the Commissioners of Trade, 27 March 1697, CO 5/714/ff. 46–51, especially his comments on the list of delegates.

3. Memorial of the Quakers received at the Board of Trade, 6 Oct. 1697, CO 5/714/f. 181; Trevor to the Commissioners of Trade, 26 Aug. 1697, CO 5/714/f. 178; Anglican clergy of Maryland to Bishop Compton, 14 May 1698, LPL, Fulham Palace Papers, American Colonial Section, II, ff. 100–103; and John H. Seabrook, "The Establishment

of Anglicanism in Colonial Maryland," *Historical Magazine of the Protestant Episcopal Church* 39 (Sept. 1970): 292–93.

4. Nicholson to the Commissioners of Trade, 20 Aug., 12 Sept. 1698, CO 5/714/ff. 256–57, 292; declaration of the grand jury at Saint Marys, 12 Sept. 1698, LPL, Fulham Palace Papers, American Colonial Section, II, f. 112.

5. Such is the evaluation of David W. Jordan, "John Coode, Perennial Rebel," *Maryland Historical Magazine* 70 (Spring 1970): 23–24. See also David William Jordan, "The Royal Period of Colonial Maryland, 1689–1715" (Ph.D. diss., Princeton University, 1966), pp. 191–92.

6. Slye to James Vernon, 26 May 1698, CO 5/714/ff. 322, 324–27; Slye to Vernon with memorandum of charges, 23 June 1698, CO 5/719/ff. 332, 334–37; Slye to Sidney Godolphin, 23 June 1697, SP 32/7/no. 79; minutes of the Lords Justices in Council, 29 June 1697, SP 44/275/p. 96; Vernon to Nicholson, 11 Oct. 1697, BL, Add. MSS 40,777, f. 267; two petitions from Slye to Nicholson, 4 Sept. 1698, HL, Elsmere Collection (Bridgewater Papers); Vernon to Nicholson, 31 Aug. 1698, CO 324/26/p. 95; and Benjamin Harrison II to Nicholson, 1 Sept. 1698, CW, Nicholson Papers.

7. Testimonial in HL, Elsmere Americana (Bridgewater Papers), EL 9698; Vernon to the Lord Chancellor, 21 May 1698, LPL, Fulham Palace Papers, XI, ff. 80–81; and Nicholson to Bishop Compton, 4 Feb. 1698/9, CW, Nicholson Papers. The decision to transfer Nicholson and to appoint another governor for Maryland was made well before Slye's second set of charges arrived in London. See Vernon to the Commissioners of Trade, 31 May, 18 July 1698, SP 44/99/pp. 516, 540.

8. Commissioners of Trade to the Lords Justices in Council, 6 Sept. 1698, CO 5/725/pp. 208–11.

9. Blakiston to the Commissioners of Trade, 5 July 1700, CO 5/715/ff. 35, 43–44; Commissioners of Trade to Blakiston, 3 Dec. 1700, CO 5/726/p. 4; Baltimore's memorial, 20 Feb. 1707/8, CO 5/716/no. 42.

10. See the protests of Edward Haistwell, John Feild, and Theodore Eccleston to the Commissioners of Trade, 17 Oct. 1699, CO 5/714/ff. 406–8; report of the Commissioners of Trade, 29 Nov. 1699, CO 5/725/pp. 436–39 (copy in LPL, Fulham Palace Papers, American Colonial Section, II, f. 132). On the opposition to this legislation see David W. Jordan, " 'Gods Candle' within Government: Quakers and Politics in Early Maryland," *WMQ*, 3d ser. 49 (Oct. 1982): 628–54.

11. Nicholson to Archbishop Tenison, 27 May, 23 July 1700, LPL, Fulham Palace Papers, XI, ff. 113, 115; Blakiston to Tenison, 28 May 1700, Fulham Palace Papers, American Colonial Section, II, f. 160; Blakiston to the Commissioners of Trade, 28 May, 5 July 1700, CO 5/715/ff. 25–26, 35–36.

12. Memorial of the Quakers, 3 Sept. 1700, CO 5/715/f. 71; memorial (probably presented by Bray), n.d., LPL, Fulham Palace Papers, American Colonial Section, II, ff. 183–84; Attorney General Thomas Trevor to the Commissioners of Trade, 11 Jan. 1700/01, CO 5/715/ff. 93–94.

13. Representations of the Commissioners of Trade, 11 Feb., 21 May 1701, CO 5/726/pp. 28–31, 66; draft bill, CO 5/715/ff. 162–83; objections by Feild, Haistwell, and Joseph Wyeth to the Board of Trade, 6 May 1701, CO 5/715/ff. 184–85; and order in council, 5 June 1701, CO 5/715/f. 201.

14. See the report by an unidentified clergyman to Nicholson, 8 Dec. 1702, CW,

Nicholson Papers; and Gilbert Parke to Thomas Coke, 10 Oct. 1702, HMC, *Twelfth Report,* app., pt. 3 (London, 1889), p. 16.

15. Sir Thomas Lawrence to the Commissioners of Trade, 25 Oct. 1703, CO 5 / 715 / ff. 294 – 95; William Popple, Jr., to William Penn, 12 Jan. 1703 / 4, CO 5 / 1290 / f. 204.

16. Baltimore to William Hunter, 14 Dec. 1704, CO 5 / 726 / pp. 359 – 60; William Popple, Jr., to Sir Edward Northey, 17 Oct. 1705, CO 5 / 726 / p. 318; Northey to the Commissioners of Trade, 18 Oct. 1705, CO 5 / 715 / f. 432; representation of the Commissioners of Trade, 29 Nov. 1705, CO 5 / 726 / pp. 343 – 44; and Popple to Northey, 5 Dec. 1705, CO 5 / 726 / p. 345. Royal officials intervened, however, to insure that priests would not be prosecuted for performing private services for Catholic families. Order in council, 3 Jan. 1705 / 6, PC 2 / 91 / pp. 60 – 62.

17. Secretary Hedges to the Commissioners of Trade, 28 June 1706, SP 44 / 105, pt. ii / p. 64; Seymour to Secretary Sunderland, 10 March 1708 / 9, Maryland Historical Society, Seymour Papers, MS 737.

18. See the memorial by Bray, n.d., LPL, Fulham Palace Papers, American Colonial Section, II, ff. 195 – 98; Jordan, "Royal Period of Colonial Maryland," pp. 281 – 82; and Samuel Clyde McCulloch, "Dr. Bray's Trip to Maryland: A Study in Militant Anglican Humanitarianism," *WMQ,* 3d ser. 2 (Jan. 1945): 15 – 32.

19. See Jordan, "Royal Period of Colonial Maryland," pp. 210 – 32.

20. For the complicated story of the Maryland secretariat see the order in council, 2 Jan. 1704 / 5 and the petition of Lawrence, CO 5 / 715 / ff. 339, 340 – 41; Lawrence to Thomas Bordley, 4 Feb. 1705 / 6, Maryland Historical Society, Bordley-Calvert MSS, no. 82; statement by Lawrence, 28 Jan. 1706 / 7, CO 5 / 716 / ff. 81 – 82; the queen to Lawrence, 15 Jan. 1707 / 8, CO 5 / 210 / ff. 38 – 39; report by Sir Simon Harcourt, 31 July 1707, CO 5 / 716 / f. 118; and orders in council, 8 Jan. 1707 / 8 and 30 March 1710, PC 2 / 81 / pp. 487 – 90, PC 2 / 82 / p. 561 – 62.

21. See the instructions to Seymour, 21 July 1703, CO 5 / 726 / pp. 265 – 67.

22. Harcourt to William Popple, Jr., 3 Jan. 1706 / 7, and Harcourt to the Commissioners of Trade, 7 June 1708, CO 5 / 716 / ff. 54, 130 – 40; Montague's report to the Commissioners of Trade, 7 June 1708, CO 5 / 716 / ff. 208 – 9.

23. Commissioners of Trade to the queen, 18 Oct. 30, Nov. 1709, CO 5 / 727 / pp. 132 – 37, 141 – 42; Commissioners of Trade to Seymour, 12 Jan. 1708 / 9, CO 5 / 727 / pp. 110 – 15.

24. Seymour to the Commissioners of Trade, 3 July, 28 Aug. 1705, CO 5 / 715 / ff. 353 – 54, 429; Secretary Hedges to the Commissioners of Trade, 27 Oct 1705, SP 44 / 105 / p. 303; William Lowndes to William Popple, Jr., 2 Nov. 1705, CO 5 / 715 / f. 444; Commissioners of Trade to Hedges, 9 Nov. 1705, CO 5 / 726 / ff. 27 – 28; Popple to Lowndes, 9 Nov. 1705, CO 5 / 726 / pp. 334 – 35; and Seymour to the Commissioners of Trade, 21 Aug. 1705, CO 5 / 716 / ff. 57 – 59.

25. Seymour to the Commissioners of Trade, 3 July 1705 and March 1706, CO 5 / 715 / f. 349, CO 5 / 716 / ff. 29 – 30; Northey to Secretary Hedges, 27 July 1706, CO 5 / 721 / ff. 34 – 35.

26. Seymour to the Commissioners of Trade, 10, 23 June 1708, CO 5 / 716 / ff. 109 – 15, 219 – 24; and Jordan, "Royal Period of Colonial Maryland," pp. 242 – 46.

27. Seymour to Secretary Sunderland, 13 Oct. 1707, Maryland Historical Society, Seymour Papers, no. 737.

28. Seymour to the Commissioners of Trade, 10 Jan., 10 March 1708/9, CO 5/716/ff. 281–83, 286–88; Seymour to Secretary Sunderland, 10 March 1708/9, Maryland Historical Society, Seymour Papers, no. 737; Sunderland to Seymour, 4 Aug. 1709, CO 5/210/f.79.

29. Marlborough to Godolphin, 19 May 1710 (n.s.), and Godolphin to Marlborough, 27 May 1710 (n.s.), Snyder, *Marlborough-Godolphin Correspondence,* 3: 1486, 1498, 1533; and Dartmouth to the Commissioners of Trade, 7 July 1710, SP 44/110/p. 10.

30. Dartmouth to Corbett, 18 Jan., 27 Jan. 1710/11, CO 389/42/ff. 69, 77–78; Corbett's petition, n.d., SP 34/28/f.37.

31. Blathwayt's narration, SP 44/110/pp. 345–49; representation of the Commissioners of Trade, 26 July 1711, CO 5/727/pp. 291–93.

32. Two undated petitions by Baltimore, but one endorsed as received 1 Feb. 1711/12, the other 8 Feb. 1711/12, Portland Papers, BL, Loan 29/285.

33. Petition of the merchants trading to Maryland, 15 Feb. 1711/12, CO 5/717/f. 115; petition of Bowles, Portland Papers, BL, Loan 29/285; representation of the Commissioners of Trade, 12 March 1711/12, CO 5/727/pp. 312–13; C. Douglas to [Dartmouth?], 7 Feb. 1712/13, CO 5/721/f. 113.

34. Lloyd to the Commissioners of Trade, 20 Nov. 1712, CO 5/717/f. 190.

35. Memorial of Charles, Baron Baltimore, to Oxford, Portland Papers, BL, Loan 29/285; Baltimore to Benedict Leonard Calvert, 14 Oct. 1713, BL, Loan 29/129; Benedict Leonard Calvert to Oxford, 22 Dec. 1713, BL, Loan 29/129; Bolingbroke to the Commissioners of Trade, 1 Jan. 1713/14, SP 44/114/n.p., n.f.; Hart to Oxford, 22 Jan. 1713/14, BL, Loan 29/285.

36. James Logan to Thomas Grey, 4 Nov. 1714, HSP, James Logan Papers, James Logan Letterbook, 1712–15, p. 271.

37. Stanhope to the Commissioners of Trade, 29 Jan., 4 Feb. 1714/15, SP 44/117/pp. 86, 87.

38. Order in council, 30 Sept. 1715, PC 1/58/B1; Guilford to the Commissioners of Trade, 16 May 1715, with a certificate of Exchequer warrant, CO 5/717/ff. 264, 266.

39. See William Popple, Jr., to John Talour, 24 Aug. 1715, CO 5/1292/f. 234, requesting papers from the Treasury relating to the possible surrenders.

40. How this was done is not clear, as much of the evidence is lacking. See Jordan, "Royal Period of Colonial Maryland," pp. 341–42; and Donnell MacClure Owings, *His Lordship's Patronage: Offices of Profit in Colonial Maryland* (Baltimore: Johns Hopkins Press, 1953), p. 35.

41. David W. Jordan, "Maryland's Privy Council, 1637–1715," in *Law, Society, and Politics in Early Maryland,* ed. Aubrey C. Land, Lois Green Carr, and Edward Papenfuse, (Baltimore: Johns Hopkins University Press, 1977), p. 80. Yet for some among the prominent families of the colony, London and England still held strong attraction. Stephen Boardley and his brother William were sent off to London by their father, one to learn the ways of a merchant, the other to study law. After the death of his father, Stephen wrote to his widowed mother begging her to allow him to remain in the metropolis, for "no where better" could business be learned. And the easiest and cheapest way of "coming to perfection" in the law "is to go to some Lawyer in London." Nowhere could it be better learned than in England. Many men had been brought up to the law in Maryland, "but what are they to the English lawyers?" Stephen Boardley to his mother, 22 Jan.

1728, and to John Beale, 22 Jan. 1728, Maryland Historical Society, Boardley Letter Book, pp. 5, 7.

Chapter 7

1. Elizabeth Hyrne to Burrell Massingberd, [1702], Lincolnshire Record Office, Massingberd Deposits, Mass 21/67.

2. Edward Hyrne to Burrell Massingberd, 16 May 1701, Massingberd Deposits, Mass 21/41; Converse D. Clowse, *Economic Beginnings in Colonial South: 1670–1730* (Columbia: University of South Carolina Press, 1970), p. 163; Stuart Owen Stumpf, "The Merchants of Colonial Charleston, 1680–1756" (Ph. D. diss., Michigan State University, 1971), pp. 70–72; and Richard Waterhouse, "South Carolina Colonial Elites: A Study in the Social Structure and Political Culture of a Southern Colony, 1670–1760" (Ph. D. diss., Johns Hopkins University, 1973), pp. 71–85.

3. Proprietors to John Ely, 21 Sept., 19 Oct. 1699, CO 5/289/ff. 38, 40; and William Thornburgh to William Popple, 21 July 1699, CO 5/1258/f. 99.

4. William Stevens Powell, *The Proprietors of Carolina* (Raleigh: North Carolina State Department of Archives and History, 1963), pp. 51, 52–53, 61–62.

5. Edward Randolph to William Blathwayt, 8 April 1699, 19 Nov. 1700, CW, Blathwayt Papers, vol. 2.

6. James Adams to the SPG, 18 Sept. 1708, *The Colonial Records of North Carolina*, ed. William L. Saunders, 10 vols. (Raleigh, N. C., 1866–90), 1:686.

7. James Adams to the SPG, 4 Sept. 1710, ibid., p. 733.

8. Pollock to Alexander Spotswood, 30 April 1713, printed in Francis L. Hawks, *History of North Carolina*, 3 vols. (New York, 1857–58), 2:434.

9. The best treatment of North Carolina factionalism is the extended introduction in Mattie Erma Edwards Parker, ed., *North Carolina Higher-Court Records, 1670–1696* (Raleigh: North Carolina State Department of Archives and History, 1968), and William Soloman Price, Jr., "The Records of North Carolina Higher Courts, 1702–1708" (Ph. D. diss., University of North Carolina, 1973). For a treatment with emphasis on the religious element see Gloria Beth Baker, "Dissenters in Colonial North Carolina," (Ph. D. diss., University of North Carolina, 1970).

10. Jennings to the earl of Sunderland, 20 Sept. 1708, HL, HM22021. See also the extracts from Thomas Pollock's letterbook printed in Saunders, *Colonial Records of North Carolina*, 1:696–98.

11. Entry for 13 Sept. 1710, Byrd, *Secret Diary*, p. 230; Adams to the SPG, 4 Sept. 1710, Saunders, *Colonial Records of North Carolina*, 1:733; and minutes of the proprietary board, 7 Dec. 1710, CO 5/292/p. 35.

12. Pollock to Hyde, 29 Aug. 1710, printed in Hawks, *History of North Carolina*, 2:38.

13. Spotswood to [the earl of Dartmouth], 31 July 1711, CO 5/1337/f. 42; [Spotswood] to Cary and Hyde, 20 June 1711, CO 5/9/f. 78; Spotswood to Cary, 21 June 1711, CO 5/9/f. 79; Spotswood to the earl of Rochester, 30 July 1711, *The Official Letters of Alexander Spotswood*, ed. Robert A. Brock, 2 vols. (Richmond: Virginia Historical Society, 1882–85), 1:108–09; Spotswood, to the proprietors of Carolina, 28 June 1711, ibid., pp. 100–101.

14. Hyde to Dartmouth with address of the council of North Carolina, 22 Aug. 1711,

CO 5/308/ff. 6, 7; Dartmouth to the proprietors, 25 Sept. 1711, SP 44/112/pp. 323, 354; minutes of the proprietary board, 8, 13, 20 Nov., 14 Dec. 1711, 15 Jan. 1711/12, CO 5/292/pp. 47–50, 52; memorandum, 24 Jan. 1711/12, CO 5/290/p. 49.

    15. Minutes of the proprietary board, 29 Jan. 1711/12, CO 5/292/pp. 54–55.

    16. Hyde to Dartmouth, 20 July 1712, CO 5/9/f. 80; Pollock and the council to the proprietors, 20 Sept. 1712, William L. Saunders, ed., *Colonial Records of North Carolina,* 10 vols. (Raleigh: North Carolina Department of Archives, 1886–90), 1:873; minutes of the proprietary board, 8 Nov. 1712, CO 5/290/p. 57.

    17. Shelton to Spotswood, 24 Nov. 1713, CO 5/290/p. 73.

    18. M. Eugene Sirmans, *Colonial South Carolina: A Political History, 1663–1763* (Chapel Hill: University of North Carolina Press, 1966), pp. 56–73; proprietors to Blake, 20 Dec. 1697, CO 5/289/f. 19; proprietors to Blake and the council, 11 April 1698, CO 5/289/f. 24.

    19. Proprietors to the governor and council, 21 Sept., 19 Oct. 1699, CO 5/289/ff. 37, 40.

    20. Minutes of the council of South Carolina, 11 Sept. 1700, CO 5/1261/f. 305; and Alexander Samuel Salley, Jr., ed., *Narratives of Early Carolina, 1650–1708* (New York: Charles Scribners Sons, 1911), p. 221.

    21. Morton to the Board of Admiralty, 23 Aug. 1701, John Ellis Papers, BL, Add. MSS 28,887, ff. 254–55; Morton to the Commissioners of Trade, 29 Aug. 1701, CO 5/1261/f. 114; the earl of Manchester to the Commissioners of Trade, 2 Feb. 1701/2, SP 44/101/p. 185; Nicholas Trott to the Commissioners of Trade, 7 April 1702, CO 5/1261/f. 293.

    22. Archdale to ———, 12 Nov. 1705, Howe to Archdale, 30 Jan. 1705/6, Library of Congress, John Archdale Papers, nos. 7, 12.

    23. On the proceedings in the upper house see HMC, *Manuscripts of the House of Lords,* n.s. 6:406–12, no. 2248. See also the report of Northey and Harcourt, 17 May 1706, and the order in council, 10 June 1706, CO 5/1263/ff. 478, 500.

    24. Order in council, 26 June 1706, PC 2/81/p. 223; and memorandum of William Killigrew, n.d., but presented in July 1706, CO 5/306/f. 5.

    25. See Howard E. Kimball, "Gideon Johnson: The Bishop of London's Commissary to South Carolina, 1707–1716," *Historical Magazine of the Protestant Episcopal Church* 42 (March 1973): 2.

    26. See Frank J. Klingberg, ed., *The Carolina Chronicle of Dr. Francis Le Jau, 1706–1717* (Berkeley: University of California Press, 1956), p. 17.

    27. Naire to Secretary Sunderland, 17 Oct. 1708, HL, Huntington Misc. 22268 (misdated copy in the Colonial Office files: CO 5/306/ff. 10–11).

    28. Minutes of the proprietary board, 10 Feb., 9 April, 3 Nov. 1709, CO 5/292/pp. 9, 14, 28; proprietors to the deputies and councilors, 2 April 1709, CO 5/289/ff. 98–99.

    29. Minutes of the proprietary board, 28 Feb. 1710/11, CO 5/292/p. 44.

    30. Sirmans, *Colonial South Carolina,* pp. 105–6; proprietors to Rhett, 31 Jan. 1712/13, CO 5/290/p. 62.

    31. Minutes of the proprietary board, 4 Sept. 1714, CO 5/292/p. 75; 8 Sept. 1714, CO 5/290/p. 79.

    32. Kettleby and others to the Commissioners of Trade, 18 July 1715, CO 5/1264/f. 301; Commissioners of Trade to Secretary Stanhope, 19 July 1715, CO 5/383/ff. 1–2.

33. Minutes of the proprietary board, 24 Feb. 1715/16, CO 5/292/p. 84; proprietors to the governor and council, 3 March 1715/16, CO 5/290/pp. 92–94; proprietors to the assembly, 3 March 1715/16, CO 5/292/p. 91.

34. Godin to the Commissioners of Trade, 25 July 1716, CO 5/1265/f. 83; proprietors to the Board of Trade, 27 July 1716, CO 5/1265/no. 62.

35. Minutes of the proprietary board, 3 Nov. 1716, CO 5/292/p. 92; Middleton, Izard, and Godin to Boone and Beresford, 30 Nov. 1716, with the address of the assembly, CO 5/387/ff. 34, 35.

36. Daniel and the council to the proprietors, 26 Jan. 1716/17, CO 5/1265/f. 151; the case of the colony, read at the Board of Trade, 4 June 1717, CO 5/1265/f. 148; proprietors to the Commissioners of Trade, 4 June 1717, CO 5/1265/ff. 157–58.

37. Extract, Brett to the Commissioners of Customs, 31 Dec. 1717, CO 5/1265/f. 253; Boone to the Board of Trade, 13 May 1718, with address, CO 5/1265/ff. 270–71, 274.

38. Minutes of the proprietary board, 10 July, 21 Oct., 21 Nov. 1718, CO 5/292/pp. 97–99, 100, 109; proprietors to Governor Johnson and the council, 4, 12 Sept. 1718, CO 5/290/pp. 121–22, 124–25; minutes of the proprietary board, 13 and 20 Feb. 1718/19, CO 5/292/p. 113; proprietors to Governor Robert Johnson, 12 March 1718/19, CO 5/290/p. 129.

39. Extracts of letters to Secretary Skraggs, 14, 18 Nov. 1719, CO 5/1265/ff. 413, 415; revolutionary council to the Commissioners of Trade, 24 Dec. 1719, CO 5/1265/ff. 429–30; and Johnson to the Commissioners of Trade with the address of the Charles Town convention, 27 Dec. 1719, CO 5/1265/ff. 432, 433.

40. Commission and instruction to Francis Nicholson, Privy Council Papers, PC 5/5/pp. 100–108, 109–25.

Chapter 8

1. See, for example, Penn to Southwell, [11 March 1676/7], BL, Add. MSS 12,098, f. 14.

2. Logan to Penn, 5 April 1705, HSP, Logan Letter Book, 1, pt. 2: 172.

3. See, for example, the tickets presented for Philadelphia, Chester, and Bucks during the election for the assembly in 1711, in Isaac Norris to James Logan, 13 Oct. 1711, *Correspondence between William Penn and James Logan . . . and others, 1700–1750*, ed. Edward Armstrong, 2 vols. (Philadelphia, 1870–72), 2:438.

4. Logan to William Penn, Jr., 29 Sept. 1715, and Logan to Hannah Penn, 10 Oct. 1715, HSP, Logan Letter Book, 1712–15, pp. 320–34.

5. See the petition of Ford's widow and children, n.d., Portland Papers, BL, Loan 29/289/no. 63; Frederick B. Tolles, *James Logan and the Culture of Provincial America* (Boston: Little, Brown, 1957), pp. 28–29; and Joseph E. Illick, *Colonial Pennsylvania: A History* (New York: Charles Scribner's Sons, 1976), p. 66.

6. Logan to Penn, 18 June 1708, HSP, Logan Letter Book, 1, pt. 3:306.

7. Isaac Norris to Daniel Zachery, 29 Jan. 1700/1, Armstrong, *Correspondence between Penn and Logan,* 1:22.

8. See the copies of letters relating to illicit trade from Nicholson, HL, Bridgewater Americana, 9583–9592; and Penn to Nicholson, 22 Nov. 1697, ibid., 9595.

9. Robert Snead to Sir John Hublon, 25 April 1698, CO 5/1257/f. 65; John Moore to Francis Nicholson, 1 July 1698, CO 5/714/ff. 267–68.

10. Quary to the Commissioners of Trade, 4 July 1698, CO 5/1257/ff. 96–98; Edwin B. Bronner, *William Penn's "Holy Experiment": The Founding of Pennsylvania* (New York: Temple University Press, 1962), pp. 195–96; affidavit of Robert Webb, enclosed in Quary to the Commissioners of Trade, 1 March 1698/9, CO 5/1258/ff. 48–50, 52; Quary to the Commissioners of Trade, 20 Oct. 1698, CO 5/1257/f. 158. Of Webb's commission Lloyd exclaimed: "This is a fine baby, a pretty baby, but we are not to be frightened of babies," according to Quary.

11. Memorial of Penn, 19 Dec. 1698, CO 5/1257/ff. 177–78; petition of Newcastle and minutes of the provincial council, CO 5/1260/f. 4.

12. Tolles, *James Logan,* p. 28; and Penn to Charlewood Lawton, 21 Dec. 1700, HSP, Penn Letter Book, 1699–1703.

13. William Popple to Blathwayt, 4, 11, 22 Aug. 1699, BL, Add. MSS 9747, ff. 17, 19, 21; Popple to Robert Quary, 22 Aug. 1699, CO 5/1288/ff. 40–41; and Commissioners of Trade to Penn, 12 Sept. 1699, CO 5/1267/pp. 98–102 (also in HSP, Penn MSS, Official Correspondence, 1:17).

14. Penn to Somers, 22 Oct. 1700, and Penn to the Commissioners of Trade, 31 Dec. 1700, HSP, Penn Letter Book, 1699–1703; Logan to William Penn, Jr., [25 June 1700], Armstrong, *Correspondence between Penn and Logan,* 1:18.

15. Penn to Charlewood Lawton, 21 Dec. 1700, HSP, Penn Letter Book, 1699–1703.

16. Norris to Daniel Zachery, 3 Oct. 1701, Armstrong, *Correspondence between Penn and Logan,* 1:57; Illick, *Colonial Pennsylvania,* p. 68; and Gary B. Nash, *Quakers and Politics: Pennsylvania, 1681–1726* (Princeton: Princeton University Press, 1968), p. 288.

17. Address of the representatives of the lower counties, 25 Oct. 1701, CO 5/1261/f. 262; two addresses to Penn, 18 Oct. 1701, CO 5/1261/ff. 272, 276–77; the charter of privileges, 28 Oct. 1701, CO 5/1263/ff. 196–97.

18. Penn to Logan, 31 Oct., 3 Nov. 1701, 4 Feb. 1701/2, HSP, Penn Collection, Penn Family to James Logan; Illick, *Colonial Pennsylvania,* p. 75.

19. See Frederick B. Tolles, *Meeting House and Counting House: Quaker Merchants of Colonial Pennsylvania* (Chapel Hill: University of North Carolina Press, 1948), p. 16.

20. Logan to Penn, 2, 7 May 1702, HSP, Logan Letter Books, 1, pt. 1: 14, 22; Logan to Penn, 18 June (with postscripts of 23 and 25 June), 29 July, ibid., pp. 31, 40–41; Penn to Logan, 6 Sept. 1702, Armstrong, *Correspondence of Penn and Logan,* 1:133.

21. Penn to Logan, 21 June 1702, Armstrong, *Correspondence of Penn and Logan,* 1:112; Penn to Logan, 28 July 1702, printed in *Pennsylvania Magazine of History and Biography* 36, no. 3 (1912): 303–4; Penn to Logan, 23 Sept. 1703, HSP, Penn Papers, Penn Family to Logan; and Nottingham to the Commissioners of Trade, 22 June 1702, with memorial of Penn, SP 44/104/pp. 57, 57–58.

22. Commissioners of Trade to the queen, 11 Nov. 1702, CO 5/1290/ff. 119–20; Penn to Logan, 24 Feb. 1702/3, HSP, Penn Papers, Penn Family to Logan; representation of the Commissioners of Trade, 21 Jan. 1702/3, CO 5/1290/pp. 143–44; and order in council, 21 Jan. 1702/3, CO 5/1262/ff. 59–60.

23. Penn to Logan, 8 March, 26 Aug. 1703, HSP, Penn Papers, Penn Family to Logan; Logan to Penn, 20, 30 April, 3, 4 May, 1703, HSP, Logan Letter Books, 1, pt. 1:85, 88, 89, 91.

24. Penn to the Commissioners of Trade, 11 May 1703, CO 5 / 1262 / f. 106; Penn's proposals of 18 June 1703, CO 5 / 1262 / ff. 121–22.

25. Penn to ———, 9 Feb. 1703 / 4, HMC, *Manuscripts of the Duke of Portland, Welbeck Abbey, 15th Report*, app., pt. 4, p. 81; Penn to the Commissioners of Trade, 3 Jan. 1704 / 5, CO 5 / 1263 / ff. 3–6.

26. William Popple, Jr., to Penn, 11 Jan. 1704 / 5, CO 5 / 1291 / ff. 44–45; Penn to the Commissioners of Trade, 12 Jan. 1704 / 5, CO 5 / 1263 / ff. 1–2.

27. Penn to the Commissioners of Trade, 9 March 1704 / 5, CO 5 / 1263 / f. 116; Popple to Penn, 9 March 1704 / 5, CO 5 / 1293 / ff. 66–67; copy of a draft patent requested by Penn with comments by the Commissioners of Trade, 23 May 1705, CO 5 / 1263 / ff. 125–37; Popple to Penn, 26 July 1705, CO 5 / 1291 / ff. 97–101; and paper by Penn read at Board of Trade on 1 Sept. 1705, CO 5 / 1263 / f. 173.

28. Logan to Penn, 13 July 1705, HSP, Logan Letter Books, 1, pt. 2:186–87.

29. Logan to Penn, 2, 18 Oct. 1702, HSP, Logan Letter Books, 1, pt. 1:47–49, 53–55; Logan to Penn, 9 July, 2 Sept., 1 Dec. 1702, ibid., pp. 56–69, 101–2, 109–18.

30. Penn to Logan, 10 March 1703 / 4, HSP, Penn Papers, Penn Family to Logan.

31. Evans to the earl of Nottingham, 10 March 1703 / 4, BL, Add. MSS 29,589, f. 384; Evans to the Commissioners of Trade, CO 5 / 1262 / ff. 279–80; Logan to Penn, 14 July 1704, HSP, Logan Letter Books, 1, pt. 2:148–50, 153.

32. Logan to Penn, 28 Sept. (with postscript of 3 Oct.) 1704, HSP, Logan Letter Books, 1, pt. 2:159–65.

33. Logan to Penn, 27 Oct. 1704, Armstrong, *Correspondence between Penn and Logan*, 1:338–39; Logan to Penn, 11, 17 Feb., 5 April 1705, HSP, Logan Letter Books, 1, pt. 2:168, 172; Penn to Mompesson, 17 Feb. 1704 / 5, HSP, Penn Family to Logan.

34. Logan to Penn, 13 July, 22 Aug., 8 Nov. 1705, HSP, Logan Letter Books, 1, pt. 2:186–87, 194–95, 207–8.

35. Logan to Penn, 28 May, 25 July 1706, HSP, Logan Letter Books, 1, pt. 2:218–20, 231–33; Logan to Penn, 6 Oct., 26, 30 Nov., 5 Dec. 1706, ibid., pp. 256, 257, 260–62.

36. Penn to the Commissioners of Trade, 29 Jan. 1706 / 7, CO 5 / 1263 / f. 585; Commissioners of Trade to the earl of Sunderland, 5 Feb. 1706 / 7, T 1 / 115 / f. 118; Sunderland to Godolphin, 24 Feb. 1706 / 7, SP 44 / 106 / p. 36; and William Lowndes to William Popple, 18 March 1706 / 7, CO 5 / 1263 / f. 616.

37. Dobrée, *William Penn*, pp. 324–25; order in council, 22 Jan. 1707 / 8, PC 2 / 81 / p. 508. For the Fords' petition and their statement to the lord chancellor see Portland Papers, BL, Loan 29 / 289 / no. 63. Penn submitted a statement of expenses for which he wanted compensation from the crown, claiming a total of £76,144 for expenses and interest incurred in his father's loan to Charles II and his own expenses (with interest) in founding and maintaining Pennsylvania (HSP, Penn MSS, Official Correspondence, 1:39).

38. Logan to Penn, 2 March 1706 / 7, 20 May 1707, HSP, Logan Letter Books, 1, pt. 3:276–77, 288–89; Roy N. Lokken, *David Lloyd: Colonial Lawmaker* (Seattle: University of Washington Press, 1959), p. 173.

39. Evans to the Commissioners of Trade, 29 Sept. 1707, CO 5 / 1264 / f. 68; Logan to Penn, 22 June 1707, HSP, Logan Letter Books, 1, pt. 3:295–96.

40. Penn to Logan, 3 May 1708, HSP, Penn Papers, Penn Family to Logan; Logan to Penn, n.d., Logan Letter Books, 1, pt. 3:307–8.

41. Logan to Penn, 3 Feb., 6 March 1708 / 9, HSP, Logan Letter Books, 1, pt. 3:323, 324–29.

42. Gookin to the secretary of the SPG, 27 Aug. 1709, Perry, *Historical Collections, American Colonial Church,* 2:52.

43. Penn to the Quakers of Philadelphia, [1710], BL, Add. MSS 35,909, ff. 1–7; Clair Wayne Keller, "Pennsylvania Government, 1701–1740: A Study in the Operation of a Colonial Government" (Ph.D. diss., University of Washington, 1967), p. 357; Tolles, *Meeting House and Counting House,* p. 17; and James T. Lemon, *The Best Poor Man's Country: A Geographical Study of Early Southeastern Pennsylvania* (Baltimore: Johns Hopkins University Press, 1972), p. 221.

44. Isaac Norris, *Friendly Advice to the Inhabitants of Pen[n]sylvania* (Philadelphia: printed by Andrew Bradford, 1710).

45. Dartmouth to the Commissioners of Trade, 31 July 1710, and the "Memorial of William Penn, Proprietor & Governor of Pen[n]sylvania in relation to his Government in that Province," SP 44 / 110 / pp. 137–38, 138–41; Penn to the Commissioners of Trade, 7 Dec. 1710, [2 Feb. 1710 / 11], CO 5 / 1264 / ff. 205–6, 217–18; Penn to the Quakers of Philadelphia, 10 Feb. 1710 / 11, HSP, Penn MSS, Private Correspondence, 1:37.

46. Logan to Hannah Penn, 14 May, 2 July 1713, and Logan to William Penn, Jr., 29 Sept. 1715, HSP, Logan Letter Books, 1712–15, pp. 107, 123, 319–20; Penn to Oxford, 22 June 1711, HMC, *Manuscripts of the Duke of Portland, Welbeck Abbey,* 5:17; Penn to the lord treasurer, 12 May 1712, T 1 / 147 / f. 143.

47. Northey to the lord treasurer, 25 Feb. 1711 / 12, CO 5 / 1265 / f. 8. There is a copy of this report in the Treasury Board papers, T 1 / 144 / f. 97, endorsed to the effect that a warrant was later signed for £1,000.

48. Penn to the Quaker elders, 24 July 1712, *Memoirs of the Historical Society of Pennsylvania,* 14 vols. (Philadelphia, 1826–95), 1:217–18.

49. Hannah Penn to Logan, 17 Oct. 1713, HSP, Penn Papers, Penn Family to Logan; report of the committee of the Privy Council, 20 March 1713 / 14, PC 1 / 58 / B1; Logan to Hannah Penn, 8 April 1714, HSP, Logan Letter Books, 1712–15, p. 181; the attorney general to the Commissioners of Trade, 22 July 1714, CO 323 / 7 / f. 78; Commissioners of Trade to the committee of the Privy Council, 2 Sept. 1714, CO 5 / 1292 / ff. 210–12.

50. Norris to Joseph Pike, 4 June 1711, and Norris to Benjamin Cole, 16 June 1711, Armstrong, *Correspondence between Penn and Logan,* 2:435, 436.

51. Isaac Norris and others to Penn, [10 April 1711], HSP, Penn MSS, Official Correspondence, 1:45; Norris to Logan, 13 Oct. 1711, Armstrong, *Correspondence between Penn and Logan,* 2:438; Logan to Evans, 5 July 1712, HSP, Logan Letter Books, 1712–15, p. 40.

52. Logan to Henry Goldney, 20 Jan. 1712 / 13, Logan to Hannah Penn, 1 June 1713, Logan to Thomas Grey, 5 March 1713 / 14, Logan to Thomas Story, 29 May 1714, Logan to Charles Eden, 5 May 1715, Logan to Hannah Penn, 15 Aug. 1715, 13, 28 Oct. 1715, HSP, Logan Letter Books, 1712–15, pp. 78, 82, 117, 198, 289, 302, 342, 351.

53. Logan to Thomas Grey, 4 Nov. 1714, and Logan and Norris to Henry Goldney,

18 Aug. 1715, HSP, Logan Letter Books, 1712–15, pp. 269–70, 307; Hannah Penn to Logan, 22 Jan. 1714/15, HSP, Penn Papers, Penn Family to Logan.

Chapter 9

1. See the Commissioners of Trade to the Lords Justices in Council, 2 Oct. 1701, CO 5/1289/ff. 122–29, and the draft of a surrender of government (intended to have been presented in April 1688, so William Dockwra, a proprietor of East New Jersey, claimed) to James II, CO 5/1261/ff. 176–77.

2. John Robert Strassburger, "The Origins and Establishment of the Morris Family in the Society and Politics of New York and New Jersey, 1630–1746" (Ph.D. diss., Princeton University, 1976), p. 124; and Eugene R. Sheridan, *Lewis Morris, 1671–1746: A Study in Early American Politics* (Syracuse, N.Y.: Syracuse University Press, 1981), pp. 19–21. On certain issues Sheridan's Ph.D. dissertation, "Politics in Colonial America: The Career of Lewis Morris, 1671–1746" (University of Wisconsin, 1972) has more detail than his published political biography of Morris.

3. See William Blathwayt to the earl of Bridgewater, 18 Oct. 1697 (n.s.), HL, Bridgewater Papers, Elsmere Collection, EL 9741; Commissioners of Trade to the Lords Justices, 27 Oct. 1697, CO 5/1287/ff. 88–93 (copy in the John Champante Papers, Bodl., Rawlinson A MS, vol. 272, ff. 10–13); order in council, 25 Nov. 1697, CO 323/2/f. 210.

4. Council of West New Jersey to the proprietors, 14 April 1697, CO 5/1257/f. 69; Sheridan, *Lewis Morris*, p. 24.

5. Strassburger, "Morris Family and Politics of New York and New Jersey," pp. 119–21, 124; Sheridan, *Lewis Morris*, p. 26.

6. William Popple to William Lowndes, 14 Dec. 1698, and Popple to John Sansom, 22 Dec. 1698, CO 5/1287/ff. 132, 142–43; order in council, 9 March 1698/9, on the petition of the proprietors of East New Jersey, CO 5/1257/ff. 221, 223.

7. Memorial of Lewis Morris to the Commissioners of Trade, 5 Aug. 1701, CO 5/1261/ff. 58–59.

8. William Popple to Dockwra, 14 April 1699, CO 5/1289/f. 201; Commissioners of Trade to the king, 18 April 1699, CO 5/1287/ff. 201–2; memorial of the proprietors of East Jersey, 19 April 1699, CO 5/1258/f. 19; Dockwra to the Commissioners of Trade, 5 July 1699, CO 5/1258/ff. 82–83; and Popple to Blathwayt, 11 Aug. 1699, Blathwayt Papers, BL, Add. MSS 9747, f. 19.

9. Penn to Hamilton, [3 April 1701], HSP, William Penn Letter Book, 1699–1703; Strassburger, "Morris Family and Politics of New York and New Jersey," p. 140; Sheridan, *Lewis Morris*, pp. 29–34.

10. Secretary Hedges to the Treasury, 19 March 1699/1700, SP 44/101/pp. 116–17; and the account of the hearing before the court, CO 5/1044/ff. 144–66.

11. Dockwra and others to the Commissioners of Trade, 9 Dec. 1700, CO 5/1260/ff. 294–95.

12. Basse to Blathwayt, 20 Aug. 1701, Blathwayt Papers, BL, Add. MSS 9747, f. 38; Morris to William Popple, 13 Sept. 1701, with enclosures, CO 5/1261/ff. 130, 131–33; Strassburger, "Morris Family and Politics of New York and New Jersey," pp. 170–71.

13. Commissioners of Trade to the Lords Justices in Council, 2 Oct. 1701, CO

5/1289/ff. 122–29; Dockwra to Morris, 13 Feb. 1701/2, Rutgers University Library, New Brunswick, N.J., Lewis Morris Papers; deed of surrender, 15 April 1702, CO 5/970/f. 102 (Privy Council Papers, PC 5/2/306); petition of Morris and others, CO 5/1261/f. 341; petition of Sonmans and Dockwra, CO 5/1261/f. 337.

14. Commissioners of Trade to Secretary Nottingham, 1 June 1702, with the form of a letter from the queen, CO 5/1290/f. 7.

15. Dockwra's list for the council, 3 Aug. 1702, CO 5/970/ff. 6–7; Clarendon to Nottingham, 1 Sept. 1702, with remarks by Basse, CO 5/980/ff. 38, 40; and Dartmouth, Cecil, Pollexfen, and Prior to Nottingham, 3 Sept. 1702, CO 5/980/f. 36.

16. Instructions for Cornbury, 21 Aug. 1702, CO 5/5/994A/pp. 43–90.

17. Morris to the Commissioners of Trade, 29 Sept. 1702, CO 5/970/f. 16; Sheridan, *Lewis Morris,* pp. 50–51.

18. See Sheridan, *Lewis Morris,* pp. 54–55. Peter Sonmans was involved in a dispute with his two sisters and their husbands, Joseph Wright and Joseph Ormston, over the terms of their father's will. The elder Sonmans had held several shares in the eastern division. For the details see Andrew Hamilton to William Penn, 21 Oct. 1702, HSP, Penn MSS, Official Correspondence, 1:36.

19. Cornbury to the Commissioners of Trade, [9] Sept. 1703, CO 5/970/ff. 20–21; James Logan to William Penn, 2 Sept. 1702, HSP, Logan Letter Book, 1, pt. 1:109–18.

20. Quary to the Commissioners of Trade, 14 Aug. 1703, CO 5/1262/ff. 156–57.

21. Quary to the Commissioners of Trade, 20 Dec. 1703, CO 5/970/ff. 26–30; Cornbury to the Commissioners of Trade, 14 Jan. 1703/4, CO 5/970/ff. 34–36.

22. Sheridan, *Lewis Morris,* pp. 61–62.

23. Cornbury to the Commissioners of Trade, 19 Feb. 1704/5, CO 5/970/ff. 64–69; Sheridan, *Lewis Morris,* pp. 64–65.

24. Commissioners of Trade to the queen, 20 April 1705, with additional instructions, CO 5/994A/pp. 190–91, 191–95; order in council, 23 April 1705, CO 5/980/f. 48; Commissioners of Trade to Cornbury, 20 April 1705, CO 5/994A/pp. 197–200.

25. Logan to William Penn, 12 April, 3 May 1707, HSP, Logan Letter Book, 1, pt. 3:279, 290.

26. Quary to the Commissioners of Trade, 28 June 1707, CO 323/6/ff. 137–39; Cornbury to the Commissioners of Trade enclosing the council of New Jersey to the queen, n.d., CO 5/970/ff. 176, 180–81; and the documents signed by Morris, Thomas Gordon, and Samuel Jennings among the Sunderland Papers, HL, HM 22301, HM 1407, HM 1969; Cornbury to the Commissioners of Trade, 7 June 1707, with his speech to the assembly of 9 April and the remonstrance of the assembly, CO 5/970/ff. 151–53, 155–56, 157–64.

27. Logan to William Penn, 2 Feb. 1708/9, HSP, Logan Letter Book, 1:321; Robert Livingston to William Lowndes, 2 June 1707, PRO T 1/102/f. 130; Sheridan, *Lewis Morris,* p. 79.

28. Cornbury to the Commissioners of Trade, 29 Nov. 1707, with resolution of the assembly of 27 Oct., CO 5/970/ff. 170, 172; Quary to the Commissioners of Trade, 10 Jan. 1707/8, CO 323/6/ff. 142–43.

29. Morris to secretary of state [Harley?], 9 Feb. 1707/8, CO 5/1091/ff. 31–35. Sunderland had just replaced Harley as a principal secretary of state. The story of Cornbury's wearing woman's apparel became embedded in the partisan mythology of colonial politics to be used by the governor's opponents. Morris claimed it was a common occur-

rence. William Smith, Jr., in his *History of the Province of New York,* ed. Michael Kammen, 2 vols. (Cambridge: Harvard University Press, 1972), 1:130, wrote that it was not uncommon for Cornbury to dress in a woman's habit and them to "patrole" about Fort Anne, the governor's residence in Manhattan. Some men attributed his wearing of female clothing as a symbol of the monarch, others to his drunkenness. Arthur D. Pierce, "A Governor's Skirts," *Proceedings of the New Jersey Historical Society* 88 (Jan. 1965): 3, concludes that "Cornbury actually appeared in women's attire at his wife's funeral," but he cites no documents for this statement.

30. Nominations for the council with objections of several proprietors, 12, 19 May 1708, CO 5/970/ff. 186, 188–89; Penn to William Popple, 26 May 1708, CO 5/970/f. 194; Sunderland to the Commissioners of Trade, 29 June 1708, SP 44/106/p. 327; Commissioners of Trade to Sunderland, 1 July 1708, CO 5/994A/pp. 449–50; order in council, 18 Aug. 1708, CO 5/970/f. 240; and instructions to Lovelace, 19 Aug. 1708, CO 5/210/f. 56.

31. Commissioners of Trade to Lovelace, 22 June 1708, CO 5/1121/pp. 282–86.

32. Coxe to [William Dockwra?], 17 Jan. 1708/9, HL, HM 22302.

33. Address of the assembly to the queen, 31 March 1709, CO 5/970/ff. 243–44; council of New Jersey to Lovelace, n.d., HL, HM 1366; Peter Sonmans to Lovelace, with petition of the grand jury of Middlesex, 8 March 1708/9, and the report of the assembly, HL, HM 1390; the council to Ingoldsby, 6 May 1709, HL, HM 1446; Lewis Morris to Sunderland, 30 May 1709, HL, HM 22282; the assembly to the queen, 10 June 1709 (signed by Thomas Gordon), HL, HM 1397; and Thomas Gordon to Sunderland, 13 June 1709, HL, HM 46, 597.

34. Ingoldsby to the Commissioners of Trade, 16 June 1709, CO 5/970/f. 246; James Logan to William Penn, 14 June 1709, HSP, Logan Letter Book, 1:338; and George MacGregor Waller, "Samuel Vetch and the Glorious Enterprise," *New York Historical Quarterly* 34 (April 1950): 117–18.

35. Nicholson and Vetch to the Commissioners of Trade, 28 June 1709, CO 5/1049/f. 355; Thomas Cockerill to William Popple, 2 June 1709, CO 5/1049/ff. 380–81; [Morris] to Sunderland, [June 1709], Rutgers University Library, Lewis Morris Papers.

Introduction to Part Three

1. David Jamison to Robert Livingston, 15 July 1701, FDRL, Robert Livingston General Correspondence, Livingston Family Papers.

Chapter 10

1. See Governor Robert Hunter to the Commissioners of Trade, 14 Nov. 1710, CO 5/1050/ff. 19–25; and Cadwallader Colden to Alexander Colden, 15 Oct. 1759, Smith, *History of the Province of New York,* 1:308.

2. David Jamison to Robert Livingston, 15 July 1701, FDRL, Robert Livingston General Correspondence, Livingston Family Papers; Jamison to Livingston, 8 Oct. 1701, ibid.; and Jamison to Benjamin Fletcher, 26 Dec. 1701, HL, Blathwayt Papers, BL 197.

3. See, for example, the analysis in Caleb Heathcote to Gilbert Heathcote, [1701], HL, Blathwayt Papers, BL 224.

4. See the statement of the younger Leisler and Gouverneur, n.d. but read at the Plantation Office 25 Sept. 1696, CO 5/1039/ff. 266–68, and the list of alleged grievances CO 5/1039/ff. 270–73 (copy in the Portland Papers, BL, Loan 29/289).

5. Shrewsbury to the Commissioners of Trade, 16 March 1696/7, SP 44/100/ p. 275.

6. Livingston to Shrewsbury, 30 Sept. 1696, and Livingston to Romney, 20 Sept., 1696, HMC, *Manuscripts of the Duke of Buccleuch and Queensbury at Montague House,* 2, pt. 2:405, 408; Bellomont to Somers, 16 Oct. 1697, Surrey Record Office, Kingston, Somers Papers, Acc 775 G1/1; James Vernon to William III, 22 Nov. 1698, Vernon Papers, BL, Add. MSS 40,772, f. 341; Somers to Shrewsbury, 15 Dec. 1698, *Private and Original Correspondence of Charles Talbot, Duke of Shrewsbury,* ed. William Coxe (London, 1821), p. 570; and Charles Lodowyck to the earl of Oxford, 4 June 1711, Portland Papers, BL, Loan 29/45c/no. 18, f. 146.

7. Kidd to———, 12 May 1701, HMC, *Report on the Manuscripts of the Duke of Portland at Welbeck Abbey, Fifteenth Report,* app., pt. 2 (London, 1897), p. 17.

8. Fletcher to the Commissioners of Trade, 22 June 1697, CO 5/1040/f. 69; Fletcher to Chidley Brooke and William Nicoll, 20 Dec. 1696, CO 5/1039/ff. 310–11; and memorandum of the council of New York, 15 Sept. 1696, CO 5/1039/f. 261.

9. Vernon's minutes of the meetings of the council for 11 July, 11 Dec. 1699, BL, Add. MSS 40,781, ff. 51, 53; Fletcher to Blathwayt, [5 Aug. 1698], BL, Add. MSS 9747, f. 5; Vernon to Bellomont, 31 Aug. 1698, CO 324/26/pp. 92–93.

10. Commissioners of Trade to the Lords Justices in Council, 19 Oct. 1698, CO 5/1116/pp. 1–34; Lords Justices in Council to Bellomont, 10 Nov. 1698, CO 324/6/ pp. 226–30.

11. Fletcher to the Commissioners of Trade, 24 Dec. 1698, CO 5/1041/ff. 395–400; deposition of John Evans, 3 Jan. 1698/9, CO 5/1042/f. 2; minutes of the Board of Trade, 30 Jan. 1698/9, CO 391/11/pp. 346–60; Blathwayt to George Stepney, 30 Dec. 1698, SP 50/52/n.p.; and Graham to Abraham DePeyster, 22 May 1699, New-York Historical Society, DePeyster Papers, 1695–1710, no. 21.

12. Undersecretary of State Robert Yard to Blathwayt, 1 Sept. 1699, Boston Public Library, Blathwayt Papers; Vernon to Shrewsbury, 21 Sept. 1699, *Letters . . . Addressed to the Duke of Shrewsbury by J. Vernon . . . ,* ed. G. P. R. James, 3 vols. (London, 1841), 2:353; Vernon to William III, 22 Sept. 1699, BL, Add. MSS 40,774, f. 193.

13. Petition of the London merchants trading to New York, 9 Feb. 1698/9, CO 5/1042/f. 26; petition of Henry Adderly and others to William Popple, 18 Feb. 1698/9, CO 5/1042/f. 28; Blathwayt to Bellomont, 11 Feb. 1698/9, CW, Blathwayt Papers, vol. 8; memorial of John Lofting, Henry Adderly, Benjamin Hackshaw, and others, 10 March 1698/9, CO 1042/ff. 63–71.

14. Bellomont to [Somers?], 12 May 1698, Bodl., Clarendon MS, vol. 102, ff. 19–20.

15. Bellomont to the Commissioners of Trade, 18 May 1698, CO 5/1040/ff. 127–28, 129, 137–38; Bellomont to the Treasury, 25 May 1698, T 1/56/no. 274.

16. Bellomont to the Commissioners of Trade, 22 June 1698, CO 5/1040/ff. 196–201, enclosing the testimony of Henry Beekman, the depositions of Edward and Hanna Earle, and the defense of William Pinhorne, CO 5/1041/ff. 203, 205, 207, 212–20.

17. Compare Bellomont to the Treasury, 21 Oct. 1698, T 1/57/ff. 24–25; Bellomont to the Commissioners of Trade, 21 Oct. 1698, CO 5/1041/ff. 209–10; and Bellomont to William Popple, 27 Oct. 1698, CO 5/1041/f. 258, with the version of the merchants cited in note 13 above.

18. Bellomont to the Commissioners of Trade, 21 Sept. 1698, CO 5/1041/ff. 46–48; Bellomont to Somers, 16 May 1699, Surrey Record Office, Kingston, Somers Papers, ACC 775 G1/3; Bellomont to the Commissioners of Trade, 27 April 1699, CO 5/1042/ff. 116–18; heads of complaints against Bellomont signed by John Key, 11 March 1698/9, CO 5/1042/ff. 150–51; and Beverly McAnear, "Politics in Provincial New York, 1689–1761" (Ph. D. diss., Stanford University, 1935), 1:173–75.

19. Bellomont to the Commissioners of Trade, 3, 15, 29 May 1699, CO 5/1042/ff. 170–72, 193, 203–8, 236–38; Bellomont to the earl of Bridgewater, 12 May 1699, HL, Bridgewater Americana, 9764; and Bellomont to the Commissioners of Trade, 15 Dec. 1699, CO 5/1116/pp. 260–62.

20. Bellomont to the Treasury, 8 Sept. 1699, T 1/63/f. 142.

21. Viola Barnes, "The Rise of William Phips," *New England Quarterly* 1 (July 1928): 288; G. B. Warden, *Boston, 1689–1776* (Boston: Little, Brown, 1970), pp. 41–46.

22. Richard R. Johnson, *Adjustment to Empire: The New England Colonies, 1675–1715* (New Brunswick, N. J.: Rutgers University Press, 1981), pp. 393–94.

23. For Dudley's connections in Massachusetts see his letters to his wife in Foxbury, 6 May 1696, 24 June 1697, 13 April 1698, Winthrop Papers, *MHSC*, 6th ser. 3:514, 515, 516, 517.

24. Bellomont to Secretary Vernon, 12 Dec. 1696, SP 63/385/no. 75, f. 183; memorial of Harrison, 1 Feb. 1696/7, CO 5/859/ff. 165–66; and the memorial of the Anglo–New England merchants in the timber trade, 1 Feb. 1696/7, CO 5/859/ff. 169–70.

25. Shrewsbury to the Commissioners of Trade, 16 March 1696/7, SP 44/100/p. 275; Bellomont to William Popple, 14 April 1697, CO 5/859/ff. 234–35.

26. Minutes of the proceedings of the Lords Justices in Council, 13, 27 July, 22 Aug. 1697, SP 44/275/pp. 126, 151–52, 179; minutes of the proceedings of the Lords Justices in Council, 3 Aug. 1697, SP 44/100/p. 179; Commissioners of Trade to Stoughton, 3 Aug. 1697, CO 5/907/p. 217.

27. Johnson, *Adjustment to Empire,* pp. 293–94.

28. Order of the Lords Justices in Council, 24 Nov. 1698, approving the representation of the Commissioners of Trade of the same date, CO 5/860/f. 86.

29. Opinion of the attorney general, Thomas Trevor, 4 April 1699, CO 5/860/f. 210; Commissioners of Trade to Bellomont, 3 Feb. 1698/9, CO 5/908/pp. 124–31.

30. Ashurst to Wait Winthrop, 25 Aug. 1697, *MHSC,* 6th ser. 5:39; Bellomont to Somers, 12 May 1698, Bodl., Clarendon MSS, vol. 102, f. 19; Wait Winthrop to Ashurst, 26 July 1698, *MHSC,* 5th ser. 8: 533; Wait Winthrop to Fitzjohn Winthrop, 9 Oct. 1699, ibid., pp. 560–61.

31. Wait Winthrop to Sir Henry Ashurst, [1699], *MHSC,* 6th ser. 5:50.

32. Sewall, *Diary,* 1:411; Bellomont to the Treasury, 8 Sept. 1699, T 1/63/f. 142.

33. Bellomont to the Commissioners of Trade, 28 Aug. 1699, CO 5/860/ff. 202–5; Bellomont to the Commissioners of Trade, 28 Nov. 1700, CO 5/1045/f. 18.

34. Bellomont to the Commissioners of Trade, 15 July 1700, CO 5/861/ff. 413–

16; James Vernon to William Blathwayt, 24 Sept. 1700, BL, Add. MSS 34, 348, ff. 96–97.

35. Blathwayt to George Stepney, 30 Dec. 1698, SP 105/52; Bayard to John Povey, 23 June 1699, CW, Blathwayt Papers, vol. 7; Bayard to Bridgewater, 23 June 1699, HL, Elsmere Collection, Bridgewater Americana, 9765.

36. Bayard to Bridgewater, 16 Oct. 1699, and Bellomont to Bridgewater, 12 Oct. 1699, HL, Bridgewater Americana, 9775, 9767; Graham to Robert Livingston, 16 Jan. 1699/1700, FDRL, Robert Livingston General Correspondence.

37. Bellomont to Abraham DePeyster, 22 Jan. 1699/1700, New-York Historical Society, Abraham DePeyster Papers, 1695–1710, f. 3; John Riggs to Robert Livingston, n.d. but endorsed 12 Feb. 1699/1700, FDRL, Robert Livingston General Correspondence.

38. Bellomont to the Commissioners of Trade, 8 July 1699, CO 5/860/ff. 149–51.

39. Bellomont to Sir John Stanley, 5 March 1699/1700, HMC, *Manuscripts of the Duke of Portland, Welbeck Abbey,* 8:69–70.

40. Bellomont to the Commissioners of Trade, 26 July 1700, CO 5/1044/ff. 168–69.

41. Hawles to the Commissioners of Trade, 27 June 1700, CO 5/1044/ff. 130–33; Montague to the Commissioners of Trade, 13 Aug. 1700, CO 5/1044/ff. 187–98; and Commissioners of Trade to the Lords Justices in Council, 19 Aug. 1700, CO 5/1117/pp. 384–85.

42. Bellomont to the Commissioners of Trade, 17 Oct. 1700, CO 5/1045/no. 1; Graham to Blathwayt, 30 Oct. 1700, CW, Blathwayt Papers, vol. 10; Bellomont to the Commissioners of Trade, 21 Feb. 1700/01, CO 5/1044/ff. 239–40.

43. Bellomont to the Treasury, 2 Jan. 1700/01, T 1/72/f. 5.

Chapter 11

1. See the account of the governor and assistants, 24 Jan. 1708/9, CO 5/1254/ff. 160–61.

2. Memorial of Ashurst, 24 July 1697, CO 5/859/f. 306; petition and case of the duchess of Hamilton, CO 5/859/ff. 244, 247–48; reply of the Hamiltons, 3 May 1697, CO 5/859/ff. 256–57; memorial of Winthrop, 30 April 1697, CO 5/859/f. 251; Brenton to the Commissioners of Trade, 30 April 1697, CO 5/859/f. 253; Winthrop to Ashurst, 24 Oct. 1697, and Winthrop to Nathaniel Coddington, 30 Oct. 1706, MHS, Winthrop Family Papers.

3. Winthrop to the Commissioners of Trade, 27 Jan. 1687/8, CO 5/1257/f. 53; Winthrop to the Commissioners of Trade, 27 Oct. 1698, MHS, Winthrop Family Papers.

4. James Mark Poteet, "Preserving the Old Ways: Connecticut, 1690–1740" (Ph.D. diss., University of Virginia, 1973), pp. 95–127, 184–89.

5. Winthrop to William Popple, 27 Oct. 1698, CO 5/1258/f. 3; petition of Palmes and John Hallam, 23 Feb. 1698/9, CO 5/1257/f. 208; remonstrance of Palmes, 11 May 1699, CO 5/1258/ff. 38–44.

6. Petition of the Hallams, 5 Dec. 1700, CO 5/1260/ff. 274–75; Henry Ashurst to the Commissioners of Trade, 13 Dec. 1700, enclosing the governor and company of Connecticut to the Commissioners of Trade, 22 Oct. 1700, CO 5/1260/ff. 301–3, 304; affidavit of the London merchant Arthur Bunyan, 28 Nov. 1700, CO 5/1260/f. 319;

William Popple to the attorney general and solicitor general, 18 Dec. 1700, CO 5 / 1288 / f. 207; Thomas Trevor and John Hawles to the Commissioners of Trade, 19 May 1701, CO 5 / 1261 / f. 13.

7. Samuel Wyllys to Winthrop, 6 Oct. 1701, 22 April 1702, *MHSC*, 6th ser. 3:80–81, 111.

8. Poteet, "Preserving the Old Ways," pp. 174–77.

9. Livingston to Winthrop, 10 Aug. 1704, *MHSC*, 6th ser. 3:254; Commissioners of Trade to the queen, 9 March 1703 / 4, CO 5 / 1290 / ff. 227–29; order in council, 23 March 1703 / 4, Privy Council Papers, PRO, PC 5 / 3 / p. 363.

10. Dudley to the Commissioners of Trade with the proceedings of the commission of inquiry, 25 Aug. 1705, CO 5 / 1263 / ff. 234, 237–77; representation of the Commissioners of Trade, 24 Jan. 1705 / 6, CO 5 / 912 / pp. 111–13; Ashurst to Fitzjohn Winthrop, 21 May 1706, *MHSC*, 6th ser. 3:324–25; Samuel Reade to Winthrop, 21 May 1706, ibid., p. 328; John Winthrop to Fitzjohn Winthrop, [June 1706], ibid., p. 334.

11. Charles Congreve to William Popple, 4 Dec. 1704, with the protest of John Rogers, CO 5 / 1262 / ff. 304–5, 306; Ashurst to the Commissioners of Trade, 4 May 1705, CO 5 / 1263 / ff. 121–23; Wyeth and Feild to the Commissioners of Trade, 5 June 1705, CO 5 / 1263 / ff. 139–40.

12. Ashurst to Harley, 5 July 1705, Portland Papers, BL, Loan 29 / 289 / no. 54; Ashurst to Wait Winthrop, 24 Aug. 1708, *MHSC*, 6th ser. 5:173.

13. See, for example, Charles Carkesse of the Customs Board to William Popple at the Plantation Office, 25 Oct. 1715, and Popple's reply of 28 Oct., CO 5 / 1265 / f. 15; also Poteet, "Preserving the Old Ways," pp. 208–13.

14. Poteet, "Preserving the Old Ways," pp. 224–51.

15. Wait Winthrop to Fitzjohn Winthrop, 24 Feb. 1696 / 7, *MHSC*, 5th ser. 8:525.

16. Wait Winthrop to Fitzjohn Winthrop, 9 Oct. 1699, ibid., pp. 560–61; Fitzjohn Winthrop to Francis Brinley, 18 Dec. 1699, ibid., p. 372; deposition of Nicholas Hallam, 31 Jan. 1700 / 1, CO 5 / 1260 / f. 371; petition of the Atherton Associates, [1701], *MHSC*, 6th ser. 5:104; order in council, 11 May 1710, PC 5 / 82 / pp. 581–82.

17. Sidney V. James, *Colonial Rhode Island: A History* (New York: Charles Scribner's Sons, 1975), pp. 117, 187, 234–35; John Graves to the Commissioners of Trade, 19 Feb. 1696 / 7, CO 323 / 2 / f. 134.

18. Jahleel Brenton to the Commissioners of Trade, 8 March 1697 / 8, enclosing Sanford to the Commissioners of Trade, 30 Jan. 1697 / 8, and Sanford, Francis Brinley, and Brenton to the king, 31 Jan. 1697 / 8, CO 5 / 1257 / ff. 61, 63, 64.

19. Address of Rhode Island to the king, 4 May 1698, CO 5 / 751 / f. 81; Cranston to the Commissioners of Trade, 8 May 1698, CO 5 / 1257 / f. 70.

20. Order in council, 5 Jan. 1698 / 9, CO 5 / 1257 / f. 181; Brenton to the Commissioners of Trade, 10 Feb. 1698 / 9, CO 5 / 1257 / ff. 195–96; memorial of Brinley, CO 5 / 1258 / f. 27.

21. Cranston to the Commissioners of Trade, 27 May 1699, CO 5 / 1258 / ff. 163–64; Commissioners of Trade to the governor and assistants of Rhode Island, 11 Aug. 1699, CO 5 / 1288 / ff. 37–40; and William Popple to William Blathwayt, 11 Aug. 1699, BL, Add. MSS 9747, f. 19.

22. Bellomont to William Popple, 15 Sept. 1699, CO 5 / 1043 / f. 1; Bellomont to Popple, 6 Nov. 1699, CO 5 / 861 / f. 75; Bellomont to the Commissioners of Trade, 27 Nov. 1699, with the journal of his proceedings at Rhode Island, CO 5 / 1259 / ff. 143–45;

147–51; Sanford to Bellomont, 8 Nov. 1699, CO 5 / 861 / f. 99; Brinley, Coddington, and Sanford to Bellomont, 23 Dec. 1699, CO 5 / 1043 / f. 86; and Addington's remarks, CO 5 / 1043 / ff. 87–88.

23. Petition of the governor and company of Rhode Island, 13 May 1700, CO 5 / 861 / f. 292; Pemberton, Lewis, and Blening to Bellomont, 20 Dec. 1699, and Christopher Almy to Bellomont, 15 April 1700, CO 5 / 1260 / ff. 224, 226; Cranston to the Commissioners of Trade, 18 April 1701, CO 5 / 1261 / f. 1.

24. Dudley to the Commissioners of Trade, 17 Sept. 1702, CO 5 / 862 / ff. 391–93; minutes of the assistants of Rhode Island, 3 Sept. 1702, CO 5 / 1302 / ff. 1–2.

25. Commissioners of Trade to the queen, 24 Nov. 1702, CO 5 / 1290 / ff. 122–24.

26. Bellomont to Popple, 7 May 1700, CO 5 / 861 / f. 284; Weston Clarke, the provincial secretary of Rhode Island, to the Commissioners of Trade, 30 June 1703, CO 5 / 1262 / f. 123.

27. Northey to the Commissioners of Trade, 24 Dec. 1703, CO 5 / 1262 / f. 213; Commissioners of Trade to the queen, 13 Jan. 1703 / 4, CO 5 / 1290 / ff. 207–8; report by Northey and Harcourt, CO 5 / 1263 / f. 299.

28. Reply of the government of Rhode Island, 1 Feb. 1705 / 6, CO 5 / 1263 / ff. 376–77.

29. James, *Colonial Rhode Island,* pp. 120, 129–30, 135–37.

30. Cranston to the Commissioners of Trade, 15 Nov. 1710, CO 5 / 1264 / ff. 211–12; William Popple, Jr., to Northey, 13 Sept. 1715, CO 5 / 914 / pp. 300–301.

Chapter 12

1. Usher to the Commissioners of Trade, 8 and 23 Oct. 1696, CO 5 / 859 / f. 111 and CO 5 / 759 / f. 123.

2. Usher to the Commissioners of Trade, 16 Feb. 1696 / 7, Story to Usher, 31 Jan. 1696 / 7, Redford to Usher, 1 Feb. 1696 / 7, Usher's account, CO 5 / 859 / ff. 186, 187, 189, 190–91.

3. Penny to Ichobod Plaisted, 17 Dec. 1697, *Documents and Records Relating to the Province of New Hampshire,* ed. Nathaniel Bouton et al., 40 vols. (Concord: New Hampshire Historical Society, 1867–1943), 2:264–65; Henry Dow and Penny to the Commissioners of Trade, 3 Feb. 1697 / 8, ibid., pp. 267–68; and Usher to the Commissioners of Trade, 20 Jan. 1697 / 8, enclosing Smith to Usher, 17 Jan. 1697 / 8, CO 5 / 860 / ff. 12, 14.

4. Allen to Blathwayt, 23 Sept. 1698, CW, Blathwayt Papers, vol. 12.

5. Bellomont to the Commissioners of Trade, 9 Sept. 1699, CO 5 / 860 / ff. 246–47; Allen to Bellomont, 1 Nov. 1699, CW, Blathwayt Papers, vol. 12; Usher to Blathwayt, 8 Nov. 1698, ibid., vol. 6. Several merchants of London had their factors at Portsmouth ship timber to Spain and Portugal, and had the proceeds in silver, wine, oil, and fruit remitted to England. See their petition in CO 5 / 861 / f. 202.

6. Bellomont to the Commissioners of Trade, 23 April and 28 Nov. 1700, CO 5 / 931 / ff. 21–22 and CO 5 / 1045 / no. 18.

7. Bellomont to Secretary Vernon, 22 June 1700, enclosing his "discovery" and an account of Allen's offer, CO 5 / 861 / ff. 372, 373–74, 375; Bellomont to the Commissioners of Trade, 22 June 1700, CO 5 / 861 / ff. 327–36.

8. Usher to the Commissioners of Trade, 12 Dec. 1700, CO 5 / 862 / f. 124.

9. Joseph Smith to John Usher, 22 Sept. 1701, CO 5 / 863A, pt. ii / f. 149; William

Ashurst to Thomas Hopkins (undersecretary of state), 13 Nov. 1701, SP 32 / 12 / ff. 250 / 51; and caveat against Dudley by Sir Henry Ashurst, 13 Nov. 1701, SP 44 / 74 / p. 12.

    10. Dudley to the Commissioners of Trade, 5 Aug. 1703, CO 5 / 863A, pt. ii / f. 267.

    11. David E. Van Deventer, *The Emergence of Provincial New Hampshire, 1623 – 1741* (Baltimore: Johns Hopkins University Press, 1976), pp. 56 – 57; Usher to the Commissioners of Trade, 27 March 1705, CO 5 / 864, pt. ii / f. 319; Paul Dudley to Blathwayt, 20 March, 3 May 1705, HL, Blathwayt Papers, BL 267, 268; Joseph Dudley to Blathwayt, 9 May 1705, ibid., BL 269.

    12. Dudley to the Commissioners of Trade, 15 Nov. 1710, CO 5 / 865 / ff. 262 – 63; Usher to the Commissioners of Trade, 20 Jan. 1714 / 15, CO 5 / 866 / f. 113.

    13. Dudley to William Popple, 3 Feb. 1709 / 10, CO 5 / 865 / f. 213.

    14. Dudley to William Blathwayt, 30 July 1705, HL, Blathwayt Papers, BL 262; Dudley to the Commissioners of Trade, 27 Dec. 1708, CO 5 / 865 / f. 41; Dudley to William Popple, 15 Nov. 1710, CO 5 / 865 / f. 297.

    15. Usher to the Commissioners of Trade, 21 March 1705 / 6, CO 5 / 864, pt. ii / f. 306; Usher to the Commissioners of Trade, [July 1709], CO 5 / 865 / f. 153; Usher to the Commissioners of Trade, [1708], CO 5 / 864 / pt. iii / f. 434.

    16. Richard R. Johnson, *Adjustment to Empire* (New Brunswick, N.J.: Rutgers University Press, 1981), pp. 355 – 57, 361, 400 – 403, 415n.

    17. John Ellis to George Stepney, 8 July 1701, Stepney Papers, BL, Add. MSS 7074, f. 37.

    18. Memorandum by James Vernon of the meeting of the Lords Justices in Council, 5, 7 July 1701, Vernon Papers, BL, Add. MSS 40,775, f. 5; William Sharpas to Robert Livingston, 24 Nov. 1701, FDRL, Robert Livingston General Correspondence; Ashurst to Wait Winthrop, 10 July 1701, *MHSC,* 6th ser. 5:89.

    19. Nathaniel Byfield to Dudley, 7 Aug. 1701, HL, Blathwayt Papers, BL 258; protest of the representatives, ibid., BL 255; the Presbyterian ministers to Mather and Willard, 28 July 1701, with attached note from Dudley to Blathwayt, ibid., BL 257; Dudley to Robert Harley, 9 Aug. 1701, Portland Papers, BL, Loan 29 / 289 / no. 18.

    20. Cotton Mather to Joseph Dudley, 25 Aug. 1701, *Selected Letters of Cotton Mather,* ed. Kenneth Silverman (Baton Rouge: Louisiana State University Press, 1971), pp. 65 – 66; Stephen Mason to Elisha Cooke, 23 Sept. 1701, MHS, Winthrop Family Papers.

    21. Caveat entered by Ashurst, 13 Nov. 1701, SP 44 / 74 / p. 12; William Ashurst to Thomas Hopkins, 13 Nov. 1701, SP 32 / 12 / ff. 250 – 51; Dudley to Harley, 1 Nov. 1701, BL, Loan 29 / 113; Dudley to Harley, 13 Nov. 1711, BL, Loan 29 / 289 / no. 25.

    22. Ashurst to Wait Winthrop, 25 March 1702, Winthrop to Ashurst, March 1702, *MHSC,* 6th ser. 5:109, 110.

    23. Memorial and addresses of the council and assembly, 9 Aug. 1701, CO 5 / 862 / ff. 259 – 60, 261 – 62; instructions to Dudley, 11 Dec. 1701, CO 5 / 910 / pp. 30 – 60.

    24. Chamberlain to Dudley, 22 Sept. 1702, *MHSC,* 6th ser. 3:530 – 31.

    25. Dudley to Godolphin, 11 Nov. 1702, T 1 / 82 / f. 225, and Johnson, *Adjustment to Empire,* pp. 341, 349.

    26. Atwood to Secretary Vernon, 29 Dec. 1701, Atwood to Sir Charles Hedges, 29 Dec. 1701, Atwood to the Commissioners of Trade, 29 Dec. 1701, CO 5 / 1047, pt. 1 / ff. 225, 227 – 28, 229 – 32.

    27. Mather, *Selected Letters,* pp. 57 – 58.

28. Sewall, *Diary*, 1:454; and David Levin, *Cotton Mather: The Young Life of the Lord's Remembrancer, 1663–1703* (Cambridge: Harvard University Press, 1978), pp. 290–92, 296.

29. Sewall, *Diary*, 1:486; Dudley to the Commissioners of Trade, 15 Sept. 1703, CO 5/863A, pt. ii/f. 291; and John Chamberlain to Dudley, 27 Oct. 1702, *MHSC*, 6th ser. 3:532.

30. Cotton Mather to the earl of Nottingham, 26 Nov. 1703, BL, Add. MSS 29,549, f. 109; Increase Mather to Nottingham, 8 Dec. 1703, Add. MSS 29,549, f. 111; Samuel Myles to the rector of St. Peter's, Cornhill, 4 Jan. 1703/4, London, SPG, Records A, Letters, I, no. 162; Sir Henry Ashurst to [Harley], [1704], HMC, *Manuscripts of the Duke of Portland, Welbeck Abbey*, 10:62; Dudley to Harley, 16 Oct. 1704, BL, Loan 29/289/no. 9.

31. G. B. Warden, *Boston, 1689–1776* (Boston: Little, Brown, 1970), pp. 61–67; Johnson, *Adjustment to Empire*, p. 402; Philip S. Haffenden, *New England in the English Nation, 1689–1713* (Oxford: Oxford University Press, 1974), pp. 184–85.

32. Dudley to the Commissioners of Trade, 19 Dec. 1703, CO 5/863/no. 66; address of the council and assembly, 12 July 1704, T 1/91/f. 169; Dudley to the Commissioners of Trade, 13 July 1704, CO 5/863B, pt. i/ff. 110–11.

33. Dudley to the Commissioners of Trade, 10 March 1704/5, 1 Nov. 1705, CO 5/863B, pt. ii/ff. 213–14, 290–91; address of the council and assembly of Massachusetts, 15 Sept. 1705, CO 5/751/f. 153.

34. Cotton Mather to Stephen Sewall, 2 May, 11 Oct. 1706, Mather, *Selected Letters*, pp. 71, 72.

35. John Winthrop to Fitzjohn Winthrop, July 1707, *MHSC*, 6th ser. 3:388–90; George MacGregor Waller, *Samuel Vetch, Colonial Entrepreneur* (Chapel Hill: University of North Carolina Press, 1960), p. 89; Dudley to the Commissioners of Trade, 8 Oct. 1706, CO 5/864, pt. 1/ff. 242–43; petition of Vetch, Borland, and Lawson and the case of Vetch, CO 5/864, pt. 1/ff. 157, 160–61; Edward Northey to the Commissioners of Trade, 28 March 1707, CO 5/864, pt. ii/f. 328.

36. Order in council, 12 June 1707, PC 2/81/p. 382; John Chamberlain to Robert Harley, 16 June 1707, Portland Papers, BL, Loan 29/289/no. 23. A printed copy of the tract is in CO 5/864, pt. ii/ff. 352–74.

37. Godolphin to Marlborough, 16 June 1707, Snyder, *Marlborough-Godolphin Correspondence*, 2:823.

38. Dudley to Godolphin, 10 Nov. 1707, T 1/103/ff. 185–86; two addresses from New Hampshire, CO 5/864/ff. 527, 528; Dudley to Godolphin, 10 Nov. 1707, and Dudley's defense and the declaration of the Hampshire clergy, 11 Nov. 1707, T 1/102/ff. 185, 187–88, 189; and Dudley to Secretary Sunderland, 10 Nov. 1707, HL, HM 22287.

39. Sewall, *Diary*, 1:578–79, 583.

40. The Boston address, dated 13 Feb. 1707/8, is in T 1/105/f. 157. For the public reaction to the decision of the Privy Council see Luttrell, *Historical Relation of State Affairs*, 6:260.

41. Sewall, *Diary*, 2:663.

42. Richard Hill to Secretary St. John, 25 July 1711, CO 5/898/f. 67; Matthew Prior to Sir Thomas Hanmer, 9 Oct. 1711, *The Correspondence of Sir Thomas Hanmer*,

Bart., ed. Sir Henry Bunbury (London, 1838), p. 131; Dudley to the Commissioners of Trade, 13 Nov. 1711, CO 5/865/f. 363.

43. Johnson, *Adjustment to Empire*, pp. 397–98.

44. Cotton Mather to Sir William Ashurst, 12 Oct. 1714, HL, HM 22309; Dummer to Benjamin Colman, 14 Jan. 1714/15, *MHSC*, lst ser. 5:198; Byfield's petition, n.d., BL, Egerton MSS 929, f. 146.

45. Johnson, *Adjustment to Empire*, pp. 352–53.

46. Commissioners of Trade to Secretary Stanhope, 3 Aug. 1715, CO 5/931/ff. 92–93; Vaughan to the Commissioners of Trade, 10 May 1715, CO 5/866/f. 117.

Chapter 13

1. See, for example, Ichobod Plaisted to the Commissioners of Trade, 12 April 1709, CO 5/865/f. 105.

2. DePeyster, Walters, Weaver, and Staats to John Champante, 19 May 1701, Bodl., MS Rawlinson A, vol. 272, f. 124; remonstrance of Livingston and Schuyler, 31 March 1701, FDRL, Robert Livingston General Correspondence; Nicholas Bayard to Sir Philip Meadows, 8 March 1700/01, CO 5/1046/f. 106; Staats, Walters, Weaver, and DePeyster to Secretary Vernon, 6 March 1700/01, CO 5/1046/ff. 92–93; William Smith, Schuyler, and Livingston to the Commissioners of Trade, 30 April, 5 May 1701, CO 5/1046/ff. 125–29, 174–75.

3. James Vernon to William III, 22, 26 Aug. 1701, BL, Add. MSS 40,775, ff. 85, 93.

4. Broughton to the Commissioners of Trade, 3 Sept. 1701, CO 5/1046/ff. 303–4. The voting in the wards for alderman and assistants that fall generally followed national lines, although some Dutch voters did support anti-Leislerian candidates. Loyalist or English candidates won in the Dock Ward, Leislerians in the North. When the returns in the East, West, and South Wards were disputed, a compromise was arranged for the Common Council. See Thomas J. Archdeacon, *New York City, 1664–1710: Conquest and Change* (Ithaca, N.Y.: Cornell University Press, 1976), p. 138, and David Jamison to Robert Livingston, 8 Oct. 1701, FDRL, Robert Livingston General Correspondence. The ethnic or national interpretation is also stressed in Archdeacon's "The Age of Leisler: New York City, 1690–1710" (Ph.D. diss., Columbia University, 1771), but questioned in Joyce Diane Goodfriend, " 'Too Great a Mixture of Nations': The Development of New York City in the Seventeenth Century" (Ph.D. diss., University of California, Los Angeles, 1975).

5. David Jamison to Robert Livingston, 8 Oct. 1701, FDRL, Robert Livingston General Correspondence; remonstrance of Thomas Willett and others, 13 Sept. 1701, and Caleb Heathcote to ———, [late 1701], HL, BL 219, 224.

6. See the "Humble Petition of the Protestant Subjects," 30 Dec. 1701, CO 5/1047, pt. i/ff. 197–98; and Nanfan and the council to the Commissioners of Trade, 20 Jan. 1701/2, CO 5/1047, pt. i/f. 247.

7. For what occurred during Nanfan's tenure see the memorial of Henry Adderly and Charles Lodowyck, 16 April 1702, CO 5/1047, pt. i/ff. 281–82, with enclosures (especially the letters of Thomas Wenham, Philip French, Nicholas Bayard, and Samuel Bayard), CO 5/1047, pt. i/ff. 291, 293–94, 295–96; abstract of several letters from

New York, CO 5/1047, pt. i/ff. 318–19; Cornbury to the Commissioners of Trade, 27 Sept. 1702, CO 5/1047, pt. i/ff. 378–79; and Beverly McAnear, "Politics in Provincial New York, 1689–1761" (Ph.D. diss., Stanford University, 1935), 1:185–96.

8. The queen to Cornbury, 3 May 1702, CO 324/27/p. 401, and Edward Northey to the Commissioners of Trade, 25 April 1702, CO 5/1047, pt. i/f. 310. A bill later passed by the New York assembly reversing the conviction was not approved by the crown for some years until Bayard would agree to a clause barring legal action against the Leislerians for false arrest.

9. Livingston to the Commissioners of Trade, 13 May 1701, CO 5/1046/f. 198–99.

10. Instructions to Cornbury, 26 Nov. 1701, CO 5/1118/pp. 440–87.

11. William Sharpas to Robert Livingston, 24 Nov. 1701, FDRL, Robert Livingston General Correspondence; Livingston to Fitzjohn Winthrop, 11, 18 May 1702, *MHSC*, 6th ser. 3:91, 93; Weaver to John Champante, 2 June 1702, Bodl., MS Rawlinson A, vol. 272, f. 159; Cornbury to Godolphin, Oct. 1702, T 1/82/f. 184.

12. John DePeyster to Abraham DePeyster, 12 July 1703, New-York Historical Society, DePeyster MSS, Letterbook of Translations of Dutch Letters to Colonel Abraham DePeyster, p. 175; Mompesson to the third earl of Clarendon, 13 Nov. 1714, John Carter Brown Library, Providence, R.I., Clarendon Papers Relating to America, 243.

13. See, for example, Cornbury to the bishop of London, Sept. 1702, Bodl., Rawlinson C, Vol. 984, f. 134; and Cornbury to the Commissioners of Trade, 27 Sept. 1702, CO 5/1047, pt. ii/f. 376.

14. Byerly to Lord Treasurer Godolphin, 30 Nov. 1703, T 1/87/f. 553.

15. Conditions improved with the end of hostilities, but the trade was still seasonal. In reporting prices for wheat and flour early in 1713 Peter Schuyler expected that they would not hold until the spring because of low demand in the West Indies and the lack of a market in Lisbon. The price offered for flour rose and fell in Manhattan chiefly according to the number of vessels loading for the West Indies. Schuyler to Robert Livingston, 2 Jan. 1712/13, FDRL, Robert Livingston General Correspondence.

16. Cornbury to the Commissioners of Trade, 30 June 1703, CO 5/1048A/ff. 163–65, 168–70; Cornbury to the Commissioners of Trade, 6 Nov. 1704, CO 5/1048B, pt. ii/ff. 220–22.

17. Cornbury to the Commissioners of Trade, 8 July 1705, CO 5/1048B, pt. ii/ff. 326–27; Cornbury to Sir Charles Hedges, 17 July 1705, CO 5/1084/ff. 89–90.

18. Francis Makemie, *Narrative of a New American Imprisonment of Two Presbyterian Ministers and Persecution of Francis Makemie* (London, 1707), pp. 3, 7, 8, 13, 25, reprinted in *Tracts and Other Papers Relating . . . to . . . the Colonies in North America*, ed. Peter Force, 4 vols. (New York, 1836–46), vol. 4, no. 4.

19. Cornbury to the Commissioners of Trade, 14 Oct. 1706, CO 5/1049/ff. 310–11; also BL, Stowe MSS 324, ff. 147–48. Cornbury's account is printed in *Documents Relative to the Colonial History of the State of New York*, ed. Edmund B. O'Callahan and Berthold Fernow, 15 vols. (Albany and New York, 1856–87), 4:1186–87.

20. Livingston to William Lowndes, secretary to the Treasury, 2 June 1707, T 1/102/f. 130; minutes of the council of New York, 27 Oct. 1708, as to charges made earlier against Cornbury, John Carter Brown Library, Clarendon Papers Relating to America, 161, 163.

21. Commissioners of Trade to Cornbury, 4 Feb. 1705/6, CO 5/1120/ff. 384–92.

22. William Anderson to Clarendon, 10 May 1708, Bodl., MS Clarendon, vol. 102, f. 166.

23. Cornbury to Clarendon, 22 Feb., 9 March 1708/9, John Carter Brown Library, Clarendon Papers Relating to America, pp. 165, 170 (also BL, Add. MSS 15,895, f. 349), and Peter Fauconnier to Cornbury, 13 Jan. 1708/9, Bodl., MS Clarendon, vol. 102, f. 195. For the list of Cornbury's creditors see BL, Add. MSS 15,895, f. 349. Cornbury did receive some money from the queen's secret service funds. See Portland Papers, BL, Loan 29/45B/no. 69.

24. Penn to James Logan, 18 May 1708, HSP, Penn Papers, Penn Family to Logan; Sir Henry Ashurst to Gurdon Saltonstall, 25 Aug. 1708, *Letters from the English Kings and Queens . . . to the Governors of Connecticut, Together with the Answers Thereto from 1639–1740,* ed. Royal R. Hinman (Hartford, 1836), p. 334.

25. Morris to Sunderland, n.d., Rutgers University Library, Lewis Morris Papers.

26. Marlborough to Godolphin, 22 Aug. 1709 (n.s.), Godolphin to Marlborough, 18, 19 Aug. 1709, Marlborough to Godolphin, 7 Sept. 1709 (n.s.), and Marlborough to Godolphin, 3 Oct. 1709 (n.s.), Snyder, *Marlborough-Godolphin Correspondence,* 3:1139, 1346, 1348, 1355, 1381.

27. Atwood's memorial, 26 Oct. 1709, CO 5/1049/ff. 435–44; Atwood to ———, 4 Nov. 1709, Bodl., MS Rawlinson A, vol. 272, f. 243.

28. James Edward Scanlon, "British Intrigue and the Governorship of Robert Hunter," *New-York Historical Society Quarterly* 57 (July 1973): 202–6.

Mary Lou Lustig in a recent study, *Robert Hunter, 1666–1734: New York's Augustan Statesman* (Syracuse, N.Y.: Syracuse University Press, 1983), at times refers to Hunter as a military imperialist and to his administration as an example of garrison government. In this she follows the thesis posed by Stephen Sauders Webb, *The Governors-General: The English Army and the Definition of Empire, 1569–1861* (Chapel Hill: University of North Carolina Press, 1979). In the present work I have attempted to present evidence against such a view. Lustig's own work both implicitly and at times explicitly (see, e.g., p. 222) recognizes that Hunter functioned in New York as an astute political manipulator rather than as a martial bully using nonexistent force.

29. William Blathwayt to the earl of Oxford, 13 Dec. 1713, BL, Loan 29/291/n.p., n.f.

30. McAnear, "Politics in Provincial New York," 1:223–45; Patricia Bonomi, *A Factious People: Politics and Society in Colonial New York* (New York: Columbia University Press, 1971), pp. 82–83.

31. Hunter to the Commissioners of Trade, 3 Oct., 14 Nov. 1710, CO 5/1050/ff. 13–14, 19–25; Commissioners of Trade to the queen, 16 Feb. 1710/11, CO 5/1084/ff. 217–18; draft bill, CO 5/1084/f. 222 (with copy approved by the law officers dated 13 March 1710/11), Newcastle Papers, BL, Add. MSS 33,028, ff. 22–31.

32. Hunter to the Commissioners of Trade, 14 Nov. 1710, 7 May 1711, CO 5/1050/ff. 19–25, 121–22; Hunter to John Hyde, 7 May 1711, Portland Papers, BL, Loan 29/289; Hunter to Swift, Williams, *Correspondence of Swift,* 1:363.

33. Hunter to the Commissioners of Trade, 12 Sept. 1711, CO 5/1050/ff. 208–9; Auditor Edward Harley to Oxford, 6 Aug. 1712, T 1/150/f. 148; Hunter to Secretary Henry St. John, 12 Sept. 1711, CO 5/1084/ff. 248–53; Hunter to Lord Treasurer Oxford, 23 June 1712, T 1/149/f. 3.

34. Eugene R. Sheridan, *Lewis Morris, 1671–1746* (Syracuse, N.Y.: Syracuse University Press, 1981), pp. 88, 175.

35. Peter Sonmans to Clarendon, 12 Feb. 1710/11, and Sonmans to Dockwra, 27 March, 30 May 1711, BL, Add. MSS 14,034, ff. 118–20, 135–36, 137–41.

36. Hunter to the Commissioners of Trade, 27 Aug. 1714, CO 5/970/f. 18.

37. McAnear, "Politics in Provincial New York," 1:247–60; Sheridan, *Lewis Morris,* p. 109. Copies of the two tracts are in CO 5/1050/ff. 477–78, 480–83.

38. Vetch to Robert Livingston, 17 June 1714, and Hunter to Robert Livingston, 30 March 1713, FDRL, Robert Livingston General Correspondence; Hunter to William Popple, 11 May 1713, CO 5/1050/f. 475.

39. Printed copy of Hunter's speech, 22 May 1713, CO 5/1050/f. 491.

40. Hunter to William Popple, 7 May 1714, CO 5/1050/f. 609.

41. Hunter to the Commissioners of Trade, 27 Aug. 1714, CO 5/1050/ff. 611–15; Sheridan, *Lewis Morris,* pp. 111–13.

42. Hunter to John Dalrymple, third earl of Stair, 18 Oct. 1714, CO 5/1051/ff. 83–87; Hunter to William Popple, 8 Nov. 1714, CO 5/1123/pp. 289–90.

43. Order in council approving a representation of the Commissioners of Trade, 6 May 1715, CO 5/1050/f. 656; Commissioners of Trade to Hunter, 22 June 1715, CO 5/1123/pp. 302–3.

44. Hunter to the Commissioners of Trade, 21 May 1715, CO 5/1051/f. 32.

45. Hunter to the Commissioners of Trade, 21 May, 25 July 1715, CO 5/1051/ff. 4–9, 32; Sheridan, *Lewis Morris,* pp. 115–16.

46. Commissioners of Trade to Secretary Stanhope, 31 Aug. 1715, CO 5/1085/f. 57; order in council, 9 Sept. 1715, CO 5/1051/f. 76.

47. Chesterfield to Solomon Dayrolles, 16 Nov. 1753, *The Letters of Philip Dormer Stanhope, Fourth Earl of Chesterfield,* ed. Bonomy Dobrée, 6 vols. (London: Eyre & Spottiswoode, 1932), 5:2059.

Conclusion

1. James Logan to Thomas Grey, 4 Nov. 1714, HSP, James Logan Papers, Logan Letterbook, 1712–15, p. 271.

2. Cadwallader Colden to Alexander Colden, 15 Oct. 1759, "The Colden Letters on Smith's History," *New-York Historical Society Collections,* Publication Fund Series (New York, 1868), 1:205; also in William Smith, *The History of the Province of New-York,* ed. Michael Kammen, 2 vols. (Cambridge: Harvard University Press, 1972), 1:308.

3. Heathcote to the Treasury, 2 Jan. 1715/16, *Calendar of Treasury Papers Preserved in Her Majesty's Public Record Office,* 6 vols. (London: Longmans, Green, 1868–89), 5:185–86.

4. Blathwayt to Secretary James Vernon, 17 Sept. 1700 (n.s.), BL, Add. MSS 40, 774, f. 305.

Index

Act: For ascertaining the Laws, 1699 (in Maryland), 84, 85; of Conformity (1662), 219; Corporation (1661), 16; for Denizenation, 1698 (in New York), 162; for the Encouragement of Trade (1663), 38; for Encouraging and Increasing Shipping (1660), 37; for Granting Revenue to Her Majesty to arise within the Province of New York in America for the support of that Gov-[ernment]t, proposed, 223, 226, 229; for the Preservation of White Pines, 1710, 42; to Prevent the Export of Woolens (1699), 39; to Prevent Frauds, 1698 (in Pennsylvania), 113; for Preventing Frauds and Regulating the Plantation Trade (1696), 24, 37, 59, 134, 168; reception in Rhode Island, 185; for the Service of Almighty God and the Establishment of Religion, 1700 (in Maryland), 80, 81; Test, 1673, 16; of Toleration, 1689, 16, 219

Adams, James (SPG missionary), 97

Addington, Isaac, 204; on laws of Rhode Island, 187

Addison, John, 79, 80

Addison, Joseph, 222

Address to the Inhabitants and Freeholders of Westchester County, 226

Admiralty courts, 24

Adventure Galley (ship), voyage of, 157. *See also* Kidd, Captain William

Africa Company, 47

Allen, James, 165

Allen, Samuel (proprietor of New Hampshire), 192, 193, 194, 195, 196, 197, 233; relations with Blathwayt, 195; death of, 197

Allen, Thomas, 196, 197, 208

Amy, Thomas, and Carolina proprietary, 93, 94

Anderson, Robert, on tobacco trade, 43, 73

Anderson, William, 220

Andros, Edmund, 6, 7; as governor in Boston, 165, 177; as governor of Virginia, 59–65, 68, 234

Aniello, Thomaso (Masaniello), allusion to, 171

Anne, Queen of England, 15, 17, 18, 26, 36, 89, 228

Appleton, John, 204

Appleton, Samuel, 207

Archdale, John, and Carolina proprietary, 93, 94, 95, 99, 101, 102, 103

Archdale, Thomas, 93

Armstrong, Robert, 197

Armstrong, Thomas, 195

Arnold, Caleb, 186

Arnold, Josiah, 186

Ash, John, 16, 101

Asheton, Robert, 115

Ashley, Maurice, and Carolina proprietary, 93, 98, 106–8

Ashurst, Sir Henry, 27, 160, 164, 166, 193, 196, 205; as colonial agent, 176, 181, 182, 189, 200; on governors, 168, 200, 201, 208, 209, 221; and naval stores, 40

Ashurst, Sir William, 196; as fiscal agent, 172; opposes Dudley, 201; on wool trade, 39

Atherton Associates, claim to Narragansett country, 183, 184, 187, 190, 191

Atterbury, Francis (bishop of Rochester), 18

Atwood, William: as chief justice of New York, 214, 215, 216, 221, 222; as judge of admiralty, 201, 203

Baltimore, Benedict Leonard Calvert, 4th baron, 90

Baltimore, Charles Calvert, 3d baron, and
Maryland proprietary, 4, 6, 25, 28, 29, 56,
76, 77, 80, 82, 89, 90, 92, 105
Baltimore, Charles Calvert, 5th baron, 90
Bank of England, 15
Barbarie, John, 24, 217
Barclay, John, 226
Barker, James, 188
Baron, Samuel, 41
Basse, Jeremiah, and New Jersey government,
133–39, 147, 149
Basset, William (councilor of Virginia), 68,
69, 70, 71
Bath, John Granville, earl of, and Carolina
proprietary, 94
Bayard, Nicholas, and New York government,
158, 159, 160, 161, 162, 171, 172, 173,
215, 216; land grant to, 161, 163
Beake, Thomas (secretary of Maryland), 91
Beaufort, Henry Somerset, duke of, as Caroli-
na proprietor, 97, 105
Bedford, Wriothesley Russell, duke of, 181
Beekman, Gerardus, 154
Belcher, Andrew, 207
Belcher, Jonathan, 209, 211
Bellinger, Edmund, and Carolina politics, 100
Bellomont, Richard Coote, earl of, 14, 32, 33,
69, 137, 139, 156, 157, 158, 159, 160,
166, 174, 188, 199, 216, 236; as captain
general, 33, 153, 157, 166, 167, 172; as
governor of Massachusetts, 153, 156, 164,
166, 167, 168, 169, 170, 175, 199, 206; as
governor of New Hampshire, 193, 194,
195, 212, 214; as governor of New York,
134, 153, 158, 159, 160, 161, 162, 168,
170, 171, 172, 173, 174, 213, 217, 229; investigates Rhode Island, 186, 187, 190; on
provincials, 163, 194; relations with Kidd,
157, 159, 169; salary for, 167, 170, 172
Bennett, Richard, 80, 85
Beresford, Richard, and Carolina politics,
104, 106, 107
Berkeley, Edmund, 69, 70, 71
Berkeley, Lord, John, 132, 137
Berkeley, Sir William, 57
Beverley, Robert, and Virginia politics, 64,
65, 66, 67
Biles, William, 123
Blackwell, John, on Quakers, 3
Bladen, William, 83
Blair, James, 59, 62, 63, 66, 69, as commis-

sary, 16; opposes Andros, 59, 61, 62, 63;
opposes Nicholson, 64, 65, 66; opposes
Spottswood, 75; and Virginia government,
58, 62, 63, 65, 67, 68, 69, 234
Blake, Joseph: as Carolina proprietor, 93; as
governor of South Carolina, 99
Blakiston, Nathaniel, 66; as colonial agent,
69, 70; as governor of Maryland, 79, 80,
81, 83, 234
Blakiston, Nehemiah, 77, 79
Blathwayt, William, 21, 32, 114, 136, 139,
159, 166, 171, 172, 201; on chartered gov-
ernments, 88, 89; on colonies, 6, 20, 21,
26, 28, 32, 33, 35, 36, 83, 87, 88, 233; re-
lations with Samuel Allen, 194, 195, 196
Blening, James, 188
Bohun, Edmund (chief justice of South Caroli-
na), 99
Bolingbroke, Henry St. John, viscount, 15,
18, 21, 89; as secretary of state, 19, 21, 34
Boone, Joseph, 16, 107; as agent for South
Carolina, 101, 105, 106
Boone, Mrs. Joseph, 103
Borland, John, 207, 209
Bowne, Andrew, 136, 138
Bowne, John, 143, 146, 147
Bowles, Tobias, 89
Boyd, Thomas, 98
Boyle, Henry, as secretary of state, 15, 19
Bradford, John, 205
Brattle, Thomas, 168
Brattle, William, 168, 203, 208
Bray, Thomas: as commissary, 16, 80; and
Maryland government, 79, 82
Brazier, Abraham, 154
Brent, George, and Northern Neck of Virgin-
ia, 58
Brenton, Jahleel: as agent for Rhode Island,
177; as collector of customs, 168, 180, 185,
186, 187, 204
Brenton, Thomas, 204
Bridger, John (surveyor of woods), 41, 42,
197
Bridges, Dr. John (chief justice of New York),
217
Bridgewater, John Egerton, earl of, as com-
missioner of trade, 60, 62, 171
Brinley, Francis, 180, 184, 185
Brooke, Chidley (collector of customs), 159,
161
Brooke, Robert (Jesuit in Maryland), 82

Brooke, Thomas, 80
Broughton, Samuel Shelton (attorney general of New York), 214, 215
Broughton, Thomas, and Carolina government, 103, 104, 106
Browne, David, 79
Buckeley, Gershom, 177
Bull, William, 107
Burges, Elizeus, 211
Burnet, William, 231
Burrill, John, 199
Burwell, Joanna, 69
Burwell, Major Lewis, 62, 63, 65
Burwell, Lucy, 63, 69
Burwell, Nathaniel, 65, 69
Byerly, Thomas (auditor of New York), 35, 217
Byfield, Deborah, 169
Byfield, Nathaniel, 164, 165, 166, 168, 169, 180, 200, 201, 202, 203, 204, 209, 211
Byfield, Thomas, 41; opposes Carolina bill on religion, 101
Byrd, William, 60, 64, 67; seeks governorship, 30; on tobacco trade, 43
Byrd, William II, 21; and Virginia politics, 60, 61, 63, 67, 69, 70, 74, 88, 97

Calvert. *See* Baltimore
Captain generalcy, 33, 174. *See also* Bellomont, Richard Coote, earl of
Carpenter, Samuel, 112; approaches to Cornbury, 118; and Pennsylvania politics, 122, 124, 130; relations with Penn, 115, 128, 129
Carr, Robert, 188
Carroll, Charles, 83
Carter, Robert, 59, 62, 66, 69, 70; in Virginia government, 63, 65, 67, 68
Carteret, Sir George, 132, 137
Carteret, John, and Carolina proprietary, 94, 97, 98, 106, 107
Cary, John: and tobacco trade, 46, 49; on wool trade, 39
Cary, Miles, 67
Cary, Thomas, and revolt in Carolina, 95, 96, 97, 98
Cecil, Robert, as commissioner of trade, 21
Chamberlain, John (secretary of SPG), 202
Champante, John, 229
Charter of Privileges (1701), 116
Cheseldyne, Kenelm, 77
Chester, John, 180

Chesterfield, Philip Dormer Stanhope, earl of, on patronage, 58, 230
Chevin, Nathaniel, 98
Chilton, Edward, 61, 62, on Virginia government, 65
Clarendon, Henry Hyde, 2d earl of: favors bishops for America, 17; and patronage, 119, 217, 220
Clark, George, 217, 220
Clark, William, 122
Clarke, Philip, 77, 78, 80
Clarke, Richard, 85
Clarke, Walter: as deputy governor, 186, 188, 190; as governor of Rhode Island, 185, 186
Clarkson, Matthew, 158
Cock, Richard, 52
Coddington, Nathaniel, 185, 186, 187
Codrington, Thomas, 219, 222
Colden, Cadwallader, 232
Cole, Michael, 52
Cole and Bean (ship), violates navigation code, 24
Colleton, Sir John, as Carolina proprietor, 94, 97, 98, 101, 106, 107, 108
Collins, Francis (timber contractor), 41, 197
Colman, Benjamin, 204, 208
Compton, Henry (bishop of London): and bishops for America, 16, 17, 61; and Virginia politics, 61, 62
Contee, John, 83
Conseillere, Benjamin, 104
Converse, James, 199
Coode, John, and Maryland government, 60, 76, 77, 78, 79, 80, 88
Cooke, Arthur, 112
Cooke, Elisha, and politics in Massachusetts, 164, 165, 166, 168, 169, 200, 201, 202, 203, 205, 236
Cooke, Elisha II, 206, 211
Copley, Lionel (governor of Maryland), 76, 77, 83, 234
Corbett, John (governor of Maryland), 88
Corbile, Dr. John, 159, 161
Corbin, Gawin, and Virginia politics, 67, 70
Cornbury, Edward Hyde, lord (later 3d earl of Clarendon): as governor of New Jersey, 139, 141, 142, 143, 145, 146, 147, 148, 149, 225; as governor of New York, 33, 171, 202, 212, 214, 216, 217, 218, 219, 220, 222, 223; and Quakers of Pennsylvania, 118, 122

Cotton, John Hynde, as commissioner of trade, 21
Council of Plymouth (Council of New England), and land claims in New England, 176, 184, 192
Coursey, William, 84
Courteen, Myndert, 154
Coutts, James, 127
Cowper, Spencer, 181
Cowper, Lord Chancellor William, 15; in Penn's case, 125
Coxe, Colonel Daniel, 137, 139, 141; and New Jersey politics, 145, 146, 148, 149, 225
Coxe, Dr. Daniel, as New Jersey proprietor, 133
Cranston, John, 186
Cranston, Samuel, 185; as governor of Rhode Island, 186, 187, 188, 189
Craven, Charles: as secretary of South Carolina, 104; as governor of South Carolina, 104, 105, 106
Cruger, John, 220
Culpepper, John, 98
Culpepper, Lord Thomas, as governor of Virginia, 57, 68
"Culpepper's Rebellion," 97
Custis, John, and Virginia government, 62, 65, 67
Cutler, Timothy, 182
Cutts, John Lord, favors Dudley, 156, 166

Daniel, Robert (deputy governor of Carolina), 95, 106, 107
Danson, John, as Carolina proprietor, 93, 95, 97, 98, 103, 106, 107, 108
Danson, Mary (Archdale), 93
Darnall, Colonel Henry, 83
Dartmouth, William Legge, earl of: as commissioner of trade, 20, 21; as secretary of state, 15, 19, 88, 97
Davenport, Francis, 139, 141
David, Benjamin, 204
Deacon, George, and government of New Jersey, 139, 141, 149
Dean, James (naval contractor), 41
Deene, Cornelius, and tobacco trade, 49
Deerfield, Massachusetts, raid on, 33
Defoe, Daniel, as pamphleteer, 16, 101
DeLancey, Stephen, and New York politics, 172, 217, 220, 222, 229

Delanoy, Peter, 156
Dellius, Godfrey, 161, 171
Dennison, George, 184
Dent, William, 84
DePeyster, Abraham, and New York politics, 154, 155, 159, 161, 214, 216, 217, 221
DePeyster, John, 215, 217
Digges, Dudley, and government in Virginia, 67, 68, 70
Dockwra, William, as New Jersey proprietor, 133, 136, 137, 138, 139, 141, 143, 147, 225
Docminique, Paul, as New Jersey proprietor, 133, 138, 147, 225
Dorset, Charles Sackwille, earl of, 62
Drummond, John, 15
Drysdale, Major Hugh, appointed deputy governor of Virginia, 75
Dudley, Ann, 203, 208
Dudley, Joseph, 33, 156, 164, 169, 180, 181, 182, 190; and Anglican church, 17; as governor of Massachusetts, 33, 42, 69, 175, 194, 199, 200, 201, 202, 203, 204, 205, 206, 207, 208, 209, 210, 211, 212, 231, 236; as governor of New Hampshire, 196, 197, 198; investigates Rhode Island, 188
Dudley, Sir Matthew: and proprietary of New Hampshire, 197; and trade in naval stores, 40, 41, 146
Dudley, Paul (attorney general of Massachusetts, 208
Dudley, Rebecca, 203
Dudley and Associates, and timber trade, 40, 166
Duke, Henry, and government of Virginia, 65, 67, 68
Dummer, Jeremiah (agent for Massachusetts), 29, 211
Dyer, Giles, 204

Earle, Edward, 161
Earle, Hannah, 161
East India Company, 15, 16, 21, 24, 47, 159
Eden, Charles, appointed governor of North Carolina, 98
Edsall, Samuel, family connections of, 154
Eldridge, Daniel, 188
Emott, James, 158
Evance, Sir Stephen, 15, 166; and naval stores, 40
Evans, John: as Penn's deputy, 119, 122, 124,

125, 126; rumored as royal governor, 129, 130

Evans, Captain John (of New York), 158, 159, 160

Eveleigh, Samuel, 104, 107

Eyre, Robert (solicitor general), on land grants in colonies, 42

Fauconnier, Peter, 149, 202

Feild, John: against established church, 80, 181; as creditor for Penn's estate, 129

Fenwick, John, 104

Finney, Samuel, 119

Fitch, James, and Connecticut government, 177, 178, 180, 190

Fitzhugh, William, and Northern Neck of Virginia, 58

Fletcher, Colonel Benjamin: and Anglican church, 17; as governor of New York, 155–60, 172, 173; as governor of Pennsylvania, 110

Florus Gessius, reference to, 147

Foley, Thomas, as commissioner of trade, 21

Fowler, Bartholomew (attorney general for Virginia), 62

Foxcroft, Francis, 204

Ford, Brigid, sues Penn, 125

Ford, Philip, relations with Penn, 111, 114, 115, 121, 124

Forster, Miles, 141, 148, 149, 158

Founce, Stephen, and Virginia politics, 64, 65

Franks, Brigadier Richard, as governor of Maryland, 90

French, Philip, 172, 215, 217

French, Robert, against Quakers, 114, 124, 127, 129, 219, 222

Fretwell, Peter, 134

Frisby, James, 79

Fryer, Nathaniel, 194

Fundamental constitutions, of Carolina, 99, 101

Gardiner, Thomas, and New Jersey politics, 135, 143, 145, 149, 226

Garton, Thomas, 219, 222

Gedney, Bartholomew, 164

Gee, Joshua, as creditor for Penn's estate, 129

Gibbes, Robert (chief justice of South Carolina), 104

Glover, William, and Carolina government, 95, 96, 104

Godin, Benjamin, 104

Godin, Stephen, 105

Godolphin, Sidney Godolphin, earl, 15; and colonial affairs, 35, 44, 48, 49, 60, 88, 222; as lord treasurer, 18, 19, 20, 21, 33, 34, 60; and patronage, 65, 66, 69, 203, 208; relations with Marlborough, 20, 30; relations with Penn, 26, 125

Gold (Gould), Nathan, 178

Goodson, John, 112

Gookin, Captain Charles, as Penn's deputy, 126, 127, 130

Gordon, Thomas, as New Jersey proprietor, 134, 141, 142, 143, 149, 226

Gorges, Sir Ferdinando, claims to New England, 176

Gouldney, Henry, as creditor for Penn's estate, 129

Gouverneur, Abraham, and government of New York, 154, 156, 162, 173, 214, 216

Graham, Augustine, 229

Graham, James, 155, 159, 160, 161, 163, 171, 173, 213, 214

Granville, John Granville, baron: as Carolina proprietor, 29, 94, 103; on establishment of religion, 101, 102

Greenberry, Nicholas, 77, 79

Greene, John (deputy governor of Rhode Island), 186, 188

Grenville, George, on colonial taxation, 232

Griffith, Alexander, 144

Growdon, Joseph, and Pennsylvania proprietary, 112, 115, 119, 124

Grove, Silvanus, as creditor for Penn's estate, 129

Guest, John, 115

Guilford, Francis North, baron: as commissioner of trade, 21; and Maryland proprietary, 90

Gwyn, Francis, as commissioner of trade, 21, 89

Haistwell, Edward, on tobacco trade, 44, 46, 47

Halifax, Charles Montague, lord, 14, 15, 62, 221

Hall, Kingley, 194

Hall, William, 148

Hallam brothers (of Connecticut), 177, 178, 179, 180, 181

Halliwell, Richard, opposes Quaker government, 114, 122, 124, 127

Hamilton, Andrew, 119, 139; as deputy governor of Pennsylvania, 119, 122; as governor in New Jersey, 133, 134, 135, 136, 138, 144

Hamilton, John, 148

Hamilton family (of Scotland), claims to New England, 177, 184

Hammond, John, of Maryland council, 79, 80, 84

Harcourt, Sir Simon (solicitor general), 15; on Carolina proprietors, 102; on colonial charters, 28, 189; on Maryland laws, 85

Harkins, William (naval stores contractor), 41

Harley, Robert. *See* Oxford, Robert Harley, earl of

Harrison, Benjamin II, on Virginia government, 59, 62, 63, 66, 68, 69

Harrison, Benjamin III, 59, 62

Harrison, Edmund, and Kidd venture, 157, 166

Harrison, Edward, and tobacco trade, 46

Harrison, John, 148

Harrison, Nathaniel, 62, 70

Harrison, Sarah, 59

Hart, Captain John, as governor of Maryland, 90, 234

Hart, Charles, 107

Hartshore, Richard, 143

Hartwell, Henry, on Virginia government, 61, 62, 65

Hawles, Sir John (solicitor general): on Carolina bill for religion, 102; in *Hester* case, 137; on land grants in colonies, 172

Heath, James, 80, 85

Heathcote, Caleb, 15, 147, 158, 172, 217, 221, 226; on chartered colonies, 29, 232, 233; land grants to, 161, 163

Heathcote, Sir Gilbert, 15, 147; on tobacco trade, 46, 47; on trade in naval stores, 41

Heathcote, Samuel, and tobacco trade, 46

Hedges, Sir Charles, as secretary of state, 15, 19, 28

Herbert, Henry Herbert, baron, as commissioner of trade, 21

Herne, Sir Joseph, and naval stores, 40

Hester (ship), case of, 137, 138

Higginson, John, 169

Higginson, Nathaniel, 169, 202, 205, 207, 208

Hill, Abraham, as commissioner of trade, 60, 79, 81

Hill, General John, and expedition against Canada, 34, 209

Hill, Richard, on Maryland council, 79

Hill, Richard, of Pennsylvania, 124, 128, 129

Hill, Colonel Richard, criticizes Massachusetts, 34, 209, 210

Hinckes, John, 193, 194, 196

Hobby, Sir Charles, 203, 207, 208, 209; and New Hampshire proprietary, 197

Hoddy, Hugh, 148

Holland, William, 84

Hollis, John, 181

Holt, John (Lord Chief Justice): on colonial charters, 28, 88; on the *Hester*, 137

Howard of Effingham, Francis Howard, baron (governor of Virginia), 57

Howe, Job, on Carolina dissenters, 101

Hudson's Bay Company, 47

Huitson, Michael, 82

Hull, Joseph, 188

Hunking, Mark, 198

Hunlocke, Edward, 139

Hunter, Elizabeth, 231

Hunter, Colonel Robert, 130, 228; on assemblymen, 224, 232; captured by French, 68, 69; named deputy governor for Virginia, 68; as governor of New Jersey, 150, 224, 225, 226, 229; as governor of New York, 22, 36, 70, 72, 208, 221, 222, 223, 224, 226, 227, 228, 229, 231, 233; calls for parliamentary taxation, 36, 223, 224, 225, 228, 229

Hunter, William (Jesuit in Maryland), 82

Hutchins, Charles, on Maryland council, 79, 81

Hutchins, John, 125, 216

Hutchinson, Elisha, 184, 200

Hyde, Edward (deputy governor of North Carolina), 98

Ingoldsby, Major Richard, 154, 171, 200; as deputy governor of New Jersey, 149, 150

Iron trade, regulations proposed for, 38, 39

Izard, Ralph, 107

Jaffries, George, 197

James II, 6, 7, 8, 30. *See also* York, James Stuart, duke of

Jamison, David, 162, 163, 226

Jeffreys, George, 127

Jeffreys, Jeffrey, and packet service, 31

Jenkins, Francis, 79

Jennings, Edmund: and Virginia government, 65, 68, 69, 70; on Quakers, 96
Jennings, Samuel, on New Jersey government, 133, 134, 135, 139, 141, 145, 146, 147, 149
Jewell, John, criticizes Quakers, 134
Jewett, Nehemiah, 199
Johnson, John, 220, 229
Johnson, Sir Nathaniel (governor of South Carolina), 100, 103, 104
Johnson, Robert (governor of South Carolina), 105, 106, 108
Johnston, Dr. John, and government in New Jersey, 141, 142, 143, 226
Jones, Griffith, in Pennsylvania politics, 112, 115, 120, 123, 124
Jones, Jeffrey, land claims of, 134
Jones, Robert, 124
Jowles, Henry, as councilor in Maryland, 77, 80, 81

Keith, George, 16, 126
Kettleby, Amos: petitions crown, 105; on rice trade, 52
Kidd, Captain William, 14, 157, 159, 169, 172
King, Peter, 181
King's Province, 176. *See also* Narragansett County
Knight, Tobias, 98
Kurbatov, Aleksei, and tobacco contractors, 48

Laconia (New Hampshire), claims to, 176, 184
Lambert, Thomas, 143, 145
Lane, Thomas, and tobacco trade, 47, 67
Lane, Sir Thomas, as West Jersey proprietor, 133, 138, 149
Larkin, George, on navigation code in Massachusetts, 202
Lawrence, Elisha, 150
Lawrence, John, 158
Lawrence, Sir Thomas, as secretary of Maryland, 77, 79, 80, 83, 84, 91
Lawrence, Thomas II, 81, 83
Lawrence, William, 217
Lawson, Robert, 207
Lechmere, Thomas, 211
Lee, Richard, 62, and tobacco trade, 49
Leeds, Daniel, and government of New Jersey, 143, 146, 147, 148

Leeds, Thomas Osborne, earl of Danby, Marquis of Carmarthen and duke of, 195
Leete, Andrew, 178
Legg, John, 204
Legg, Samuel, 204
Leinster, Meinhardt lord (duke of Schomberg), 195
Leisler, Jacob, 154, 161, 171, 200, 215
Leisler, Jacob II, opposes Fletcher, 156
Leonard, Samuel, 139
Letchmore, Richard, and naval stores, 41
Leverett, John, 200, 203, 204, 209
Lewis, John, 67, 188
Lightfoot, John, on Virginia council, 63, 65, 66, 67
Linton, John, on tobacco trade, 48
Liveen (ship), dispute over, 179
Livingston, Alida (Schyler), 154
Livingston, Captain John, 180, 181
Livingston, Robert, 154, 155, 158, 159, 160, 161, 163, 171, 173, 180, 181, 216, 217; on Cornbury, 219; as creditor, 32; land grant to, 173; relations with Bellomont, 157, 172; relations with Fletcher, 156, 157, 158, 159; relations with Kidd, 157
Lloyd, David, 112, 114, 116, 117, 124, 125, 127, 130, 234, 236; attacks royal government, 113; opposes proprietary government, 111, 112, 115, 116, 121, 122, 123, 124, 125, 126, 129, 131; opposition to, 127
Lloyd, Edward, 84; as Maryland councilor, 87, 89
Lloyd, John, 41
Lloyd, Philemon, 84
Locke, John: as commissioner of trade, 60, 61, 62, 79; on colonial policy, 62
Lodowyck (Lodwyck), Charles, 157, 172; and naval stores, 41
Lofting, John, 135
Logan, James (agent for Penn), 115, 117, 118, 121, 122, 125, 126, 127, 128, 129, 130; on Cornbury, 119; on Evans, 122; on politics in Pennsylvania, x, 124; on Quakers, 110, 122, 146
Lonsdale, John Lowther, viscount, 195
Lords Justices in Council, 18, 79, 167
Louis XIV: war against, 19; on English succession, 33
Lovelace, Lady Charlotte, 222
Lovelace, Colonel John: as governor of New

Jersey, 147, 148, 149; as governor of New York, 220, 221

Lowe, Charles, and Maryland proprietary, 90

Ludwell, Philip, 58

Ludwell, Philip II, opposes royal governors, 63, 65, 66, 67, 68, 69, 70, 74, 75

Luke, George, 65

Lumley, George, 97

Lurting, Robert, 158, 229

Lyle, Edward, 169

Lynes, Philip, 83

Magna Carta, 78, 165

Makemie, Francis, confronts Cornbury, 219

Manley, John, and Carolina proprietors, 105

Mark, James, 41

Markham, William, as Penn's deputy, 112, 114

Marlborough, John Churchill, duke of, 15, 21, 34, 62, 88, 222; on campaigns in America, 34; and colonial patronage, 20, 30, 65, 66, 68, 69, 148, 208, 220, 221

Marlborough, Sarah Churchill, duchess of, 34

Marshall, Peter, 47

Martindale, Isaac, 188, 190

Masham, Mrs. Abigal (Hill), 34

Mason, Captain John (of Connecticut), 180

Mason, John (of New Hampshire), 176, 192

Mason, Robert, 78

Mason, Samuel, 178, 180

Mason, Stephen, 201, 208, in timber trade, 41

Massaniello. *See* Aniello, Thomaso

Mather, Cotton, 201, 204, 205, 209, 219; relations with Dudley, 199, 201, 203, 208, 209, 211

Mather, Increase, 163, 165, 166, 168, 201, 203, 205, 209; as agent, 204; relations with Dudley, 201, 211; relations with Phips, 199, 202

Mayor of New York and Company, as political club, 162

Meadows, Sir Philip, as commissioner of trade, 20, 21, 26, 60, 62, 79, 89, 139

Memorial of the Present Deplorable State of New England, 208

Merritt, William, 158

Methuen, John, as commissioner of trade, 20

Mico, John, and timber trade, 41, 197

Mico, Richard, and naval stores, 41

Middleton, Arthur, and government of South Carolina, 104, 107, 236

Milbourne, Jacob, 154, 161, 171

Minvielle, Gabriel, 158, 160, 162

Mohegan lands, claims to, 180

Mompesson, Roger, 24, 119, 122, 123, 145, 217

Monckton, Robert, as commissioner of trade, 21, 42

Montague, James (solicitor general), 36, 85

Montague, John, 172

Moore, Arthur, as commissioner of trade, 21, 89

Moore, James, and Carolina politics, 100, 104, 108

Moore, John, and Pennsylvania politics, 113, 121, 124

Moore, Throwgood, criticizes Cornbury, 146

Morris, Anthony, 113, 114, 123

Morris, John, 158

Morris, Lewis, 132, 155, 236; aids Hunter, 150, 223, 225; and Anglican church, 17; and government in New York, 221, 223, 226, 229, 230, 231; in New Jersey politics, 134, 136–45, 147–50, 225, 226

Morton, Joseph, 100

Mosely, Edward, 96

Mott, Gershon, 150

Mulford, Samuel, 222, 228, 229

Muscovy Company, on tobacco trade, 46, 47

Myles, Samuel, 205

Naire, Thomas, in Carolina politics, 103, 104

Namier, Sir Lewis, 235

Nanfan, Captain John, as deputy governor of New York, 162, 213, 214, 215, 216, 217

Narragansett country, dispute over, 183, 184, 189, 190, 191. *See also* King's Province

Naval stores, 40, 41, 42

Navigation code, 23; violations of, 24, 35, 37. *See also* Acts

Nelson, John, 204

Newbury, Massachusetts, Anglicans of, 17

New Cambridge, "county" of, claims to, 176, 184

Newcastle, John Holles, duke of, 20; and patronage, 21, 148, 220

Newcastle, Thomas Pelham-Holles, duke of, and colonial policy, xi

Nicoll, William, 158, 159, 160, 161, 162, 163, 171, 172, 173, 174, 214, 215, 217, 218, 222, 223; opposes New Jersey proprietors, 134

Nicolls, Colonel Richard (governor of New York), 133

Nicholson, Colonel Francis, 61, 62, 65, 198, 224, 228, 234; and Anglican church, 17, 80, 113; campaigns against French, 33, 34, 149, 209; as deputy governor of New York, 59; as governor of Maryland, 59, 60, 77, 78, 79, 82; as governor of Virginia, 62–68, 81; opposes Andros, 59, 60, 61

Norris, Isaac, and politics of Pennsylvania, 116, 121, 123, 124, 127, 128, 129

Northern Neck of Virginia, 58

Northey, Edward (attorney general), 223; on colonial charters, 27, 28, 89, 102, 189; on laws of Maryland, 86; on Narragansett country, 191; on sale of Penn's proprietary, 128

Nott, Major Edward (deputy governor of Virginia), 66, 67, 68

Nottingham, Daniel Finch, earl of, 15, 16, 19, 20, 21, 217, 235; on government for New Jersey, 139; presents Occasional Conformity bill, 18

Noyes, Oliver, 211

Oade, Thomas, as creditor for Penn's estate, 129

Oakes, Doctor Thomas, and politics in Massachusetts, 165, 205, 206

Oates, Titus, 172

Oaths, Quakers on, 141

Occasional conformity, 18

Oliver, James, 199

Orford, Edward Russell, earl of, 14, 15, and Bellomont, 159; backs Kidd, 157

Orkney, George Hamilton, earl of, as absentee governor of Virginia, 30, 66, 68, 69

Ormston, Joseph, as New Jersey proprietor, 137, 138, 225

Owen, Griffith, and politics in Pennsylvania, 115, 121, 122, 128

Oxford, Robert Harley, earl of, 14, 15, 18, 19, 21, 29, 34, 36, 49, 89, 90, 157, 182, 205, 211, 222; and Dudley, 201; relations with Penn, 110, 128, 226; and tobacco trade, 49, 50

Packer, Thomas, 194, 198

Page, Mann, 70

Paget, Lord Henry, 182

Paggen, Peter, on tobacco trade, 44

Paige, Nicholas, 204

Palmer, John, 155

Palmes, Edward, as dissident in Connecticut, 177, 178, 179, 180, 181

Parke, Colonel Daniel, 66; assassinated, 97

Parke, Lucy, 69

Partridge, Richard (agent for Rhode Island), 29

Partridge, William, as deputy governor of New Hampshire, 193, 194, 195, 208, 212, 233

Peartree, William, 221

Pemberton, chief Justice Francis, on claim to New Cambridge, 177

Pemberton, Joseph, 188

Pemberton, Phineas, 112

Penhallow, Samuel, 196, 211

Penn, Hannah, 129, 130

Penn, William, 3, 4, 25, 26, 27, 56, 80, 92, 105, 110, 111, 112, 115, 116, 119, 121, 122, 123, 127, 216, 217, 221; attempts to sell government, 27, 119, 120, 121, 125, 128, 130; claim to lower counties, 111, 127, 128; his connections, 20, 26, 128; holdings mortgaged, 29, 114, 115, 121, 125; loses government, 25, 28, 56, 76; as a proprietor of New Jersey, 136, 148; as proprietor of Pennsylvania, 25, 28, 114, 116, 117, 123, 124, 125, 126, 129, 189, 234; on Quakers, 127; suffers stroke, 128

Penn, William II: behavior of in Philadelphia, 120, 122; as political agent, 26

Pennsylvania and Carolina Company, 41

Penny, Henry, 194

Perry, Micajah, 67, 70, 73; opposes bill on religion, 101; and tobacco trade, 46, 47

Perth Amboy, New Jersey, as port, 134, 136, 137

Peter, czar of Russia, 46, 48

Philipse, Adolph, 217

Philipse, Frederick, 155, 158, 159

Phips, Sir William: Bellomont on, 194; as governor of Massachusetts, 153, 163, 164, 166, 167, 170, 199, 202, 236; relations with Mather, 199

Pickering, John, 193, 194

Pinhorne, William, and government in New York, 139, 158, 159, 160, 161

Plaisted, Ichobod (timber contractor), 41, 194, 197

Plaisted, John (timber contractor), 41, 194, 197

Pollexfen, John, as commissioner of trade, 20, 21, 60, 62, 79, 81
Pollock, Thomas, and government in North Carolina, 96, 97, 98
Popple, William, 110; at Board of Trade, 20, 21
Popple, William II, at Board of Trade, 21, 229
Porter, John, and Carolina politics, 95, 96, 97, 98
Portland, William Bentinck, duke of, 171
Portlock, Edward, 115
Povey, John, 61
Povey, Captain Thomas, deputy governor of Massachusetts, 180, 201
Powys, Sir Thomas, on act for religion, 102
Prior, Matthew, as commissioner of trade, 21, 26
Proprietary government, 4; in Carolina, 94ff.; in Maryland 76ff.; in New Jersey, 132, 136, 140; in Pennsylvania, 110ff.
Pulteney, John, as commissioner of trade, 21
Puritans, 3; Usher on, 193
Pusey, Caleb, and politics in Pennsylvania, 112, 115, 122, 124, 128
Pytts, Samuel, as commissioner of trade, 21

Quakers, x, 4, 16, 205; complaints against, 3, 27, 35, 112, 117, 122, 127, 134, 139, 140, 141, 143, 179, 181; in England, 80, 81; on military affairs, 127, 144, 218; in New Jersey, 132, 133, 135, 137, 138, 140, 142, 145, 146, 148, 149, 225, 226; in North Carolina, 95, 96, 97; and oaths, 116, 119; in Pennsylvania, 110, 115–20, 123, 127, 130, 234; in Rhode Island, 185, 188
Quary, Robert (surveyor general of customs), 24, 35, 122, 141, 233; criticizes proprietary governments, 112, 113, 119, 141, 142, 146; on tobacco trade, 48, 49
Queensberry, William Douglas, duke of, promised governship of Maryland, 89
Quinebaug lands, claims to, 177

Randolph, William, 67
Rawle, Francis, and Pennsylvania politics, 112, 115, 124
Raymond, Robert (solicitor general), 223; on colonial assemblies, 36
Redford, William, 193
Reed, William, 98

Revell, Thomas, and politics in New Jersey, 134, 141, 143, 146, 147, 148
Rhett, William, and government in South Carolina, 103, 105, 106, 107
Rice, trade in, 52, 93; regulations for, 52
Richards, John, 164
Richardson, Samuel, 123, 124
Richier, Edward (New Jersey proprietor), 138
Roach, Richard, 97
Roberts, John, 124
Robinson, Christopher, 71
Robinson, John (bishop), 75
Robinson, John (of Virginia), 71
Robotham, George, 79
Rochester, Laurence Hyde, earl of, 15, 16, 139
Rogerenes, in Connecticut, 183
Rogers, John, 181
Romney, Henry Sidney, earl of, 159, 167; backs Kidd, 157
Rouse, William, 207
Royce, John, 136

Sacheverall, Henry, 17
Saffin, John, 200, 215
Salter, Richard, 143, 145, 146, 147
Saltonstall, Gurdon, 178, 180; as governor of Connecticut, 182, 183
Saltonstall, Nathaniel, 164
Sanders, William (attorney general of South Carolina), 104
Sanford, Peleg, and politics of Rhode Island, 185, 186, 187
Saturday Night Club, 162
Schenectady, New York, raid on, 33
Schism bill, 18
Schuyler, Colonel Peter, 160, 161, 172, 173, 214; land grant to, 163, 173
Searle, Jonathan, and tobacco trade, 49
Secretariat, jurisdiction of, 18
Selleck, John, 178
Selling of Joseph, The, 204
Sergeant, Peter, 164, 205
Sewall, Samuel, 164, 169, 202, 203, 204, 205, 208
Seymour, Sir Edward, on wool trade, 39
Seymour, John (governor of Maryland), 82, 83, 85, 86, 87, 234
Shaftesbury, Anthony Ashley Cooper, earl of, and Culpepper's rebellion, 98

Sharp, John (archbishop of Canterbury), 17, 59
Sharp, John, as commissioner of trade, 21
Sheafe, Sampson, 194
Sheffield, Joseph, 188, 189, 190
Sheffield, Nathaniel, 190
Shelton, Richard (secretary of Carolina proprietary board), 98, 105
Shenkingh, Benjamin, 107
Shippen, Edward, 112, 121, 122; approaches Cornbury, 115, 118; relations with Penn, 128
Shippen, John, 40
Shrewsbury, Charles Talbot, duke of, 14, 19, 60, 61, 159, 166, 167, 172, 235; backs Kidd, 14, 156, 157; relations with Bellomont, 157, 167
Shute, Colonel Samuel (governor of Massachusetts), 211
Silvester, Giles, 180
Skipworth, Sir Fulworth, and Carolina proprietary board, 94, 106
Slocum, Giles, 188, 190
Sloughter, Colonel Henry (governor of New York), 154
Slye, Gerard, criticizes Nicholson, 60, 78
Smith, George (Carolina dissenter), 103
Smith, John, 67
Smith, Joseph (of New Hampshire), 194, 198
Smith, Robert, on Maryland council, 79, 84
Smith, Thomas (Carolina dissenter), 103, 104
Smith, William: as chief justice, 214, 215, 217; and government of New York, 158, 160, 232; land grant to, 161, 163, 173; as president of council, 214
Snead, Robert, 113
Society for the Propagation of the Gospel, 17; missionaries for, 15, 97; Norris and, 138
Somers, John, baron and later viscount, 14, 15, 61, 166, 167, 172, 221; and Bellomont, 159, 163, 172; and Kidd, 156, 157; relations with Penn, 115
Somerset, Charles Seymour, duke of, 181
Sonmans, Peter, as New Jersey proprietor, 137, 141, 149, 225
Sothell, Seth (Carolina proprietor), 103
South Sea Company, 16, 21
Southwell, Sir Robert, 110, 159
Spotswood, Alexander (deputy governor of Virginia), 69, 70–75, 234–35; on Cary's Rebellion, 97, 98

Staats, Dr. Samuel, and politics in New York, 159, 161, 214, 216, 221, 222, 226
Stamford, Thomas Grey, earl of, as commissioner of trade, 26
Stanhope, James (secretary of state), 19, 22, 90, 211
Stepney, George, as commissioner of trade, 20, 21, 81
Stoddard, Solomon, on church membership, 203, 208
Story, Charles, 193
Story, Thomas, 122, 129; as Quaker missionary, 81
Stoughton, William, 164, 166, 169, 200, 209; Bellomont on, 168, 169; as deputy governor of Massachusetts, 167, 168, 170, 200, 202; and Dudley, 200
Stuart, James Edward (the old Pretender), 26; recognized by Louis XIV, 33
Suffragan, for America, 17
Sunderland, Charles Spencer, 3d earl of, 15, 21, 69; as secretary of state, 19, 21, 87, 147, 220, 221
Sunderland, Robert Spencer, 2d earl of, 7
Sutton, Colonel Richard, proposed governor of Massachusetts, 208
Swift, John, 124
Swift, Dean Jonathan: relations with Hunter, 224; as suffragan for America, 17, 222

Talbot, John, 17
Tasker, Thomas, 79, 81
Tatham, John, 134
Taylor, John, 41, 197
Taylor, William (deputy governor of Massachusetts), 209
Tench, Thomas, 84
Tenison, Edward (archbishop of Canterbury): Anglicans appeal to, 60, 80; and Virginia politics, 61, 62, 64
Thornburgh, William, and Carolina proprietary, 93
Thrale, John, 65
Tilly, Sir Joseph, on wool trade, 39
Timber, trade in, 194, 197. *See also* Naval stores
To All Whom These Presents May Concern, 226
Tobacco, trade in, 45, 53, 74, 81; regulation of, 47, 48, 49, 84, 85, 86; taxes on, 43, 45, 49, 50, 51, 52, 57, 58

Tobacco Adventurers (Company of Contractors with the czar for the sole importation of Tobacco into Russia), 46

Tothill, Jeremiah, 158

Tothill, William, 158

Townley, Mary, 83

Townley, Richard, 145

Townshend, Charles (secretary of state), 19, 22

Treat, Robert (governor of Connecticut), 178, 182

Trevor, Thomas (attorney general), 78; in case of *Hester*, 137

Trewhitt, Levi, 97

Trott, Nicholas, and proprietary government in South Carolina, 93, 99, 103, 104, 105, 106, 107, 108

Trott, Nicholas (proprietor of Carolina), 93, 94, 103

Trumbull, Sir William (secretary of state), 14

Turner, Sir Charles, as commissioner of trade, 21, 89

Turner, Robert, relations with Penn, 112, 115

Tynte, Major Edward (governor of Carolina), 96, 104

Usher, Elizabeth (Allen), 195

Usher, John: as deputy governor of New Hampshire, 193, 196, 197, 198, 211, 212, 233; and proprietary of New Hampshire, 193, 194, 195; on Puritans, 222

Van Cortlandt, Jacobus, 222

Van Cortlandt, Stephen: land grant to, 173; and New York politics, 154, 155, 158, 160, 173, 213

Van Dam, Rip, 215, 220, 221

Van Renssaeler, Kiliaen, 217, 221

Vaughan, George, 197; as deputy governor of New Hampshire, 21

Vaughan, William, and New Hampshire politics, 193, 194, 198, 212

Vermillie, Johannes, 154

Vernon, James (secretary of state), 14, 19, 33, 78, 159; encourages Bellomont, 172

Vesey, John (archbishop of Tuan), 90

Vesey, William, 160

Vessels, Dirck, 214

Vetch, Samuel, 34, 149, 207, 209, 227; seeks governorship, 88

Waldron, Richard: and government of New Hampshire, 196, 198; opposes New Hampshire proprietor, 193, 194, 195

Walker, Henderson, and Anglicans in North Carolina, 95

Walker, Sir Hovenden, 108; and expedition against Canada, 34, 209

Wallace, James, 65

Wallis, William, and timber trade, 41

Waln, Nicholas, 123

Walpole, Sir Robert, xi, 21, 75, 233

Walters, Robert, and politics of New York, 161, 214, 216, 221, 222, 226

Ward, Collingwood, 97

Warwick, Robert Rich, earl of, 176

Waterhouse, David, 201, on naval stores, 41; opposes bill on religion, 101

Watts, Robert, 229

Weare, Peter, 194

Weaver, Thomas, and politics in New York, 162, 173, 214, 215, 216

Webb, Robert, 113

Wenham, Robert, and politics of New York, 158, 173, 215, 216, 217, 221, 236

Wenham and Company, as political club, 162

Wentworth, John, 211

West Jersey Society: as proprietor, 133, 137, 138, 148, 149, 225; Lewis Morris and, 140, 141

Weymouth, Thomas Thynne, viscount, as commissioner of trade, 20, 189

Wharton, Philip Wharton, baron, 15, 169

Wharton, Richard, 40

Wharton, Thomas Wharton, baron, 14

Wharton, William, 26, 189

Whiting, William, 180

Wiggington, Henry, 104

Wilcox, John, 123, 124

Willard, Samuel, 165, 168, 199, 201, 204

Willett, Richard, 218

William III, 7, 14, 15, 18, 19, 20, 26, 32, 33, 61, 161; on colonial governors, 30, 158

Williams, Thomas, 154

Willocks, George, and politics of New Jersey, 135, 137, 141, 142, 216, 226

Willson, Ebenezar, 158, 162

Winchilsea, Charles Finch, 3d earl of, as commissioner of trade, 15, 21, 89

Winthrop, Anne, 179

Winthrop, Fitzjohn, 26, 160, 176, 177, 200;

as Connecticut major general, 33, 177, 183, 184; as governor of Connecticut, 178, 179, 182, 184, 189, 190
Winthrop, John II, 176, 180
Winthrop, John IV, 208
Winthrop, Waitstill, 164, 166, 191, 200, 201, 203, 205, 208, 209; and Ashurst, 201; and Bellomont, 168; as chief justice of Massachusetts, 200, 208; as judge of admiralty, 170; and Narragansett country, 184
Wise, John, 165
Wood, Joseph, 123
Woods, John, as creditor for Penn's estate, 129
Wool trade, regulation of, 39, 40

Wormeley, Ralph, 58
Wragg, Samuel, 104
Wright, Joshua, 143, 145
Wyeth, Joseph, 181
Wyllys, Samuel, 178, 179, 180

Yale, Elihu, 169
Yeates, Jasper, 111; opposes proprietary government, 122, 130; opposes Quakers, 117
Yonge, Francis, 107
York, James Stuart, duke of, 4; and government of New Jersey, 132; and Penn, 110, 111, 128; as proprietor of New York, 218. *See also* James II